HUMAN SYSTEMS

and the environment

Robert Prosser

Making good use of this book

This book is a collection of case studies stretching across the field of human geography and the relationship of people and systems to the natural environment. The aim of the materials is to add breadth and depth to your understanding of topics on population, housing, industry, shopping, farming and the environment, tourism, transport and aspects of development by applying the general principles which you will cover in classes or find in other texts to specific examples.

Each case study is free-standing and so you can select the materials in any sequence to fit your syllabus. Most of the case studies are made up of four elements:

1 A **background** element sets the example within the broader context, e.g. if the case study is illustrating aspects of population movement in a specific area, then this background links it to the general topic of population studies. It sets the scene and jogs your memory.

2 The **key understandings** are the key points which you should gain from working through the case study.

3 The **case study** element is the core of the book and makes up the bulk of the materials. A range of resources are presented to give opportunities for you to become practised in the use of varied data and written material. Many of the case studies are adapted from articles in geographical periodicals. Using them should improve your confidence to seek out and use such academic sources for yourself.

4 The **activity** element is intended to first, allow you to check and review your understanding, second, to give you exam practice, and third to suggest ideas for coursework assignments and projects

The use you make of the activities may depend upon the type of coursework and examination questions you are preparing for.

The best way, then, to use these case studies, is in conjunction with class notes, textbooks and other reference materials, to enrich and vary your learning.

(Please note: where some case studies have been adapted from US publications, measurements such as feet, yards and miles have been retained.)

To Wendy, Simon and Samantha

Thomas Nelson and Sons Ltd
Nelson House   Mayfield Road
Walton-on-Thames   Surrey
KT12 5PL   UK

58 Albany Street
Edinburgh
EH1 3QR   UK

Thomas Nelson (Hong Kong) Ltd
Toppan Building 10/F
22A Westlands Road
Quarry Bay   Hong Kong

Thomas Nelson Australia
102 Dodds Street
South Melbourne
Victoria 3205   Australia

Nelson Canada
1120 Birchmount Road
Scarborough   Ontario
M1K 5G4   Canada

CONTENTS

CHAPTER 1

Peopling the earth

Introduction

Assuming it takes you five minutes to read this Introduction, by the time you reach the end there will be 250 more Indians in the world. One every 1.2 seconds. Seventy thousand a day. Rather more than the entire population of Australia in one year.

At the end of the century, there will be certainly be one billion Indians ... According to one recent study, the population will surpass China's to reach 1 680 000 000 by the year 2050. (The Guardian, 23 February 1990)

*In Europe, population **decline** is emerging as a serious problem; except for Ireland and most Eastern European countries, birth rates have dropped to a level that is too low to keep the size of the population stable in the long run. (The Guardian, 23 February 1990)*

The British Green Party Manifesto for a Sustainable Society states: There is general agreement that the United Kingdom could not reasonably support its present population into a doubtful future. (Autumn 1989)

The brief quotations above and the images and information in resources 1.1 and 1.2 and 1.3 are convincing evidence that pop-ulation totals, trends and distributions and the demands these billions make upon the global system are *the* major world issue. The case studies in this chapter focus upon two aspects of **demography** (the study of population) which are of particular interest to geographers: **population change** and **migration**. By examining the processes which trigger population change, whether it be growth or decline – and the forces which cause people to move, we can begin to understand more fully the **spatial distribution of population**, i.e. where people live.

Population in a region or country results from two principal processes: first, the relationship between births and deaths, known as the **net reproduction rate (NPR)**. The 'growth rate' figures given in resource 1.1 are largely the outcome of an excess of births to deaths per year. One important component in this NPR is the number of children a woman is likely to have in a given society. This is combined with the number of female children born, and the numbers who survive to adulthood. The significance of this 'fertility rate' is illustrated in case study 1.2.

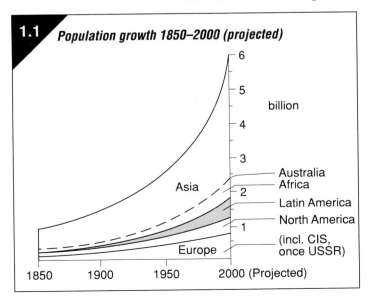

1.1 *Population growth 1850–2000 (projected)*

billion

- 6
- 5
- 4
- 3
- 2
- 1

Asia

Australia
Africa
Latin America
North America
(incl. CIS, once USSR)
Europe

1850   1900   1950   2000 (Projected)

Crowds of people on the Howrah Bridge in Calcutta, one of the world's most densely populated cities

Population growth, 1965 to 1986, and projected to 2000

Country group	1986 population (millions)	Average annual growth (per cent)				
		1965–73	1973–80	1980–86	1986–90	1990–2000
Developing countries	3528	2.5	2.1	2.0	2.1	1.9
Low-income countries	2374	2.6	2.0	1.9	2.0	1.8
Middle-income countries	1154	2.5	2.4	2.3	2.2	2.0
Oil exporters	475	2.6	2.6	2.6	2.5	2.3
Exporters of manufactures	2081	2.5	1.8	1.6	1.7	1.5
Highly indebted countries	570	2.6	2.4	2.4	2.3	2.2
Sub-Saharan Africa	399	2.7	2.8	3.1	3.3	3.2
High-income oil exporters	20	4.8	5.5	4.2	4.0	3.4
Industrial countries	742	1.0	0.7	0.6	0.5	0.4
World	4290	2.2	1.9	1.8	1.8	1.7

The second process, that of **migration**, is measured in terms of the **net migration rate (NMR)**, the balance between **emigration** (out-migration) and **immigration** (in-migration). The complex causes of migration are commonly grouped into 'push' and 'pull' factors. The movements generated may be internal or international, individual or communal, economic or social, voluntary or involuntary, one-stage or stepped. However, underlying all but truly 'enforced' moves is a straightforward motive:

'Migration occurs because migrants believe that they will be more satisfied in their needs and desires in the place that they move to than in the place from which they come'.

When examining official population statistics we must remember a third possible factor which influences the figures, namely **boundary change**. Figures are usually collected for administrative units, and so, if the boundaries of these units change, e.g. cities, counties, provinces or even countries, then the population included will alter.

Case studies 1.1 and 1.3 examine changes in population distributions within countries. The African countries in case study 1.3 (Sudan and Sierra Leone) illustrate the core-periphery and urbanisation patterns of economically developing countries. Case study 1.1 on the other hand, uses England and Wales to illustrate an opposite process, that of **counterurbanisation**. This shift of population away from large cities is a growing trend in a number of industrialised, urbanised countries and is caused by a mixture of social, economic and environmental motives. People seek an improved quality of life and believe they can find it within smaller scale communities and settlement systems.

Case study 1.4 focuses on the third major theme of the chapter: the deep-seated individual and group desires for freedom and cultural identity. Such feelings unleash vigorous forces both for migration and for staying within one's 'homeland'.

The example illustrates how the long-running civil war in El Salvador causes internal displacement of population and is one factor 'pushing' people to attempt to enter the USA as refugees. The question is though, are they refugees or 'economic migrants'.

CASE STUDY 1.1 *Regional population change and counterurbanisation in Britain*

Background

Population census figures for most advanced Western countries show that from the late 1960s, population growth rates have been declining, but rates of population redistribution have been accelerating. The main trend has been **decentralisation** or **deconcentration**, with population moving from cities to suburbs, from metropolitan areas to surrounding non-metropolitan districts, from national core areas to peripheral regions. This is a reversal of the agglomeration and concentration processes associated with industrialisation and urbanisation, where centripetal forces attract people to major cities. The centrifugal movements have several names: 'rural rejuvenation', 'population turnaround', 'migration reversal', and, most commonly, 'counterurbanisation'.

Counterurbanisation involves a complex set of movements, but a useful basic definition is: *population deconcentration and the resurgence of population growth in the nation's rural areas*. It is important to understand that it is a much broader concept than suburbanisation, as you can see in this second definition: 'a process of demographic deconcentration, beyond that of suburbanisation or metropolitan decentralisation'. Metropolitan sprawl and commuter village growth is seen as 'spillover'; a further stage in the urbanisation process. Genuine counterurbanisation, however, is seen as a 'clean break'; a different type of settlement system, based not on 'new agglomeration in a different location, but diffused development based upon smaller-scale systems' of settlements (resource 1.4)

Three main causes energising counterurbanisation are usually given. First, changing values and preferences by migrants, for example those desiring a 'rural' way of life and people of retirement age who want to live in a more peaceful, less

Estate of 40 houses added to the village of Orleton, N Herefordshire.

threatening environment (resources 1.5 and 1.6). Second, government regional policies, such as New Towns, Small Industry grants for rural areas, and the economic advantages of peripheral areas – for example lower labour costs and land prices. Third, job and industrial locational decisions. Except for retirement migration, this last factor is regarded by many as most important: 'The mainspring of counterurbanisation is the location of employment'. Remember that decisions on jobs are taken at four levels:

- **individuals** – for example a person decides to move for a new job;
- **separate business establishments** – an individual factory is moved;
- **corporate structures** – multinational companies relocate their operations;
- **the role of the state** – regional policy and relocating government agencies.

Working together, these four factors 'have favoured the more accessible and environmentally attractive parts of non-metropolitan space'.

The materials in this case study focus on two key issues concerning population distribution in Britain: first, is the counterurbanisation trend accelerating, and second, does it mean a permanent rearrangement of our settlement pattern? Are we, for example, moving towards what Professor Peter Hall has called 'Spread City' ?

Key understandings

- ◆ Counterurbanisation is more than the continued growth of suburbs. It is a distinctive movement of population to smaller-scale settlement systems, affecting particularly, non-metropolitan and rural population trends.

- ◆ The rate of counterurbanisation in Britain has varied over time and from region to region since the late 1960s.

- ◆ The rapid loss of population from large metropolitan areas during the 1970s slowed down during the 1980s.

In 1983, a survey of over 400 people of working age, i.e. non-retirees, who had migrated to West Cornwall, showed that 'quality of life' was more important than economic opportunity (see table). The 'image' of the county was an important motive and approximately one-third were attracted by a preferred lifestyle. About 75 per cent came from the SW, SE, and W Midlands regions, popular origins of holidaymakers to Cornwall, and generally prosperous regions. The stories below are typical, but as (resource 1.6) illustrates, the rural life does not work for everyone.

Success stories

A couple moved in 1967 from Essex, 'for a new beginning'. Both had worked in London, and had no previous connection with Cornwall. They were able to buy their house outright, following which the husband set up his own building and decorating business. Now they 'don't even wish to leave Cornwall for long to visit relatives.'

Another family moved 'to get away from Tyneside and make a fresh start'. The husband was previously a welder, and his wife in medical research. Since moving they have both had short term or part-time jobs, but are 'not seeking any more work'.

A former city lecturer had had two full time jobs and several spells of self-employment (building and fishing) since arriving. He said he had 'no money, but I enjoy living here – I don't want to move away'.

1.5

Crucial factors determining the decision to move to Cornwall (% of respondents)

Reason	Return migrants	Non-return migrants	Total numbers
Previously lived in Cornwall	78	0	30
Previous holidays in Cornwall	20	49	38
Relatives living in Cornwall	67	60	40
Job prospects	28	38	34
Better climate	6	27	23
Better housing	4	3	3
Cheap housing	10	12	11
Better wages	1	4	3
Quality of environment	33	47	42
Child education and welfare	22	20	21
Health reasons	6	9	8
Retirement in the future	6	11	9
To avoid the 'rat-race'	28	46	39
Other (including being sent by an employer)	8	13	11

N.B. An individual respondent may have recorded more than one item as 'important'

1.6

Commuters come back to town

The great middle-class love affair with country life may be over. Thousands of city dwellers who moved to villages in the 1980s are abandoning their rustic retreats and returning to town.

Rising commuting costs, falls in city house prices and disappointment with rural life are pushing growing numbers of people back to the urban territory they left.

One estate agent in west Wales said this weekend that almost a third of the buyers who arrived from towns last year had sold up and gone.

There is evidence that in most remote areas people are becoming disillusioned. When houses in the countryside become as expensive as those in towns, there are not the economic incentives to move out that there were 10 years ago.

A Bristol study of 1000 commuters from the West Country to London found rising rail fares were deterring long-distance travellers.

Since 1986 the cost of standard-class season tickets has increased by up to 85 per cent putting the annual charge from Bristol to London at £4028.

When Hamish and Trisha Bell left London four years ago to live in Norfolk with their four children and nanny, they thought they would never go back. But their dream of a slow life in the country lasted two years, and now they are in Stockwell, south London.

'We wanted to get out of the rat race, but it was unrealistic,' said Trisha, a film production buyer. 'We bought a huge old rectory on four acres with a tennis court but we had to keep working to pay for it. We spent most of our time on the M11 going to or from work.

'I didn't realise what life in the country would be like. I'm a terrible romantic and plunged in. I missed the theatre and cinema, and we couldn't buy ginger or garlic in the local shops.'

The Bells' two teenage sons found country life boring and had difficulties at school. 'They were different from the yokels, and spent most of their weekends trying to escape from the country, staying with friends in London,' she said.

John Humphries, presenter of Radio 4's *Today* programme bought a 134-acre dairy farm in Trelech, west Wales, 10 years ago. 'I underestimated the effort involved,' he said. 'Even with a manager it proved impossible to run it without living there full-time.

He has sold all but 20 acres, which he keeps for holidays. The history of a small-holding nearby tells its own story. 'Nearly every six months a different family moves there from London or Manchester,' he said. 'They think they will live the good life, but as soon as they realise it is not all roses round the door they up and go and a different family moves in.'

(Source: *The Sunday Times* 3 June, 1990)

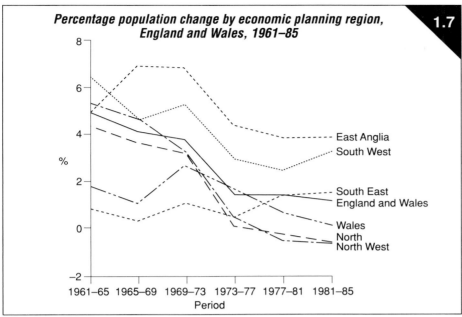

Percentage population change by economic planning region, England and Wales, 1961–85

1.7

Cornwall, Breckland, mid-Suffolk. Third, resort and retirement areas with rapid 1980s growth (3), e.g. South Devon, Monmouth. Fourth, rural areas associated with the 1970s counterurbanisation surge, whose growth rates had slackened by the 1980s (4), e.g. Radnor and Ryedale.

(Source: adapted from A G Champion, 'Recent changes in the pace of population deconcentration in Britain', *Geoforum*, 18(4), 1987, pp. 379–401)

Activities

Resources 1.8 and 1.9 compare trends in rates of change between time periods. For example, (2) on resource 1.9 indicates districts which recorded higher rates of growth 1971–81 than 1961–71; (4) indicates districts which increased 1971–81 after losing population 1961–71.

With a partner, use the maps to support or criticise these statements:

(i) The 1970s witnessed a surge of counterurbanisation in England and Wales (resource 1.8(b)).

(ii) During the 1980s, districts with the highest rates of increase were in non-metropolitan areas and predominantly in a zone 70–140 km from London (resource 1.8(c)).

(iii) The pattern of counterurbanisation has changed, with the growth locations shifting to the more accessible districts of south-east England and away from the peripheral locations that were prominent in the 1960s and 1970s (resources 1.8 and 1.9).

Are we all going to live in the country?

Part I: Regional population trends in England and Wales, 1961–85

From 1961, absolute population growth was slow (resource 1.7). For example, in mid-1985, the total population of England and Wales was 49.9 million, only 300 000 more than in 1971. However, the regions south of the Severn/Wash divide (South-West, South-East, East Anglia) performed consistently better than the rest. The three maps in resource 1.8 make it clear that the detailed pattern of these changes varied over time. For instance, in the 1961–71 decade (resource 1.8(a)) there was a broad zone of high increases across south and east England, focused around London, but during the 1971–81 decade (resource 1.8(b)), high growth was more restricted. Several high growth sectors led from London and there was a scatter of rural areas, e.g. peripheral districts such as Cornwall and Radnor, or districts accessible to cities, e.g. Wychavon and much of Norfolk. By the 1980s (resource 1.8(c)) the high increases were even more fragmented, e.g. later New and Expanded Towns such as Milton

Keynes and Peterborough; resort and retirement areas in Cornwall, New Forest, Bournemouth; metropolitan 'spillover' districts such as Woodspring (near Bristol) and South Staffordshire. Notice that a number of rural districts which had shown significant growth in the 1970s had slackened, suggesting a less powerful decentralisation drive after 1981.

Resource 1.9 gives a summary picture of the patterns of change since 1961. It is based upon (a) **ranking** the subregional districts in terms of growth rates for each period (1961–71; 1971–81; 1981–91), (b) **subdividing** the ranking list into six equal parts (sextiles); (c) **examining** which districts were in the top sextile during which periods, i.e. had the highest growth rates; and (d) **plotting** the districts according to the time periods they were in the top sextile. For non-metropolitan districts, four major features of change can be seen: first, the consistently high growth districts (1) were mostly growing towns in the outer ring of the South-East region, e.g. Basingstoke, Newbury, Milton Keynes. Second, a series of rural areas with accelerated growth from the early 1970s (2), e.g. North

Part II: Is counter-urbanisation running out of steam?

There is clear evidence of counterurbanisation in England and Wales since 1961, but since the late 1960s, this growth has become increasingly focused within south-

1.8

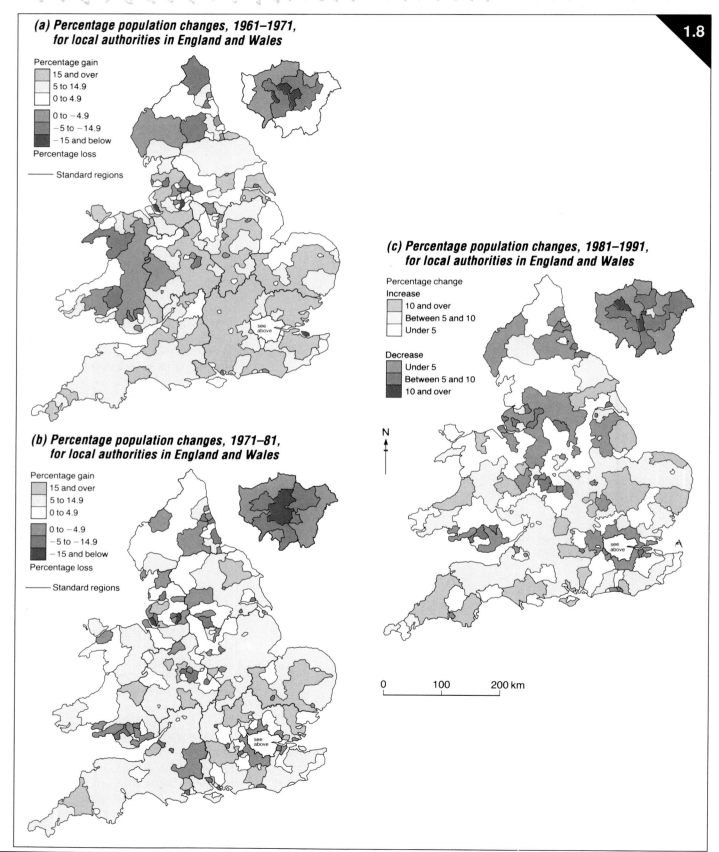

(a) Percentage population changes, 1961–1971, for local authorities in England and Wales

Percentage gain
- 15 and over
- 5 to 14.9
- 0 to 4.9

- 0 to −4.9
- −5 to −14.9
- −15 and below

Percentage loss

—— Standard regions

see above

(b) Percentage population changes, 1971–81, for local authorities in England and Wales

Percentage gain
- 15 and over
- 5 to 14.9
- 0 to 4.9

- 0 to −4.9
- −5 to −14.9
- −15 and below

Percentage loss

—— Standard regions

see above

(c) Percentage population changes, 1981–1991, for local authorities in England and Wales

Percentage change

Increase
- 10 and over
- Between 5 and 10
- Under 5

Decrease
- Under 5
- Between 5 and 10
- 10 and over

N

see above

0   100   200 km

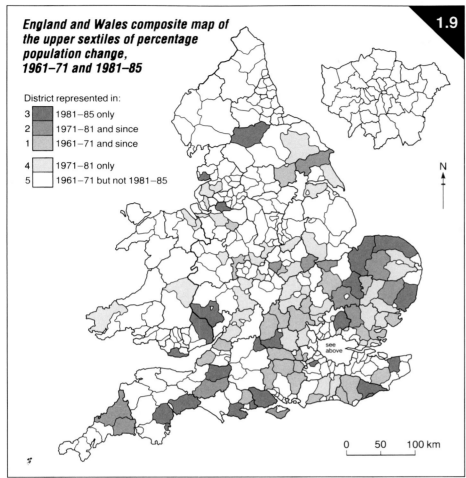

England and Wales composite map of the upper sextiles of percentage population change, 1961–71 and 1981–85

1.9

District represented in:

3	1981–85 only
2	1971–81 and since
1	1961–71 and since
4	1971–81 only
5	1961–71 but not 1981–85

N

see above

0   50   100 km

may involve far more people than a 0.5 per cent shift in, say, rural Wales).

If counterurbanisation is at work, non-metropolitan and rural areas should record the most rapid growth. At first glance, the pattern of population trends shown by the graphs of resource 1.11 did not seem to alter greatly between 1971 and 1984, i.e. 'Metropolitan Britain' continued to decline, while the 'Non-Metropolitan Districts' continued to grow. A closer look, however, reveals some significant shifts: first, the rates of population loss in Greater London and the Metropolitan Districts were much reduced. Second, population loss spread into the 'large' and 'smaller' cities and 'industrial areas' of non-metropolitan Britain, but at low rates of decline. Third, while other types of non-metropolitan district continued to increase, they did so at lower rates. (The extent of these changes can be identified clearly by making a table for the settlement categories and the four time periods, then entering the change into each box of the table.) Overall, the outstanding feature was the

east England. Furthermore, even within this high growth region, two quite distinct trends have been emerging (resources 1.10 and 1.11). First, counterurbanisation has continued, but at slower rates than in the 1960s, e.g. the outermost zones (outer south-east and peripheral south-eastern England) show highest growth, but at slower rates. The second trend, again suggesting a slow-down in the counterurbanisation flow, has been the much improved performance of London (Outer London; Inner London), where population decline has become much less severe (see also the London inset maps on page 6). Further evidence of this trend comes from data for other major cities (resource 1.14). (NB the maps and graphs show rates of change, not absolute numbers. Thus, a 0.5 per cent change in the south-east

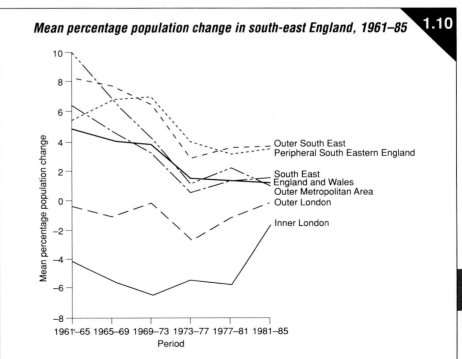

Mean percentage population change in south-east England, 1961–85

1.10

Mean percentage population change

Outer South East
Peripheral South Eastern England

South East
England and Wales
Outer Metropolitan Area
Outer London

Inner London

1961–65 1965–69 1969–73 1973–77 1977–81 1981–85
Period

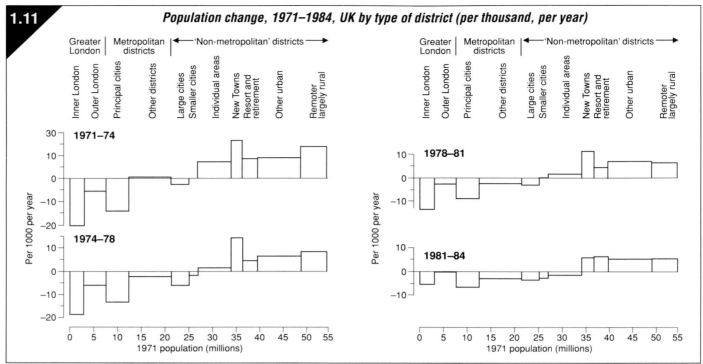

1.11

Population change, 1971–1984, UK by type of district (per thousand, per year)

1971–74

1974–78

1978–81

1981–84

Per 1000 per year

1971 population (millions)

Greater London | Metropolitan districts | ◄—— 'Non-metropolitan' districts ——►

Inner London | Outer London | Principal cities | Other districts | Large cities | Smaller cities | Individual areas | New Towns | Resort and retirement | Other urban | Remoter largely rural

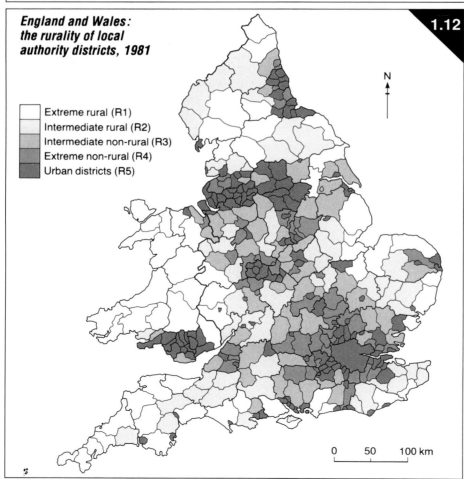

England and Wales: the rurality of local authority districts, 1981

1.12

N

- Extreme rural (R1)
- Intermediate rural (R2)
- Intermediate non-rural (R3)
- Extreme non-rural (R4)
- Urban districts (R5)

0   50   100 km

remarkable transformation experienced by the nation's largest cities, particularly London.

A further way in which counterurbanisation can be assessed is by subdividing districts as 'urban' or 'rural', and then comparing their populations. Cloke and Edwards (1968) have constructed an Index of Rurality, based on characteristics of the area and the population, classifying districts from 'Urban' to the 'Extreme Rural' (resource 1.12). The graph in resource 1.13 reveals that of the five categories it is the rural districts (R1, R2, R3) which record the best growth rates, thereby supporting the counterurbanisation hypothesis.

(Source: D F W Cross, 'Counterurbanisation in England and Wales context and development', *King's College London Department of Geography*, O.R. 28, May 1987)

1.13

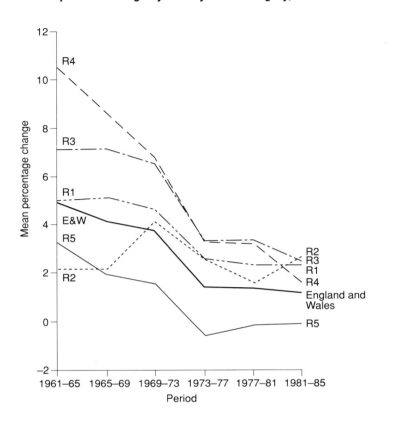

Population change by rurality index category, 1961–85

(y-axis: Mean percentage change; x-axis: Period)

Periods: 1961–65, 1965–69, 1969–73, 1973–77, 1977–81, 1981–85

Labels: R4, R3, R1, E&W, R5, R2, R2, R3, R1, R4, England and Wales, R5

Activities

Group discussion

From the data provided in this case study:

1 Present evidence which (a) supports the operation of counterurbanisation in England and Wales, and (b) identifies sub-periods of distinctive trends within the 1961–85 period.

2 Select one region and (a) summarise the main population trends, 1961–85, and (b) suggest the principal reasons for these trends.

3 It is possible to up-date the figures by reference to government annual publications such as *Regional Trends, Social Trends; Annual Abstract of Statistics, Registrar General's Annual Returns.* (Reference sections of larger public libraries often stock at least some of these.) From the early 1990s, the results of the 1991 Population Census will be published. Using such sources, you can compare trends since 1985 with those you have identified in this case study.

1.14

| | Rates of population loss in major cities, 1971–84, (percentage per annum) | | | |
	1971–74	1974–78	1978–81	1981–84
Manchester	−2.49	−1.71	−1.02	−0.57
Glasgow	−2.55	−2.56	−1.67	−1.29
Liverpool	−2.44	−1.37	−1.11	−1.26
Birmingham	−0.72	−1.07	−0.51	−0.37
Newcastle upon Tyne	−1.18	−0.71	−0.91	−0.35
Sheffield	−0.51	−0.65	−0.45	−0.43
Leeds	−0.16	−0.49	−0.58	−0.25

Background

Efforts by developing countries to control the numbers of children born and so to reduce their population growth rates have been well publicised e.g. China's 'one child per family' campaign (resources 1.15 and 1.17). Population growth rates in excess of 3 per cent a year, the doubling of a country's population within a 25 year period, and age-structures where more than 50 per cent of the population are under 21 years of age, are common indicators of the problems African, Latin American and Asian nations face in the struggle for development. Less well known is the emerging problem of developed nations where too few children are being born to prevent populations from falling. The basis for this is the low level of fertility of women, i.e. the number of children they bear.

The data in this case study, for the United Kingdom and thirteen other developed countries, shows that in all but one case (the Irish Republic), fertility rates are below the critical replacement level. In the medium term, therefore, unless there is net in-migration, or a change in the number of children each woman bears, populations in these countries will fall. Governments and employers are aware of, and responding to this possibility. For instance, since 1989, the British government has been encouraging people to stay in employment longer, to counteract the fall in young people entering the labour market in the 1990s. Employers such as banks and insurance companies have run campaigns and incentives to recruit young people, encouraging them not to go into higher education. As the figures in this case study show, one factor in West Germany's initially enthusiastic welcome of migrants from East Germany in the surge of autumn 1989, was West Germany's concern over growing labour shortages. The largely young, often highly educated and skilled East German migrants have been valuable recruits to the West German economy (resource 1.16).

Key understandings

◆ Fertility rate is a vital component of population change.

◆ Most developed countries have fertility rates below replacement level.

◆ Women are tending to have their children later in life.

◆ Increasing proportions of children are being born outside marriage.

◆ These changes have important implications for social and economic policies.

1.16

The Second Miracle

West Germany steams into the 1990s aboard a powerful economic boom

West Germany has become the high-performance engine that regulates European growth, with businesses that bestride the Continent and are Japan's most dynamic competitor for many world markets. The economy is so strong and expansive that it will have no trouble absorbing the nearly 200 000 East Germans who are expected to flood across the border by the end of this year.

West Germany is churning out automobiles, machinery, electronic components and chemicals at record rates. Many factories are running at more than 90 per cent of capacity, and their managers are crying out for more skilled workers. The more than 70 000 East Germans who have flooded refugee camps since August have been besieged by job recruiters, and so far there have been more employment offers than new arrivals.

Certainly there are jobs galore for those with the appropriate skills. The construction industry, where one-quarter of the labour force is older than 50, needs some 100 000 additional workers. The nation's textile plants, which suffered mass layoffs during the 1960s and 1970s are crying for master craftsmen, engineers and technicians. 'You can't get staff for love or money,' said Walter Holthaus of the Knitwear Industry Association.

The East German refugee wave is especially welcome because among the newcomers are the welders, machine operators, electricians, construction laborers and other workers that West Germany needs most.

(Source: *Time*, 13 November 1989)

1.15

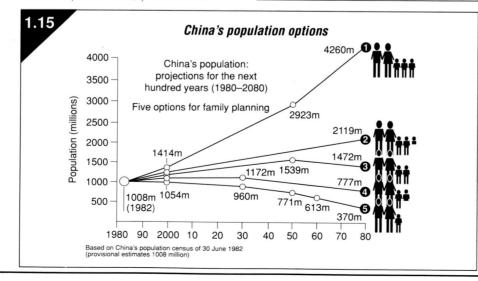

China's population options

China's population: projections for the next hundred years (1980–2080)

Five options for family planning

Based on China's population census of 30 June 1982 (provisional estimates 1008 million)

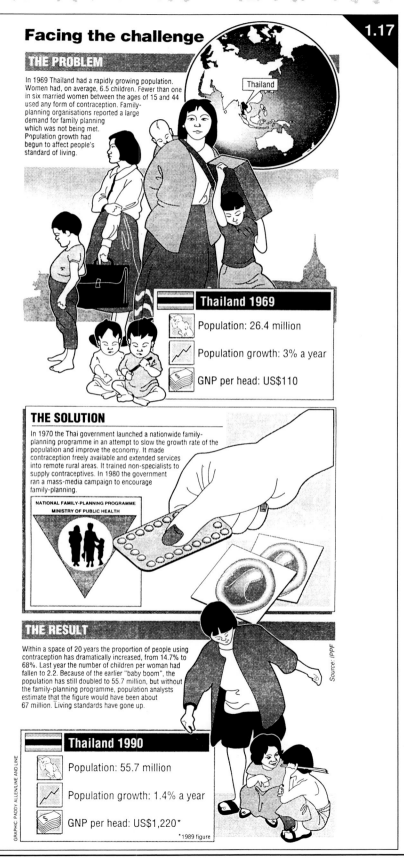

Facing the challenge

1.17

THE PROBLEM

In 1969 Thailand had a rapidly growing population. Women had, on average, 6.5 children. Fewer than one in six married women between the ages of 15 and 44 used any form of contraception. Family-planning organisations reported a large demand for family planning which was not being met. Population growth had begun to affect people's standard of living.

Thailand 1969

Population: 26.4 million

Population growth: 3% a year

GNP per head: US$110

THE SOLUTION

In 1970 the Thai government launched a nationwide family-planning programme in an attempt to slow the growth rate of the population and improve the economy. It made contraception freely available and extended services into remote rural areas. It trained non-specialists to supply contraceptives. In 1980 the government ran a mass-media campaign to encourage family-planning.

NATIONAL FAMILY-PLANNING PROGRAMME
MINISTRY OF PUBLIC HEALTH

Source: IPPF

THE RESULT

Within a space of 20 years the proportion of people using contraception has dramatically increased, from 14.7% to 68%. Last year the number of children per woman had fallen to 2.2. Because of the earlier "baby boom", the population has still doubled to 55.7 million, but without the family-planning programme, population analysts estimate that the figure would have been about 67 million. Living standards have gone up.

Thailand 1990

Population: 55.7 million

Population growth: 1.4% a year

GNP per head: US$1,220*

*1989 figure

GRAPHIC: PADDY ALLEN/LINE AND LINE

How many children are we having?

A key to population forecasting and hence long-term planning is to know how many children are being born and what future trends will be. To do this, we need to know trends in the numbers of women of child-bearing age, and how many children each one will have. One popular measure is called the **total period fertility rate** (TPFR): the average number of children each woman will bear. (Many countries use the age-range 15–50 years in their calculations.) In order for a population to remain stable (ignoring migration), the TPFR needs to be 2.1 children. At this rate of 2.1, a group of women is likely to replace itself with the same number of daughters, i.e. potential mothers. (The fact that the TPFR needs to be 2.1 rather than 2.0 is explained by (a) a slightly higher number of male than female births and (b) some women die during their child-bearing period, and so have fewer children.)

During the early 1960s concern centred on the shortage of houses, schools etc. which would result from continuing population growth. Central government policy responses included the creation of new urban settlements, and increases in the numbers of teachers being trained. During the 1980s, however, concern shifted to the implications of the reverse situation in which the numbers of young people in the population were falling. In such circumstances, problems were likely to arise from the shrinking of the national labour force at the same time as the elderly population, needing income and health care support, was still growing.

The underlying cause of this turnaround in policy concern was the substantial falls in TPFRs, and hence in numbers of annual births, which have occurred in many countries since the 1960s (resource 1.18). West Germany saw the sharpest decline in fertility. The TPFR has now been below 1.5 for over ten years. As a result, annual numbers of deaths in West Germany already substantially exceed annual numbers of births. In contrast, in Italy and Spain, countries with traditionally high levels of fertility, the much more recent sharp falls in the fertility level to the surprisingly low TPFRs of 1.5 or 1.6 have been widely welcomed.

'Although the level of fertility in the UK fell substantially for ten years after the mid 1960s, there has been a small net increase over the past decade. As a result, whilst the TPFR in the UK is still about 15 per cent below the long term replacement level, the current level of fertility is higher than in most other developed countries. If the tendency for women to have more children in their late twenties and thirties continues, the level of fertility in the UK will increase further over the next twenty years, possibly to a TPFR of about 2.0. Should this happen, the problems of a rapidly falling population size, which can arise from prolonged, very low fertility levels, may be avoided. However, the fall in fertility which has already occurred will lead to a period of

ageing of the labour force bringing with it difficulties arising from the falling numbers of young recruits to the labour force during the 1990s .

Trends in total fertility rates

1966–76

In 1966 the TPFR in the UK was 2.79 and had just started to fall from the maximum level of 2.93 reached in 1964. This TPFR lay towards the upper end of the range 2.5 to 3.0 which included the TPFRs of most of the countries considered in this case study. The exceptions are Japan and Sweden, where the TPFRs were lower, and Northern Ireland and the Irish Republic, where the TPFRs were higher. The very low TPFR of 1.6 seen in Japan in 1966 was exceptional, although the prevailing level of about 2.1 in Japan in the years immediately before and afterwards was well below the equivalent TPFRs of all the other countries. This explanation for the 1966 drop in fertility in Japan is that this was the year of 'Hinoeuma', or 'Year of the Horse'. According to a legend, a girl born in the Year of the Horse (which returns every 60 years) will kill her husband. In 1966 the power of the legend, coupled with

the modern availability of contraceptive techniques and abortion, led to the avoidance of about half a million births (about 25 per cent) during 1966.

TPFRs in all the countries of this case study fell between 1966 and 1976. The steepest falls (42 per cent) occurred in West Germany and the Netherlands, with the UK fall (38 per cent) next. The fall in the TPFR for the USA between 1966 and 1976 was also high at 36 per cent, but fertility in the USA had peaked (at 3.77) almost a decade earlier in 1957 and had already started to decline steeply during the 1950s and early 1960s when fertility rates in Europe were still rising. At the other end of the scale, the falls in the TPFRs between 1966 and 1976 in the predominantly Catholic countries of Italy, the Irish Republic and Spain were all below 20 per cent; in Spain the decline was as little as 5 per cent. In Japan also the fall in the TPFR between 1966 and 1976 was relatively small at 14 per cent.

1976–86

By 1976 the TPFR in almost all the countries had fallen below the level of 2.1. Exceptions were the Irish Republic, Northern Ireland, Spain

---

1.18 Total period fertility rates (TPFR) for developed countries, 1966 – 1986

Year	United Kingdom	England	Wales	Scotland	Northern Ireland	France	West Germany	Italy	Spain	Irish Republic	Denmark	Netherlands	Belgium	Sweden	Australia	Canada	USA	Japan
1966	2.79	2.75	2.70	2.89	3.49	2.78	2.53	2.62	2.91	3.95	2.62	2.89	2.53	2.36	2.88	2.79	2.74	1.60
1967	2.70	2.63	2.58	2.87	3.53	2.64	2.49	2.54	2.94	3.84	2.40	2.79	2.42	2.28	2.84	2.59	2.57	2.22
1968	2.62	2.55	2.57	2.82	3.45	2.57	2.38	2.49	2.87	3.78	2.12	2.69	2.31	2.07	2.89	2.46	2.48	2.12
1969	2.52	2.45	2.48	2.67	3.33	2.53	2.21	2.51	2.86	3.84	2.00	2.74	2.24	1.93	2.88	2.45	2.45	2.12
1970	2.45	2.41	2.44	2.57	3.25	2.48	2.02	2.42	2.84	3.87	1.95	2.58	2.20	1.92	2.85	2.40	2.48	2.13
1971	2.41	2.37	2.44	2.53	3.14	2.50	1.92	2.41	2.86	3.98	2.04	2.38	2.21	1.96	2.91	2.22	2.27	2.16
1972	2.21	2.17	2.23	2.27	3.00	2.43	1.71	2.36	2.84	3.87	2.03	2.17	2.09	1.91	2.67	2.01	2.01	2.14
1973	2.05	2.01	2.07	2.13	2.96	2.32	1.54	2.34	2.82	3.74	1.92	1.92	1.95	1.87	2.44	1.96	1.88	2.14
1974	1.92	1.89	1.97	1.97	2.77	2.12	1.51	2.33	2.87	3.62	1.90	1.79	1.83	1.87	2.34	1.88	1.84	2.05
1975	1.81	1.77	1.84	1.90	2.67	1.93	1.45	2.19	2.80	3.41	1.92	1.66	1.73	1.77	2.17	1.89	1.77	1.91
1976	1.74	1.70	1.78	1.78	2.69	1.83	1.46	2.08	2.79	3.32	1.75	1.63	1.72	1.68	2.08	1.84	1.74	1.85
1977	1.69	1.66	1.69	1.71	2.58	1.86	1.41	1.95	2.66	3.28	1.66	1.58	1.71	1.64	2.02	1.81	1.79	1.80
1978	1.76	1.73	1.77	1.75	2.64	1.82	1.38	1.85	2.53	3.24	1.67	1.58	1.69	1.60	1.96	1.76	1.76	1.79
1979	1.86	1.83	1.90	1.85	2.80	1.86	1.38	1.74	2.35	3.23	1.60	1.56	1.69	1.66	1.91	1.76	1.81	1.77
1980	1.89	1.87	1.95	1.84	2.78	1.95	1.45	1.66	2.18	3.23	1.55	1.60	1.69	1.68	1.90	1.75	1.84	1.75
1981	1.81	1.78	1.86	1.83	2.54	1.95	1.44	1.57	2.00	3.08	1.44	1.56	1.67	1.63	1.94	1.70	1.82	1.74
1982	1.78	1.75	1.84	1.73	2.46	1.91	1.41	1.57	1.87	2.95	1.43	1.50	1.60	1.62	1.94	1.69	1.83	1.77
1983	1.77	1.75	1.82	1.70	2.44	1.79	1.33	1.53	1.72	2.75	1.38	1.47	1.56	1.61	1.93	1.68	1.80	1.80
1984	1.77	1.75	1.81	1.68	2.44	1.81	1.29	1.50	1.65	2.58	1.40	1.49	1.52	1.65	1.85	1.69	1.81	1.81
1985	1.80	1.78	1.84	1.71	2.44	1.82	1.28	1.42	–	2.49	1.42	1.51	1.50	1.73	–	1.67	1.84	1.76
1986	1.78	1.77	1.82	1.68	2.45	1.84	1.36	–	–	2.43	1.48	1.55	1.53	1.79	–	1.67	1.81	–

Notes: The total period fertility rate (TPFR) is the average number of children which would be born per woman if women experienced the age-specific fertility rates of a given year throughout their childbearing years.

and Italy, although in Italy the TPFR was only just above the replacement level. In the UK the TPFR reached a minimum in 1977 and a fairly sharp recovery up to 1980 followed. The USA, France and West Germany also experienced short-lived recoveries in fertility during the late 1970s, but in none of these countries was the up-turn so strong as in the UK. During the early 1980s, after a fairly sharp fall between 1980 and 1981, fertility in the UK fluctuated less than at any time since the 1950s. In other countries there were much greater changes and, because fertility trends in several of these countries behaved differently in the late 1970s as well, the clearest comparisons are provided by looking at changes over the decade from 1976 to 1986 as a whole.

(Source: B Werner, 'Fertility trends in the UK and in thirteen other developed countries, 1966–86', *Population Trends*, 51, Spring 1988, pp. 18–24)

Activities

1 From resource 1.18, (a) record the year in which each country's fertility rate fell below the replacement level; (b) list countries where fertility rates are sufficient to sustain population, and the three countries where populations decline is likely to be most severe.

2 From resource 1.18, plot graphs for the several parts of the United Kingdom. Compare and contrast the trends shown, and attempt to account for observed differences.

3 How do the graphs of resource 1.19 support the claim that there is a trend for women to delay having their children?

4 Summarise the key differences in fertility patterns shown by resource 1.20.

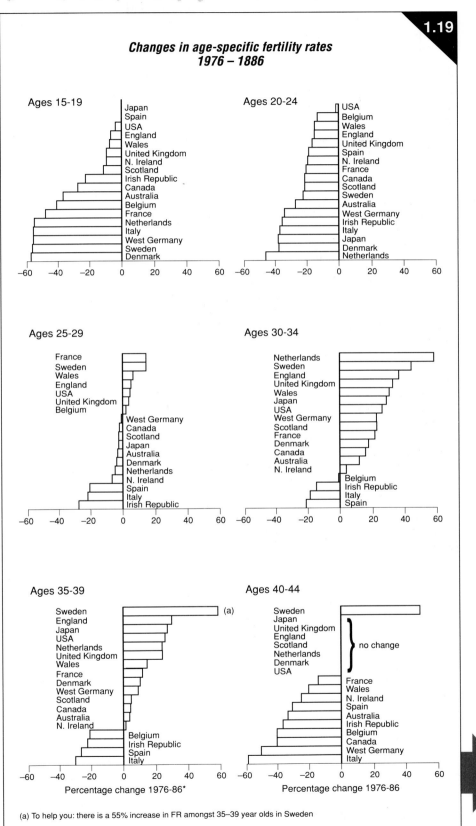

1.19

Changes in age-specific fertility rates 1976 – 1886

(a) To help you: there is a 55% increase in FR amongst 35–39 year olds in Sweden

CASE STUDY 1.2 *Fertility trends and their effects on population trends – examples from the developed world*

1.20

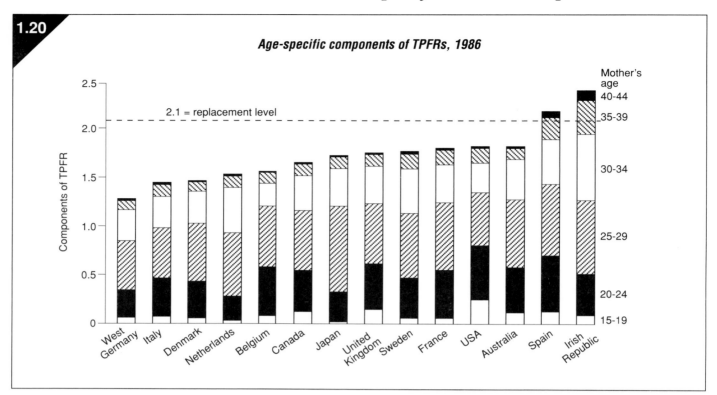

Age-specific components of TPFRs, 1986

1.21

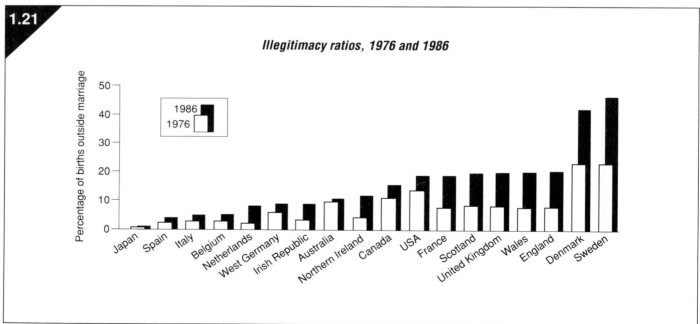

Illegitimacy ratios, 1976 and 1986

5 Group discussion

(i) Why have fertility rates fallen?

(ii) Why are women having their children later in life?

(iii) Why are more children being born outside marriage? (Resource 1.21.)

(iv) What implications do the trends shown in this case study have for

(a) government policy (social and economic),

(b) employers, and

(c) families and their lifestyles?

CASE STUDY 1.3 *Population change in the developing world – examples from the Sudan and Sierra Leone*

Background

Whereas in developed countries, imminent population decline is emerging as a threat to further development (see case study 1.2), in the developing world, rapid population growth remains a critical problem. Many developing countries still endure population growth rates of well over 2 per cent a year, figures frequently higher than their average economic growth rates (resource 1.22). As one measure of 'development' is the improvement in quality of life for an ever-growing proportion of the population, it is clear that such a process is impossible to attain while population growth exceeds economic growth.

A second common demographic characteristic of developing countries is that while a majority of their people remain 'rural', the highest rates of population increase occur in and around towns and cities. The growth rates are sustained by a combination of high natural increase rates (excess of births over deaths) and continued net in-migration (excess of arrivals over departures). The process of urbanisation, and especially the emergence of a 'primate city', tends to accentuate the contrasts between a rapidly growing 'core' and a less dynamic 'periphery'. Governments are trying to break down this core-periphery structure for a number of reasons: to promote economic growth; to exert social control; to improve political stability; to establish a national identity in place of what may be a traditional 'tribal' system; to reduce pressures on the main cities and to prevent or cure ecological and environmental damage.

The patterns and trends of population change observed for a particular country will be the outcome of the complex interaction between these various environmental, political, economic, social and cultural motives and factors. Remember, however, that your study of the demography of a developing country may be blurred by the inaccuracy and non-comparability of the statistics you have available. The Sudan, the main focus of this case study, exhibits certain of these problems. For instance, the first census (1955–56) took almost a year to complete; it did not count the population at a single day in time; the 1973 census results have not been published; the definition of a 'nomad' varies from census to census; and an arbitrary north-west segment of the country is regarded for census purposes as 'uninhabited'. Nonetheless, there is sufficient data to be able to plot population 1955–83 and to try to account for the patterns and trends shown. It was a period of recurrent droughts (the Sudan is part of the Sahel zone), periodic political unrest and civil war, agricultural development using the waters of the Nile basin, extensive urbanisation, and inward migration from countries to the west, such as Chad. Across this disturbed period, the population doubled, with an average annual growth rate around 3 per cent.

	Average annual population growth rate 1980–85			Per capita GNP 1983	Percentage growth rate of GNP 1980–85
Country	**%**	**%**	**%**		
	Urban	Rural	Country		
Ghana	5.2	2.0	3.25	320	−1.1
Nigeria	5.8	2.7	3.34	760	−0.3
Sierra Leone	4.6	0.8	1.77	380	1.8
Sudan	6.3	1.6	2.86	400	3.3
Bolivia	3.3	2.2	2.89	510	−1.4
Guyana	3.0	1.5	1.95	520	−2.9
Venezuela	3.8	0.2	3.26	4100	0.7
Bangladesh	5.4	2.4	2.74	130	4.9
Malaysia	3.7	1.7	2.29	1870	7.3
Nepal	5.3	2.2	2.33	170	2.9
Papua New Guinea	4.5	2.4	2.69	790	1.2

Economic and population change in selected developing countries — 1.22

Key understandings

◆ The Sudan and Sierra Leone exhibit many demographic features typical of developing countries – high growth rates and rapid urbanisation.

◆ Population trends vary regionally in developing countries and may be related to core-periphery structures.

◆ Internal and external factors, human and natural processes combine to influence the pattern of population change.

1.23

	Numbers 1955	('000) 1983	Increase (%) 1955–83	% of population 1955	1983	% change 1955–83
Urban	854	4154	386	8	20	+12
Rural sedentary (settled)	8003	14 219	79	78	69	−9
Rural nomadic	1406	2192	56	14	11	−3
Total	10 263	20 565				

Part I: On the move in the Sudan

A quick look at resource 1.24 and then resource 1.25 gives an immediate impression of both concentration and dispersal in Sudan's population change, 1955–83. Population densities grew in every census district and the population doubled overall. However, as resource 1.26 shows, there were significant regional variations. Resource 1.23 suggests strong urbanisation, with urban populations rising from 8 to 20 per cent of the total, although the rural numbers (sedentary and nomadic) did almost double from 8.4 million to 16.4 million.

Which areas have increased their population most – and why?

Return to resources 1.24, 1.25 and 1.26 and compare them more closely. You should be able to identify four main areas of particularly rapid population growth. First, Khartoum province grew by 250 per cent to a total of 1.8 million people. This was the result of persistent in-migration and urbanisation associated particularly with the capital city, Khartoum. (Notice that 'Khartoum' is actually three distinct urban units – Khartoum, Khartoum North and Omdurman. In this case study, the term 'Greater Khartoum' will be

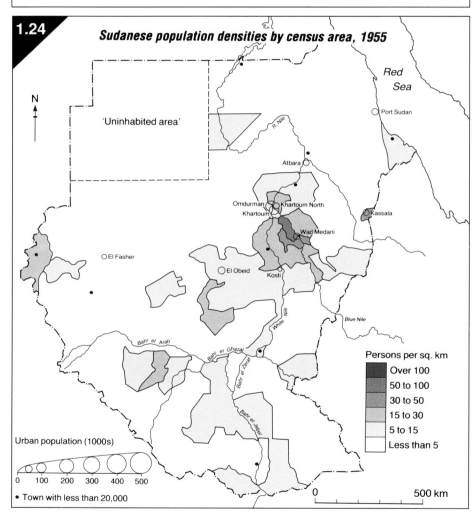

1.24

Sudanese population densities by census area, 1955

Persons per sq. km
- Over 100
- 50 to 100
- 30 to 50
- 15 to 30
- 5 to 15
- Less than 5

Urban population (1000s)

0 100 200 300 400 500

• Town with less than 20,000

0   500 km

used to cover all three.) The second area was Gezira province, stretching south from Khartoum along the Blue Nile. Most of the increases here were caused by extensions to the great Gezira Scheme, e.g. some 535 000 hectares of land were bought under irrigation, from 1955–83.

Away from this central zone, Kassala province in the east was the third growth area. This province benefited from extensive irrigation projects along the River Atbara, e.g. 148 000 hectares irrigated by the Khasm el Girba scheme, whose main purpose was to resettle 35 000 Sudanese Nubians displaced by the lake created behind the High Aswan dam in Egypt. Further increases came from refugees fleeing from famine and war in Eritrea and Ethiopia. Finally, two linear belts of growth can be discerned running west and south-west from El Obeid. These were the result of improved accessibility created by the extension of railways to Nyala and Wau. The westerly belt was further strengthened by migrants moving eastwards from Chad, another country suffering from recurrent political unrest.

In contrast, much of southern Sudan and Northern province astride the River Nile showed very low population growth rates. In the south this was due largely to the long-running civil war between the central government and southern tribal groups. Economy, services and infrastructure have suffered badly. Northern Sudan is arid, there are few opportunities for irrigation and the resource base is poor. Remember too that inundation by the lake behind the High Aswan dam displaced many thousands of people.

Is urbanisation the main cause of growth?

In 1955, only 18 towns, in addition to Greater Khartoum, had populations greater than 10 000. By 1983 this number had increased to 61. As resource 1.23 shows, the urban component increased from 8 per cent to 20 per cent of Sudan's population, with urban settlements growing more rapidly than most rural districts. The highest growth rates of all were recorded in Greater Khartoum, thereby accentuating the primate city structure in the Sudan. The changes in the size ranking list (resource 1.27) reflect the country's changing economy. The reasons for these urban shifts have been explained in this way:

'Sudan's attempts to develop, its dependence upon foreign aid, the needs for imports and the increased role in the country's life of the Arabian peninsula have all

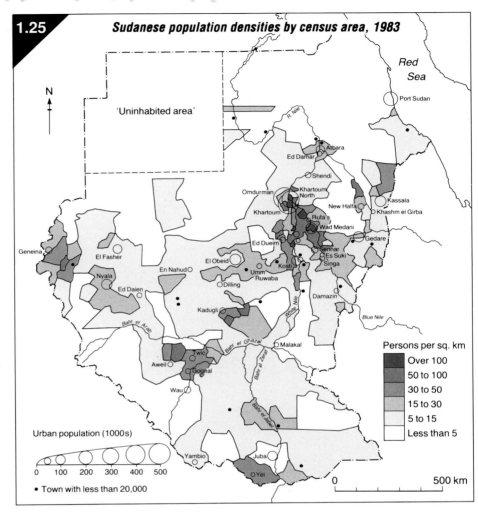

1.25   *Sudanese population densities by census area, 1983*

Urban population (1000s)

0   100   200   300   400   500

• Town with less than 20,000

Persons per sq. km

Over 100
50 to 100
30 to 50
15 to 30
5 to 15
Less than 5

0   500 km

contributed to the growth of Port Sudan. The increased importance of eastern Sudan in general, through development schemes and the influx of refugees, has contributed to the rise of Kassala, and to Gedaref with a six-fold increase from 18 000. The relative decline in the fortunes of Wad Medani and El Obeid also reflect the development process. The Gezira is no longer the only large irrigation scheme, and El Obeid is no longer the western terminus of the railway. Nyala, the new western terminus, has grown from 12 000 to 114 000.'

Some of the highest percentage urban growth rates occurred in southern Sudan, e.g. greater than 600 per cent in five of the six provinces of the south. Yet the south

remains the country's least urbanised region as the high proportional growth was achieved from a very low 1955 base-line.

Is the nomadic population growing?

Nomadism remains the main form of human occupance across the extensive semi-arid and arid environments of the Sudan. Despite government settlement programmes, the numbers of nomads increased from 1.4 to 2.2 million between 1955 and 1983. The largest increases occurred in semi-arid, ecologically fragile western Sudan, e.g. in Kordofan and Darfur, the numbers grew from 660 000 to 1.25 million. This growth coincided with a series of drought years across the Sahel zone of Africa. The combination of

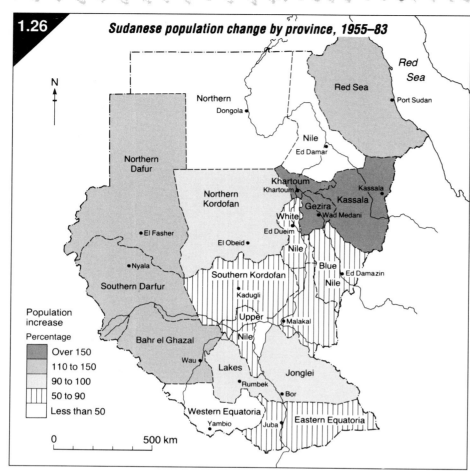

1.26 *Sudanese population change by province, 1955–83*

Population increase
Percentage

- Over 150
- 110 to 150
- 90 to 100
- 50 to 90
- Less than 50

0   500 km

drought years and increasing human and animal populations produced environmental stresses which have led to accelerated desertification and suffering.

(Source: adapted from H R J Davies, 'Population change in the Sudan since independence', *Geography*, 73(3), June 1988, pp. 249–255)

1.27 Sudan's urban ranking

1955	1983
1 Greater Khartoum	1 Greater Khartoum
2 El Obeid	2 Port Sudan
3 Wad Medani	3 Kassala
4 Port Sudan	4 Wad Medani
5 Atbara	5 El Obeid

Activities

1 Write brief answers to the following:

a To what extent are population trends in the Sudan controlled by environmental resources? (NB Remember to consider *other* factors);

b Does the Sudan illustrate a core/periphery structure, and if so, was it being strengthened or weakened during the 1955–83 period?

2 With a partner, consider these two questions arising from your understandings of the Sudan:
(a) Do the demographic patterns and trends of the country support or fit into general models proposed for developing countries, e.g. primate city structures; rapid urbanisation?
(b) Are the changes unique to

the country or are they typical of developing countries? What factors influence the similarities or differences? To answer the second question, you need information on other countries. As a start, study the following report on Sierra Leone: first, list the characteristics of change and the factors influencing them; second, compare them with the Sudan. Now you are in a position to discuss the key question.

Part II: Changing population distribution in Sierra Leone, 1963–85

Basic trends 1963–74–85

Sierra Leone is a small and, by tropical African standards, densely populated country with an overall density of 30 persons per square kilometre in 1963, 38 per sq. km in 1974 and 49 per sq. km in 1985. The major feature of the 1963 population distribution was its relatively even spread, although the capital city Freetown made the density of Western Area more than ten times the national average. Freetown is also the country's main industrial centre and chief port. Relatively high population density in the north-west of the country was also based on the commercialisation of swamp rice cultivation in the lower valleys of the Great and Little Scarcies rivers. Higher density in the south-east was related to cash-crop production, especially of coffee and cocoa, and diamond mining.

The population of Sierra Leone increased by 25.8 per cent between 1963 and 1974. At the provincial level, the Western Area and the Eastern Province had higher rates of increase, the Southern and Northern provinces lower (resource 1.28), leading to some redistribution of population. The district-level analysis shows that during 1963–74 population concentration occurred in favour of the Western Area, which includes Freetown, and Kono District, which contained the large-scale diamond mining activity (resource 1.29).

The 1974–85 intercensal increase in population was 28.9 per cent. At the provincial level only the Western Area's population grew faster than the national average rate. On the one hand there was continuing, and intensifying, spatial polarisation of population in Freetown, whilst on the other hand the diamond mining Eastern province's strong increase of 1963–74 faded during 1974–85. The Western Area increased its share of national population from 11.5 per cent in 1974 to 15.7 per cent in 1985; in 1963 it had been only 8.9 per cent (resource 1.28). By contrast, Kono, the district with the largest diamond mines, increased its population by 95.4 per cent in the first intercensal period, but only by 18.8 per cent in the second.

The reversal of the tendency to concentrate in the provincial diamond mining areas between 1974 and 1985 has resulted in a more even distribution of population in the provinces in 1985 than had been the case in 1974 but less so than in 1963 (resource 1.29).

Trends in diamond mining areas

Diamond mining is significant in influencing population redistribution in two ways. First, by offering wage employment at better levels of income, potentially much higher than those in agriculture, it induces migration. Permanent movement to a mining village or company camp affects national and regional distribution whilst seasonal migration between farm and mining areas can affect distribution at these scales as well as more locally. Second, because of the multiplier effect, the impact of diamond mining is greater than the numbers directly employed in it.

The industry consists of a large-scale or company sector and a small-scale sector divided into licensed and illicit operators. The company sector is relatively insignificant in employment terms with a maximum labour force of around 5000 in 1970.

Throughout the 1970s the National Diamond Mining Company (DIMINCO) struggled to survive in the face of increasing depletion of the alluvial deposits and rising costs of working them. By 1977 employment had fallen to 3250. In August 1982 it decided to close twelve plant operations and make 1500 workers redundant.

The small-scale sector of the industry, working under the Alluvial Diamond Mining Scheme (ADMS), also has been in decline for much of the period under consideration. The number of licences issued declined annually from 1965 to 1975 when it recovered slightly to a level about one-quarter of that in the 1960s. Similarly the number of contributors (the mining labourers who are employed by the licence-holders) has also declined to a level at the end of the 1970s only one-sixth that of the late 1960s and one-third that of the early 1970s. It is notoriously difficult to estimate the number of illicit miners and thus to gauge its significance in influencing changes in the distribution of population.

1.28

Sierra Leone: changing population distribution by province and district, 1963–85

	1963		1974		1985		Intercensal population increase (%)	
	'000	%	'000	%	'000	%	1963–74	1974–85
SOUTHERN PROVINCE	524	24.9	596	21.6	741	21.0	12.1	24.3
Bo	210	9.6	217	8.0	269	7.6	3.6	23.6
Bonthe	80	3.7	87	3.2	105	3.0	9.6	23.5
Moyamba	167	7.7	189	6.9	251	7.1	11.3	24.7
Pujehun	85	3.9	103	3.8	116	3.3	21.1	11.6
EASTERN PROVINCE	546	25.0	775	28.4	961	27.4	41.7	19.4
Kailahun	150	6.9	181	6.6	234	6.7	20.2	29.5
Kenema	227	10.4	265	9.7	337	9.6	16.4	27.2
Kono	168	7.7	329	12.0	390	11.1	95.4	18.8
NORTHERN PROVINCE	898	41.2	1045	38.5	1262	35.9	16.4	17.2
Bombali	199	9.1	233	8.5	316	9.0	23.3	35.5
Kambia	138	6.3	155	5.7	186	5.3	12.6	20.1
Koinadugu	129	5.9	158	5.8	183	5.2	22.4	16.0
Port Loko	247	11.3	293	10.7	329	9.4	18.3	12.5
Tonkolili	184	8.5	206	7.6	248	7.0	11.9	19.8
WESTERN AREA	195	8.9	314	11.5	554	15.7	61.2	76.3
SIERRA LEONE	2180	100.0	2730	100.0	3518	100.0	25.2	28.9

CASE STUDY 1.3 *Population change in the developing world – examples from the Sudan and Sierra Leone*

Urbanisation

Between 1963 and 1974 the larger towns in the urban system – Makeni, Kenema and Bo – grew rapidly and their continued rapid growth between 1974 and 1985, concealed in the data for districts, may explain partly the performance of the districts in which they are located.

The continued trend towards concentration of population in the Western Area, and more particularly metropolitan Freetown (resource 1.30), can be partly explained in terms of urban bias which, through the operation of tax and investment policies, leads to a transfer of resources and population from the rural to the urban areas, for example, the levying of export duties on agricultural crops, the levying of import taxes and excise duties on purchases made by peasant farmers, the pricing policies of the Sierra Leone Produce Marketing Boards (SLPMB) and the former Rice Corporation. SLPMB has consistently offered producer prices considerably below world market prices. The surpluses are transferred to the State and are then expended on consumption and investment but since the 70 per cent of the population who are rural receive only 16 per cent of the public investment, most is expended in the urban areas. Similarly, in order to keep urban food prices down, particularly in the largest market (Freetown), producer prices of rice are controlled and the shortfall in production which results is made good by imports. Thus the peasant farmer subsidises the urban consumer.

Conclusions

Two trends in the spatial redistribution of population in the intercensal period 1963–74 can be identified: a redistribution from rural to urban characterised by increased concentration in the primate, capital metropolitan area; and a redistribution in favour of the diamond mining areas at the

expense of the remainder of the country. Analysis of the 1985 census suggests that the first trend has continued and intensified. The second, however, has been replaced by a much more diffuse pattern of change resulting in a more even distribution of population in the provinces in 1985 than had been the case in 1974. The explanation for these changes is to be found in combined urban bias in policies on the one hand, and a major downturn in the fortunes of the diamond mining industry on the other.

(Source: M B Gleave, 'Changing population distribution in Sierra Leone, 1974–1985, *Geography*, 73(4), October 1988, pp. 351–354)

Metropolitan Freetown

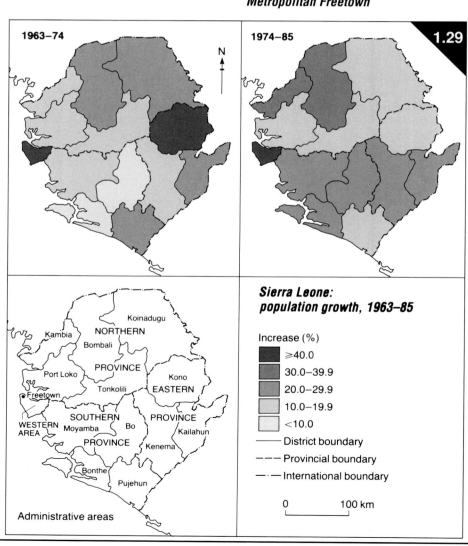

1963–74

1974–85

N

Sierra Leone: population growth, 1963–85

Increase (%)

- ≥40.0
- 30.0–39.9
- 20.0–29.9
- 10.0–19.9
- <10.0

——— District boundary
----- Provincial boundary
—·— International boundary

0   100 km

Koinadugu
Kambia   NORTHERN
Bombali
PROVINCE
Port Loko   Kono
Tonkolili   EASTERN
Freetown
SOUTHERN   PROVINCE
WESTERN Moyamba   Bo
AREA
PROVINCE   Kailahun
Kenema
Bonthe
Pujehun

Administrative areas

CASE STUDY 1.4 *Political conflict and migration – an example from El Salvador*

Background

Wars between countries and internal political and cultural conflicts within countries produce large-scale population displacement. The small Central American country of El Salvador, where civil war has rumbled on since 1979 provides a graphic example of population shifts. At least 250 000 people are believed to have left. As this is largely involuntary, unplanned movement by relatively poor people, the majority have sought refuge in neighbouring countries such as Belize, Honduras and Mexico. In such migrations, many may intend to return to their homeland once a more acceptable and stable political system is in place, a further factor which influences the contemporary short distance moves to nearby countries.

A second type of movement is internal displacement. Political unrest and civil war rarely flare up across a whole country, but are concentrated in certain regions, e.g. where opposition to the ruling government is strongest, perhaps energised by cultural pride, as with the Sikhs in the Punjab, India, or in peripheral districts where rebel groups can obtain supplies and support from across the border, as with the 'Contras' in Nicaragua. People move away from these conflict zones, most intending to return when they feel safe to do so.

A proportion of the displaced people, however, intend to emigrate permanently, either directly, i.e. 'jump' migration, or via an internal move before emigrating, i.e. 'step' migration. For instance, in the case of El Salvador, the primary intended destination is the USA (resource 1.31). This case study assesses whether political unrest alone accounts for this 'push' migration, or whether we also need to consider other factors. In other words, do Salvadoran nationals seeking entry to the USA come only from the regions of intense civil conflict?

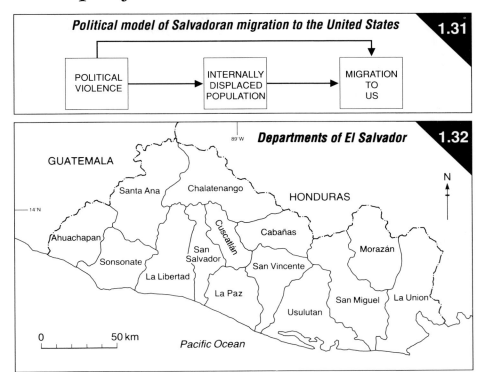

Political model of Salvadoran migration to the United States 1.31

POLITICAL VIOLENCE → INTERNALLY DISPLACED POPULATION → MIGRATION TO US

Departments of El Salvador 1.32

GUATEMALA — Santa Ana — Chalatenango — HONDURAS — Ahuachapan — Cuscatlán — Cabañas — Morazán — Sonsonate — San Salvador — San Vincente — La Libertad — La Paz — San Miguel — La Union — Usulutan — Pacific Ocean

0 50 km

Key understandings

◆ Political unrest may cause involuntary population movements.

◆ Complex migration flows may result from the interaction of political and economic forces.

◆ Official policies make the distinction between 'refugees' and 'economic migrants', which may cause distress to many people.

Patterns of migration in El Salvador

El Salvador is divided into 14 administration areas, called departments (resource 1.32). Resource 1.33 gives the 1981 population (column (b)) of these departments, and four measures which influence the migration pattern. Column (c) is a measure of the level of civil war activity, based on the number of violent incidents e.g. fighting, assassinations, related to the political struggle.

If the level of political unrest was the sole cause of out-migration, then the figures of columns (d) and (e) should correlate directly and positively with column (c). If you rank the departments at 1–14 according to their figures in columns (d) and (e), i.e. according to migration rates, it is clear that the rank orders differ from each other and from that of column (c). Resource 1.34(a), (b) and (c) demonstrates the patterns more simply by plotting extreme values of the figures in the three columns. Again, it can be seen that the departments shaded do not match up neatly.

Thus it appears that political unrest alone is not the cause of migration. For this reason column (f) of resource 1.33 attempts to provide a measure of factors which reduced economic performance. These economic setbacks include 'economic sabotage', particularly the destruction of dams, bridges, roads and electricity stations, strikes, attempts to enforce land reform programmes. Further, the influx of

1.33 El Salvador – Population and aspects of migration

Department	Population (1981 '000)	Nos of violent political incidents 1982–85	Displaced persons resident in October 1983 (rate/hundred thousand pop.)	Migration to USA: 1982–85 (rate/hundred thousand pop. picked up by US immigration service)	Economic setbacks 1982 (nos of incidents which significantly damaged economic performance)
a	b	c	d	e	f
San Salvador (includes the capital city)	1161	32	4500	3.88	18
Morazán	204	20	31 000	1.96	10
Usulutan	419	12	5400	1.91	14
Chalatenango	230	11	9400	0.87	3
San Vincente	208	9	13 800	0.00	5
Cuscatlán	207	8	9600	2.42	6
San Miguel	443	7	2500	4.51	12
Cabañas	182	6	5300	0.00	2
La Union	330	4	1400	5.16	12
Santa Ana	453	2	500	2.07	1
La Paz	253	2	2900	0.79	3
La Libertad	401	1	4200	0.25	3
Sonsonate	337	1	800	0.30	2
Ahuachapán	244	0	600	0.82	1

displaced people may put stress on the economy of a department. Resource 1.34(d) and, in more detail, column (f) above, show that economic conditions were deteriorating most seriously in the eastern half of the country. Comparison of resource 1.34(c) with 1.34(d), and columns (e) with (f) indicate that the majority of unauthorised migrants trying to gain entry to the US were from these economically disrupted departments, only some of which were enduring intense political unrest. Notice, however, that many of the so-called 'economic setbacks' were connected to politically motivated incidents, e.g. the blowing up of bridges by opponents of the government.

It seems, therefore, that the migration can be accounted for by a combination of political conflict and deteriorating economic conditions. People may be affected differently, and make different decisions, but the main types of movement are summarised in resource 1.35. Three main migration streams have been identified:

'Poor villagers from the northern zones who migrated to Honduras and Belize; poor villagers from the northern and central regions who became internal refugees in the departmental capitals; and better-off, more urbanised persons from eastern departments and San Salvador who went to the United States'.

The stream of emigrants from El Salvador to the USA illustrates the complex distinction between a 'refugee' and an 'economic migrant.' Most countries, including the United States, have signed international conventions whereby they give asylum to refugees. However, the US Immigration and Naturalisation Service (INS) generally operates a tight definition before refugee status is granted: the person must prove that he or she faces 'a clear probability of persecution for reasons of race, religion, nationality, membership of a particular social group, or political opinion'. Throughout much of the 1980s, the INS turned away more than 90 per cent of would-be Salvadoran migrants because they failed to prove this possibility. The INS regarded them as economic migrants seeking a better quality of life, and therefore subject to the quota system operating. This created controversy through opposition from action groups including Churches, the American Civil Liberties Union and

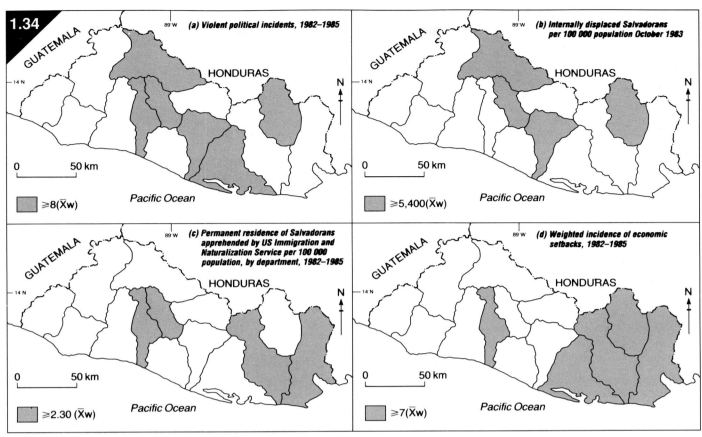

1.34

(a) Violent political incidents, 1982–1985

GUATEMALA
HONDURAS
89°W
14°N
N
0   50 km
Pacific Ocean
■ ≥8(X̄w)

(b) Internally displaced Salvadorans per 100 000 population October 1983

GUATEMALA
HONDURAS
89°W
14°N
N
0   50 km
Pacific Ocean
■ ≥5,400(X̄w)

(c) Permanent residence of Salvadorans apprehended by US Immigration and Naturalization Service per 100 000 population, by department, 1982–1985

GUATEMALA
HONDURAS
89°W
14°N
N
0   50 km
Pacific Ocean
■ ≥2.30 (X̄w)

(d) Weighted incidence of economic setbacks, 1982–1985

GUATEMALA
HONDURAS
89°W
14°N
N
0   50 km
Pacific Ocean
■ ≥7(X̄w)

the US Committee for Refugees, who claimed a much higher proportion were genuine refugees. Clearly, danger and threat are not always easy to prove, and there are many other examples, e.g. Tamils from Sri Lanka seeking residence in the UK; the Vietnamese 'Boat People' using Hong Kong as an intended stepping stone to Europe, North America or Australia; until 1989, people from Eastern Europe seeking asylum in 'the West'.

(Source: adapted from R C Jones, 'Causes of Salvadoran migration to the United States', *Geographical Review*, 79(2), April 1989, pp. 183–194)

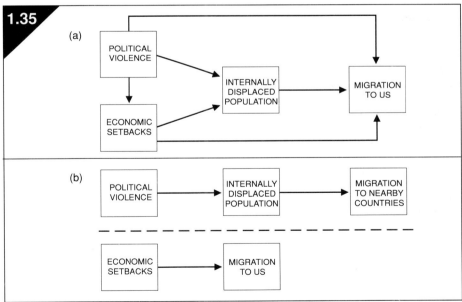

1.35

(a)

POLITICAL VIOLENCE → ECONOMIC SETBACKS
POLITICAL VIOLENCE → INTERNALLY DISPLACED POPULATION
ECONOMIC SETBACKS → INTERNALLY DISPLACED POPULATION
INTERNALLY DISPLACED POPULATION → MIGRATION TO US
POLITICAL VIOLENCE → MIGRATION TO US
ECONOMIC SETBACKS → MIGRATION TO US

(b)

POLITICAL VIOLENCE → INTERNALLY DISPLACED POPULATION → MIGRATION TO NEARBY COUNTRIES

ECONOMIC SETBACKS → MIGRATION TO US

Activity

Use the data in resource 1.33 to test these hypotheses:

a There is no relationship between level of political unrest and migration rates.

b Migration can be explained by economic conditions in a region.

Select appropriate scattergraph/regression techniques and correlation methods to test the direction and strength of relationships. Remember to test for statistical significance. (Check the availability of micro-computer statistical packages helpful in your calculations and plotting.)

CHAPTER 2

Making spaces for places – the decision making process

Introduction

In small, crowded countries such as Britain and Japan, where every hectare is owned and used, land and water space are scarce resources. Stated simply, scarcity exists when demand exceeds supply. Scarcity leads to competition and the greater the resource scarcity the more intense the likely competition, e.g. when there is a housing shortage, with more buyers available than there are houses for sale, house prices rise, as does the price of land. (See Chapter 3.) It is in such conditions of resource scarcity that 'resource management' becomes vital (resource 2.1).

Management of land and water resources operates through a fluctuating tension between **market forces** (what competitors are prepared to pay) and the **planning system**. When it was introduced in the 1940s by several major acts of Parliament, the British planning system was meant to control and direct development in our cities and countryside. Today it still aims to do so, but actually works through a process of negotiation and 'deals' between the various interested parties. This process has been based upon three main changes in the planning system since the 1940s:

1 **Planning gain** Local authorities are increasingly able to secure some public advantage from granting planning permission to a developer, e.g. a private housing developer may be required to provide sufficient land for a new school.

2 **Public participation** Town and Country Planning Acts passed in 1968 and 1972 have made it possible for the public to have a much stronger voice in the planning process, e.g. individuals and pressure groups can make representations to planning committee meetings.

3 **Developer participation** Since the late 1970s, developers have been given the right to work with planning departments in identifying land suitable for development.

The term 'development' means some change in the way land is used, e.g. from farming to housing, from one type of industry to another, and so requires planning permission. The case studies in this chapter identify the individuals, groups and institutions involved in this process and the roles they play in decision-making within the framework of the planning system.

Resource 2.2 is a typical example which illustrates the complexity of planning

Management
The rational allocation and organisation of resources in accordance with a consistent set of principles, priorities and procedures.

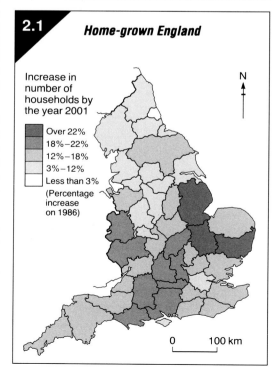

2.1 *Home-grown England*

Increase in number of households by the year 2001

- Over 22%
- 18%–22%
- 12%–18%
- 3%–12%
- Less than 3%

(Percentage increase on 1986)

N

0   100 km

Waterside haven or 'cesspool'?

A conservation group opposes plans to build a barrage across Cardiff Bay and replace the tidal mudflats with a freshwater amenity lake.

The bay at low tide is haunted by a few wading birds, such as tern and dunlin. Ornithologists say these species would not take kindly to their brackish hunting ground becoming a freshwater marina and leisure water park.

The 500-acre lake's water will not be fresh, even though it is fed by the rivers Taff and Eley, for both are heavily polluted by raw sewage, industrial effluent and phosphoric overflows from treatment works along the way.

The new lake would require 'slurp' machines to harvest green algae, and oxygenation to stop it smelling. The lake would also raise the local water table level, endangering cellars in Cardiff.

The Cardiff Bay Development Corporation claim: 'Water-buses may ply their trade across the 500-acre freshwater lake created by the Cardiff Bay Barrage, expected to start building in 1991 following its passage through Parliament this year.'

Opponents of the scheme, led by the Royal Society for the Protection of Birds, agree that the whole of this area of South Wales, urgently needs

to be redeveloped. They have produced an alternative plan which would provide a 'quality living waterfront to attract developers, leisure boat facilities, sea front, access and a nature reserve.' The RSPB's proposal includes a barrage, to create a waterfront venue for restaurants, but this one is a tenth of the size of that proposed by the CBDC.

The waterfront factor is what attracts housing developers. The new lake is clearly intended to hype property values, but the protesters say that the cost of the barrage has already risen from an estimated £85 million to £140 million, bringing the infrastructure bill to £547 million of Government money.

Broadly speaking – barrage or no barrage – the whole urban regeneration scheme will provide 6000 new homes, of which 25 per cent will be low-cost housing, the CBDC claims; and there will be 30 000 new jobs created over the next decade.

Volume builders are already committed to the area. A consortium, consisting of Beazer, Barratt and Westbury, promise that the Windsor Quay development – the first major housing scheme on the western side of Cardiff Bay – would be opening show houses in July. One-bedroom flats will be around £55 000; four-bedroom town houses, £160 000.

(Source: Michael Dineen, *The Observer*, 22 April, 1990)

issues, the intensity of feelings generated and the totally opposed perceptions of single proposals. This summary of the Cardiff Bay barrage proposal identifies the four main elements involved in most planning and environmental issues: (i) the State – central and local government and their agents, committees etc; (ii) commercial companies; (iii) special-interest societies; (iv) environmental conservation groups. (The last two elements often work as a single pressure group.)

The purpose of the planning system is to provide a consistent, democratic and fair framework within which decisions can be taken (resource 2.3). The case studies in this and later chapters make it clear that reality is much less straightforward: government policies fluctuate or favour some interests rather than others; people and institutions vary in their ability to influence the decisions. The lack of clarity is illustrated in case study 2.1 by recounting the problems met by a football club in the apparently simple task of finding a new ground. Case study 2.2 sets out a model which may help you in analysing planning issues and in improving your skills in decision-making exercises. Case study 2.3 focuses upon one of the most important elements of post-1945 planning strategy – the Green Belt, and assesses its effectiveness in the zone of most intense conflict, surrounding London. Case study 2.4 uses Manchester to examine the part played by land-ownership and availability in inner city redevelopment.

The planning procedure

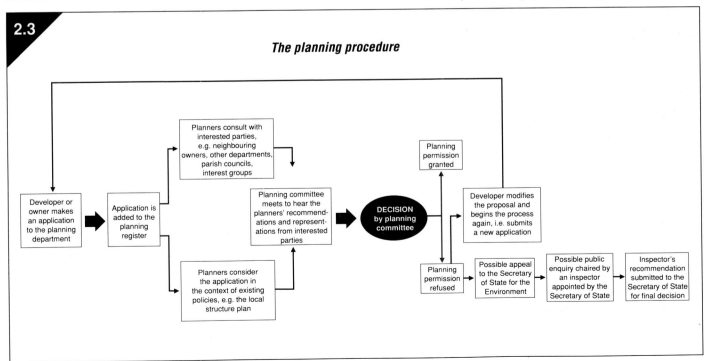

CASE STUDY 2.1 *The planning system at work – an example from Southend*

Background

In a crowded country like Britain, owning land does not automatically mean that you can develop it as you wish. Your neighbours, other interested parties, one or more local councils, or even central government, may each have opinions about how the land should be used. They can express these views through the planning system, and so influence the decision-making process. Planning laws, regulations and procedures are intended to ensure that valuable land resources are used sensibly, so that the proposed development will fit into the surrounding pattern of land uses, will not damage the environment nor the quality of life for neighbouring people unnecessarily.

For these reasons, development proposals must go through the planning process outlined in resource 2.3. Major schemes may require an Environmental Impact Assessment (EIA), measuring the likely economic, social and environmental effects of the proposal.

This may seem a good example of democracy at work: decisions arrived at as a result of discussions in which everyone has an opportunity to participate. There is, however, a reverse side to the coin. What seems a straightforward and sensible scheme may become bogged down for years as different interest groups use the system to achieve their own ends.

Key understanding

◆ When land is scarce, obtaining permission for development is likely to be a complex process, involving people with different interests and responsibilities.

Activities

1 Construct a table of events. Begin with the initial proposal, its nature, location and reasons. Then set out each stage in turn, identifying what the proposal was; where it was located; who were the 'players' (who objected or supported the proposal) and what were their views and attitudes.

2 What appear to be the strengths and weaknesses of the system for allocating land resources illustrated by this case study?

2.4

Playing the planning game: the struggle to build a football stadium for Southend United

Last week, in the aftermath of Hillsborough, *The Sunday Times* called for a radical programme to effect the rebuilding of Britain's crumbling soccer stadiums. Fundamental to our proposals was the establishment of a body which we called the Football Development Agency, which would be able to cut through the red tape of local-government bureaucracy. If ever proof was required of the need for such an agency, it is surely provided by the case of Southend United, who have been trying to get permission to build an improved stadium for four years, during which time the price has increased by £4m.

Vic Jobson, the Southend chairman, committed the club to the building of a stadium on a greenfield site when he took over the club five years ago. He found the Roots Hall stadium – which was built in 1955, and therefore, at least chronologically, was the most modern in England – in a state of desperate disrepair. Terraces were subsiding. Seats, where they existed, were cramped and wooden. Exits were narrow and restricted. The crush barriers were constructed out of ageing, splintering wood or hollow steel tubing that shook to the touch, and two sides of the ground had roofs clad in asbestos.

Rebuilding was a matter of survival. Since Southend were already deeply in debt, the only way to finance the rebuilding was to sell the Roots Hall site and use the proceeds to build another stadium elsewhere.

The easy part was designing the stadium. A firm of Canadian consultants designed a multi-purpose all-seater stadium to the latest safety standards. It would be concrete, with wide exits, cantilevered stands, extensive car parking, and a moat that would stop pitch invasions and serve as a safety route out of the ground. Finance would come from selling Roots Hall to the Tesco group and developing sports and social facilities underneath the new stadium.

Then, as Jobson, a property developer knew it would, the local-government nightmare began. Southend had found a suitable greenfield site near Southend airport. Rochford borough council expressed approval for the scheme, but objections were soon raised. The proposed site was too near the airport. And mineral-excavation rights had not been adequately respected.

Reluctantly, Jobson agreed to find another site. Enter Southend borough council, Rochford's neighbours, who suggested a disused site a mile from Roots Hall. Johnson re-submitted his plans, with additional proposals for an athletics track and market alongside the stadium. Then Rochford council objected. The site as a whole straddled the Rochford and Southend boundaries, but the football ground was entirely within Southend, which meant a loss of prestige, and rates, for Rochford. Jobson therefore relocated the scheme on the Southend side of the boundary. It was too near the crematorium, several Southend councillors protested. So Jobson re-located again, moving the site half a mile from the crematorium.

Enter Essex county council highways department. The site which solved the airport problem, the mineral-rights problem, the Rochford rates problem and the crematorium problem, had inadequate roads. Jobson found yet another solution. The club would pay for improved roads.

Southend council finally approved the project. But nothing could be done to implement this victory. By then a Department of the Environment inquiry had started, and was being vigorously lobbied by parties interested in archaeology, farming and graveyards. All these groups were adamantly opposed to Southend's new stadium.

There was even opposition within the local football community, from a group of Southend fans who believed Jobson was using the stadium scheme for his own financial benefit. In vain did he point out that his company was not involved in the scheme, and that Tesco had long since been replaced by a housing scheme, thereby diminishing the amount that could be realised from the sale of Roots Hall.

Some time this summer, the DoE inquiry will report, and Jobson and Southend may get their dream stadium. The delay has added £4m to the cost.

(Source: Chris Lightbown, *The Sunday Times*, 30 April 1989)

CASE STUDY 2.2 *Do the good guys always finish last? A model for comparative study*

Background

The model set out here presents the planning process as a competitive 'game' with a set of 'players'. Each of the players has a role and strategies which they adapt according to the nature and stage of the game, i.e. they 'play the system'. Sometimes certain players will co-operate to out-manoeuvre another player. The model suggests that while the planning process is supposed to provide all interested parties (players) in the competition with an equal change of winning, it is how skilfully and powerfully the game is played which determines the outcome. Actual planning applications become decision-making exercises played for real, where the strategy is as important as the proposal. Remember, that like any generalised model, it provides only a framework, not a detailed structure, to assist the examination of specific planning issues.

The model is based on a study of housing development pressures in Central Berkshire between 1976 and 1986 (resource 2.5). This area was given 'growth area' status in the 1970 South-east Regional Strategy, which was a signal from central government that local plans should

include opportunities for extra employment and housing. With its proximity to London, Heathrow airport and the M4 axis, this part of Berkshire has been subjected to intense development pressures. In 1961, the population was 251 000, by 1981, it was 400 000. During the early 1980s, central government was insisting that by 1990, land for at least 40 000 additional houses should be made available through local planning policies. This has led to a series of fiercely fought battles, from which the key players in the 'development game' are easily identified.

Key understandings

◆ The key interest groups involved in planning development issues are: (i) the state, (ii) commercial developers and associated professionals, and (iii) voluntary pressure groups, local and national.

◆ The planning process can be manipulated by skilful or ruthless players.

◆ Identification of the roles, objectives and strategies of the important players is essential for an analysis of planning issues.

The players and their strategies

I The developers

Their goal is to obtain planning permission. These speculative builders and development companies submit planning applications for particular parcels of land to the local planning authority. They hope to obtain planning permission with the minimum limitations and conditions. After local residents and other interested parties have been given an opportunity to submit their opinions on the application, the local planning committee comes to a decision. If planning permission is denied, the developer may give up, or modify the scheme and resubmit or appeal against the decision. If the developer appeals, then central government appoints an inspector and an enquiry is held at which all the interested parties may present evidence. The inspector presents the decision in the form of a report which may reject the proposal, approve it with conditions, or approve it subject to the agreement of the Secretary of State for the Environment.

Clearly, the first tactic of the developer is to identify parcels of land where the opposition to development from other players is likely to be weak. Once the land has been identified, however, developers fall into four major types, according to the strategies they adopt. Resource 2.6 summarises their tactics and character.

A crucial factor then, is how the developer probes the system and what carrots they are prepared to offer, such as environmental improvements, infrastructure and so on, i.e. planning gain.

II The volunteers

Local people join together into 'action groups' with the intention of influencing planning decisions. They

2.5 Central Berkshire in a regional context

N

Bedford
Banbury
Saffron Walden
Stevenage
Colchester
Luton
Aylesbury
Hertford
Harlow
Clacton
Hemel Hempstead
St. Albans
Chelmsford
Oxford
Watford
High Wycombe
Basildon
Slough
Greater
Southend
M4 Reading
Heathrow
London
Margate
Central Berkshire
Bracknell
Staines
Dartford
Chatham Gillingham
Newbury
Aldershot
Canterbury
Basingstoke
Reigate
Maidstone
Guildford
Ashford
Tunbridge Wells
Dover
Folkestone
Crawley
Winchester
Southampton
Hastings
Chichester
Brighton
Eastbourne
Poole
Portsmouth
Bournemouth

0   50 km

––– Outer metropolitan area, post 1974
------- Outer south east, post 1974

2.6 Model showing types of developers

HIGH

CAUTIOUS
These players adopt cautious tactics and are usually small companies who buy and submit applications for fairly safe sites, especially ones with existing outline planning permission. Risky or controversial applications are rare. These players lack the skills and resources to interact closely with the planning system beyond submitting the application. Their competent yet cautious tactics give them a fairly high success rate.

NEGOTIATORS
These are highly skilled and well-equipped players, they are mostly large firms with resources which allow them to probe and interact with the planners, councillors and opposition groups at all stages. They prefer large sites and are prepared to persist with risky applications. They use the appeals mechanism well and are quick to adapt their strategy when opposition is met, e.g. by the use of the 'planning gain' tactic. Their skills and patience then give them a high success rate.

APPLICATION RATE

EXTENT TO WHICH PLANNING POSSIBILITIES ARE PROBED

LITTLE ←→ **A GREAT DEAL**

PLANNING SUCCESS

NAIVE
There are only a few of these players, who lack the skills necessary to play the game successfully. They are very small companies who submit hopeful or careless applications without sounding out the 'opposition' or the planning application carefully beforehand. Their lack of skills and resources prevents them from using the appeals system effectively. Their 'work rate' in attempting to influence the planning process, and their success rate are both low, but their costs too, are low.

AGGRESSORS
These are energetic, but relatively unskilled players. Although they have considerable knowledge of the game, and push hard upon the planners and councillors, they are impatient and often lack the resources to persist. They may choose unusual and risky sites and may be content with obtaining outline planning permission before selling on a profit, e.g. to 'cautious' or 'negotiator' players. Their overall success rate is low.

LOW

2.7 Green belt test for Patten

A plan to release 800 acres of land for development around Chester has presented a direct challenge to the Government's green belt policy. The Council for the Protection of Rural England, has asked Mr Chris Patten, the Environment Secretary, to review the proposals put forward by the city council, and backed by Cheshire county council. His decision will be important as the choice, which will be watched by local authorities and developers everywhere, is between housing estates and business parks, and the need to preserve features which make Chester an international heritage city – its Roman walls, cathedral, medieval Rows, and Tudor buildings.

Mr Tony Burton, the CPRE's planning officer, said: 'If you continue to expand the city, the people … in the green belt have to go in to shop, and the traffic congestion would cause serious problems.'

But a senior city council planning officer said: 'If we don't get that land, there will be deterioration of the urban environment, high-density development in the city, a lack of funds for transport improvements, and pressure for building in villages, open countryside and North Wales

Planners also fear Chester will lose job opportunities, and housing will become more scarce and expensive.

However, the CPRE doubts that the plan covering parts of the green belt would create jobs for local people, 'Because vacancies will be filled by incomers.

(Source: Michael Morris, *The Guardian*, December 2, 1988)

may encourage the involvement of national special-interest lobbies such as the Royal Society for the Protection of Birds (RSPB), or the Council for the Protection of Rural England (CPRE) (resource 2.7). These group players usually focus their game plans around one or more of the three aspects of environment: the **physical environment**, which is the form and distribution of buildings, roads, open spaces, woodlands; the **social environment** which is the social and demographic characteristics of the local population; the **resource environment** which is the location and accessibility of facilities such as schools, shops, and recreation areas.

These group players fall into three types according to their objectives and strategies: stoppers, getters and stopper-getters (resource 2.8).

III The state

These players fall into two categories: central government, which is concerned with directing overall policy through laws, guidelines and financial targeting, and local authorities who adopt tactics to interpret government policy to suit local needs. Both categories contain two types of player, each with their own roles and priorities. First there are the elected representatives such as MPs and local councillors, and second there are the professionals, the civil servants and local authority officers. Central government agents tend to act as coaches or referees, and so it is the local officers who become the key players, along with the elected councillors who sit on the planning committee.

This planning committee, made up of local officials and elected councillors, with the councillor chairperson as the key play-maker, adopts five main tactics:

1 Resist the growth

They try to reject the application outright. This is often difficult because of the appeal procedure. Thus, this may be used as a delaying

2.8

Stoppers

They are concerned with preventing further development and with protecting the quality of their local environment. They tend to be found in the more 'exclusive' urban neighbourhoods and especially in rural villages, and to have moved in within the last 20 years. They see further enlargement of their settlement as bringing noise, traffic and perhaps people of a different type, thereby threatening their property prices and 'way of life'. They are the NIMBYs, the 'Not-in-my-backyard' viewpoint, which believes in development, but somewhere else! In Berkshire, they were found to be 'middle-class, middle-aged, owner occupiers'.

Getters

Their game plan is built around gaining improvements in their social and resource environments. They are found most commonly on recently-built housing developments and their aim is to generate community unity and involvement by campaigning for the provision of community and health centres, schools, bus services an so on. If they get what they want, they may become 'stoppers'.

Stopper-getters

Their game plan is flexible, they aim to stop growth but are prepared to compromise if they get something in return, such as amenity woodland or improved services. These players are scattered in different environments and tend to be opportunists.

All of these group players base their strategies on keeping a close check on the planning system locally: for example monitoring local papers and planning committee meeting minutes. Once a planning application to which they object is submitted they will gather together and submit a formal objection to the planning authority. They may maintain telephone contact with planning officers to obtain more details, they may lobby local councillors, they may bombard the local press with letters. Clearly, these groups are not popular with the other players.

---

tactic while negotiations go on for a better 'deal'.

2 Deflect the development

Here, the tactic is to accept the inevitability of development, but try to move its location or alter its character. This shifting of growth may bring neighbouring district councils into conflict, where the one district is trying to push unwanted development into the territory of the other. This, in turn, is likely to anger the 'volunteers'.

3 Deflect the blame

If the planning committee opposes an application, but is forced to give consent, despite the views of individual concillors (players), then the blame must be shifted. Speeches, reported in the local newspapers, are made, condemning the decision and transferring the blame to central government or civil servants.

4 Control the development

This tactic by the planning committee is based on the premise: 'If it can't be altered, then it must be planned'. The planning committee becomes involved in the details of the development, such as density, layout and design. Again, it benefits councillors to get publicity for these efforts so that they can show that they are doing their best to control development, even if they can't stop it.

5 Planning gain

This is an extension of the previous tactic, in that the committee tries to extract some sort of gain or recompense from the developer in view of the costs and losses imposed on a local community. This could include for example, offsite drainage, road improvements, amenity woodland, footpaths, and free site provision for schools.

Developers are aware of this tactic and may include it in their original submission if they think it will help their changes of success (resource 2.9).

Activity

With a partner: Resource 2.9 mentions Rainham Marshes, which lie along the Thames Shoreline, east of London. This issue is the focus of resource 2.10.

(i) Read the two extracts carefully.

(ii) Analyse this issue in terms of the model set out in the case study, e.g the players and their tactics.

(iii) What is the proposed 'planning gain' in the Rainham Marshes issue?

2.9

Building conservation into the planning equation – are planning 'gains' all that they seem?

The rise of 'green consciousness' towards the end of the 1980s meant that environmental issues became a much more potent factor in the planning stakes. Added to the ever-increasing difficulty which developers have in getting planning permission, the conservationists would appear to be gaining the upper hand. The need to discover ways of combining conservation and development at a local level is becoming ever more pressing.

But as with most issues involving the environment, these apparent planning gains made by the conservationists have other costs.

County nature conservation trusts are already becoming involved at early stages in proposed developments. For example, the Berkshire, Buckinghamshire and Oxfordshire Nature Trust (BBONT) has acquired a number of reserves, particularly gravel pits, from developers. They are approached by developers before they lodge a planning application, and asked if they would like to take on the management of a site as a nature reserve. The trouble is that if they agree, it could imply that they support the application. It could be assumed that a conservation body has endorsed the scheme and that the development is 'friendly' to the environment and wildlife. This is rarely the case.

The gains are frequently less than they seem at first. For example, turning a disused gravel pit into a reserve is not a gain as the site was unlikely to be useful anyway – a number of conservationists feel that they just get the awkward bits of land that developers can't use.

BBONT now looks for more solid evidence of commitment from developers. For example, at a site near Wokingham, where ARC wants to develop a golf course and some retirement homes, the trust has agreed to manage a meadow and woodland, with a £75 000 fund which allows the site to be opened up for educational purposes.

The Council for the Protection of Rural England would like environmental concerns to be incorporated into planning conditions. Commitments would be required from applicants, before permission is given, rather than conservation being attached subsequently as a marketing ploy or a public relations exercise.

The Rainham Marshes scheme has put the conservation aspects of planning at the top of the agenda. British Urban Development's plan to develop a large area of the marshes – a site of special scientific interest, also proposes a trust fund to acquire and manage other grazing and sites beside the Thames (see resource 2.10). The environmental and wildlife bodies do not believe that the wildlife and special flora of Rainham Marshes should be bargained for with protection of other areas. Protection of the area itself must be absolute.

2.10

Conservationists lose battle over theme park

A £2 billion theme park and film studio on Rainham Marshes, east of London, can go ahead, allowing the destruction of an important wild life site, Chris Patten, the Environment Secretary, decided yesterday.

The development, which MCA International says will create 20 000 jobs, will destroy 70 per cent of the 1200-acre Site of Special Scientific Interest, the largest near London. Conservation groups were appalled by the decision, saying it created a precedent which encouraged developers to cast aside environmental issues.

The development, called Universal City, has already been approved in outline by Havering district council. It includes 110 acres of film and television studios and theme park; four hotels; 2.4 million square feet of business park and industrial development, offices and shops; 2000 houses and flats; and a 175-acre riverside nature and leisure park.

MCA and their partners, British Urban Development and the Rank Organisation, have begun site evaluation. The company said the development could still go to northern France if the site was not suitable.

Tony Young, the company president, said he was delighted by the decision and hoped that conservationists would now co-operate with the development of a 428-acre nature reserve on the site.

Philip Hurst, of London Wildlife Trust, said: 'This decision makes a mockery of the protection of SSSIs afforded by the Countryside and Wildlife Act. These safeguards are now seen as pretty meaningless. This is a premeditated destruction of a vital habitat. Mr Patten is fast losing his green veneer.'

David Pritchard, of the Royal Society for the Protection of Birds, said: 'Six hundred acres of this SSSI will now be destroyed at a stroke, but Mr Patten has not called this in for a public inquiry. Issues of principle have been raised, it is a matter of national importance and yet it has been left to the local authority to make a decision when it has a vested interest in it going ahead.

Michael Spicer, Planning Minister, said Mr Patten had noted that development in the area would be consistent with his strategy to redress the economic imbalance between the east and west of London, and with the Greater London Development Plan. He had considered carefully the significant effects for nature conservation of the development, in particular within a SSSI, but had concluded that it was appropriate for the application to be decided by the local planning authority.

(Source: Paul Brown, *The Guardian*, 6 April 1990)

CASE STUDY 2.3 *Watch this space! Policies and perceptions in Green Belts*

Background

Green Belts have been an element of national and local planning policies since the 1940s. They have always aroused controversy, as their goal is to control development around the fringes of major towns and cities – those zones where pressures for and against development are strongest. Three important issues arise. First, what does Green Belt policy set out to do? Second, has it worked, and if not, why not? Third, what are people's perceptions of the Green Belt, and what do they think its purpose should be?

In April 1989, *Which?* magazine 'interviewed a representative national sample of 2300 adults in their homes, to find out about their attitudes to the Green Belt.' The August 1989 edition included the results of this survey as part of an article which explored the three issues raised above, and which is included in the first part of this case study.

Here are two suggestions to help you make best use of the case study materials:

1 *Which?* magazine represents the 'consumer lobby' and hence presents a distinctive viewpoint, i.e. that of the 'ordinary citizen'. So, remember that planners or developers may have different viewpoints.

2 The *Which?* article provides an excellent basis for an **individual or group project** or a **decision-making exercise** on your local, or an accessible, Green Belt. It gives pointers to sources and to components of the study. Remember – do not be too ambitious. Select a sector or even an individual development proposal for examination.

The second part of the case study focuses upon the Colne Valley, a linear strip in London's Green Belt, with particularly complex pressures, where policy has been based upon the creation of a Regional Park.

Key understandings

◆ Green Belts surround many major British cities, and aim to prevent urban sprawl, protect the countryside and help urban regeneration.

◆ Green Belt policy aims are difficult to achieve because of the intense competition for these attractive urban fringe land resources.

◆ There is much public support for a strong, protective policy, but equally strong pressures for development.

◆ Most Green Belt land is privately owned, and public access is limited.

◆ There are a number of sites of low environmental quality scattered across the Green Belts.

◆ There are opportunities in the planning process for people to participate in the decision-making.

2.11

The city of Oxford is surrounded by precious Green Belt land

Activities

1 Make two lists:

a Those who are likely to support a strongly protective Green Belt policy, and why. (Consider individuals, groups, institutions.)

b Those who are likely to press for development on Green Belt land, what type of development, and why.

2 Why are areas in the Green Belt liable to become neglected?

3 a In a small group:

Discuss whether you think Green Belts are a good idea, and what are the alternatives?

b Discuss ways in which public access to Green Belt land could be increased.

4 Construct a labelled flow diagram describing the planning process, indicating clearly where members of the public can become involved.

5 Use the example of the Colne Valley Regional Park (pages 35 – 36) to illustrate:

a The problems created by the diversity of land uses crowded within the Green Belt.

b How the chosen plan attempts to solve the above problems.

Part I: Attitudes to Green Belts

The facts

- There are fifteen Green Belts in England, covering almost 4½ million acres or 14½ per cent of the country. Their size varies from 2000 acres (Burton-on-Trent) to 1 200 000 acres (London). In Scotland there are five, covering almost 335 000 acres (resource 2.13). Northern Ireland has Areas of Special Control, which are now being replaced by Green Belts – so far there are two.
- Not all open land around a city or separating towns is Green Belt – only if it's been given that status in local authority plans. The Government approves their broad outlines, but exact boundaries are defined by local authorities.
- It's not impossible to build on Green Belts. But the policy is not to allow it, unless it can be shown there are exceptional circumstances or if it's for a use considered suitable for a rural area.
- Not all Green Belt land is green and pleasant – some areas are neglected and run-down.
- Most Green Belt land is not open to the public. It's mostly privately-owned, and the public has no special rights of access.

The aims

The Government currently lists five aims for setting up Green Belts. These are to:

- check the sprawl of large built-up areas
- safeguard the countryside around towns from further building
- stop neighbouring towns merging
- make sure the character of historic towns isn't spoilt by too much modern building
- help urban regeneration (the idea is that by preventing the outward expansion of towns and cities, more developers will invest in declining inner-city areas).

Track record

Green Belts seem to have been successful in their primary aims of preventing urban sprawl and saving open land on the edge of cities from development. But they may be a mixed blessing in other respects.

Development is pushed out to the countryside … Since controls on building in the Green Belt are so strict, development must happen elsewhere. The rest of the countryside doesn't have the same kind of protection as the Green Belt, so developers are attracted to build there instead. Restricting building in the Green Belt means a greater likelihood of development in the rest of the countryside.

… and into the city Green Belt restrictions also mean more pressure on space in the city. Developers, particularly in London, are building houses and flats on patches of open land such as back gardens and playing fields. High property values encourage this trend. Open space disappears and people live at higher densities.

Higher property prices? It's argued that the Green Belt makes property prices higher by restricting the supply of land. So people who couldn't afford to buy houses in the city have had to move out to towns beyond the Green Belt. In turn, this means longer and more expensive journeys to work. (Remember, though, that property prices are decided by a number of complex factors; Green Belts may be one reason for them going up.)

So what's the answer?
For Green Belts to work, there need to be other policies to plan where people, jobs and houses should go. One solution, promoted by the Town and Country Planning Association, is that instead of adding to existing towns and villages, completely new settlements should be built. This has had some support from the Government, developers and other organisations. But if any such scheme is to work properly, it must fit into a broad, long-term, plan.

Public support for Green Belts
As resource 2.12 shows, our survey results show strong public support for continuing strict controls on Green Belts – and little support for the arguments of people who want

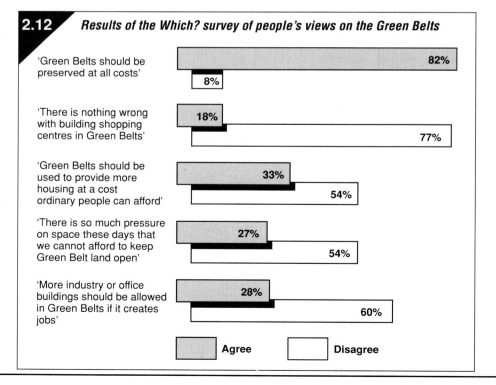

2.12 *Results of the Which? survey of people's views on the Green Belts*

'Green Belts should be preserved at all costs'
- Agree: 82%
- Disagree: 8%

'There is nothing wrong with building shopping centres in Green Belts'
- Agree: 18%
- Disagree: 77%

'Green Belts should be used to provide more housing at a cost ordinary people can afford'
- Agree: 33%
- Disagree: 54%

'There is so much pressure on space these days that we cannot afford to keep Green Belt land open'
- Agree: 27%
- Disagree: 54%

'More industry or office buildings should be allowed in Green Belts if it creates jobs'
- Agree: 28%
- Disagree: 60%

☐ Agree   ☐ Disagree

to relax them to provide new homes and jobs.

We also gave people different reasons for setting up Green Belts and asked them how important they thought they were. They said the two most important reasons were to preserve the special character of the countryside, and to provide green space for people to enjoy. They gave these higher priority than the principal aims of the Green Belt.

The threat from development

Simply because land has been designated Green Belt doesn't mean it can never be built on. Planning permission may be given if a sufficiently good case is made.

In the south-east the main pressures for development are:

- **New housing** The number of households is expected to rise by 14 per cent between 1986 and 2001. 570 000 new houses or flats will have to be provided between 1991 and the end of the century
- **Major development projects** These include the Channel Tunnel, Stansted airport and further development of Heathrow. They will bring more business to the south-east, increasing demand for housing and services
- **The M25** It's already had an impact, cutting right through the Green Belt for almost all its length. Further land will be taken to widen it and to build service stations, and new shopping and business development is likely
- **Disused hospitals** As a result of Government policy to close hospitals for mentally ill and handicapped people, large sites will become vacant over the next few years. It's estimated that there are 20 of these sites in the London Green Belt.

And it's not only in the south-east that there's pressure on the Green Belt. In Chester, the local authority has proposed rolling back its Green Belt to supply land for housing and light industry (see resource 2.7 on

2.13

Green Belts in England and Scotland

N

0   100   200 km

page 28). York plans to cut its Green Belt to allow for more housing and factories.

Changes in farming

Green Belts throughout the country will be affected by major changes in farming. The Government is asking farmers to produce less food. It's encouraging farmers to take land out of production and to look at new ways of adding to their incomes – for example, by providing recreation facilities, or setting up farm shops or craft industries.

Government policy

The Government has said that it has a strong commitment to Green Belt policy. This commitment is tested when developers who are refused planning permission by local

authorities appeal to the Secretary of State for the Environment. He has turned down several appeals that have attracted a lot of public interest.

The threat from neglect

Problems like pollution and vandalism can make land on the edge of the city difficult to farm or manage, and some Green Belt landowners have allowed their land to get run-down and neglected. Parts of the Green Belt are spoilt by eyesores such as:

- rubbish tipping
- derelict buildings
- gravel pits, open mines and quarries
- disused railway lines.

People in our survey took a hard line on the responsibilities of landowners to clear up their property; 86 per cent agreed they should be forced to tidy up derelict land.

The majority of people in our survey agreed that Green Belts should be used more for recreation, even if this means they become less peaceful.

Taking action

The Countryside Commission has helped local authorities set up country parks in Green Belts to encourage people to visit. It's now promoting the creation of 'community forests' – woodland open to the public, on former run-down land.

Groundwork Trusts restore derelict or poorly used land with the help of volunteers and business sponsorship. The land is turned into parks, nature reserves, play areas, and so on. Local people can get involved in work such as planting trees and clearing ponds, mapping guided walks and designing leaflets.

Local authorities can have an important role in improving Green Belts, even when they don't actually own the land. The Countryside Commission helps them do this by paying part of the salary of project officers, who work with local landowners to improve the landscape and facilities for the public.

Local authorities can also help by:

- maintaining public footpaths
- providing public transport
- negotiating for public access
- providing information on places to visit.

But who pays?

Finding the money for improvements is a problem. One way is for local authorities to work with developers, using the cash from a commercial project for the benefit of the community. An example is Stockley Park in Hillingdon, West London. Part of a derelict site is being developed into a business park while the rest is to become a golf course, park and playing field.

Objecting to a proposed development

If you are unhappy about a proposed development, you can object to planning permission being granted.

When the application is made

1 The developer puts in an application to the planning authority. It's placed on the planning register open to the public. The local authority doesn't have to inform the public directly except in very limited circumstances, although some do by advertising in the local press, writing to those affected or putting up notices near the site.

2 If you want to object, find out from the planning department when the deadline for objections to reach them is. Give the facts about how it will damage the area; for example, it may increase traffic.

Check if the application fits in with policies in the structure plan, and the local plan, which defines exact Green Belt boundaries. These plans are available at the town hall or the planning department. They also show whether the site has any other official designation, such as Area of Outstanding Natural Beauty. If so, point this out.

Try to get support from other people and organisations and encourage them to object too. Contact your local councillor and the chaiman of the council's planning committee – the planning department will give you their names and addresses.

3 The planning committee, made up of councillors, will consider the application. You should be allowed to attend the meeting, although not speak. Your objections should be considered.

4 If permission is given, there's nothing you can do.

5 If the application is refused, the developer can appeal to the

Secretary of State for the Environment. If either side insists or there's a lot of public interest – probable in the case of a proposal to build on the Green Belt – then a public inquiry is usually held.

If there's a public inquiry

6 At the inquiry the developer and the planning authority put their cases, call witnesses and cross-examine each other. As a third party you don't have the automatic right to appear and cross examine witnesses but in practice the inspector will let you.

7 Prepare your case thoroughly. You can carry out your own research – for example, a survey of the number of people using an open space. You can employ professionals, such as planners or lawyers, either as expert witnesses or to present your case. This can be expensive. The other side will probably have batteries of professional advisers – your evidence will have to stand up to their cross-examination.

8 At the end of the inquiry, the inspector considers all the evidence and writes a report. It's usually about nine months before you'll hear the decision.

(Source: 'The Green Belt', *Which?* August 1989, pp. 388–391)

2.14

Chester Business Park. The local authority has put forward proposals to use its Green Belt land for new housing and light industry

Part II: The Colne Valley – a close look at the struggles within London's Green Belt

Surrounding London is Britain's largest and most complex rural-urban fringe zone, where competition and conflict between different users are most intense. The outcome is a complex mixture of land uses which has been called 'the mess on the fringes'. The segment of London's western fringe shown on resource 2.15 shows that despite more than 30 years of 'protection' by the Green Belt, extensive areas are 'damaged' or 'threatened'. Yet within this 'mess', there are areas where great efforts have been made to control change, provide public access and to maintain environmental quality. One such area is the Colne Valley Regional Park (X on resource 2.15).

The principal motive behind the setting up of the Colne Valley Regional Park in 1967 was to make more positive use of the urban fringe, and to rehabilitate the landscape. In 1971 a plan for the 'future landscape' of the park was published (resource 2.16). It was an attempt to organise the confused land uses in this 25 km north-south strip, tightly hemmed in by urban development, Heathrow airport and crossed by the M4 and M40. Emphasis was placed upon providing public access and recreation opportunities, e.g. water recreation on reservoirs and upgraded disused sand and gravel pits. A second emphasis was to be on landscape quality and conservation, e.g. woodland, wildfowl sanctuaries, maintenance of agriculture.

Resource 2.17 shows the situation in the mid-1980s: despite 15 years of planning, the park remained under intense pressure. The most fundamental change has been the construction of the M25, which sliced through the length of the park. It dominates the landscape and disrupts local patterns of accessibility, but, of course, the park provided the only relatively open,

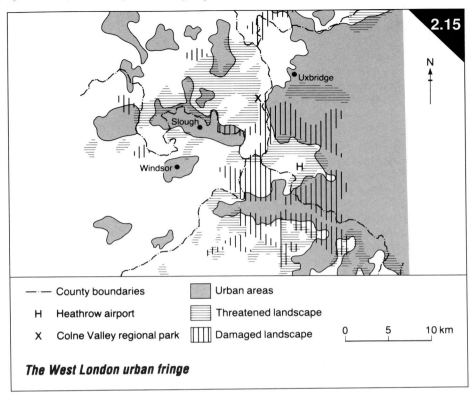

2.15

--- · — County boundaries

H Heathrow airport

X Colne Valley regional park

Urban areas

Threatened landscape

Damaged landscape

0   5   10 km

The West London urban fringe

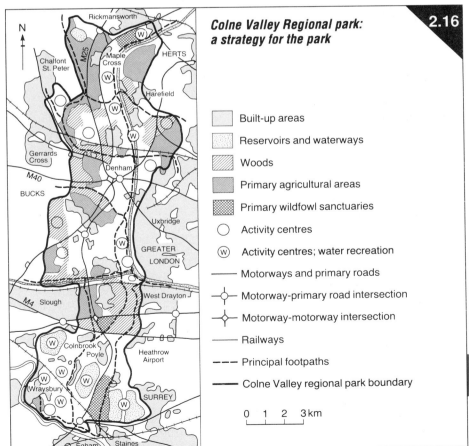

2.16

Colne Valley Regional park: a strategy for the park

Built-up areas

Reservoirs and waterways

Woods

Primary agricultural areas

Primary wildfowl sanctuaries

◯ Activity centres

Ⓦ Activity centres; water recreation

—— Motorways and primary roads

—◇— Motorway-primary road intersection

—◈— Motorway-motorway intersection

—— Railways

--- Principal footpaths

—— Colne Valley regional park boundary

0   1   2   3 km

undeveloped, corridor around the western fringe of London. Motorway construction and the south-east's building boom led to extensive new sand and gravel workings. Yet there had been successes, for example, water-based recreation on old gravel pits, wildfowl reserves and footpath networks.

A survey of a small area in the north of the park (A on resource 2.17) reveals the extent of the change even in areas not crossed by the M25 (resource 2.18). Despite designation and protection as a Regional Park within the Green Belt, change has been considerable, especially urban development and enlarged sand and gravel working at the expense of agriculture. The net effect is one of immense disorder and confusion, with rapid transition from rural tranquility to urban industrial chaos in a very short distance. Notice how limited is public access, although there are several private open spaces.

(Source: adapted from A M Blair, 'Future landscapes of the rural-urban fringe', in D G Lockhart and B Ilbery (eds) *The future of the British rural landscape*, Geobooks, 1987)

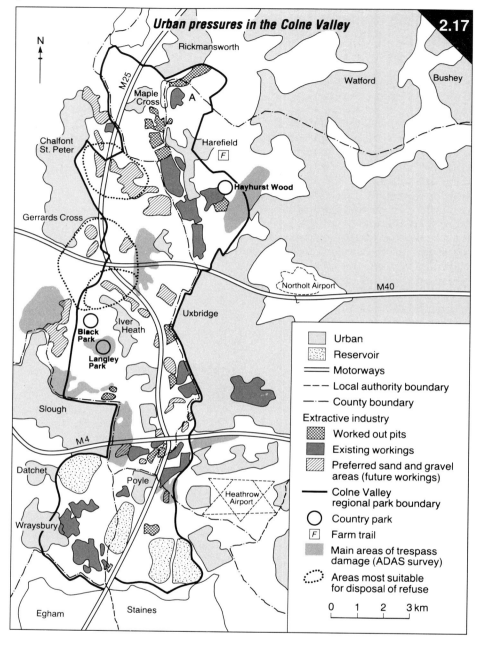

Urban pressures in the Colne Valley 2.17

Legend:
- Urban
- Reservoir
- Motorways
- Local authority boundary
- County boundary
- Extractive industry
  - Worked out pits
  - Existing workings
  - Preferred sand and gravel areas (future workings)
- Colne Valley regional park boundary
- Country park
- F Farm trail
- Main areas of trespass damage (ADAS survey)
- Areas most suitable for disposal of refuse

0 1 2 3 km

Activities

1 'The rural-urban fringe … has elements of traditional agricultural landscape next to rapidly urbanising landscape, and new agricultural landscape is only a road's width away from disturbed and neglected waste. Planning has certainly not solved the urban-fringe landscape problem'.

Use the evidence in this case study to illustrate what this statement means and suggest reasons why planning seems to have failed in such areas.

2 **Group discussion**

The model in resource 2.19 explains the types of rural-urban fringe in terms of four main forces which generate change

and character: urban economy, agricultural economy, agricultural policy, and countryside planning. As shown around the outside of the diagram, each of these forces can range from 'strong' to 'weak', and will fluctuate over time. By using combinations of the relative strengths of the forces, the model identifies four types of urban fringe: Sector 1 – disturbed landscapes, Sector 2 –

neglected landscapes, Sector 3 – simplified landscapes, Sector 4 – valued landscapes.

In a group: study the model carefully, and then discuss how the model may be used to help explain the patterns, trends and problems revealed in the Colne Valley Regional Park.

NB You may find this model useful as the basis for a coursework/fieldwork project.

2.18

Land use change, south of Rickmansworth, Colne Valley Regional Park, 1949–82

USE	1949 (hectares)	1982 (hectares)	% Change
Agriculture	769	640	−17
Urban	246	307	+25
Woods	111	106	−45
Open space	76	87	+14
Water	72	102	+42
Public utilities	47	64	+36
Derelict	33	43	+30
Extractive	30	23	−23

2.19

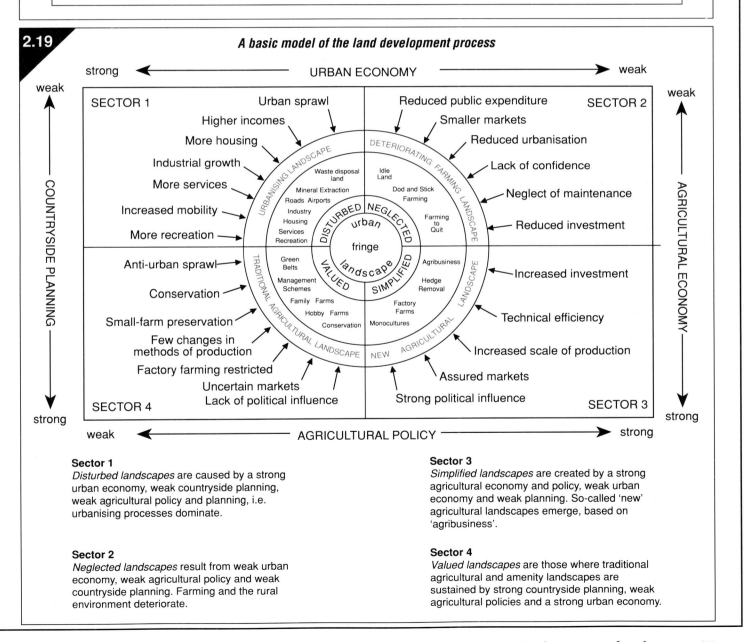

A basic model of the land development process

Sector 1
Disturbed landscapes are caused by a strong urban economy, weak countryside planning, weak agricultural policy and planning, i.e. urbanising processes dominate.

Sector 2
Neglected landscapes result from weak urban economy, weak agricultural policy and weak countryside planning. Farming and the rural environment deteriorate.

Sector 3
Simplified landscapes are created by a strong agricultural economy and policy, weak urban economy and weak planning. So-called 'new' agricultural landscapes emerge, based on 'agribusiness'.

Sector 4
Valued landscapes are those where traditional agricultural and amenity landscapes are sustained by strong countryside planning, weak agricultural policies and a strong urban economy.

Background

In a small, crowded country like Britain there is intense competition for space. Demand for land is greater than available supply, and land prices rise (see case study 2.3, pages 31-37). Yet as you travel into a city centre, and sit gazing out of the window of the car, bus or train, you may see the tracts of empty land and wonder why they are there. At any moment in time, there is a surprisingly large area of vacant land in many inner cities. Making the same journey perhaps a year later, you may still see the same block of land lying empty, or under temporary use – as an open car park or a waste dump. While it is inevitable that there will be some time lag between the ending of one use on a block of land and the development of a new use, one of the most difficult problems in many inner city areas has become the length of time sites lie vacant (resource 2.22). When a site is vacant it is not producing income, providing jobs, homes or access and is likely to downgrade the local environment, although a few derelict sites have become valuable nature reserves or informal recreation areas (resource 2.20).

During the 1980s local authorities and their planning committees were being squeezed by twin pressures: on the one side the construction industry demanded the release of land for development; on the other side, residents were mounting increasing resistance to further land release. One problem has been that the greater pressures both for and against development are on peripheral, greenfield, sites (resource 2.21). One government response has been to emphasise the Green Belt policy in parallel with a relaxation of planning controls and support of developments in inner cities, with schemes such as Urban Development Grants, Enterprise Zones, Derelict Land Grants, and Urban Development Corporations in London's Docklands and Merseyside.

2.20

Urban farm, Small Heath, Birmingham

Despite such encouragements, most industrial cities still have considerable totals of vacant land in their inner areas. One influential factor is whether the land is easily available. In the planning context, 'available land' is defined as land which 'is free from, or can easily be freed from, ownership, planning and physical constraints'. The study of six wards in inner Manchester in this case study illustrates the influence and effects of the four main hurdles a developer has to overcome:

- Ownership of the site.
- Planning policies and requirements.
- Physical characteristics of the site.
- Land prices.

2.21

Developers look north for bites at the green belt

Large tracts of countryside in England's North and Midlands are coming under intense pressure from developers looking for alternatives to the overcrowded southeast.

In the West Midlands four councils, Birmingham, Solihull, Warwickshire, and Hereford and Worcester, have chosen three 100-acre pieces of attractive Green Belt land which they want to use to entice hi-tech industry.

Alan Weban-Smith, Birmingham's assistant director of development, said: 'We know the Green Belt is an emotive and sensitive issue and developing it causes resentment. But we have grasped the nettle to try to give the area a future. 'We wouldn't fritter away these premium locations for anything less than excellent reasons.'

Coventry, like other boroughs in the West Midlands, has been asked by the government to find 100 acres of land for hi-tech development on a prime location. Harry Joble, Coventry's director of planning, insists that the city has 'run out of land' so that it too is having to look at 100 acres of Green Belt for development.

Other areas are under similar pressures. Barnsley is facing a request from one of its most prestigious businesses, Mercedes Benz, to extend its northern distribution depot by taking up 25 acres of Green Belt. Wakefield has just allowed Coca-Cola Schweppes to built part of its newest and largest bottling plant in Europe on Green Belt land.

York, one of the North's most fashionable cities, is creating special problems for authorities controlling its hinterland, such as Ryedale and Selby. A planning application exists for 400 houses to be built on Green Belt to the south of the city. The residential pressure on York has also prompted a building firm to propose a 4500-home development for nearly 15 000 people on the edge of the city. A similar plan to build a new town of 6000 homes near Wetherby threatens to destroy the tranquility of villages between Leeds, York, and Harrogate.

The proposal has drawn angry opposition from local pressure groups and Spencer Batiste, Conservative MP for Elmet. 'What it would mean is the beginning of the end of the rural communities between Leeds, York and Harrogate,' he said.

(Source: *The Sunday Times*, 20 November 1988)

2.22

The scandal of Britain's wasteland

State industries leave thousands of acres derelict, while the Green Belt areas are turned into building sites

Less than half a mile from Nottingham city centre, old rolling stock defaced with graffiti stands idle on a rusting line in 30 acres of abandoned railway sidings.

For the past 10 years, mattresses, burnt sofas and tyres have been strewn over the lines that once formed the nerve centre of the Great Eastern Railway.

Nottingham city council despaired of ever encouraging British Rail to release the land, which includes two listed buildings. Its planning officials lobbied MPs, cabinet ministers and the chairman of BR. Yet all their efforts failed to result in action.

So, after three years of tortuous negotiation and letters that never received replies, the council decided to make a compulsory purchase order.

Within three weeks, BR submitted four planning applications to transform the site with housing, light industrial units and parkland.

The sudden change of heart came as no surprise to Richard Blenkinship, the city's chief planning officer. 'British Rail is a past master of the art of delay,' he said. 'But you have to keep trying'.

The bureaucracy of British Rail and other public sector bodies is particularly frustrating for city planners who want to attract new light industries and create jobs.

'We have new business asking us for sites, yet British Rail, the Central Electricity Generating Board, British Coal and British Gas have all refused to sell us land,' said Blenkinship.

The public utilities, the old nationalised industries, and the newly-privatised companies are among the biggest landowners in Britain. But they also have thousands of acres of wasteland because of decades of lax management.

Since the early 1980s, when the government set up a register of unused public land, the spotlight has been thrown on the six biggest landowners – British Rail, with an estimated 7500 acres of derelict land, British Coal (9500 acres), British Steel (2000 acres), British Waterways (2000 acres), British Gas (1500 acres), and the Ministry of Defence (2500 acres).

The disposal of the land has been a laborious process often complicated by a lack of demand, local planning rows and the cost of removing toxic substances or other contaminants.

At Bell Green in south London, the people of Selworthy Road know all about the problems of contamination. The smell from a partly disused gas works near their houses hangs heavy in the air and over their lives.

British Gas, which owns 1500 acres of derelict land, says that 18 acres of the site is surplus to requirements. But Lewisham council has ruled that it may not sell it until it cleans up pollution which is endangering the health of children who play nearby.

Scientists commissioned by the council have found that poisons including lead, cadmium, arsenic and cyanide, from coal tar used at the gas works have seeped into the river bed and bank, but residents' attempts over the past three years to get the land cleaned up have come to nothing.

Susan Smith is anxious about her daughter Zoe, 12, who plays in the park by the river. 'You get a lot of kids throwing each other in,' she said. 'Occasionally I walk the dogs, but now I won't let them off the lead in case they head for the water.'

A couple of hundred miles away Thornton Briggs, a retired miner, stares out of his lounge window down the valley at a blackened scar of 20 acres where Cortonwood colliery used to stand in Rotherham, South Yorkshire.

'There's nothing more depressing than having a useless wasteland on your doorstep. The heart's been torn out; surely someone can put it back,' he said.

British Coal, which abandoned the colliery in 1985, has sold the land to a private developer who will do nothing with it unless he can get government money to restore it.

The blight of Cortonwood is repeated all over Rotherham, with more than 40 eyesores covering 700 acres. Two-thirds of the land designated for industry is derelict.

Rotherham council is receiving several million pounds of government money to restore much of this land. Yet, a few miles down the road, it has been trying to put new factories on 165 acres of green belt because reclamation takes so long and the developers prefer greenfield sites.

In some cases the government itself has prevented the sale of sites owned by nationalised industries to maintain the apparent value of their assets in the run-up to privatisation. Staffordshire county council was prevented from buying a derelict sewage works near Cannock because the DoE did not want to take land from Severn Trent Water Authority before it was privatised.

(Source: *The Sunday Times*, 4 February 1990)

Key understandings

◆ Vacant inner city land is a dynamic phenomenon, part of the continuous flow of land through the development process.

◆ Sites vary in their **dynamism** – the speed with which they move through the process.

Vacant land in inner Manchester

Once one of Britain's most prosperous industrial and commercial cities, Manchester has endured several decades of increasing unemployment, especially in manufacturing industry. Many industrial premises are of poor quality and there are numerous vacant plots previously occupied by now demolished factories and warehouses (resource 2.23). In addition, there are extensive areas of former terraced housing, removed under slum clearance programmes of the 1960s and 1970s, and because of the tightening of the city's finances, never replaced. Resource 2.24 shows the vacant land situation starting in 1978, when the Inner City Partnership programme, organised by central government and local authorities, was set up. Notice that although by 1984 the total area of vacant land had been reduced from 695 hectares to 530 hectares, this reduction was due entirely to environmental improvement and open space schemes on publicly owned land. The total of privately owned land remained stubbornly around 100 hectares (1 hectare = 2 hockey or football pitches)

Most land vacancy lay in an area to the north, east and south-east of the central business district. A survey of six wards in this zone for 1978–84 identified 384 sites greater than 0.2 hectares vacant **at some time** during this six year period. By the end of the survey period, one third (135 sites), totalling 157 hectares had been developed, while two thirds (249 sites), on 294 hectares still lay

2.23

Is developing vacant land creating new jobs?

In March 1990, Norman Willis, the president of the TUC launched an inter-union recruitment drive in Trafford Park.

Trafford Park, covering around 1200 acres, a couple of miles west of Manchester, is one of eleven Urban Development Councils (UDCs) which were given greater financial and planning power by the government during the 1980s in order to revitalise derelict areas.

Founded in 1896, Trafford Park employed 75 000 people during the second world war. By the 1980s, although more than 600 companies still employed 24 000 people, large patches of derelict land blighted the area.

Large tracts of land are still empty, shops are tatty or boarded up and the few public buildings (two churches, a school, baths and a public washhouse) have been closed.

A recent report on the north-west economy concluded that the gain of 47 new companies and around 700 new jobs, was 'not spectacular', especially given the closures and redundancies which have continued across the area.

At present, the busiest sectors of the local service industry appear to be the King Arthur's Court takeaway, and a church made of corrugated tin which offers confessions at any time by appointment.

Despite the unprepossessing material to hand, in 1990 the Trafford Park Development Corporation forecast optimistically that thousands of new jobs would flow into a revived 3000 acres, fuelled by £160 million of public money, at the centre of an unrivalled academic, business and communications network.

However, a think-tank study published at the same time, suggested that UDCs had 'barely scratched the surface of relating physical development to the pressing needs of the local labour market' and that they have paid more attention to the quantity of dereliction cleared than to the jobs created as a result.

vacant. The survey analysed all of the sites in terms of the four obstacles to development set out on page 38 to try to find out why certain sites stayed vacant and why others were developed. Resource 2.25 sets out the basic framework of the processes in terms of a systems model. Notice that the speed with which the vacant land moves through the process is influenced by the demand-supply relationship. If demand from industry is high, then the energy in the system is great, and drives vacant plots over the 'hurdles' relatively quickly.

The land ownership hurdle

The ownership of a vacant plot of land clearly has great influence on its fate. In trying to understand how owners will behave, we need to examine their motives. There seem to be two basic types of owners. First, **passive owners** are those who

do not hold land for a specific development purpose but might be persuaded to sell if circumstances (mainly price) are correct – people such as historic landowners and speculators. Second, **active owners** are those who hold land for the purpose of development. A vacant plot is likely to be developed more quickly if it is owned by an active owner or can be bought by one.

As resource 2.26 shows, 240 hectares out of a total of 294 hectares of vacant land in the six ward study area were owned by public bodies. As predominant land owner, Manchester City Council policies become crucial. The survey found that the council is an 'active' owner:

'Manchester City Council owns almost 60 per cent of all vacant land in the study area ... Between 1978 and 1984, the local authorities combined disposed of

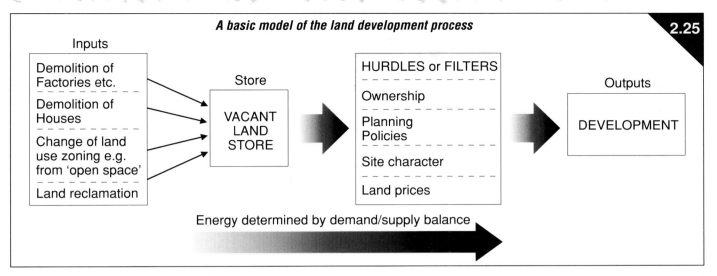

A basic model of the land development process

2.25

Inputs

| Demolition of Factories etc. |
| Demolition of Houses |
| Change of land use zoning e.g. from 'open space' |
| Land reclamation |

Store

VACANT LAND STORE

HURDLES or FILTERS
- - - - - - - - - -
Ownership
- - - - - - - - - -
Planning Policies
- - - - - - - - - -
Site character
- - - - - - - - - -
Land prices

Outputs

DEVELOPMENT

Energy determined by demand/supply balance

Vacant land, 1978–1984 (hectares) 2.24

	1978	1984
Publicly owned	598	426
Privately owned	97	104

26 hectares of vacant land in the six wards for new development and acquired a further 28 hectares of vacant land, primarily for reclamation. Indeed, the City Council in particular has played a major role in recent years in recycling inner city land and buildings. This involves the acquisition of some of the worst examples of industrial dereliction from existing owners in the private sector, followed by clearance and the provision of infrastructure and subsequent marketing for new development. Any loss is financed by derelict land grants. The City Council is therefore … a major factor in the inner city land market, both as a purchaser and a vendor.'

Within this policy, there are three key decisions. First, whether to **release** vacant land to private sector developers. The survey found that while the Council makes land readily available for industry and commerce this is less true for housing: 'The large scale City Council ownership of vacant land in Inner Manchester now acts as a constraint to private residential development'. Second, the **terms and conditions** on which the Council releases land. Usually the Council retains the freehold and releases land on 99-year leases. This has not deterred industry, but has discouraged private house developers. Third, the **price** at which the land will be sold.

For privately owned vacant land, a major factor in determining its real availability has been uncertain or multiple ownership. The complexities of locating and negotiating with several owners may deter a potential developer. Also, small, awkwardly shaped sites, each separately owned, may occur next to each other, requiring further complex negotiations. Manchester City Council has played an important role in sorting out such problems and assembling blocks of vacant land for purchase.

The planning hurdle

All developments are subject to planning permission. The Conservative government which came to power in 1979, believed that one factor influencing inner city decay nationwide was over-rigid use of planning regulations. In consequence, a series of guidelines and directives were sent to local authorities. For instance, a DoE circular in 1980 stated:

2.26

Vacant land ownership in inner Manchester, 1984 (Six Wards)

Public	Area (Hectares)	Private	Area (Hectares)
Manchester City Council	173	Housing Associations	1
		Companies	46
Greater Manchester Council	15	Charities/Trusts/ Churches	5
British Rail Property Board	39	Private individuals	1
Gas/Electricity Boards	12	No information	1
Other	1		
Total public	**240**	**Total private**	**54**

'Development Control must avoid placing unjustified obstacles in the way of any development, especially if it is … relevant to the economic regeneration of the country.'

The 1978–84 survey in inner Manchester found that local policies were not holding back development of vacant land:

> Although … grandiose road proposals and large scale slum clearance programmes in the 1960s and 1970s contributed to the creation of extensive land vacancy in the inner city, there is little evidence that current planning policies are responsible for its continued existence. The City Council has adopted a flexible and informal approach to land allocation in contrast to the rigidity of the original development plans. … Informal land allocation decisions are effectively made by a working party of council officers which meets regularly and which reports to the City Planning Committee.

This informal system of land allocation is helped by the Council's extensive land ownership, and in 1984, more than 50 per cent of the vacant land was allocated for either industry or housing, and there was no shortage of available land, in planning terms. However, 'few major proposals have come forward from the private sector in the study area for industrial or commercial development, apart from those involving … out-of-centre shopping. Only in attempting to control this particular form of new development can current planning policies be described as a constraint.'

The physical site hurdle

A developer of a 'brownfield' inner city site often faces two major problems not found on a 'greenfield' urban fringe site. ('Brownfield' is a term used by planners to describe sites which have experienced at least one previous urban/industrial land use.) First the developer may need to remove the legacy of previous

2.27

Site	Problems
1 Ground conditions	e.g. foundations; subsidence
2 Site size and shape	e.g. too small or the wrong shape.
3 Buildings	e.g. presence of existing buildings, of unsuitable character
4 Services	e.g. absence of connections to water, sewage, gas, electricity supply
5 Internal access	e.g. no roads within the site
6 External access	e.g. poor connections to the district highway network
7 Adjacent site uses	e.g. noisy or noxious industries on neighbouring sites

uses, and second the new development must be fitted into the existing urban fabric. Resource 2.27 lists seven internal and external physical constraints typical of inner city sites. In inner Manchester a detailed survey of 50 sites (25 which remained vacant; 25 which had been developed) was made, using the seven factors. As resource 2.28 shows, the sites remaining vacant suffered from twice as many site constraints as the developed sites, (1.2 constraints/site, compared with 0.6/site). The survey concluded that the longer a site remained vacant before development, the more likely was it to have been physically constrained.

The land price hurdle

When a seller of land sets a price higher than prospective developers are willing to pay, then the site will remain vacant, unless there is some kind of government grant or subsidy available. Furthermore, it seems reasonable to suggest that when the supply of land exceeds demand, prices will fall. As the 1978–84 period 'was one of unprecedented decline for the Manchester economy' and by 1984 'demand for land in the study area had reached an all-time low', it was surprising 'that despite the mounting supply of industrial land on the market and the evident lack of demand, little downward

2.28

Number of sites affected by constraints

	Sites now developed (Total: 25 sites)	Sites still vacant (Total: 25 sites)
Ground conditions	7	11
Site size and shape	–	4
Buildings	4	3
Services	2	1
Internal access	2	3
External access	–	3
Adjacent site users	–	5
Total	15	30

movement in industrial land prices was identified for the study period.'

Both private owners and the Council rely on professional valuers to set the asking price, and these valuers were slow to recommend lower valuations: for most of the 1978–84 period, land prices remained at £35–45 000/acre. As a result, this 'unrealistic approach to inner city land pricing … can delay the inner city development process'. In inner Manchester, therefore, this time-lag between a fall in demand and a drop in land prices arose from an understandable reluctance by the seller to lower the price, and the tendency of the valuation system to quote unrealistically high values. Hence, land price was a significant constraint upon the development of vacant land. This has been an important factor during the 1989 – 1992 economic recession.

The following conclusions were reached by the survey:

1 'In Inner Manchester, the main constraints to the availability of land for development appeared to be the reluctance of passive owners to part with their land at other than relatively high prices and the existence of problematic site conditions, rather than any restrictions imposed by land planning policies'.

2 'Whereas in Inner Manchester, the public sector dominates the pattern of land ownership, and is involved in most land transactions, public land policies are critical in setting land prices … and in ensuring the availability of land for development through recycling vacant and derelict sites'.

3 'Irrespective of policies adopted, low levels of demand by industrial companies 'would still deter many developers from the inner city'.

(Source: adapted from C D Adams, A E Baum and H D McGregor, 'The availability of land for inner city development: A case study of Inner Manchester', *Urban Studies*, 25 (1), February 1988, 62–76)

Activities

1 Why should the City Council not wish to discourage large new shopping developments in the inner city?

2 A visitor to many of Britain's cities could well be struck by the amount of land lying empty.

   Use the Manchester materials to: (a) write a summary of the reasons for this, and (b) suggest how the 'recycling' of derelict land could be speeded up.

3 **Coursework project**. Investigate a local 'derelict' or 'disused' site, using the elements indicated in the Manchester study as the basis for your investigation. What questions would you need to ask, and from whom would you seek answers?

CHAPTER 3

Places for living – housing in the UK

Introduction

The character, distribution and availability of housing stock remain vital elements in our quality of life. The two providers are the private and the public sectors, and individuals can rent or buy dwellings within either of these sectors. The revolution in the relative distribution of the three main types of home tenure is summarised in resource 3.1.

Since the end of the Second World War, governments have stressed improvement in the quality and quantity of housing for all groups in society, as a central element of policy. Until the late 1970s such policy had two major thrusts. First, the private sector was encouraged to provide dwellings for ownership. Thus, the private rental sector, which had been so important was squeezed by strengthened controls. Second, the public sector would provide for rental tenure, through local authority housing programmes and the building of large council estates, supported by massive, though fluctuating, financial aid from central government.

From the late 1970s, as the case studies in this chapter show, this basic framework has been fundamentally disrupted. The principal reasons have been the Conservative government's strong belief in home ownership and a shift away from the large-scale provision of housing by local authorities. The results are seen clearly in resource 3.2, where all regions of the UK show the increasing dominance of the private owner-occupied sector, and reductions in the local authority and private rental sectors.

Housing Associations are organisations which receive government financial support for building or renovating dwellings for rental, usually giving priority to targeted groups such as the young.

The bases of the policy change have been as follows:

- The Right to Buy legislation of 1980, which gave council tenants the opportunity to buy their homes at discounted prices (see case study 3.1).
- A reduction in central government funding for public housing.

- Restrictions placed on local authorities to use the money raised from swelling sales to build new homes or renovate existing stock.

The outcome of this legislation is shown starkly in resource 3.3. Nationally, annual building rates in the private sector rose by more than 50 per cent while completions in the public sector were down by 61 per cent. Furthermore, regions varied widely in their rates of building, the extent of change and the balance between the private and public sectors (compare the figures for the four parts of the UK).

Demand remained high throughout most of the 1980s, especially in economically prosperous areas such as London and south-east England. As a result, house prices rose more rapidly than inflation (resource 3.4, columns (e) and (f)), fuelled partly by escalating land costs (columns (a) and (b)), making buying the land an increasing component of the total house price (columns (c) and (d)). The combination of economic prosperity, demand and competition for land, planning policy and environmental protests cause startling regional contrasts, for example between the Yorkshire/Humberside area and London and the south-east.

The case studies in this chapter explore these regional trends and differences, and allow us to examine in particular, three popular perceptions about the 1980s:

1 That there was a widening in the differences between London and the south-east and the rest of the country (the north/south divide, and Britain as a land of 'two nations').

2 That housing problems were increasingly concentrated in London and the south-east.

3 That there was greater polarisation between the 'haves' and the 'have-nots'. The 'haves' were those people who could afford to buy into private ownership. The 'have-nots' were the poor and deprived whose only opportunity was in the shrinking housing stock of local authority renting (resource 3.5).

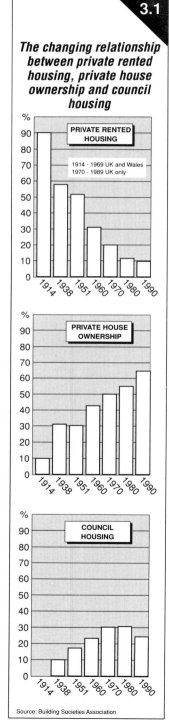

3.1

The changing relationship between private rented housing, private house ownership and council housing

PRIVATE RENTED HOUSING

1914 - 1969 UK and Wales
1970 - 1989 UK only

PRIVATE HOUSE OWNERSHIP

COUNCIL HOUSING

Source: Building Societies Association

Housing Tenure in the UK 1981 and 1987 (% of total) — 3.2

Area	Owner occupied 1981	Owner occupied 1987	Local authority rental 1981	Local authority rental 1987	Private rental & housing association 1981	Private rental & housing association 1987
United Kingdom	57	64	31	26	12	10
Wales	63	68	27	22	11	9
Scotland	36	43	54	48	10	8
N. Ireland	54	62	38	32	8	6
England	59	66	28	24	13	10
Regions of England:						
North	49	57	39	33	12	10
Yorkshire and Humberside	57	64	32	28	11	9
East Midlands	61	69	28	22	11	9
East Anglia	60	68	25	20	14	12
South West	65	71	21	17	14	12
West Midlands	59	65	32	27	10	8
North West	61	67	29	25	10	8
South East	59	66	26	22	15	12
Greater London	50	57	31	28	19	15
Rest of S E	65	72	23	18	12	9

New dwellings completed in the UK, 1981 and 1987 — 3.3

Area	Private sector 1981 ('000)	Private sector 1987 ('000)	Private sector % change 1981–87	Public sector 1981 ('000)	Public sector 1987 ('000)	Public sector % change 1981–87
United Kingdom	118.5	178.2	+50	88.0	34.3	−61
Wales	5.0	8.0	+59	4.1	1.3	−69
Scotland	11.0	13.8	+25	9.0	3.8	−57
N. Ireland	3.6	7.5	+109	3.2	2.2	−31
England	98.9	148.9	+51	71.8	27.0	−62
Regions of England:						
North	4.9	6.7	+37	4.4	1.7	−61
Yorkshire and Humberside	8.5	12.2	+43	6.6	2.7	−59
East Midlands	9.5	17.1	+81	5.4	2.2	−59
East Anglia	6.6	10.9	+66	3.2	1.4	−54
South West	14.1	19.5	+39	4.1	2.0	−49
West Midlands	10.3	13.8	+34	8.2	2.4	−71
North West	10.2	12.8	+35	11.3	4.6	−59
South East	34.9	54.9	+58	28.6	9.7	−66
Greater London	4.0	9.5	+136	15.4	2.6	−83
Rest of S E	30.8	45.4	+47	13.2	7.2	−46

Land and house price changes in the UK, 1981–87 — 3.4

Area	Housing land, £'000/hectare 1981	Housing land, £'000/hectare 1987	Land price per plot as % of new dwelling price 1981	Land price per plot as % of new dwelling price 1987	Average new dwelling price (£'000) 1981	Average new dwelling price (£'000) 1987
	a	b	c	d	e	f
United Kingdom	← No		Data →		28	50
Wales	32	76	7	12	26	38
Scotland	← No		Data →		27	41
N. Ireland	← No		Data →		26	35
England	118	359	18	29	29	52
Regions of England:						
North	92	152	17	19	25	41
Yorkshire and Humberside	67	117	10	12	25	39
East Midlands	79	173	14	18	25	43
East Anglia	41	205	10	17	26	50
South West	79	245	16	26	27	52
West Midlands	123	258	19	26	26	49
North West	95	186	17	17	27	50
South East	211	690	21	39	33	65
Greater London	327	883	20	53	36	61
Rest of SE	186	534	21	35	33	66

Caroline's one room in Bayswater

'Before I became homeless I was living with my mum. At that time I had my daughter with me. I was on Westminster's housing list but I wasn't given anywhere.

Then I went to a friend's in Yorkshire, where I became pregnant. I'd lived in Westminster all my life but I went to Leeds because I'd had problems and I went to get away from them. I would have stayed but the Yorkshire housing officer told me London was my home town and they weren't going to rehouse me. So they more or less sent me back to Westminster.

I couldn't get a place of my own. I'd been on Westminster's list for eight years when I was living with my mum, so I went to them. This was in 1986.

They said they had nothing to offer me. The only alternative was to put me in B&B, which they told me was for nine months, then another two months, then another five.

I stayed in Earls Court for a year and a bit, then they moved me out because it was too expensive. Now I'm in one room in a hotel in Bayswater. There's a kitchen in the basement – two cookers for a hundred and odd families, and even they've broken down.

I was pregnant when I was put in bed and breakfast. My son, Glenn, was born while I was in the Earls Court hotel. At the time I felt really depressed, but I decided I've just got to help myself, keep occupied take him out, go round to my mum's at weekends. If I don't keep myself occupied I can see myself having a nervous breakdown in here. I've already seen one person have a nervous breakdown in my hotel.

Because Glenn was brought up in a hotel I've seen him grow up to be a very aggressive boy – throwing things around, shouting, kicking. What can I do? I can tell him off but it doesn't seem to be working because the pressure of living in one room is what's really doing it.

After this interview I've got to go up to the council because they're no longer using this hotel for homeless families.

I've had no help from officials. They just tell you to wait your turn. They say wait another two months, another five months … I'm not asking for much, just a flat where I can settle down and live a proper life.

Something should be done, especially when there are children locked up in rooms for so long. Thank God mine's at the age where he doesn't understand. At least I haven't got the difficulty of getting proper schooling for him as well.

I tried to get a housing association place when the council couldn't help. They ask you, 'Why do you want a housing association flat?' and look at your background to see if you are a problem family. I don't think that's right.

Some people look at homeless people as problem families. We're not problem families. We just haven't got anyhere to live.'

(Source: *New Statesman & Society* 3 November 1989)

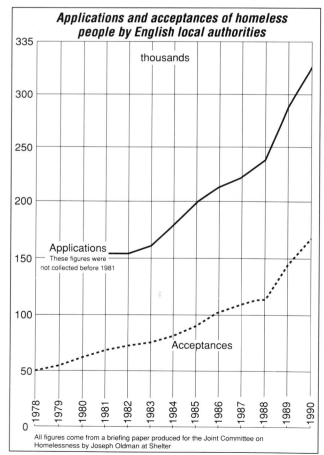

Applications and acceptances of homeless people by English local authorities

thousands

Applications
These figures were not collected before 1981

Acceptances

All figures come from a briefing paper produced for the Joint Committee on Homelessness by Joseph Oldman at Shelter

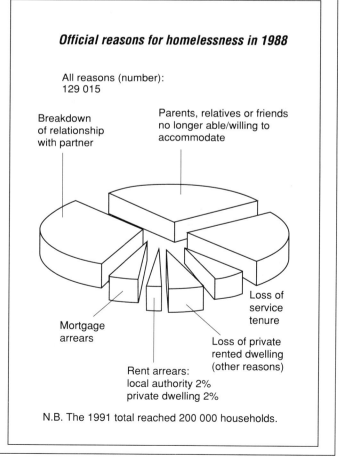

Official reasons for homelessness in 1988

All reasons (number): 129 015

Breakdown of relationship with partner

Parents, relatives or friends no longer able/willing to accommodate

Loss of service tenure

Loss of private rented dwelling (other reasons)

Rent arrears: local authority 2% private dwelling 2%

Mortgage arrears

N.B. The 1991 total reached 200 000 households.

CASE STUDY 3.1 *The changing geography of council housing*

Background

Since the 1920s, local authorities have been major providers of housing. All urban and rural areas have 'council estates', ranging from huge developments to small clusters of houses (resource 3.6). The morphology and social geography of cities are influenced significantly by their location and character. Their fundamental purpose has always been to provide homes at affordable rents for those less affluent groups in society who find it difficult to buy homes of their own, or for those who choose not to buy a home. Traditionally, this public sector housing has been dominated by rental tenure, but with the priority given to social justice rather than economic returns. Since the late 1960s however, government policy has generated a revolution in this public sector resulting in a reduction in total numbers of dwellings available and an increase in ownership by individuals and private companies.

By 1970, local authorities could obtain permission from the minister to sell council housing, and under this discretionary policy, sales fluctuated through the 1970s, reflecting economic and government changes (resource 3.7). Sales also varied according to local authority policy, some councils refusing to sell and others, such as Nottingham and Birmingham, actively encouraging existing tenants to buy their homes. The real revolution, however, dates from the Housing Act of 1980, which introduced the 'Right to Buy' policy, making council house sales **obligatory not discretionary** for local authorities. Tenants are entitled to buy, at substantial discounts below the open market value, and have a right to a mortgage. The impact shows up vividly on resource 3.7. By 1991, almost one and a half million dwellings had been sold from the stock of public housing. Despite this policy, council house sales vary regionally, according to the enthusiasm of the local authority, the socio-economic and demographic characteristics of the population and the characteristics of the housing stock. For example, families with children at home and where there is at least one member in employment are most likely to buy; districts where house prices are relatively low are likely to see high levels of sales; districts where the council housing stock is old, or has a high proportion of flats and maisonettes, are likely to have low levels of sales. The resulting pattern is complex, as shown by resources 3.8 and 3.9. Notice the distinctive pattern in London: large numbers of sales but which represent a low proportion of the total council housing stock.

A second major shift in public sector housing has been the severe drop in the number of dwellings built (resource 3.7), the outcome of changed government policy. As a result, home ownership today includes over 60 per cent of all households, but there has been a reduction in the housing stock available for those who wish to, or have no option but to seek rented accommodation (resource 3.11, page 49). Remember too, that the amount of property available for renting by private landlords has been falling for many years, and that alternative paths such as renting and ownership through Housing Associations and co-operatives, have remained fairly small. This case study examines the impact of these trends upon the public sector housing supply and the chances of people getting council rented accommodation. If you apply for a council rented property, and are put on the waiting list, the chances of being offered a home depend first upon what vacancies are available, and second the allocation policy operated by the local authority. Part I of the case study examines the former and Part II the latter hurdle. Resource 3.10 on page 49 summarises the system.

3.6

Council housing replacing an orchard, N Herefordshire

Large housing estate, Newtown, Birmingham

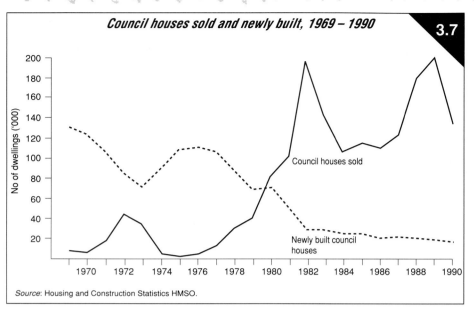

Council houses sold and newly built, 1969 – 1990

3.7

Source: Housing and Construction Statistics HMSO.

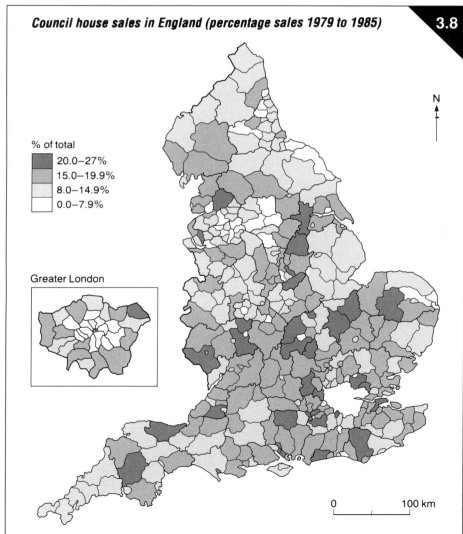

Council house sales in England (percentage sales 1979 to 1985)

3.8

% of total
- 20.0–27%
- 15.0–19.9%
- 8.0–14.9%
- 0.0–7.9%

Greater London

0   100 km

N

Key understandings

◆ The 1980s saw a major shift in public sector housing policy by both central and local governments.

◆ Where you live, as well as who you are, affects your chances of obtaining a council dwelling to rent.

Part I: Changing chances of getting a council house

Changes in supply

As resource 3.10 shows, vacancies occur in two ways: by the completion of new homes, known as the **new-build** supply, and by people vacating existing dwellings, this being the **re-let** supply. If we examine figures for the period 1976–1985 (resources 3.11, 3.12 and 3.13) it is clear that the supply of vacancies, as indicated by the numbers of lettings, peaked in 1977 and fell 15 per cent by 1985. The crucial trend however was the 60 per cent drop in the new-build supply, especially after 1980. The overall supply was maintained until 1983 by increases in the re-let supply, when this component too began to shrink. The collapse of the new-build programmes means that more than eight out of ten vacancies occur in the re-let, (older) property sector, a much higher proportion than in the past.

The drastic reduction in the new-build supply is the direct result of central government exerting an increased influence over house building by local authorities through financial controls. First, the Housing Investment Programme (HIP), introduced in 1977, requires each local authority to put in bids to the government for money to invest in housing. Central government assesses the bids in terms of local housing needs and other government policies, such as inner city initiatives, then allocates money.

Regional distribution of council house sales 1979–85

DOE region	All sales	Sales as % stock
South East	140 468	16.7
East	36 844	15.5
South West	54 305	15.0
East Midlands	63 658	14.6
West Midlands	78 379	12.5
North West (including Cumbria)	84 234	11.1
North (excluding Cumbria)	46 291	11.0
Yorkshire and Humberside	59 290	9.7
Greater London	86 954	9.6
Total	650 414	12.5

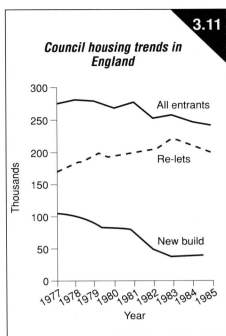

Council housing trends in England

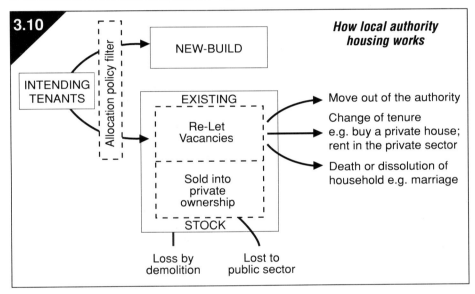

How local authority housing works

Second, although local councils are required, under the 1980 Right to Buy programme, to sell houses, central government has steadily reduced the proportion of the money raised which can be spent by an authority on building new homes: in 1981–2 it was 50 per cent; in 1985–6 it was 20 per cent. Third, under the 1980 Housing Act, other subsidies which local authorities could claim for their building programmes have been reduced or withdrawn.

The size and nature of the re-let supply depends upon the existing housing stock (resource 3.10). By 1986 more than 650 000 council dwellings had been sold under the Right to Buy programme, either individually to 'sitting tenants' or as whole estates to private companies. The fact that this huge loss to the public rental sector did not have an immediate impact upon the size of the re-let supply is explained by more vacancies occurring in the remaining rental stock. On many long-established estates, there are ageing populations, and so vacancies rise because people die or may move to some form of 'sheltered' accommodation. Increasing numbers of tenants have moved out as they become able to buy homes in the private sector. Other factors, such as rising council rents, perceptions of the low 'social status' of being a council tenant, also energise 'push' and 'pull' movement out of the public rental sector.

Changes by urban hierarchy

Resource 3.14 divides local authorities into four categories and shows clearly that London has been affected more severely than any other type of authority. This is the result of London's unusually high dependence on new-build supply to provide vacancies:

'The 'London effect' has been caused primarily by the hitherto greater dependency in the capital on lettings from new building, and hence a greater vulnerability to cutbacks in the capital (investment) programme. In 1976–77, more than half of lettings to new tenants in London originated in the building programme, while in the rest of the country the proportion was more like one-third.'

In the three other categories in resource 3.14 the new-build element declined severely, thereby increasing the importance of the re-let supply. Thus, in the conurbations and in

CASE STUDY 3.1 *The changing geography of council housing*

3.12

Council lettings to new tenants in England (thousands)

	76/77	77/78	78/79	79/80	80/81	81/82	82/83	83/84	84/85
New-build	105	100	84	85	81	52	38	42	41
Re-lets	168	181	194	181	194	199	218	204	199
Total supply	273	281	278	266	276	251	256	246	240
% of total supply from re-lets	61.5	64.4	69.8	68.0	70.3	79.3	85.2	82.9	82.9

3.13

Lettings to new tenants by urban hierarchy (thousands)

	76/77	77/78	78/79	79/80	80/81	81/82	82/83	83/84	84/85
London									
All	49.6	51.1	48.6	43.6	50.1	47.9	40.4	36.9	33.8
New-build	25.0	24.0	21.1	19.6	21.8	16.4	9.3	7.8	6.7
Re-lets	24.6	27.1	27.1	24.0	28.3	31.5	31.1	29.1	27.1
Conurbations									
All	59.9	60.6	64.4	65.2	69.0	62.4	65.7	61.7	60.8
New-build	19.0	18.4	15.5	16.6	15.5	10.8	6.2	7.5	8.2
Re-lets	40.9	42.2	48.9	48.6	53.5	51.6	59.5	54.2	52.6
Cities and large towns									
All	65.3	67.0	66.6	65.2	68.0	59.8	64.7	63.4	61.5
New-build	24.3	21.3	19.4	20.8	19.8	10.0	8.6	10.3	10.2
Re-lets	41.0	45.7	47.2	44.4	48.2	49.8	56.1	53.1	51.3
Small towns and rural areas									
All	98.0	102.2	99.0	92.3	88.5	81.2	84.8	83.6	84.1
New-build	36.8	36.4	27.8	28.2	24.2	15.2	13.8	15.8	16.3
Re-lets	61.2	65.8	71.2	64.1	64.3	66.0	71.0	67.8	67.8

the figures for the South and London were 103 per cent and 110 per cent respectively. This seems to be because lower house prices in the north enable more tenants to become owner-occupiers, by buying into the private sector.

(Source: based on M P Kleinman, 'Where did it hurt most? Decline in the availability of council housing in England', *Policy and Politics*, 16(4), October 1988, pp. 261–276)

Activities

Two important issues raised by the survey provide useful topics for class or group investigation and discussion:

1 As London appears to be the focus of housing pressure, can public housing policy influence the situation? The survey presents two alternatives:

a 'London is the one area of the country where the major housing problem is one of **access**, as is shown by the levels of homelessness. ... Arguably, therefore, it should have been the area where access opportunities into the council sector were most protected: in practice over the period analysed ... the reverse has occurred.'

b 'Public policy should seek to accommodate rather than counter market forces. That is, if access problems are concentrated in London, while other regions have (overall) surplus of housing, policy should not seek to provide for much 'excess demand' in London, but rather encourage such households to move elsewhere, particularly if they are outside the market and therefore do not 'need' to be in London.'

2 Is the role of the council rented housing sector increasingly to accommodate vulnerable and disadvantaged groups? If so, what are the social implications?

cities and large towns, chances of obtaining a council rented home changed little over the 1976–85 decade. Small towns and rural areas, on the other hand, suffered a 15 per cent drop in lettings.

Changes by region

The four regions in resource 3.14 all 'peaked' by 1981 and suffered a severe fall in building programmes, but there are significant regional differences, suggesting a north-south divide:

'The more northern authorities have been able to maintain roughly the same number of lettings in the mid-1980s as in the 1970s, while the further south one goes the greater the reduction ... with London being the worst of all. The greater ability of the north to maintain overall levels probably relates to the fact that in the 1970s a smaller proportion of lettings ... arose from new construction, i.e. the reverse of the 'London effect'.'

Furthermore, the north-south divide is identifiable in terms of the re-let supply: in 1984–85, re-lets in the north and Midlands were at 128 per cent of their 1976–77 level, whereas

Lettings to new tenants (thousands)

	76/77	77/78	78/79	79/80	80/81	81/82	82/83	83/84	84/85
The North									
All	92.1	94.5	96.8	102.3	106.9	97.1	103.0	98.9	96.5
New-build	27.3	24.6	22.6	25.8	26.3	17.0	11.4	13.4	13.8
Re-lets	64.8	69.9	74.2	76.5	80.6	80.1	91.6	85.5	82.7
The Midlands									
All	58.2	59.3	62.3	56.4	57.1	50.8	54.6	52.3	53.3
New-build	21.8	21.8	17.7	17.7	14.1	6.7	6.0	7.2	6.8
Re-lets	36.4	37.5	44.6	38.7	43.0	44.1	48.6	45.1	46.5
The South									
All	72.3	75.9	70.4	54.0	61.5	55.4	57.5	57.5	56.6
New-build	31.1	29.7	22.3	22.0	19.3	12.2	11.3	13.1	14.2
Re-lets	41.2	46.2	48.1	32.0	42.2	43.2	46.2	44.4	42.4
London									
All	49.6	51.1	48.2	43.6	50.1	47.9	40.4	36.9	33.8
New-build	25.0	24.0	21.1	19.6	21.8	16.4	9.3	7.8	6.7
Re-lets	24.6	27.1	27.1	24.0	28.3	31.5	31.1	29.1	27.1

'Although some mainstream demand for council housing has declined (because of the increased preference for owner-occupation), new sources of housing need have also arisen from factors such as the continuing decline of the private rented sector, the rise in divorces and in the numbers of elderly living alone, increased demands from single persons, the growth in mortgage default, and the discharge of those with special needs from institutional care. Council housing departments have found themselves facing widening demands but a declining supply.

… As supply reduces, councils will increasingly house only those to whom they have a statutory (legal) duty, and who are in the most obvious housing need. Inevitably, council housing is seen to become … a 'welfare' tenure.'

Part II: Does it matter where we live?

Look again at resource 3.10. All local authorities have more prospective tenants than vacant properties. Therefore there are waiting lists. Local authorities operate various schemes by which people on their waiting lists are given housing. On the diagram, this is termed the 'allocation policy filter'. Most schemes involve the awarding of points to establish priority based upon the urgency of the need for housing. However, as the following examples show, the area they live in has a significant influence when and where people are housed. (NB remember that the wages quoted in the example are for 1983.)

'The process seems, at first sight, straightforward enough: you register on the waiting list, the council awards points based on your needs, and when you have more points than anyone else, you are offered a house. The reality is often quite different. Your application to go on the list

may be refused; even if the application is accepted, you may be told you are not eligible for rehousing. Some councils do use a points system to assess need, but others use quite different allocation schemes … There will be different queues for different areas and types of houses. Finally, the actual offer of a property will be made by a housing officer who may well depart from the official scheme.'

Points schemes work by taking into account a number of factors, giving them a certain weight, and adding them together to decide who should be housed first. They make it possible to consider date-order (date of entry to the waiting list) or 'merits' (how 'deserving' you are) as only one or two factors out of many which might be considered. We will concentrate on points schemes in this section. The problem is to decide which factors should be included, which weights are appropriate, and how combinations of factors compare. Is it worse, for example, to live in a damp house with no bathroom or a modernised bedsit when you have a young child?

Three examples

The following cases, which are fictional, may help to show how this problem is dealt with in practice.

1 Mark, 21, and Jean, 20, are living with Jean's parents in a three-bedroomed council house. They sleep in one bedroom with their child, who is a year old. Jean's parents sleep in the largest bedroom, and their son Tim, aged 16, has the third, smallest, bedroom. Both Mark and Jean are unemployed. There is friction between Mark and Jean's parents, and there have been many arguments. Mark and Jean have been on the housing list for two years, and have lived in the area since birth.

2 Sandeep, aged 30, and Manda, aged 28, have bought their own two-bedroomed house, through a

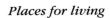

private arrangement. They have one daughter, aged six. Sandeep works in a local factory and earns a low wage (£85 a week). The house has no bathroom, no hot water, and an outside toilet. They cannot afford repairs, even with an improvement grant, and the house is in a dilapidated state. There are large patches of damp on the wall in the living room, and mould in the bedroom. They have been on the housing list for three years, and have lived in the area for four years.

3 Edward, 25, and Diane, 23, rent a modern two-bedroomed flat, on the first floor of a small block,

from a private landlord. They have a son, aged 4. The flat is in good order and centrally heated with all modern facilities. They would like to move because they do not feel the flat is suitable for a young child. Edward earns an average wage of £150 a week. They applied at a time when financially they were less well off, and have not been able to save a deposit for a house. They have been on the waiting list for four years, and have lived in the area all their lives.

Three large urban authorities have been selected to illustrate the differences in policy: Liverpool,

Manchester and Birmingham. These authorities take different factors into account, and give different weight to the problems (resources 3.15 to 3.17).

It is difficult, if not impossible, to explain the difference in local needs. There are significant differences between areas – Liverpool, for example, has a high number of properties and of vacancies, which should mitigate the worst effects of an otherwise limited allocations policy – but this does not explain the inclusion of different factors, or the weight given to them. These seem to reflect, rather, a difference in attitudes towards different kinds of

3.15

LIVERPOOL								
Mark and Jean			**Sandeep and Manda**			**Edward and Diane**		
Family	3		Family	3		Family		3
Subtenant	3		Condition	2				
Shared living room	3		No bathroom	1				
Overcrowding	3							
Total	10		Total	7		Total		3
Position	First		Position	Second		Position		Third

NB Figures indicate points given according to policy guidelines

3.16

BIRMINGHAM								
Mark and Jean			**Sandeep and Manda**			**Edward and Diane**		
Bedroom shortage	150		No bathroom	50		First floor flat		250
Shared accommodation	150		Waiting time	2		Waiting time		200
Waiting time	90		No bathroom	1				
Total	390		Total	80		Total		450
Position	Second		Position	Third		Position		First

MANCHESTER

Mark and Jean		Sandeep and Manda		Edward and Diane	
Overcrowding	10	Condition	9	Children living at a height	4
Shared amenities	5	Amenities	4	Time in need	50
Time in need	35	Time in need	45		
Total	50	Total	58	Total	54
Position	Third	Position	First	Position	Second

housing need. Points schemes are a method of achieving consistency while taking different factors into account, but they are not in themselves a guarantee of fairness.

(Source: adapted from P Spicker, 'The allocation of council housing', *Shelter*, October 1983, pp. 1–43)

Activities

1   Analyse the three examples given and identify how priorities and need are measured in each of the authorities.

2   Which scheme seems to you the fairest?

3   Obtain information from your local Housing Department on their allocation scheme (NB Only one of your class – or your tutor – should approach the Housing Department!) Analyse the scheme and compare it with the examples given. How would the three examples rank on your local scheme?

4   **Group discussion**: Work out a housing allocation scheme which you believe is fair, socially just, and workable, what are the arguments against the first come, first served policy?

Available to rent – but is it what you want?

Background

The size, character and location of the housing stock in a region are important factors influencing house availability, whether through private purchase or local council rental (see case study 3.1). There is no doubt that there is great pressure for building land and that the supply of new homes has declined over the past 20 years (resource 3.19). At the same time, the existing housing stock in both the private and public sectors is incurring greater maintenance costs. The deterioration of existing homes and the shortages of new houses which have helped to push up land and house prices, are now of crisis proportions. A 1987 report by the Association of Metropolitan Authorities (AMA), a body representing all major cities, stated 'that the extent of the crisis is such that it could cost £74 billion to put right the existing problems and build an extra 500 000 new houses estimated as the minimum required to satisfy immediate needs' (resource 3.20).

However, the nature of the problem varies regionally. If you are house-seeking in south-east England, your problem is quite different from the situation you face in Wales, Scotland or northern England. The two examples used in this case study: Berkshire and South Wales, highlight the contrasts, and put the housing crisis into its economic, social and environmental context.

Key understandings

◆ There are regional variations in the nature of housing supply and shortage.

◆ Housing and housing supply are related to the social, economic and environmental character of a region.

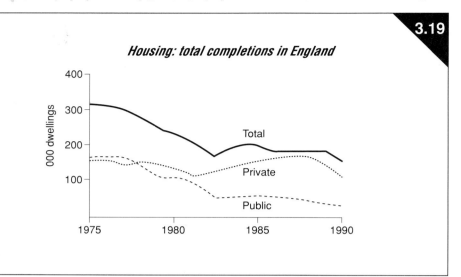

3.19

Housing: total completions in England

000 dwellings

Total

Private

Public

1975   1980   1985   1990

3.20

TOMORROW THEY COULD LEARN THEY'LL NEVER OWN THEIR OWN HOME.

The government estimates that up to two million families and single people will need homes by the year 2001. Yet we are planning to build fewer than at any time since the war – nowhere near enough to meet the predicted demand.

This means that today's school children will face a serious shortage of homes they can afford when they grow up. And first time buyers will find it almost impossible to get onto the housing ladder.

Fortunately, the problem can be solved. But only if we start to plan now for the number of homes we know we are going to need.

That means making land available – not just in the open countryside, but also in neglected areas on the edge of towns and villages, and the unused land that some public bodies still own.

Space can be found to provide all the homes we need. But unless we act now, the class of 1990 will face some very tough lessons in the future.

For more information, write to: "More Land For Homes", 82 New Cavendish Street, London W1M 8AD.

MORE LAND FOR HOMES

This campaign is supported by members of House Builders Federation, New Homes Marketing Board, Building Employers Confederation, National House Building Council, Federation of Master Builders, National Council of Building Material Producers and leading Building Societies.

Berkshire and South Wales – two faces of the housing crisis

1 Berkshire

As long ago as the 1930s Berkshire managed to ride out the economic crisis by attracting light engineering, food processing and drugs companies, which used pools of un-unionised labour. The government of the day promoted transfer schemes to relocate labour from 'distressed regions' such as South Wales. Today, the emphasis is on the professionalised, exclusive world of the small high-tech firm, although the growth of this sector began in the 1960s with an influx of large electronics firms. By the 1980s about 30 000 people, slightly over ten per cent of the workforce, were employed in the high-tech sector. Unemployment has risen partly because 'traditional' industry has moved out of the region in order to cash in on revenue from redevelopment as land prices soared. And while there has been expansion in services in recent years, as with the electronics industry, it has been socially extremely uneven, with much of the increase occurring at management level.

How has this long-term polarisation between a high growth and a declining sector been reflected in local housing provision? Historically, the emphasis has been on speculative owner-occupier building, but in recent years there has been an almost total reliance on this form of provision. For the housebuilders, under pressure to build for the more expensive 'trade-up' market, the incoming professional workers seem to have fitted the bill perfectly. Since the late 1970s there has been a remarkable expansion of the housing stock. Some 38 000 houses were added between 1976 and 1984, and in March 1985 there were outstanding commitments for a further 23 000 houses. Virtually all these have been built for owner occupation, mainly on very large

3.21

New housing at Lower Earley in Reading

sites such as that of Lower Earley, for 6000 (resource 3.21). Developers have been very successful in pushing for land release in large blocks and have used central government to override the conservationist local authorities. Much of the pressure for extra land release in Berkshire came from the large volume builders and resulted in the modification of the Central Berkshire Structure Plan in the early 1980s to make available land for an extra 8000 dwellings.

But it is clear that massive housebuilding has not eased the problems of many Berkshire residents. House prices have increased faster than in the rest of the south-east, for example by 19 per cent between 1983 and 1984. In 1984 the average price of houses was 22.5 per cent more than the rest of the south-east. Given the rate of new building in recent years, these prices probably reflect the very high salaries paid to some employees rather than any absolute shortage of housing space. The high prices have been hitting local employers, with almost a quarter of firms indicating that their workforce was experiencing difficulties in finding adequate housing.

As the private sector has moved towards the construction of trade-up housing, availability in the public sector has been rapidly eroded by privatisation of public housing. Berkshire already has the lowest proportion of public sector completions in the south-east and large amounts of council housing have been sold, especially in Bracknell.

It appears that the recent growth has increased, rather than eased social tensions in the area. The conservationist lobby has become extremely vociferous in the area, and the County Council's approved strategy is now to 'preserve the rural character of the County as a whole'. Whilst there is a growing consensus between existing owner occupiers that growth should be limited, this does not square with the demands of the housebuilders, who disagree with the population projections and estimates of future housebuilding needs. Nevertheless, there has now been a reconsideration of housebuilding commitments which has led to the removal of some 3000 houses from the Structure Plan provision. Some districts have been noticeably more successful (e.g.

Bracknell) than others (Newbury) in securing a reduction in the land allocation for housing.

Tight development control only tends to shift growth around the county, not necessarily to places of actual need. Slough for example, with some of the more acute housing problems, has Berkshire's largest local authority housebuilding programme and has won land, but is restricted by the Green Belt. Furthermore the inability of local authorities to control the price of new owner-occupied housing will mean that house prices may continue to rise rapidly. This would bar even more local people from access to new housing.

2 South Wales

In recent years, South Wales has undergone a fundamental restructuring of its economic base. This has left it highly polarised, both spatially and socially. The traditional manufacturing base is being lost as the coal and steel industries have shrunk. New jobs have been created in the electrical engineering, motor vehicle and service industries, but these have failed to match the losses from traditional industry. Growth in service sector employment has tailed off or even dropped, as in Mid Glamorgan. In both the service and manufacturing sectors there has also been a distinct shift towards low and unskilled employment, frequently part-time and taken by women.

Spatially, this economic restructuring has left South Wales polarised between the Valleys and the coastal belt. The employment structure of Mid Glamorgan for example, is distributed extremely unevenly. Districts in the south tend to be more service-sector oriented and the manufacturing workforce is dominated by men and skilled manual workers. These districts also contain more professional workers. The Valley communities, however, are overwhelmingly dominated by unskilled manual manufacturing jobs and female service sector jobs. Unemployment is extremely high in

some districts: in September 1985, Cynon Valley, with 29 per cent male unemployment, had the highest unemployment rate in Wales.

All counties place great emphasis on the attraction of new jobs to the region. This stress on 'production' policies, has a long history in the South Wales region. This comes either through direct investment by state enterprises or indirectly through the provision of infrastructure. By contrast 'consumption' issues, including housing provision, have traditionally remained very much the province of the trade unions and working-class community organisations. The Valleys in particular have achieved high levels of owner-occupation through the use of 'building clubs' to enable workers on a modest income to become homeowners. Today Rhondda is unique in the area, with over three-quarters of households owner-occupiers, but other districts also have high proportions of owner-occupation. Recently, there has been a substantial drop in the amount of new housebuilding, both public and private. The Valleys have been most severely hit by this decline.

The housing problem is one of massive and appalling urban deprivation in the valley communities, deprivation which is increasingly unlikely to be tackled given the tight financial resources of local authorities. Even though there has been considerable renovation of the housing stock, Cynon Valley, Merthyr Tydfil and Rhondda were identified as the three most deprived districts in England and Wales in a 1985 study (resource 3.23). In housing terms this means that 92 per cent of the stock of private housing in Cynon Valley – some 40 000 houses – are in an unsatisfactory condition, whilst 48 per cent have actually been labelled as unfit for human habitation. The cost of rehabilitating the stock in this valley alone is estimated to be £121 million. The Welsh Office has tried to persuade the building societies to make more funds available for rehabilitation (resource 3.23).

The speculative housebuilding industry cannot be relied upon to resolve this situation. High unemployment and the large low-paid workforce make places such as Merthyr Tydfil an unattractive proposition for the housebuilders. The housing needs of the Valleys are clear, yet it has proved very difficult to persuade private builders to develop land allocated for housing.

Housing associations have been important in fulfilling local housing needs in recent years, but

3.22

Typical housing stock in the Valleys. Is enough being done to improve and extend housing for people in this area?

increasingly, money is only available from the government funded Housing Corporation for sheltered housing (i.e. housing for the elderly and infirm). Other strategies include self-building on council-owned land and joint ventures with private developers whereby land is provided in return for an agreement on the price of the completed housing.

Virtually all new private sector housing development has been in the south, especially in areas with easy access to the M4. This development has not, however, been starter housing, the House-Builders' Federation (HBF) arguing that demand has been choked by the extensive availability of cheap old terraced housing. The emphasis on more expensive housing, bolstered by a forceful campaign over the lack of suitable 'executive' housing has led to conflicts over land availability which contrast with Berkshire. In South Wales the builders want smaller (ten to 100 unit) sites, arguing that demand for expensive housing is highly localised. The county councils, however have tended to prefer the release of land in large blocks, e.g. 4000 units at North Pentwyn, in response to growing conservationist pressure in the desirable Vale of Glamorgan.

(Source: adapted from J Barlow, 'The housing crisis and its local dimensions', *Housing Studies* 2(1), 1988, pp. 28–41)

Activity

1 Group discussion

a From the evidence in this case study, how would you define the term 'housing crisis' in (i) Berkshire, and (ii) South Wales?

b Are your definitions the same? If not, in what ways do they differ?

c What are the causes of the 'crisis' and what are the possible solutions? (Think in terms of the 'actors' involved in the decision-making.)

3.23

End to the Welsh valleys exodus

For two generations, the people of the South Wales mining valleys have been voting with their feet. It is no surprise that the trickle of new settlers from across the Severn Bridge is a curious enough phenomenon to attract recent headlines in local papers.

The valleys experienced explosive growth in housing during the first two decades of this century, and virtual standstill in the two that followed. Nearly half the housing stock in the three counties above the South Wales coalfield was completed before 1919. Although the valleys harbour some of the worst housing in Western Europe, home ownership accounts for 66 per cent and is still rising.

Coal mines have been closing at such a rate that less than a dozen are working today, compared with more than 200, 40 years ago. Most of the new jobs in kit-assembly factories have been for the wives and daughters of former miners and steelworkers. Cardiff's travel-to-work area has vastly improved road and rail links and now extends through the Glamorgan and Gwent valleys right to the edge of the Brecon Beacons.

There are some 130 000 pre-1919 terraced brick and stone miners' houses between the Lougher Valley to the west and almost as far as the Usk to the east. The greatest concentration is in the five more easterly valleys. These are the Rhondda, Cynon, Taff, Rhymney and Ebbw. Some 70 000 sub-standard houses will have been improved to a virtually new standard of structural condition. Some schemes ('enveloping') improve whole streets, while 'pepper-pot' improvements are going on where individual householders apply for grants.

Near Ebbw Vale, Marine Street in the village of Cwm is in the second phase of its improvement. Paul Gittings bought his house for £11 000 four-and-a-half years ago. With a new roof, doors and windows and re-rendering, he still reckons the property is only worth around £19 000.

In the next Gwent valley, the Ebbw Fach, Abertillery is one of five towns recently chosen to share £2.1m of Welsh Office urban-development money. Half a mile further down the valley, the village of Six Bells has another Blaenau-Gwent enveloping scheme.

Jenny Lewis and her husband Chris bought one of these improved, terraced houses in July for £24 000. It is three-bedroomed, with three floors at the rear and a kitchen and dining room in the 'basement' looking out at the back of a garden falling steeply away to a service road. The narrow valley is wooded and a real attraction to the Lewises, coming as they did from an industrial Bristol suburb. Houses like this would have cost £90 000 in Bristol, says Jenny. Her husband still travels to work in his home city. And even though Jenny brought her bespoke knitwear manufacturing business with her, the output from her eight valleys outworkers still travels back to Bristol to be sold.

The most celebrated row of terraces in Six Bells is in Graig Road. It is a row of 120-year-old stone, two-up, two-down cottages running straight up the side of a secluded wooded gorge, with the partly-closed village pit just about visible on the valley bottom. Four houses out of a dozen are owned by newcomers. The first occupant to move in was a Cambridge divorcee on a small income who paid just £7000 two years ago and is still making internal improvements. Even so, she says, houses like hers are worth nearer £30 000 now. A recent visitor was so impressed that she bought another cottage further down the road for £20 000.

(Source: Brian Morgan, *The Independent*, 10 December 1988)

---

2 The housing market reacts closely to economic conditions and government policy. The materials in this case study review the situation in the 1980s. The economic recession and stagnation of land and house prices and sales in the early 1990s have created different conditions. What effects might such changes have upon the housing situation in Berkshire and South Wales?

Background

In recent years, much government policy and funding has been focused on the problems of the inner cities. There is increasing evidence, however, that levels of poverty and social stress may be even higher on council-built peripheral estates. Furthermore, on many such estates, built largely in the 1950s and 1960s, the physical fabric of the buildings is deteriorating, and the environmental quality of the streets and open spaces is poor, causing escalating maintenance costs (resource 3.24). The scale and intensity of the social, physical and environmental problems have become so great that demolition is being adopted increasingly as the only practical answer (resource 3.25).

It all seemed such a good idea at the time: to use green-field sites to build large estates and provide decent homes and improved standards of space and amenities for hundreds of thousands of inner city dwellers. To conserve land and build quickly, various types of systems building, such as assembling pre-built components on site, and high-rise blocks were included. Almost all large cities have examples of such estates on their fringes. In support of these estates, regional development policies, supported by central government, encouraged industries to locate nearby, thereby creating employment opportunities.

Not all of these large-scale developments have been failures, and each estate has its own set of factors influencing its health or sickness. Nonetheless, certain themes recur. This statement by a Middlesbrough councillor in 1987 brings out some of these themes:

'We failed on a number of fronts. In planning the houses and the physical environment, we created areas the size of towns but without either the facilities of towns or the necessary links to other centres of social and commercial services. Perhaps if a little more time had been spent

Deteriorating housing from the late 1950s

talking to those who were to be the residents of these estates, more care would have been taken to provide such services. Less foreseeable were the changes in production and employment which would undermine the role of the peripheral estates in providing a workforce for nearby industries'.

(Source: R Brady, 'Ripe for Action', *Housing and Planning Review*, 42(6), December/January, 1987/88, p. 4)

Certain types of accommodation common on many peripheral estates, in particular, flats and maisonettes, have not proved popular under the Right to Buy Schemes (see pages 44 and 47), or contain relatively high numbers of people who are not in a position to buy, and so, the majority of dwellings have remained in rental tenure. One result has been that such estates may contain above average proportions of the more vulnerable groups in society: low-income households, the unemployed, the elderly. The various physical, social, economic and environmental needs combine

to create complex and expensive problems, yet most peripheral estates fall outside areas qualifying for government Urban Programme funds. The following examples illustrate both the problems and alternative strategies for improving the quality of life on such estates.

Demolition of deteriorated housing stock

Part I: Middlesbrough – improving the housing may not improve the lifestyle

East Middlesbrough has the largest concentration of peripheral estates in Middlesbrough. Within an area of just over two miles square are eleven estates containing more than 10 000 dwellings. Although 12 – 15 per cent of the dwellings are now privately owned, the great majority remain in Council ownership.

Unlike many similar areas, East Middlesbrough was the result of a continuous planning process started in the 1930s. Now, however, a bleak environment is much in evidence. The Council has made considerable efforts to give priority to the improvement of the housing stock. This has of course become increasingly difficult as a result of reduced government funding. Apart from five tower blocks, the housing is predominantly two-storey terraced and semi-detached houses with gardens. Although some estates need modernisation and central heating installation, most of the houses are in sound condition. The really bad housing – three and four storey flats and maisonettes – has now been removed and the tower blocks have been improved to an acceptable, standard. Some system-built housing with damp and poor internal layout still remains.

Problems are not visible because they belong to the people rather than the buildings. There are 36 000 people living in East Middlesbrough estates. Overwhelmingly, their biggest problem is unemployment. Male unemployment varies from 30 per cent to 40 per cent in all the estates and youth unemployment is similarly severe.

Many of the workers in East Middlesbrough were employed in the steel, chemical and heavy engineering complexes along the River Tees. Since the mid-1970s, there has been a continuous reduction in the workforce as more advanced technology has been applied in new and existing plants and old works have been closed down. Shipbuilding has disappeared locally, reflecting a national and European decline and heavy engineering works, and chemicals plants have closed and been demolished. The only good news on the industrial front over the past ten years has been in the oil rig module yards, but their several hundred new jobs have not been able to offset the many thousands of jobs lost in the other industries.

It is East Middlesbrough and other similar areas in Teesside which have borne the brunt of these industrial changes, because it is there that the manual workers in these industries live. There is a large concentration of former industrial workers, many unskilled and semi-skilled for whom unemployment is a long term prospect. Unemployment means of course, low income and if we add in the 17 per cent of households who are retired, it is not surprising to find that 70 per cent of Council tenants are receiving housing benefit.

Low incomes and lack of work can often be correlated with a higher than average incidence of other problems. From the accounts of professional workers in the area, mental and physical sickness, marriage problems, lower academic attainment and aspirations, petty crime and violence, vandalism and glue sniffing are present to a greater extent than elsewhere.

What is new about this? Society has always had such problems. What is different about East Middlesbrough and the other large peripheral estates around our towns and cities is the isolation. East Middlesbrough is between two and five miles from the centre of Middlesbrough. This might not have been a problem in days of full employment, but for the 70 per cent of households without a car, the return bus fare to town (average £1 per adult or £3 for a family of four) is now an unaffordable luxury. Does this matter? After all most of the estates have their own local shops, there is a modern swimming baths, two branch libraries and two community centres. In fact, there is very much missing that a normal town of 36 000 inhabitants would have. There is little choice or competition between shops, so higher prices are charged compared with superstores, there are no doctor's surgeries or health centre, no dentist, no police station and no job centre. Until recently there were no football pitches with changing rooms and only a handful of churches, pubs and clubs. There are few halls and meeting places, no sixth form college, no sports hall and relatively few voluntary and amateur organisations.

The widespread absence of such facilities adds a social dimension to the isolation of East Middlesbrough. Few people who do not live or work there will have cause to visit the area.

Peripheral estates have also tended not to easily attract private sector investment because of the perceived difficulties in acquiring land owned almost entirely by the District or County Councils.

The task of turning round an area like East Middlesbrough is clearly formidable. A start has been made: the former Southlands Secondary School has been converted to a community centre providing employment opportunities, a sports hall and meeting rooms. A former Building Department depot has been converted to provide opportunities for community business.

(Source: D Wright, Group Planning Officer, Middlesbrough Borough Council, 'East Middlesbrough: the impact of unemployment, *Housing and Planning*, 42(6), December/January 1987–1988, p. 5)

Part II: Glasgow – from centralised control to local solutions

Glasgow has received substantial media coverage as the role model for urban renewal, the principal example of a UK city which has

'made it back' as an acceptable part of the urban fabric. The urban renewal issue still figures high on Glasgow's agenda, only it has been transformed and displaced from the inner to the outer city.

Glasgow's problems can be traced back to the rapid growth in the 19th century and the industrial revolution. The pace and scale of development over that period effectively sowed the seeds of the housing problems now being experienced.

Between 1850 and 1900 for example, private enterprise built over 100 000 houses in the inner city – mainly 1–2 bedroom flats in 4-storey tenement blocks. Within particular developments, population density exceeded 1500 per hectare. Overcrowded housing, poor sanitation, ill-health and poverty were characteristic of much of the inner city.

A variety of legislative changes brought local authority intervention in the housing market. Thus between 1919 and 1939, the Glasgow corporation built nearly 52 000 houses. Nevertheless, in 1939 over 82 000 families still lived in overcrowded, substandard conditions.

The post-war response to Glasgow's housing problems was established by the 1946 Clyde Valley Plan. The Plan estimated that 500 000 people would have to be moved out of the inner city to allow redevelopment at lower densities: 250 000 to other areas within the city, 250 000 outside the city boundary.

The Town and Country Planning (Scotland) Act 1947 provided the framework to implement these proposals, principally through the powers to designate Comprehensive Development Areas (CDAs). The designation of East Kilbride and Cumbernauld as New Towns provided the mechanism for the Clyde Valley Plan to be put into practice.

The solution adopted was planned overspill (to the New Towns and various other reception centres) and the development of peripheral housing schemes. By the mid-1950s, the development of the principal schemes – Drumchapel, Easterhouse, Pollok and Castlemilk was well underway, each with between 10 and 15 000 houses in a fairly uniform 3–4 apartment tenement-block style.

Throughout this period the process of urban renewal and the pressure for improvement dictated a rapid response. Renewal was seen as a physical issue, the narrow aim of providing new housing overriding the broader objectives of creating thriving communities. The Corporation became a large centralised machine for acquiring and clearing land, building very large-scale housing schemes and transferring large populations from inner to outer city.

In retrospect it is clear that this was the outcome of many compromises e.g. cost cutting on the provision of facilities, adoption of untested design and construction solutions in terms of layout appearance and density. Throughout the process, scant regard was given to the impact of the physical approach on social and economic relations. Provision of community facilities did little to alter the fundamental social problems which were developing within the schemes – e.g. the lettings policy of the time which gave the poorest people the worst housing.

During the 1970s, substantial investment was made in an attempt to ease the acute lack of social and community facilities. In Easterhouse, for example, this included a new shopping centre, local shops, swimming pool and library and a sustained attempt to 'create' a community through a range of community development initiatives.

The main impetus for change came with the publication of the 1978 District Council Report which predicted a major vacancy problem in the peripheral estates as the

younger, more mobile sections of the population moved out. In the same year, the Council agreed that the principal objective for the peripheral estates should be to try to reproduce the character and spirit of a medium-sized town.

In 1980 the Council adopted the 'Alternative Housing Strategy' which acknowledged the need to maximise the use of existing resources against the likelihood of no additional resources from central government. The approach since then has been selective and experimental, often focused on smaller areas within the larger schemes. It has included a wide range of comparatively resource intensive housing and environmental improvements, improved approaches to housing management (including decentralisation) and a variety of new approaches to the balance of tenure (including ownership co-operatives and tenant management co-operatives).

Hand in hand with local community representatives in these peripheral schemes the aim is to reduce unemployment and poverty, improve health and housing conditions, and improve the quality of service and facilities.

In essence, the approach now being pursued by the Council has shifted radically from the physical to giving explicit emphasis to the self-determination of the communities involved. The Council, now rejects universal solutions in favour of a development strategy which recognises the individuality of a particular area. It is developing a range of initiatives in line with, and sympathetic to, local conditions.

(Source: D Wiseman, Deputy Leader of Glasgow City Council, 'The Glasgow Context', *Housing and Planning*, 42 (6), December/January 1987–1988, pp. 8–9)

Part III: Knowsley – problem-solving by collaboration between the public and private sectors

Stockbridge Village Trust

The freehold of that part of the Cantril Farm estate lying within the boundary of Knowsley Metropolitan Borough Council was transferred by the Council to the Stockbridge Village Trust on 6 April 1983. The Trust had bought the estate for £7.42 million with the purchase being financed by mortgage loans from the Abbey National Building Society (£3 million), Barclays Bank (£2 million) and Knowsley Metropolitan Council (£2.42 million).

The estate of some 3000 dwellings was deteriorating and was expected to be more than 50 per cent vacant by the early 1990s. It had been built in the 1960s by the former Liverpool CBC to house people displaced in slum clearance schemes in inner Liverpool. It comprised two-storey houses, low and medium rise maisonettes and low, medium and high rise flats.

The Trust was established, not as a housing association, but as a non-profit-making company.

The aims and objectives of the programme coordinated by the Stockbridge Village Trust to prevent the possible evacuation and subsequent demolition of the estate were as follows:

(i) demolition of the most unpopular dwellings,

(ii) refurbishment of the remaining housing stock,

(iii) development of new private housing for sale and rent via the Stockbridge Village Housing Association,

(iv) redevelopment of the central area of the estate to provide improved shopping facilities and a new leisure centre.

A large number of factors conspired to enable the Stockbridge Village programme to be launched. Broadly, the ground for this initiative was laid by the Secretary of State for the Environment, who had been charged to mount new state initiatives on Merseyside. A special allocation of urban programme funds had been reserved for Merseyside and the Merseyside Task Force had been established to coordinate central government programmes for the area.

Stockbridge Village Trust commenced operations in April 1983. Initially, the intention had been that the Trust should complete its programme within five years. Unfortunately the Trust was unable to maintain the pace of development achieved in the early months of its existence. In April 1985, an evaluation of the Trust's achievements showed that unit costs for dwelling improvements had risen quite dramatically from an original estimate of £3000 per house to £6700. Refurbishment had been completed on only 288 properties against a target of 1372. More than three-quarters of the properties remained to be refurbished. Only 98 houses had been built for sale to owner-occupiers against a target of 429 and a total programme of 600. The cost of redeveloping the central area had risen from an original estimate of £2 000 000 to a revised cost of £6 000 000.

A fundamental weakness in the position of the Trust was that it had no flexibility to adjust its programme or to raise additional capital. Rents which were virtually the only real source of income to the Trust, were subject to the Fair Rents Legislation and the improvements which were carried out to the housing stock did not always lead to higher rents.

Many residents of Stockbridge Village were unable financially to purchase their houses under the Right to Buy Scheme, so RTB sales never reached the annual projected figure of 120.

By mid-1985 it was becoming clear that the Trust's financial position was giving cause for considerable concern. Projections indicated that it would not be able meet its financial targets for a variety of reasons. The cost of the maintenance and refurbishment programmes were underestimated. Inflation was not adequately taken into account in original projections, nor were the high interest rates which had prevailed.

Knowsley Council and the DoE provided £5 million extra to save the project. So in August 1987, the Trust had refurbished 1240 dwellings with 900 remaining. The Stockbridge Village Housing Association had developed 267 new dwellings for rent. A major private developer had built 127 homes of which all had been sold. The Trust had built a new retail shopping centre at a cost in excess of £1 million and Knowsley Borough Council had commenced work on a new Leisure Centre costing £4 million and had demolished one of three 22-storey blocks of flats to be demolished in the Central Area.

The Trust has made considerable progress in achieving its physical and social objectives. Crime and vandalism have declined by 20 per cent over the period 1983–1987 and are still falling.

The future objective of the Trust continues to be the completion of its housing programme to 1990–91. It aims to continue to improve housing management, its response to repairs and to widen the type of tenure of dwellings. The Stockbridge Village Housing Association plan to build a further 260 dwellings for rent and to provide shared ownership for dwellings for sale whilst private developers propose to add additional new dwellings.

(Source: Richard Penn, Chief executive of Knowsley Borough Council, 'Stockbridge Village Trust', *Housing and Planning,* 42(6), December–January 1987–1988, pp. 18–19)

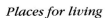

CASE STUDY 3.3 *Problem solving on peripheral estates – can we correct past mistakes?*

Part IV: Solihull – offering greater variety and more involvement

The Kingshurst Hall Estate – blueprint for a better life

The Kingshurst Hall Estate was built by the City of Birmingham in the 1950s on a site some 7 miles outside the city in Warwickshire, 1600 properties were built, most of them flats and maisonettes in walk up blocks interspersed with traditional houses and multi storey blocks.

As early as 1959 the Birmingham Mail featured the plight of 'The Lonely Exiles of Kingshurst' who lived a considerable distance from the city in an area with few shops, few social amenities and poor public transport. In 1980 the estate was taken over by Solihull MBC, in whose area the estate is situated. This presented a considerable challenge to Solihull, whose previous housing management experience had been in suburban and rural housing. Kingshurst Hall exhibited all the hallmarks of a difficult to let peripheral estate, severe vandalism, high turnover, a large number of empty properties and high rent arrears. The area was also socially disadvantaged with a high proportion of residents dependant on income support, a high child density and a marked lack of social amenities.

Amongst the first steps taken by Solihull was the appointment of estate supervisors and cleaners and the establishment of a local housing management office on the estate. In April 1981, a hard-to-let block of maisonettes was sold to first time buyers who were either existing council tenants or registered on the waiting list.

It was obvious, however, that to improve conditions on the estate generally, an ambitious programme of redevelopment and refurbishment would be needed. The money for such a programme would not be available from Solihull's limited HIP allocation or from capital receipts, given the constraints on spending these (see page 44). Consequently attention was turned to the possibility of attracting private finance. During 1982, a plan for redevelopment and refurbishment was produced, called the Kingshurst Action Plan. This plan involved refurbishment of some existing homes, the sale of difficult-to-let housing to the private sector, and the selective demolition of some blocks and replacement with traditional houses for rent and for sale, thus improving the tenure mix on the estate. In March 1983 Solihull's Housing Committee gave its approval to the Plan and consultation with residents began.

By this time a Neighbourhood Centre had been established on the estate, which became the focus for consultation about the Plan. On the whole residents were happy with the Plan, but wanted to see more blocks of maisonettes demolished.

By 1988, 254 maisonettes had been demolished and replaced by a total of 127 new houses for rent. Six blocks of maisonettes were sold to Wimpey for refurbishment, to provide 128 flats and maisonettes for first time buyers. Wimpey were also responsible for the topping of maisonettes to provide 34 traditional three bedroomed houses for sale as well as building some two bedroomed houses for sale on infill sites.

These properties attracted considerable demand from both first time buyers and existing council tenants, demonstrating a large and previously unmet need for homes for sale in the area.

In 1985, a pilot refurbishment scheme of one block of maisonettes was carried out. This included improvements to the exterior appearance and communal areas as well as rewiring and improved fitments. Detailed consultation with tenants on these improvements took place and their favourable comments resulted in a further six blocks being refurbished. Consultation with tenants is seen as a crucial part of these refurbishment schemes so that tenants choices are taken into consideration and inconvenience is kept to a minimum.

In 1988, plans were in hand to sell five blocks of flats and maisonettes to Blue Boar for refurbishment for sale. Refurbishment of the remaining blocks was planned and further applications made for Estate Action funding to these projects.

(Source: C Hodson, Research and Development Officer in Housing, Solihull Borough Council, 'The Kingshurst Hall Estate – blueprint for a better life', *Housing and Planning*, 42 (6), December–January 1987–1988)

Activity

With a partner

For the four areas in the case study:

a Why were the estates built, for whom, and in what form?

b Compile a list of the principal problems which have emerged. (Identify physical, economic and social issues.) Are there any which seem common to all estates?

c Compile a second list, setting out the various solutions being tried, and the parties involved. Again, note how the **physical**, **economic** and **social** issues are being tackled. (Pay particular attention to the role of the residents themselves.)

d What appear to be the principal obstacles to the success of the improvement schemes?

CASE STUDY 3.4 *Private sector housing – are there two Britains?*

Background

Where you live has a significant influence upon your quality of life. A key factor in this quality is the type of home, usually determined by what the family or individual can afford, and the housing stock that is available. Thus, variations in house prices from place to place and from time to time influence access to houses, the ability to buy into the private sector and the type of property available. For example, a particulary rapid surge in house prices took place between 1984 and 1988. This focused attention upon the marked regional differences, especially between the expensive London/south-east England and the rest of the country. In July 1988, the average price of a house in Greater London reached £100 000, up 29 per cent in a year; in the south-east region, the average was £90 000, up 25 per cent: in the north, the average price of £36 000 had risen only 9 per cent. Areas with good rail links to London – such as Grantham saw prices rise rapidly in this period (resource 3.26).

Such price gaps raised the spectre of 'two nations' and the 'north-south divide' in society. Further, the disparity was constraining unemployed people from moving to the jobs available in the south. Conversely, managers and executives were reluctant to move north in case they could not afford to buy into the southern market again.

This case study, based on a study of the private housing market over the period 1969 – 1988, suggests first that these regional price differentials are not a new phenomenon, and second that they follow a cyclical pattern – a surge, followed by a 'flatter' period. Since 1969 there have been three surges in house prices nationally. In each case, the surge began in London and the south-east, with the impact rippling steadily outwards. Similarly, the slackening of house prices began in

London, gradually reaching other parts of the country. This pattern was vividly illustrated in the 1988 – 1992 collapse of the housing market, during which London and the south-east were hit first, and most severely (resource 3.30 on page 66).

Key understandings

◆ House prices vary regionally, with London having consistently higher prices.

◆ Regional differences in house prices vary over time.

◆ The regional house price gap is highly cyclical, i.e. varies rhythmically over time.

◆ There is a two-way relationship between house price fluctuation and social, political, economic and environmental processes.

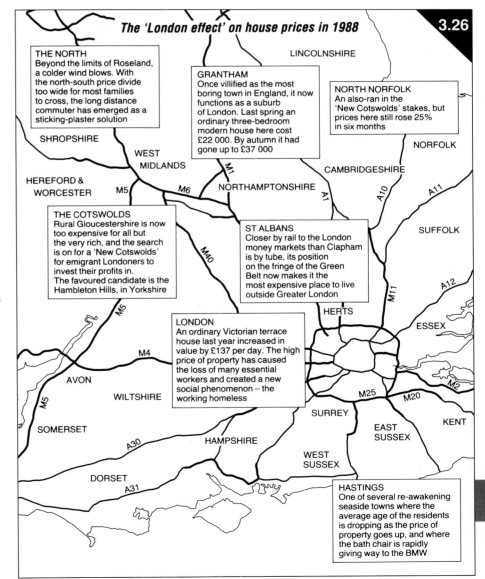

The 'London effect' on house prices in 1988 3.26

THE NORTH
Beyond the limits of Roseland, a colder wind blows. With the north-south price divide too wide for most families to cross, the long distance commuter has emerged as a sticking-plaster solution

GRANTHAM
Once villified as the most boring town in England, it now functions as a suburb of London. Last spring an ordinary three-bedroom modern house here cost £22 000. By autumn it had gone up to £37 000

NORTH NORFOLK
An also-ran in the 'New Cotswolds' stakes, but prices here still rose 25% in six months

THE COTSWOLDS
Rural Gloucestershire is now too expensive for all but the very rich, and the search is on for a 'New Cotswolds' for emigrant Londoners to invest their profits in. The favoured candidate is the Hambleton Hills, in Yorkshire

ST ALBANS
Closer by rail to the London money markets than Clapham is by tube, its position on the fringe of the Green Belt now makes it the most expensive place to live outside Greater London

LONDON
An ordinary Victorian terrace house last year increased in value by £137 per day. The high price of property has caused the loss of many essential workers and created a new social phenomenon – the working homeless

HASTINGS
One of several re-awakening seaside towns where the average age of the residents is dropping as the price of property goes up, and where the bath chair is rapidly giving way to the BMW

LINCOLNSHIRE · SHROPSHIRE · WEST MIDLANDS · HEREFORD & WORCESTER · NORTHAMPTONSHIRE · NORFOLK · CAMBRIDGESHIRE · SUFFOLK · HERTS · ESSEX · AVON · WILTSHIRE · SOMERSET · HAMPSHIRE · SURREY · WEST SUSSEX · EAST SUSSEX · KENT · DORSET · M5 · M6 · M1 · M40 · M4 · M11 · M25 · M20 · M2 · A1 · A10 · A11 · A12 · A30 · A31

The ups and downs of house prices

Resource 3.27 shows that house prices for the regions of the UK rose by as much as ten-fold between 1969 and 1987. The figures reveal first, persistent rises everywhere, second consistent regional differences in absolute price levels and third, regional variations in relative rates of price inflation. The pattern is made clearer by resource 3.28, where individual regional averages for each year are plotted as a percentage of the UK average. Thus, at the top end, house prices in London have run at 25–60 per cent above UK averages, while Yorkshire and Humberside has had lowest house prices, 65–80 per cent of the average. This regional pattern remained basically stable over the 19-year period. One significant exception was the province of Northern Ireland, which fluctuated strongly, (it was lowest in 1973; third in 1977–79; lowest in 1984). The main cause of these swings was shifting lending policies by building societies in the province.

Although the rank order of house prices remained relatively stable, a closer look at resource 3.28 reveals that there were consistent fluctuations in the size of regional price differentials. First, the gap between London and the south-east and the lower price regions opened up sharply during the first surge in house prices, in 1970–73. For example, in 1970 London house prices were 130 per cent of the UK average, but in 1972 were 150 per cent. In the south-east the 1970–72 rise was from 120 per cent to 135 per cent. There were small increases in the south-west and East Anglia, but all other regions showed a marked decline relative to the UK average. Second, the size of the gap narrowed considerably 1973–1978. By 1978 the gap between the high and the low price regions was back to the pre-price surge scale. Third, while London and south-east prices relative to the UK average peaked in 1972, in the south-west in 1973 and East Anglia in 1974, prices relative to

the national averages continued to rise until 1977 in the lower price regions. In other words, there was a time-lag in price movements between high price and low price regions. Fourth, this cyclical pattern was repeated, 1977–81 in a less marked fashion, e.g. in the 1977–79 house price boom, the gap between the four southern regions and the rest opened up, but narrowed again by 1981. In the 1983–1988 house price surge, the same pattern seemed to be emerging.

Resource 3.29 sums up this cyclical structure by plotting regional house prices as percentages of London prices. Two points stand out: (i) the consistent gap between London and the south-east and the rest of the country, and (ii) marked cyclical variations in regional house prices relative to London prices. Thus, between 1969 and 1972 average house prices fell sharply in relation to London prices, which meant that the regional price gap widened. From 1972 to 1978 the gap narrowed as regional house prices

3.27

Average regional house prices at mortgage completion stage (£000's)

	Northern	Yorks and Humber	East Midlands	East Anglia	Greater London	South East (Excl GLC)	South West
1969	3.7	3.4	3.8	4.3	6.2	5.8	4.5
1970	3.9	3.6	4.0	4.5	6.9	6.2	4.9
1971	4.4	4.0	4.4	5.0	7.4	7.3	5.6
1972	5.4	4.9	5.6	7.0	11.1	9.9	7.8
1973	7.4	7.1	8.2	9.8	14.4	13.2	10.9
1974	8.4	8.3	9.2	11.0	14.9	13.9	11.6
1975	9.6	9.1	10.0	11.5	14.9	14.7	12.1
1976	10.5	10.0	10.6	11.9	15.6	15.5	13.0
1977	11.8	10.7	11.4	12.2	16.7	16.5	13.6
1978	13.0	12.1	12.8	14.0	19.2	18.9	15.5
1979	15.4	15.0	15.8	18.5	25.8	24.7	20.5
1980	17.7	17.7	18.9	22.8	31.0	29.8	25.3
1981	18.6	19.2	19.5	23.1	30.8	30.0	25.4
1982	18.7	18.2	19.5	23.4	30.7	29.7	25.5
1983	20.0	20.9	22.0	25.8	34.6	33.8	28.0
1984	22.6	22.4	24.4	28.3	39.3	37.3	30.6
1985	22.8	23.3	25.5	31.7	44.3	40.5	32.9
1986	24.3	25.6	28.5	36.1	54.9	48.5	38.5
1987	27.2	27.2	31.8	42.7	66.0	57.4	44.7

	West Midlands	North West	Wales	Scotland	Northern Ireland	United Kingdom
1969	4.3	3.9	4.2	4.6	3.9	4.6
1970	4.5	4.2	4.4	5.0	4.4	5.0
1971	4.9	4.9	4.8	5.4	4.7	5.6
1972	6.2	5.7	5.9	6.2	4.9	7.4
1973	8.8	7.8	8.4	8.6	6.2	9.9
1974	10.3	8.9	9.4	9.8	8.7	11.0
1975	10.9	9.8	10.1	11.1	10.0	11.8
1976	11.6	10.5	11.1	13.0	12.9	12.7
1977	12.5	11.5	11.7	14.2	15.7	13.7
1978	14.3	13.4	13.4	16.1	18.4	15.6
1979	18.5	16.9	17.0	19.4	21.8	19.9
1980	21.7	20.1	19.4	21.8	23.7	23.6
1981	21.8	20.6	20.2	23.0	19.9	24.2
1982	21.0	20.8	19.7	22.5	20.2	23.6
1983	23.1	22.8	22.6	23.7	20.9	26.5
1984	25.0	24.4	23.9	25.6	21.4	29.1
1985	25.9	25.1	25.3	26.7	23.0	31.1
1986	28.4	27.5	27.4	28.2	25.7	36.3
1987	32.7	29.5	29.7	29.6	27.8	40.6

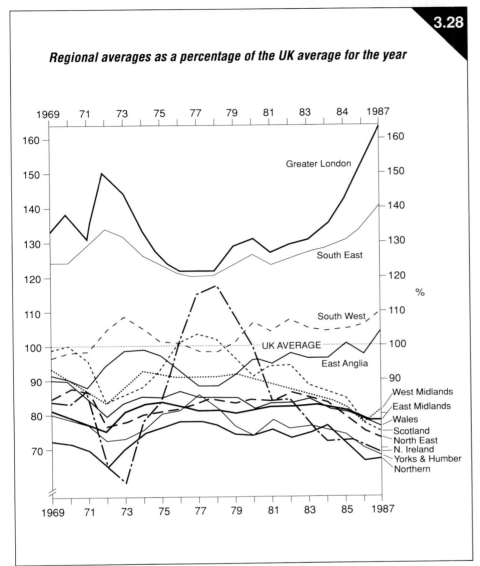

3.28

Regional averages as a percentage of the UK average for the year

rose proportionally more rapidly than London prices. Between 1978–80 the gap widened again, narrowed slightly 1982–83, and widened 1983–86, and by 1988 was narrowing again.

These changes in the difference between house prices in a particular region and the London figure are the result of variations in house price changes regionally. Resource 3.31 sets out the percentage rates of house price change and shows the violent fluctuations from year to year as well as indicating national rhythms of price surge and stagnation. But a closer examination of the figures brings out a further

important understanding: the four highest priced regions led the process of house price inflation. They were the first to rise, they rose most sharply and they were the first to fall back to slower rates of increase (resource 3.30). This is the regional time-lag effect. For example, notice the 50 per cent increases in Greater London in 1971–72, while the northern and Midland regions had much lower rates of increase. By 1972–73, when London and south-east increases had subsided to just over 30 per cent other regions were surging to 37–46 per cent increases. By 1973–74, price inflation in London and the south-east had all but ceased, but in Yorkshire and

Humberside, the region of lowest overall house prices, rises remained at 17 per cent. The same pattern is recognisable in more recent years.

Critical questions for the future, especially in the light of the 1988–92 stagnation of house prices are whether the north-south divide in house prices will continue, and whether the cyclical pattern of regional differences is a long-term feature. It is easy to be pessimistic, but note that both of the following extracts were written in mid-1988:

'It could be argued, on the basis of the regional incidence of jobs loss and unemployment over the past few years, that house prices in the northern regions will continue to remain depressed … While long term rates of price inflation have been similar between regions, this pattern may have come to an end as a result of the growing importance of banking, finance and insurance in the economy and its concentration in the south-east, the prosperity brought to the south-east as a result of the M25 and the proposed channel tunnel, the lower levels of unemployment … and resistance to the new housing building in the Green Belt.'

(C Hamnett, *The Royal Bank of Scotland Review*, 1988, p. 38).

'The current bout of house price inflation has proved so prolonged, and the north-south division so marked, that some are beginning to wonder whether we are now seeing a permanent change. The north-south gap has never been wider – a Yorkshire property, for example, is now worth just 36 per cent of one in London. Even at their previous worst, in 1973–74, Yorkshire properties were still worth around 53 per cent of the London ones.'

(J Counsell, *The Independent*, 3rd June, 1988).

These 1988 predictions were shattered by the stagnation of the

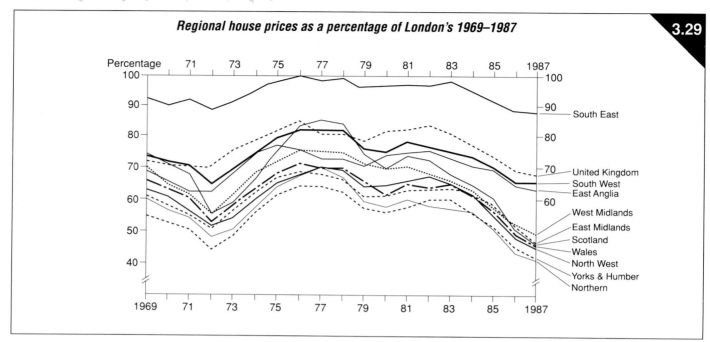

Regional house prices as a percentage of London's 1969–1987

3.29

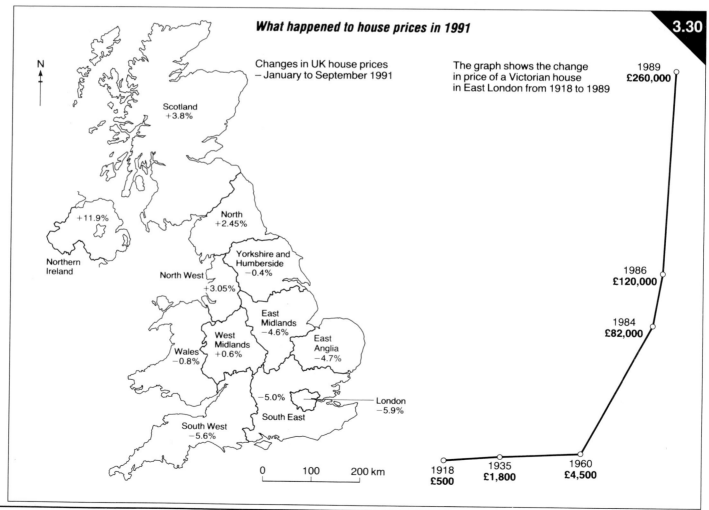

What happened to house prices in 1991

3.30

Changes in UK house prices
– January to September 1991

The graph shows the change
in price of a Victorian house
in East London from 1918 to 1989

Scotland
+3.8%

+11.9%

Northern
Ireland

North
+2.45%

North West
+3.05%

Yorkshire and
Humberside
−0.4%

East
Midlands
−4.6%

West
Midlands
+0.6%

East
Anglia
−4.7%

Wales
−0.8%

−5.0%

South East

London
−5.9%

South West
−5.6%

0   100   200 km

1989
£260,000

1986
£120,000

1984
£82,000

1918
£500

1935
£1,800

1960
£4,500

	Northern	Yorks and Humber	East Midlands	East Anglia	Greater London	South East	South West
1969–70	6.1	5.8	4.6	5.0	11.1	7.4	8.5
1970–71	11.3	10.7	10.7	10.0	7.5	17.0	14.0
1971–72	23.3	21.3	28.0	41.5	50.2	36.1	39.7
1972–73	37.0	44.6	45.7	40.7	30.0	32.8	39.8
1973–74	13.9	17.4	12.2	11.6	2.8	5.9	6.8
1974–75	13.7	9.3	8.7	4.8	0.4	5.1	4.2
1975–76	8.9	10.3	6.6	2.8	4.3	6.0	7.5
1976–77	12.6	7.3	6.8	2.7	7.6	5.9	4.2
1977–78	10.8	12.8	12.7	14.7	14.4	14.9	14.4
1978–79	18.4	24.0	23.6	32.2	34.6	30.4	32.2
1979–80	14.7	17.9	19.5	23.5	20.1	20.9	23.4
1980–81	5.0	8.5	2.8	1.1	–0.7	0.5	0.3
1969–81	401.0	459.0	413.0	436.0	396.0	417.0	464.0
1981–82	–2.8	–5.3	0.1	–1.3	–0.1	–1.0	–0.6
1982–83	10.8	14.8	13.0	10.6	12.8	13.8	9.7
1983–84	11.4	7.1	10.7	9.5	13.6	10.6	9.3
1984–85	0.8	4.4	4.8	11.9	12.6	8.4	7.6
1985–86	6.8	9.7	11.5	13.9	23.8	19.9	17.0
1986–87	12.1	8.4	11.7	18.4	20.3	18.2	16.1
1969–87	634.0	707.0	739.0	893.0	966.0	891.0	895.0

Average regional rates of house price inflation 1970-87 (%) 3.31

	West Midlands	North West	Wales	Scotland	Northern Ireland	United Kingdom
1969–70	3.3	6.7	6.4	8.5	11.3	7.2
1970–71	4.7	18.3	8.3	8.1	6.0	13.2
1971–72	26.5	15.7	23.6	15.3	6.1	30.9
1972–73	40.8	36.9	41.2	37.9	25.3	34.8
1973–74	16.8	13.4	12.1	13.7	40.9	10.5
1974–75	6.0	9.9	7.2	13.9	15.0	7.2
1975–76	6.9	7.5	10.4	16.5	28.3	7.8
1976–77	7.8	9.7	4.9	9.7	22.2	7.4
1977–78	14.5	16.4	14.6	13.4	17.0	14.2
1978–79	28.9	26.0	27.6	20.0	18.6	27.9
1979–80	17.1	18.9	13.5	12.3	8.4	18.4
1980–81	0.4	2.3	4.1	5.8	–15.9	2.5
1969–81	400.0	424.0	383.0	399.0	404.0	421.0
1981–82	–3.5	1.1	–2.4	–2.1	1.4	–2.2
1982–83	10.2	7.9	14.7	5.3	3.4	11.9
1983–84	8.0	6.9	6.2	8.0	2.9	9.9
1984–85	3.5	2.9	5.6	4.2	7.3	6.9
1985–86	10.0	9.5	9.4	4.8	11.9	16.6
1986–87	14.8	7.4	8.6	4.8	7.9	11.3
1969–87	651.0	653.0	613.0	542.0	605.0	770.0

housing market in 1989. As resource 3.30 shows, the time-lag model seems to have returned, with house prices falling in the south while continuing to rise in the north. We need to remember too, the close relationship between house prices and economic prosperity (resource 3.32).

3.32

With attractive price decrease

A spacious detached house with possible commercial use is on the market in the village of Bircher, near Leominster. And its attractiveness has been increased by a substantial decrease in the asking price.

Shrewsbury-based estate agency Cooper and Green, which covers South Shropshire and North Herefordshire from its Church Stretton office, urged the vendor that the original asking price around £159 000 was too optimistic in the present market place. Sensibly, the starter was adjusted down to £129 000.

(Source: Hereford Times, March 1992)

Activities

1 Construct graphs from resources 3.27 and 3.31 and label them to indicate where they illustrate or support key points made in this case study.

2 Use the materials to assess this statement: What you pay for a house depends as much on when you buy it as where you buy it.

3 **Suggested project**: update the figures used in this case study and attempt to determine whether the patterns and trends are still identifiable. (The property and finance sections of newspapers are useful sources, as are materials put out by building societies.)

CASE STUDY 3.5 *Do we really want to live together?*

Background

Social segregation – the clustering together of people with similar characteristics into separate residential neighbourhoods – has been one of the most persistent characteristics of cities. It is a sensitive aspect of geography as it raises the issues of social class, prejudice, snobbery, and the possibility of the ghetto. On the other hand, it includes the positive elements of community and neighbourhood, a feeling of belonging, as portrayed in soaps such as *Coronation Street* and *EastEnders*. At one extreme it is argued that people live among 'their own kind' by choice, and at the other extreme, that the 'system' forces them to do so. Reality is more complex, with the degree of choice people have about where they live varying widely

Income is the key factor in determining the type of home and its location, but other variables are used as we attempt to explain the process of social segregation, for example age, the stage in the family life-cycle, ethnic and cultural origins, educational level and occupation. These are aspects of demand, but there is also the supply side of the equation. This includes the housing stock made available by the private and public sectors, and the physical separation of council estates from private developments. The policies of estate agents and building societies also have an effect, for example the tactic of 'red lining', the drawing of a boundary around an area within which mortgages are unlikely to be granted.

Over the years, government and planning policies have attempted to reduce such segregation. These social policies have aimed to break down class and cultural barriers, to improve social and economic fairness and to create a less hierarchical and prejudiced society. For instance, several of the Phase I New Towns of the 1950s attempted to create socially mixed communities by building planned neighbourhoods which contained both private and public housing and homes of varying sizes, e.g. Hemel Hempstead. Such experiments proved unpopular and later New Towns were based on more homogenous, and hence socially segregated residential areas, towns such as Telford, and Redditch, where the Vietnamese immigrant families are tending to create clusters.

In recent years, the strength of the segregation forces has been exhibited in the 'gentrification' process. Traditionally 'working class' streets are invaded and progressively taken over by more affluent middle-class groups (the 'yuppies') and are upgraded. Sometimes this happens naturally, according to fashion. In other cases it is part of planned regeneration policies for inner city areas. The largest such scheme in Britain is the Docklands development of London's East End. Traditionally the East End has been a collection of tightly-knit working class communities. As the docks and other traditional industries declined from the 1950s, and housing schemes displaced thousands of families to peripherial estates, large areas became derelict. Then in the 1980s came the massive Docklands project, a massive multi-purpose series of commercial, leisure and residential developments, with a high-tech transport infrastructure including an airport and the new 'Docklands Light Railway'.

The marketing of this ambitious project has been decidedly up-market. Some traditional East End communities have felt that they were being pushed aside and their needs ignored by these huge projects. As a result of their protests, more lower cost or council homes have been included in some developments. In several cases, development permission has been granted on the understanding that some housing would be available for less affluent and more needy families, and those areas would become socially mixed. As the materials in this case study show, however, the attitudes and perceptions which help to generate social segregation remain powerful.

Key understandings

◆ Attitudes, perceptions and prejudices influence social segregation.

◆ The difficulty of supplying adequate housing for all socio-economic and cultural groups in locations of great land scarcity and high values.

'And ne'er the twain shall meet'

In late 1989, the Sir Thomas More Court estate near Tower Bridge was being marketed hard by its developers. It was just one of the Docklands developments which was experiencing difficulties as a result of the stagnation of the housing market caused by high London house prices and rising mortgage interest rates. The newspaper article makes it clear that further problems were emerging for this estate, generated by the policy of mixing housing tenure types and hence types of families (resource 3.33).

Activities

With a partner:

1 Identify the problem.

2 List the factors which influence the tensions.

3 List the various 'interested parties' (families and organisations) and summarise their attitudes and viewpoints.

4 In what ways does this issue illustrate the meaning of 'prejudice'?

5 Who is to blame, and what alternative solutions are there?

6 Group discussion: is social segregation (a) desirable, and (b) inevitable?

3.33

When neighbours become good enemies

Sue Poeton and Sofina Khatun spent last week being good mothers but they will never be good neighbours. It's nothing personal, says Poeton, who owns her own home on a London docklands estate. She just wishes that the man who sold her the house had warned her she would soon be living opposite a council house tenant.

It is not an atmosphere to encourage a natter over the garden fence. Until a year ago, Poeton was more than happy to pass the time of day with her neighbours. The advertising brochure had promised her 'a village atmosphere and friendly community that will echo the traditions of yesteryear', and the friendliness, at least, certainly seemed to have been delivered.

Then, one weekend last December, five months after she and her family had settled in to their £186 000 home overlooking a canal, she watched as 'seven or eight of them' moved in to her close on the Sir Thomas More Court estate in Wapping. As more council tenants moved into other parts of the estate over the next few weeks, the friendly community suddenly became very unfriendly.

Last week, neighbourly relations reached a new low. Claiming that the price of their homes had dropped because of the presence of their new neighbours, Tim and Sue Poeton, with nine other families, issued writs claiming that Heron Homes, the development company, had failed to tell them that part of the estate had been earmarked for council housing.

About 20 more home-owners are expected to issue writs over the next few weeks, with the legal arguments focusing on an arrangement reached between the London borough of Tower Hamlets and Heron Homes in which the council sold the land to the developer in return for 50 of the 190 homes on the estate.

It is, says Stephen Jakobi, the lawyer acting for the home-owners, an unprecedented row. In its implications, it is also a stark and rather unnerving demonstration of how the British middle-classes view the predominantly working class as both owners of property and possessions, and also as parents: there has been much criticism of the 'wayward' behaviour of some of the children.

Gordon Millar, managing director of Heron Homes, says no legal obligation existed for his company to 'provide a character description of prospective neighbours' and points out that 'no matter where you go in London, you are going to be adjacent to council houses'.

If a description of prospective neighbours had been issued, it would have shown that 25 of the 35 council families now living on the estate – 15 more will shortly be moving in – are Bengali, with just under a quarter of those coming from bed-and-breakfast accommodation. The remainder, mainly white, come from council houses in the borough that were either too small for their growing families or were falling down.

Such a social mix had not been anticipated by Peter and Heather Freeman, who bought their £145 000 home on the estate because 'it was the best part of docklands and we were told it was 100 per cent private'. Peter, a 44-year-old textile manufacturer, says the house is now probably worth £150 000, £40 000 less than a valuation carried out before the tenants moved in.

He said: 'It may sound trite but my parents lived in a council house in the early 1950s and there is no shame in that. I'm a left-wing Tory who firmly believes that the country should look after those in need and I also support the sale of council houses. However, the council children are running riot round here and damaging the common parts. I would not have bought the house if I had known I would be living on a council estate.'

Freeman stresses that the home-owners' objections are not racially inspired. When he and his wife discovered the 'disastrous' news after returning from a holiday last January, they helped set up an action committee with a 'fighting fund' to finance the legal action. One member of that group is Harris Yee-Chong, a 57-year-old Chinese dentist, produced by the home-owners as evidence that this is not a racial issue.

Yee-Chong is not, however, a convincing standard-bearer for the case. In common with many Chinese in Britain, he is outspoken about racial groups who do not 'attempt to blend in with the British way of life'. He said: 'I tried to talk to one of the council tenants the other day. He said he was on the dole and had never worked in his life. It's not very encouraging, is it, to know that one of your neighbours is on the dole and from a foreign country?'

While few of the other home-owners would express themselves in this way, particularly to a newspaper, there is no doubt that Yee-Chong's comments do reflect a certain view. It is that somebody who is foreign and unemployed, such as Alu Hassan, a 33-year-old Cypriot who has been out of work for three years, is not likely to contribute to the professional ethos of an estate like Sir Thomas More Court. When investments, like homes, are involved, feelings run high.

They are equally high, however, on the council tenants' side. Hassan's next door neighbour, Sofina Khatun, the woman now unlikely to be befriended by her fellow mother Sue Poeton, is angry that her colour and culture could be held against her.

She said: 'We like to live in this area and have as much right to live here as they do. The other day, I heard one of the women shouting at a council tenant to keep her children quiet. She said she paid a mortgage and the council tenant only paid £65 a week. It was very upsetting. I just wish everyone here could be friends.'

If the Poeton and Khatun families were to call on each other's homes, they would discover many common interests. They share a professional background – Sofina's husband, Afzal, is a teacher while Tim Poeton is a Lloyd's insurance broker – and a strong desire to 'strive hard in God's cause with your possessions and your lives', in the words of an Arabic saying pinned up in the Khatun sitting-room.

Any rapport is impossible, however, in the present climate on the estate. One white council tenant described how a woman home-owner took video film of his son who was cycling round the estate. 'She said she was taking the film because my son was not allowed to bicycle where he was and she wanted the evidence. My family have lived in the East End of London all our lives and yet we are now being made to feel like invaders. We hate it here and want to get out.'

Ironically, such a lament should not have been necessary if officers at Tower Hamlets had been given their way. Ian Orton, chief executive of the Wapping Neighbourhood branch of the council, said the officers had decided the estate did not fit in with the council's housing plan but had been overruled by the councillors.

'In the year before last, we were paying out £30m on bed-and-breakfast bills for homeless families and there was a lot of pressure to reduce this amount.

Having said that, we did not consider this estate to be suitable for the council tenants.'

Some council tenants are happy with the estate, however, and many of them are now planning to buy their homes.

It could be the final straw for the present home-owners, who according to one council spokesman, are 'just a little bit jealous'.

The reason: while some home-owners were buying their investments for well over £100 000, some tenants could now be getting a £100 000 house for as little as £30 000 under the right-to-buy legislation.

One of the tenants said: 'It's the least we deserve after all we have been through this year.'

(Source: Charles Oulton, *The Sunday Times*, 5 November 1989)

CHAPTER 4

Places for living – housing in the developing world

Introduction

Obtaining a secure home is a fundamental need for all but the most nomadic peoples. A growing population means a growing demand for housing, and the more rapid the population increase, the more difficult it is to keep pace with demand. As the case studies in Chapter 3 show, even rich, industrialised countries with slow population growth such as the United Kingdom, have housing problems. Furthermore, it is not simply the quantity of available housing but its quality and location and finally those who have access to it, which are important issues. For millions of people across the world, simply obtaining some form of legal right to their dwelling and the land on which it stands, is still a dream or a struggle only recently won.

Countries vary too, in their ability to build homes, and some of the countries with the most rapidly growing populations, are among the world's poorest nations. These countries find it difficult to raise funding for, and to provide the organisation and infrastructure for industries and services which are required to support a large-scale house-building industry. As a result of the inadequacy of this 'formal' sector, many countries have a thriving 'informal' sector of self-build activity. People have proved remarkably resourceful in providing themselves with homes. However these are often of a very low standard, lacking in facilities and are deemed 'illegal' (resource 4.1).

The case studies in this chapter illustrate a variety of strategies for providing homes, from illegal squatter settlements in Manila (case study 4.1), through self-help, upgrading and site-and-services schemes in Zambia (case study 4.3), to city and central government housing projects in Thailand (case study 4.2) and China (case study 4.4). Part II of case study 4.4 illustrates how settlements can be made more efficient and 'liveable' by integrating housing with economic activity and transportation.

4.1

Mexico City is the most populous conurbation in the world. These people live in Borde de Vias colony. Peasants from poor communities reach the city at a rate of 1000 a day and usually end up in places like this

CASE STUDY 4.1   *A metropolis in the developing world – Manila, Philippines*

Background

Economically developing countries in the Third World are experiencing explosive urban growth (resource 4.3). This growth, in both absolute numbers and in percentage terms, is especially rapid in the larger cities and in metropolitan areas (resource 4.2). As many developing countries have difficulty in sustaining consistent economic growth, such urban expansion may outstrip the ability of a country to support it. For instance, resource 4.4 shows that countries with low rates of GNP growth or even falling GNP, tend to have relatively rapid urban growth. As we can see from the map in resource 4.3, many of these are developing countries. All too often, the outcome is low incomes and poverty at the individual and family level. This is made worse by the inability of the city authorities and the infrastructure (roads, water supply, health services etc.) to cope with the rate and scale of growth.

Yet as we shall see, local communities and local authorities are making enormous efforts to improve the quality of life.

Clearly, every city is unique, and it is dangerous to make generalisations. Nonetheless, there are certain inter-related characteristics and problems common to many cities in developing countries. Manila, the capital city of the Philippines, is used here to illustrate how the low quality of housing is related to both poor economic opportunities and inadequate infrastructure. These combine to downgrade environmental quality and hence the quality of life for millions of people. The materials identify the major aspects of the problem, and you may find it helpful to use them as a basis for comparative studies of other cities.

4.2

Population growth rates in cities of developing countries (percentage per year)

Population	1960–70	1970–80	1980–90
20 000–99 999	1.2	0.1	−0.5
100 000– 499 999	3.5	4.4	2.6
500 000–999 999	4.1	5.4	4.4
> 1 million	5.4	5.6	5.6

4.3

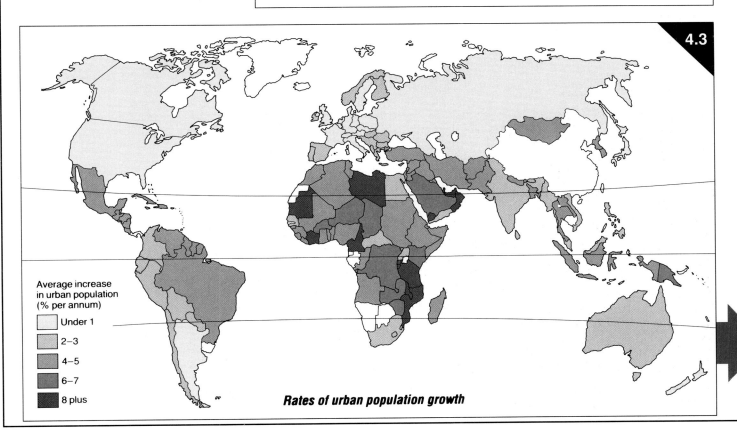

Average increase in urban population (% per annum)

- Under 1
- 2–3
- 4–5
- 6–7
- 8 plus

Rates of urban population growth

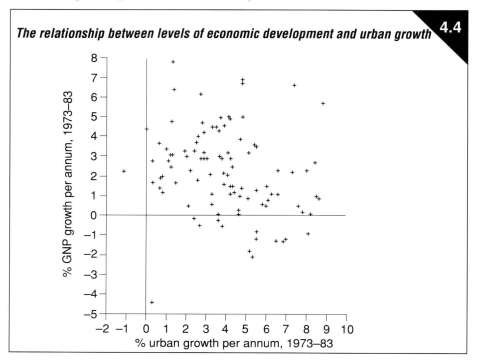

The relationship between levels of economic development and urban growth 4.4

y-axis: % GNP growth per annum, 1973–83

x-axis: % urban growth per annum, 1973–83

Key understandings

◆ In many large cities in the developing world the rate of growth, from in-migration and natural increase, threatens to overwhelm the ability of the city authorities to cope

◆ The weakness of the planning system combined with the rapidity of the growth and the poverty of the majority of the people may lead to environmental deterioration and further lowering of the quality of life

◆ Some or all of the issues present in Manila may be found in other cities in the developing world.

Manila – the growing pains of a metropolis

As in many of the major cities in the developing world, Metropolitan Manila has grown rapidly into a very large agglomeration with an inadequate planning framework and infrastructure and services needed to maintain the environmental quality. Metropolitan Manila has some 8 million people with an area of 636 square kilometres and includes the city of Manila, three nearby cities (Caloocan, Quezon and Pasay) and 13 adjacent municipalities (resource 4.5). Almost half of the population is estimated to be poor. With rapid population growth likely to continue, with a serious economic crisis and a deteriorating urban environment, the prospects for the future are not encouraging. At present, a large proportion of the population already suffer serious threats to their health, safety and well-being, as a result of their housing and living environments.

Background – a brief history of Metropolitan Manila

In the 16th century, prosperous villages along the shores of Manila Bay, appealed to the Spanish conquerors as a good site for a capital. The site of Manila provided excellent anchorage for ships and its virtually land-locked nature could easily be defended.

Population movements to Manila began during the early years of the Spanish conquest, but it was during the period under the rule of the United States that Manila grew into a large city. From 2000 inhabitants in the 16th Century, it grew to 329 000 in 1903 (when the first modern national census was taken). At the end of the Second World War in 1945 Manila expanded very rapidly, with the urban area spreading to what had previously been peripheral areas such as Pasay, Quezon City, Caloocan and Mandaluyong, all of which became part of what is now known as the Metropolitan Manila area. By 1949, after the Philippines had been granted independence, the population had reached around 1 million inhabitants. By 1970, it had 4 million inhabitants; 6 million in 1980 and some 7.35 million in 1988.

Located along the eastern shore of Manila bay and delta plains of the Pasig River, it is bounded by the swampy delta of the Pampanga River in the north, by the Bataan peninsula in the east and by the Laguna de Bay, a freshwater lake to the south-east.

The average population growth rate between 1970 and 1980 was 4.1 per cent per annum compared to a national average of 2.7 per cent for the rest of the nation. This implies that a substantial proportion of Manila's population growth during this period was a result of net in-migration. Metropolitan Manila had the highest population growth rate of any region in the Philippines in this decade.

Environmental problems of housing

The economic crisis faced by the Philippines has hit Metropolitan Manila more severely than other regions. A 1988 report on Urban Poor reports that about 44 per cent of Metropolitan Manila's residents live below the poverty line. The threshold for this poverty line is set at roughly US$156 a month per family which is far above the mean monthly family income of US$91. Although 80 per cent of the labour force is employed, 28 per cent of these are underemployed. With a low income for most families and a high cost of real estate in Manila, most people find the cost of purchasing a house or flat beyond their means. The result of this gap between what people can afford and the cost of the cheapest reasonable quality unit has been a large number of house room renters and the growth of squatter areas. House room renters represent 44.1 per cent of total families in the region. An additional 16 per cent were 'sharer/visitors' which is the term given to those who double up with other families to rent rooms or who stay and share rooms for free, indefinitely (for instance, sons or daughters and their spouses and children staying with their parents). On average, there are 12 persons per household with this large average size being explained by the proportion of people who are 'sharers/visitors'.

There is a very large and growing number of squatters in Metropolitan Manila and local government officials working in the cities or municipalities which make up Metropolitan Manila admit to being overwhelmed by the problems. In Quezon City, of the total population of 1.5 million, one estimate suggests that 50 per cent are squatters. Uncontrolled migration has contributed much to swelling the urban population.

The Philippines Government has not succeeded either in implementing policies which would moderate the flow of migrants into Metropolitan Manila or which would lower birth rates and thus the rate of natural increase.

In 1986, immediately after the February revolution (with the overthrow of the Marcos Government), thousands of people occupied vacant public and private land. In Metropolitan Manila, there was the 'invasion' of the Pasig development property in Ortigas and several government housing projects in Quezon City, Pasig and Dagat-Dagatan.

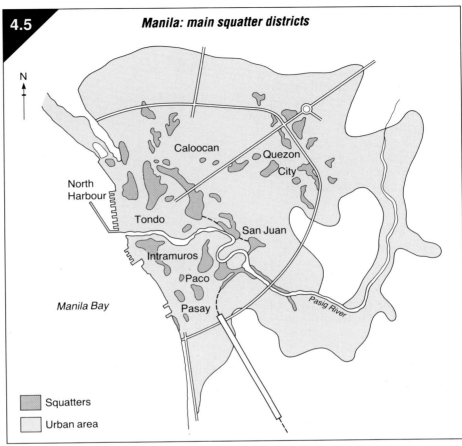

4.5 **Manila: main squatter districts**

- Squatters
- Urban area

One of the best examples of this move by squatters is the occupation of 51 hectares of reclaimed land along historic Roxas boulevard. It is now home to some 10 000 families and represents a challenge to the Public Estates Authority which cannot implement plans for the area because of the difficulties in ejecting the squatters. This is one reason for the reluctance of foreign investors to invest in this location. It is now called Pobres Park (the word 'pobre' meaning poor in Spanish) – to contrast it with Forbes Park where millionaires live. The 1988 report on Urban Poor has reported the existence of a syndicate which controls entry into the area, charges fees depending on the financial capacity of households and manages the affairs of the community. Electricity is tapped illegally from a government building and water supply is provided through door-to-door vendors.

Government attempts to enforce laws have had little impact on the development of squatter settlements. Government officials have apparently postponed decisions about ejecting squatters since they probably feel that moving these people to new sites without assurance of economic opportunities in the areas to which they are relocated would simply make the problem worse.

Solid waste

Metropolitan Manila can hardly cope with the 3500 tons of waste generated daily by domestic, commercial, industrial and institutional sources. The inability of local governments and the metropolitan administration to develop a policy on solid waste disposal and management is illustrated by a garbage dump known as 'Smokey Mountain' which covers some 22.6 hectares, with an elevation at its highest point of 18 metres. The rotting mass of organic material also produces a haze over the dump, coming from methane gas produced by the decomposition process (resource 4.6).

Some 20 000 people live in this area and some have lived here for 40 years or more. These people refuse to be relocated since they claim that they would lose their sources of livelihood by doing so. Most of these people make a living by scavenging on the garbage dump and many are children who sort through the garbage with their bare hands.

Water pollution

The two main sources of water pollutants in Metropolitan Manila are domestic and industrial wastes. Only 15 per cent of Metropolitan Manila's population is served with sewers or individual septic tanks. In addition rubbish, silt and other solid wastes find their way into 'esteros' (canals) and flood drainage mains.

Sewage, industrial wastes and rubbish, and other solid wastes washed into water bodies greatly lower their level of dissolved oxygen to the point where marine life is damaged or killed, and the water becomes anaerobic, turbid and foul smelling, unfit for use.

Inadequate or no safeguards in the disposal of toxic wastes from industry have contributed to high levels of heavy metals e.g. copper, cadmium in some river systems in Metropolitan Manila. The problems of water pollution are made worse by high levels of pesticide use in the region, as surface run-off water washes the pesticides off the crops and farmlands into waterways.

One illustration of the consequences of uncontrolled dumping of wastes is the so-called 'red tide' phenomenon. Since September 1988, bays in the Philippines have been suffering from a condition said to be brought about by the abnormal and uncontrolled growth of phytoplanktons caused by the high organic load in water bodies. This has rapidly engulfed the entire 90 000 hectares of Manila Bay. By

4.6

Children and animals on a garbage dump. Many people use dumps like these in order to scavenge for a living

October 1988, eight other bays had been affected – and all were rich fishing grounds. Eight deaths have been reported from 73 cases of poisoning from eating contaminated shellfish. As a result, the authorities have prohibited the eating of shellfish and other marine products from these areas, which has brought more hardship to many fishermen. In addition, it has removed an important source of protein from the diets of many Manila residents.

Flooding

About 2034 cubic metres of rubbish are thrown daily into Metropolitan Manila's waterways which clog them and contribute to flooding during the rainy season. In addition, some 4600 hectares are prone to flooding and affect some 1.9 million people.

Three major causes of flooding have been the overflowing of Manila's heavily silted rivers during intense rainfall; the insufficient capacity of inland drainage facilities; and the disappearance of 35 out of an estimated 95 'esteros' (canals) which, prior to World War II, were transportation arteries. Furthermore, illegal construction of dykes and the conversion of traditional fishponds

along the shores into residential areas have made the flooding worse.

Air pollution

In Manila, as in most cities, motor vehicles, industries and thermal power stations are the major sources of air pollution. The average concentrations of sulphur dioxide in the atmosphere for the years 1973 to 1980 (73 microgrammes per cubic metre) exceeded those in New York, Los Angeles and Chicago and were comparable to those in Frankfurt and London. The average concentration of particulate matter was 85 microgrammes per cubic metre, far exceeding that of Tokyo (61), New York (65) and London (31). The study also showed a significant correlation between high lead concentrations in the blood and proximity of the household to dense traffic. Mental retardation is the most devastating effect of exposure to lead.

A framework for sustained development

It is clear that municipal, city and national governments in many countries have been unable to manage city growth and guarantee adequate infrastructure and services. Metropolitan Manila is no exception, despite the fact that the economic activities within it account for 32 per cent of the nation's gross domestic product and that local governments there receive one-third of all local government revenues. The poverty of so many of its inhabitants also limits the scale of local taxation to fund any major investment programme.

Responses to urban problems have been piecemeal. They have included traffic management experiments in certain areas, a revised system of rubbish collection and efforts to revive some rivers. But there is a need for a long term strategy.

First, there must be a recognition of the scale and nature of current urbanisation and an assessment of the extent of deterioration so that the resource base can be rehabilitated and preserved. Urban communities must develop a diversity of land uses so that areas can be broken up into smaller self-contained communities, functionally related to one another. This can be made possible through the following actions:

- defining residential areas in relation to sources of employment to simplify economic activities and journey-to-work patterns;
- encouraging urban farming and urban forestry in areas where these are traditional and/or feasible;
- restoring water bodies to their natural condition so that once again they become sources of food and water and places of recreation as well as receivers and carriers of sewage and surface run-offs.

Second, there should be manageable population densities in relation to physical, financial and natural resources so as to minimise environmental stress This can be done through:

- promoting awareness of the advantages of smaller families;
- guiding the location of residential

areas through zoning and other developmental control measures as well as locational incentives;

Third, integrate rural and urban development with the aim also of minimising rural/urban differences. Among possible measures are:

- implementation of agrarian and urban land reform programmes so that social justice may prevail; without government measures to offer alternative land sites to squatters, there is little chance of major improvements in housing. Similarly, without agrarian reform, there is little possibility of slowing the migration from rural areas to cities;
- promotion of activities which are environmentally sound or which have built into them measures to minimise pollution.

Fourth, encourage local community involvement.

A study undertaken in 1984 looked into cases involving land-use conflicts at the local level. This level was the 'barangay' which is the smallest political unit within the Philippines. The study concluded that, by and large, there was a lack of community organisation to allow residents within the 'barangay' to work together to achieve common goals.

The level of the 'barangay' can provide the opportunity for community issues and problems to be discussed for the following reasons:

- it is small enough to allow first-hand knowledge of any important event or activity affecting the community;
- it is the smallest unit of government where planning may take place since its legislative assembly has the power to make decisions on matters which affect the community such as health and safety, enhancing prosperity and general welfare, maintaining peace and order;
- through its residents, there is a reservoir of workers who may be

willing to devote time to organising discussions about matters affecting their community.

(Source: adapted from R D Jimenez and A Velasquez, 'Metropolitan Manila – a framework for sustained development', *Environment and Urbanization*, 1(1), April 1989, pp. 51–58)

Activities

1 From resource 4.3, make a list of the countries with urban growth greater than 4 per cent. How many of these can be classified as economically developing countries?

2 a Identify the main categories of 'illegal' residents in Manila.

 b How are they solving their housing problems?

 c Why are they proving so difficult to deal with?

3 In what ways might 'community involvement' be able to improve the quality of life for the poorer residents of Manila?

4 List the enviromental problems occurring in Manila, suggest their causes, and possible ways of reducing them.

CASE STUDY 4.2 *Can housing supply meet demand?*

Background

In Thailand, the Bangkok metropolitan area dominates all other cities and towns in size and function – giving a primate city structure. As is typical of primate cities, Bangkok, straddling the Chao Phraya river, some 33 km north of the Gulf of Thailand, is a magnet for migrants, especially for young people (resource 4.7). This results in a youthful population structure and high birth rates. The combination of inward migration and high birth rates has produced explosive population growth (resource 4.8), and is continuing to grow by 2.5–3.0 per cent a year. In 1984, the built-up area of the metropolitan region exceeded 1300 sq.km, with approximately 32 sq.km a year being converted from agricultural to urban land uses. Between 1984 and 2000, it is estimated that the built-up area will expand by 40 per cent.

Cities in the developing world with such characteristics of size and growth are likely to experience severe housing shortages. This often leads to a large and expanding informal housing sector, including slums and squatter settlements. In addition, as the built-up area spreads, so the zone of most rapid development will ripple outwards from the central city. The materials in this case study reveal that there is a large slum and squatter element in Bangkok, and that maximum growth rates are moving outwards. However, the city seems to be sustaining high rates of housing supply, which is helping to prevent a rapid rise in the numbers and proportion of people living in inadequate accommodation. A further aspect of city change in the developing world is looked at critically: figures show that, in Bangkok at least, it is not simply the enormous inflow of people from the countryside which is generating the population explosion.

4.7

Crowded street in Bangkok. Increasing numbers of people moving to the city put severe strain on housing stocks

Key understandings

◆ A set of factors interact to determine the rate and character of housing provision.

◆ Cities in the developing world with high rates of population growth, have distinctive housing problems and responses to these problems.

◆ It is possible for the formal housing sector to sustain rapid housing supply, but the informal sector is likely to remain an important element in the housing market.

◆ Natural increase (excess of births over deaths) may be as important as in-migration in the population growth of developing world cities.

◆ Great care must be taken in making generalisations about the characteristics of developing world cities.

4.8

Population growth in Bangkok, 1960–1991 (millions)

	1960	1970	1980	1991 (estimate)
Bangkok Metropolitan City (BMC)	2.14	3.19	4.86	6.48
Bangkok Metropolitan Region (BMR)	3.30	3.79	6.87	9.25

The example of Bangkok, Thailand

Part I: Finding homes in Bangkok

Resource 4.9 lists the six main elements of Bangkok city's housing market, and how each contributed to the supply, 1974–84. Two features stand out: first, the addition of almost 350 000 dwellings in a decade, a remarkable achievement, and second, the dominance of the private sector in this provision.

Almost half of the additional housing has been in the suburban ring 10–20 km from the city centre (resources 4.10 and 4.11). In the already densely developed inner zone (0–5 km), the only substantial building was of shophouses, indicating the commercial emphasis around the CBD. As the middle ring becomes developed, so the zone of maximum growth will ripple outwards, drawn particularly by lower land prices, e.g. in 1986, land in the 20–30 km zone costs only one third as much as in the 10–20 km zone. The impact of

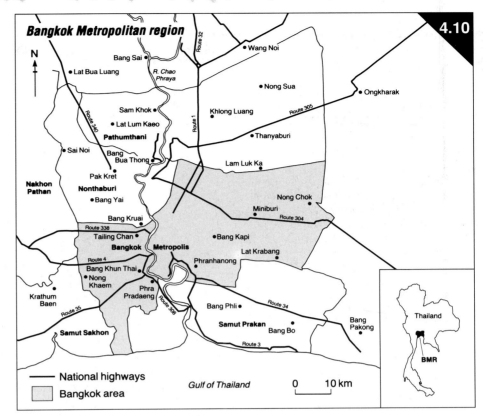

4.10

Bangkok Metropolitan region

— National highways

▨ Bangkok area

Gulf of Thailand

0   10 km

Thailand

BMR

4.9

Bangkok BMR housing stock, 1974–84

Type of housing	1974 ('000)	1984 ('000)	Share of change (%)
Private developer housing	20	114	27
Shophousing (1)	135	248	32
Land sub-division (2)	31	70	11
Individual (3)	209	271	18
Slum and squatter (4)	139	160	6
Institutional (5)	19	39	6
Total	553	902	100

(1) Shop/Workshop on to the street, with dwelling attached.
(2) Break-up of plots of land for private building, sometimes on public land.
(3) Individuals build on separate plots, with legal rights.
(4) Illegal and unauthorised building.
(5) Army, health, education etc.

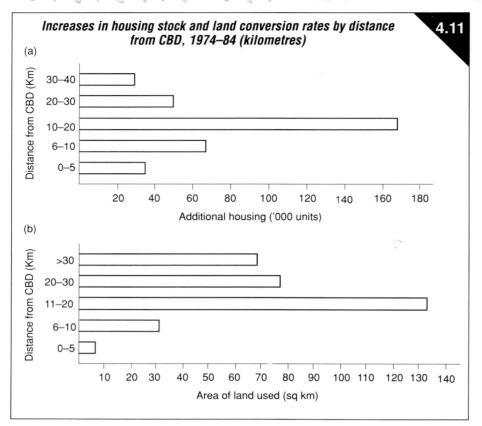

Increases in housing stock and land conversion rates by distance from CBD, 1974–84 (kilometres)

4.11

(a)

Additional housing ('000 units)

(b)

Area of land used (sq km)

prices rise even further; high land prices force housing costs up; the infrastructure is not developed, (there are few access roads, a poor water supply and sewage removal); government bureaucracy is inefficient; local construction industry cannot supply the materials.

Yet the picture in Bangkok, at least until 1984, was optimistic. Ample land was being made available by government and private owners, roads and water supply were being put in rapidly, there was little sign of land hoarding or widespread land speculation. In consequence, land prices within 10 km of the CBD rose by less than two per cent a year, and at 15–20 km the rise was only three to four per cent a year. These figures are no higher than US cities with similar growth rates, and lower than comparable British cities. Thus, a 1974–84 survey concluded that although the numbers of slum and squatter dwellings did grow from 139 000 to 160 000 (+6 per cent), this was relatively small when compared with the population explosion (resource 4.8).

the development upon the built-up area can be seen in the pie graphs of resource 4.12 with proportional rises increasing as distance from the CBD increases. Over 40 per cent of the total land conversion, 1974–84, took place in the 10–20 km zone.

Despite this growth, an important question arises: has this building

kept pace with housing demand, and has it made housing available to all groups of people? Housing crises are common in rapidly growing cities, as demand outstrips supply, and several reasons are given for such shortages, e.g. not enough land is made available, and land prices rise; speculators 'hoard' land until land

House building can only continue of course, especially in the private sector, if people can afford to buy or rent the dwellings. This has proved to be a problem in many cities with significant numbers of low income households. Resource 4.13 suggests that in Bangkok developers and

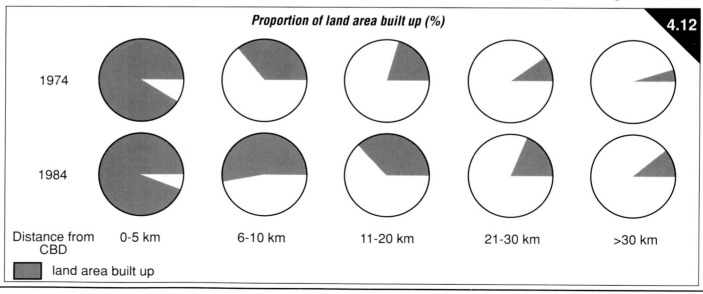

Proportion of land area built up (%)

4.12

1974

1984

Distance from CBD: 0-5 km | 6-10 km | 11-20 km | 21-30 km | >30 km

▨ land area built up

builders have been successful in keeping costs down and making housing 'affordable'. Notice how in 1986 the proportion of cheaper housing had increased from 1980. Conversely, the emergence of a wealthier middle class is indicated by 28 per cent of new buildings falling into the $28 600 – $33 800 price range. Most of the lower cost housing is on medium-scale projects, averaging 5 hectares and 180–200 dwelling units.

This is how the system works:

'Land developers acquire the land, add fill (NB This is flat floodplain land), lay out plots, provide infrastructure and contract with builders to construct housing. ... In some instances, particularly in the case of low-priced housing projects, the developer designs only one model for sale ... and may not allow the buyer to make any changes in the construction design or in the finish work. This allows the developer to control builder costs by building a standard unit at a fixed price. Materials costs can also be lowered by volume purchasing.'

A further strategy for keeping down costs is to reduce plot size. For example, in 1980, the majority of detached and semi-detached house plots were 164–200 sq.m; in 1986, the most common size was 40–80 sq.m. Finally, mortgages have become easier to obtain.

Thus, it is possible to conclude that 'the Bangkok land market is performing well. The private land and housing development sector is shifting into the low- and moderate-price range. The relative size of the informal housing sector is declining as the formal private sector expands production 'downmarket'. Moreover, house affordability has improved.'

(Source: adapted from D E Dowall, 'Bangkok: A profile of an efficiently performing housing market', *Urban Studies*, 36(3), June 1989, pp. 327–339)

4.13

Selling prices of new dwellings on private projects ($ US, 1986 value)

Price range	1980	1986
	(% of units)	
>10 400	6	10
10 401 – 13 000	10	26
13 001 – 18 200	32	18
18 201 – 23 400	18	5
23 401 – 28 600	13	10
28 601 – 33 800	10	28
>33 800	11	3

Part II: So who are the slum dwellers and squatters?

A 1985 survey estimated that approximately one million people (18 per cent of the population) lived in 10 290 slum and squatter settlements in Bangkok. Individual settlements ranged in size from tightly packed clusters of less than 100 households, to Klong Toey near the harbour and port industries, with at least 7500 households, amounting to 30–35 000 people. Slum dwellers mostly rented land from private owners and built their own dwellings, while squatters simply occupied land, paid no rent, and built their dwellings. Both types were outside the formal housing sector, and there was a growing threat of eviction from private owners or the city government, and so there had been few improvements via public projects. On public lands, where most squatter settlements were found, at least 40 per cent of the people faced eviction pressure, while in the slum settlements rented from private landlords, only 15 per cent were recorded as 'threatened'. The pressures were greater near to the CBD where land prices are high.

Where do they come from?

'One concept of slums is that they serve as a 'reception centre' for migrants who come to join their relatives and friends, and become socialised to urban life'. The 1985 report showed that Bangkok did not fit this picture, and although migration had been a significant factor in Bangkok's growth, natural increase (excess of births over deaths) was more important (resource 4.14). Even in newly developing slum and squatter settlements, there were twice as many incomers from other parts of the city as there were migrants from the countryside. The scale of intra-city movement was a reflection of the growing eviction pressures and the impermanence of many squatter settlements. The report concluded: 'the level of migration into Bangkok tends to be exaggerated. Various other urban places ... absorb many migrants, most of whom move from place to place'.

The report makes an important connection between migration and the deforestation issues. Thailand has significant areas of tropical rainforest, but the government has become alarmed about the rate of deforestation, and has begun to restrict further clearance. The report comments: 'encroached forest land absorbs millions of people. If there were no forest for encroachment, the level of migration into Bangkok would be higher'.

Are slum dwellers and squatters all poor?

While in 1985, slum dwellers had below average incomes, a sample survey showed that only 23 per cent regarded themselves as 'poor', while over 70 per cent saw themselves as having 'moderate' economic conditions. Resource 4.15, from a survey of four slum settlements, show that although most adults are 'unskilled', a very high proportion have some form of employment. Notice the importance of the 'informal sector' as a source of jobs, e.g. street traders, labourers hired by individuals rather than companies. Also, although slum and squatter settlements often grow up near job opportunities, and further opportunities are generated by a settlement as it grows, many people travel considerable distances to work. Poverty is relieved in many households by the **presence of several income earners** (resource 4.15(b)). Finally, the figures reveal considerable differences between the four settlements and warn us of the dangers of generalising about slums and slum dwellers.

(Source: adapted from S Pornchokchai, 'Bangkok slum and squatter settlements', *Planning and administration*, 16(2), Autumn 1989, pp. 104–114)

Activities

1 From the materials in this case study, assess the role played by the formal and informal housing sectors in the growth of Bangkok.

2 Using standard textbooks, identify:

a a model of urban morphology, and

b the growth characteristics of large cities in the developing world.

To what extent does Bangkok fit such a model of structure and growth in terms of housing development?

4.14

Factors influencing the growth of Bangkok

Annual rate (%)	1972	1974	1976	1978	1980	1982
Natural increase	2.4	2.2	2.6	2.1	1.6	1.4
Net migration	0.9	1.8	1.8	0.6	1.5	1.1
Overall increase	3.3	4.0	4.4	2.7	3.1	2.5

4.15

(a) Occupation of residents of four slums

Bodindaecha:	craftsman (13)	apprentice (10)	factory worker (8)
Bangsue:	vendor (41)	apprentice (13)	soldier (6)
Chongnonsee:	factory worker (16)	construction worker (11)	dressmaker (9)
Bonkai:	vendor (18)	dressmaker (9)	apprentice/ construction worker (8)

(b) Income earners per average household

	Settlements			
	A	B	C	D
average household size (persons)	5.4	5.5	5.8	4.0
persons in labour force	3.8	4.3	4.3	3.0
number of income earners	2.2	2.4	2.6	1.8
% of earners/household	41.8	43.6	46.1	47.7

(c) Locations of workplace %

	Settlements			
	A	B	C	D
at home	8.1	19.5	1.28	4.3
in the settlement	1.8	16.3	2.4	7.6
nearby (within .5 km)	11.7	19.5	14.4	7.6
outside the settlement	61.3	38.2	65.6	64.1
abroad	1.8	1.6	–	1.1
no certain place	15.3	4.9	4.8	15.2

(d) Settlement-to-workplace distances (km)

	Settlements			
	A	B	C	D
less than 2 km	34.2	45.8	29.8	50.0
2–4 km	15.8	4.2	27.4	27.3
4–7 km	5.3	18.1	22.6	7.6
7–10 km	18.4	16.7	11.9	3.0
more than 10 km	26.3	15.3	8.3	12.1
average distance	7.1	5.6	5.3	4.2

(Note: 'less than 2 km' excludes those working at home, in the settlement, and nearby less than .5 km).

CASE STUDY 4.3 — *Upgrading as a method of tackling urban housing problems in developing countries – Zambia*

Background

Squatter settlements are a common element of urban morphology in developing countries (resource 4.5, page 73). They are the outcome of urban population growth outstripping the capacity of the government and the construction industry, – the **formal** housing sector – to supply the housing need at affordable prices or rents. So, families simply occupy a plot of land wherever they can, often on the fringes of a city, and build accommodation for themselves – the **informal** housing sector (resource 4.16). This so-called 'unauthorised' housing is illegal, in that the settlers have neither rights of ownership nor hold legal lease on the land. For this reason, some governments have tried to remove these settlements, but then find they cannot rehouse the displaced families who seek out other sites and begin again.

Where the unauthorised settlements are not removed, they tend to develop through a consolidation process, by self-help among the community. For instance, dwellings are made more substantial, and where possible, extended; a rough street pattern evolves; community groups and activities emerge; shops

4.16

Informal shanty housing

and markets develop; workshops spring up. Nonetheless, the people do not have the wealth or power to install drinking water or electricity supplies and to provide health and education facilities, without outside help, and so living standards remain desperately low.

Gradually, during the 1960s and 1970s, governments and city authorities in developing countries recognised the impossibility of resettling or rehousing the growing numbers in these unauthorised settlements. Supported by the availability of funds from the World Bank, they began to adopt policies which involved **upgrading** of unauthorised settlements. The basic elements in such programmes are:

(i) making the settlements legal and giving security of tenure (either ownership or lease) to the residents;
(ii) providing physical and social infrastructure, e.g. roads, water supply, clinics, schools;
(iii) improving housing standards.

Notice, however, that the building of the dwelling remains the responsibility of the occupier. This approach has succeeded in a number of countries and can achieve considerable improvements at relatively low cost. Yet some schemes have been criticised for displacing poorer families as rents rise, the dwellings being taken up by better-off families. This case study follows the settlement of Chawama on the fringe of Lusaka, the capital of Zambia, through the development process of **establishment** → **consolidation** → **upgrading** → **assimilation into the formal urban system**. In using the materials, think particularly about these questions:

1 How did the scheme evolve and work?
2 Did upgrading displace the existing population?
3 Did all residents benefit?

Key understandings

◆ The official acceptance and upgrading of unauthorised settlements can be an effective way of tackling urban housing shortages.

◆ Upgrading schemes may displace families who then need resettlement, and so must be accounted for in the schemes.

◆ Security of tenure for the occupants is the most important element of the upgrading process.

◆ There are four main phases in the evolution: establishment/consolidation/ upgrading/assimilation.

A right to live in Lusaka

When Zambia gained its independence in 1964, Lusaka had over 21 000 households, and at least one-third of these were in 'unauthorised' squatter, settlements. During the 1960s, the new government of Zambia had an official policy of 'site and service' schemes in which a new settlement would be laid out with the infrastructure of roads, water sanitation and so on, provided, and settlers allocated a plot on which they could then build a home. These schemes could not keep up with population growth, and the government came to accept the presence of unauthorised areas such as Chawama, where a basic water supply was installed, and some control on growth was maintained.

The 1971 Second National Development Plan for Zambia adopted a combination of site-and-service schemes and squatter upgrading as the basis for tackling the housing needs of poorer members of the population. The country obtained a World Bank loan in 1973, and produced the plan for Lusaka shown on resource 4.17.

CASE STUDY 4.3 *Upgrading as a method of tackling urban housing*

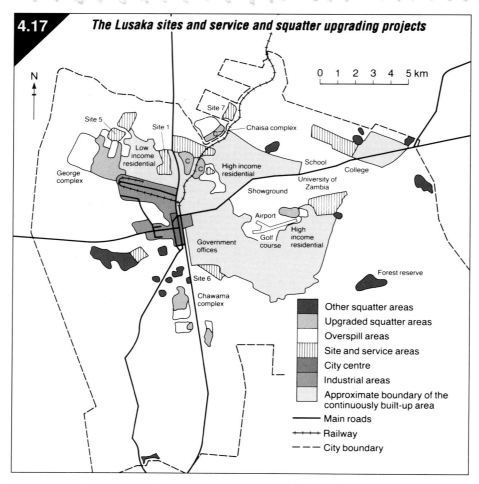

4.17 **The Lusaka sites and service and squatter upgrading projects**

N

0 1 2 3 4 5 km

Site 7
Site 5
Site 1
Chaisa complex
Low income residential
George complex
C
C
High income residential
School
College
Showground
University of Zambia
Airport
Golf course
High income residential
Government offices
Forest reserve
Site 6
Chawama complex

Other squatter areas
Upgraded squatter areas
Overspill areas
Site and service areas
City centre
Industrial areas
Approximate boundary of the continuously built-up area
Main roads
Railway
City boundary

Three large unauthorised settlements, including Chawama, were designated as Upgraded Squatter Areas. The plan for Chawama (resource 4.18) indicates the framework of the physical and social infrastructure. The notes below the map sum up the characteristics of the project. In many ways the crucial element is the security of tenure, which has the added advantage of allowing the occupier to use the dwelling as security against a loan. Notice the 'overspill' areas. These were for resettlement of families displaced by the upgrading process, e.g. houses removed in the laying out of new roads, reducing densities etc. The Chawama overspill area was for 1925 houses, with an average plot size of 210 sq.m. If a family did not wish to move, or could not afford to, they had the opportunity to exchange with a neighbour. Across the three main projects in Lusaka, by 1980 about 20 000 plots had the basic infrastructure and 5500 households had been resettled, affecting about 30 per cent of the city's population.

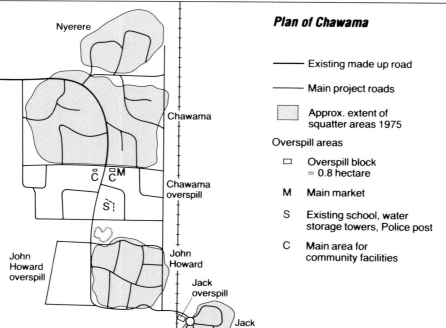

Plan of Chawama

Nyerere
Chawama
C C M
S
Chawama overspill
John Howard overspill
John Howard
Jack overspill
Jack

0   0.5   1 km

Existing made up road

Main project roads

Approx. extent of squatter areas 1975

Overspill areas

☐ Overspill block = 0.8 hectare

M Main market

S Existing school, water storage towers, Police post

C Main area for community facilities

4.18

Land
Zambian socialist government policy has discouraged private land ownership. Security of tenure is given by issuing 30-year occupancy licences: 'a permanent house number and a licence entitling the occupier of the area of the house and one metre surrounding it in all directions to continue to use the land for that purpose, subject to fulfilling the terms of the licence, including the payment of service charges'. The remaining land remains in council ownership, its use decided by the community or agreed by neighbours.

Infrastructure standards
* Communal water supply – one standpipe per 25 households
* Through roads tarmac, gravel access roads to each block of 25 houses.
* Storm water drainage.
* Pit latrines as in existing settlement.
* Refuse collection from block access road entrances.
* Basic street lighting.

Housing
* Loans for building materials.
* Loans for building to families in overspill areas To be repaid over 15 years at 7.5% interest
* Technical advice available to assist better house building.
* World Bank encourages house extension to increase income by renting out extra rooms, but Zambian socialist policy is reluctant to support this 'private landlord' approach.

4.19

Housing characteristics of Chawama, 1974–78

	1965	*1974*	*1978*	
Owner–occupied buildings	–	77%	85%	
One–room buildings	42%	11%	–6	
Less than three-room buildings	85%	62%	50%	
Four to six room buildings	9%	33%	40%	
Average buildings size (no. of rooms)	–	3.6	4.02	
Tenants (percentage of total households)	–	50%	59%	(1)
Average number of households/building	–	1.6	2.18	
Average number of people/building	–	8.5	6.36	
Average dwelling size (rooms/household)	–	2.0	1.88	
Percentage of households in one room	–	40%	50%	(2)

(1) Higher where there is a *female* head of households.
(2) 78% of *tenants* lived in one room.

What changes did the upgrading programme bring?

We must be careful not to assume that all changes and improvements were the result of the upgrading programme. Evidence from many unauthorised settlements shows the resource and energy of the occupants in creating their own improvements. For example, in Chawama, by 1974, many of the original huts of poles with 'dagga' (mud and straw) walls and thatch roofs were being replaced by dwellings of sun-dried mud brick and corrugated iron. In 1980, at least 75 per cent of all buildings were of this type, in part due to the stimulus of the upgrading programme. Resource 4.19 shows the changes in living conditions during the first part of the programme.

It is clear that the average size of building and the proportion owned had increased. Yet the proportion of the total population who were tenants had risen, with 78 per cent of these renting a single room. This helps to account for the fall in the average number of rooms/household from 2.0 to 1.88. However, this does not necessarily mean increased crowding, as the average household size had fallen from 4.24 to 3.50 persons, and although building size rose, the number of people/building dropped (8.5 to 6.36). Two things seemed to have happened: first, the improved services and facilities proved attractive, so many owners enlarged existing buildings or constructed new larger buildings, with the intention of subletting. (38 per cent of buildings had been extended or rebuilt.) New tenants were often one- or two-person households, able to cope in small spaces. Second, existing family groups were able to subdivide and become separate households by modification of existing or the building of new buildings.

A survey summed up the situation in 1980:

'House rebuilding and improvement had taken place in the upgraded area, but there was not an immense surge of house improvement. Instead, a more gradual process could be perceived. … Much of the house improvement seemed to have been undertaken by landlords and there had been a substantial increase in the amount of rental accommodation in Chawama. The ability of supply to keep pace with demand, however, had prevented rents from rising, and renting out of rooms was predominantly on a small scale, generally by owner occupiers (not by absentee landlords).'

It is important to note the apparent lack of rent rises because one danger of upgrading schemes is that they force up rents. Improvements add value to a house and the owner feels justified in putting up the rent. Thus, a poor household – the very people such projects are meant to help – may have to leave. In time, the settlement may be dominated by the relatively wealthy. In Chawama,

CASE STUDY 4.3
Upgrading as a method of tackling urban housing problems in developing countries – Zambia

4.20

The progress of Chawama

1952	A retired farm foreman is given permission by the landowner to settle on unused land at the edge of a large commercial farm.
1952–62	Other families join the retired foreman.
1962	The landowner gives permission for people to settle her land, providing they pay rent.
1964	**Zambia gains independence from Great Britain.**
1965	Population at Chawama reaches 5000. Problems over rents cause the landowner to begin to evict the squatters, and to offer to sell the land to the government.
1966	Government buys the land, and assures the people they will not be evicted, but they have no formal tenure rights.
1966–69	Government policy remains that these unauthorised settlements are illegal, but government does install some basic water supply, improved road access, a primary school, and controls new building and land allocation.
1974	Chawama is selected as one of the squatter settlements to be upgraded, because of its size (7550 households, i.e. around 40 000 people), its semi-recognised status, and government ownership of the land.
1975	Meetings are held between officials and residents at which the development of the infrastructure, i.e. roads, water supply, are explained. The need for some families to be moved and resettled is made clear. Upgrading begins.
1975–77	2000 households resettled as the upgrading process goes on – new roads and reducing housing densities cause houses to be removed.
1979	Chawama is declared an Improvement Area (an officially approved upgraded squatter area) and all land ownership is transferred to the Lusaka City Council.
1980	Occupancy licences begin to be issued to the settlers. These give families the right of occupancy of their plot and dwelling on a 30 year lease.
1982	Three primary schools, two of the three community centres, two of the five markets are complete, and the health centre is built but not in use. By the end of the year, less than 10 per cent of all occupancy licences have actually been issued. Home improvements and new building by resettled families are still being held up by a shortage of materials. The local industry cannot cope and imported materials cost more.

there is evidence that two groups may have suffered by the upgrading programme. They are poorer small households and households with a female head, who were less numerous in 1978 than in 1974 both in the upgraded area and the overspill resettlement areas. It seems that these vulnerable groups lacked the physical and financial resources to take advantage of the project, and so moved on.

(Source: adapted from C Rakodi, 'Upgrading in Chawama, Lusaka: displacement or differentiation?', *Urban Studies*, 25, 1988, pp. 297–318)

Activities

1 Follow the progress of Chawama through the 'diary' in resource 4.20. Identify the four main phases: establishment → consolidation → upgrading → assimilation, and summarise the key characteristics of each.

2 **Group discussion:**

a Use the materials in the case study to discuss the three questions introduced on page 81.

b What has been the role of:

(i) the national and city governments, and
(ii) the local people?

c Produce a summary report on Chawama settlement under these four readings – establishment; consolidation; upgrading; assimilation.

CASE STUDY 4.4 *Planned housing in a communist society – examples from China*

Background

Two essential features of housing supply in communist countries are first, that the public sector is the dominant or even the only provider, and second, that formal planning of the residential environment is strongly developed at all scales from the individual house to the massive urban estate. One result is a greater standardisation of dwellings and estate design than is found in 'capitalist' societies. Equally, many developments reflect the ideals of the British New Towns movement which dominated planning in the UK from the 1940s through to the 1970s. For example, a concern with the total living environment and not simply the housing, is evident in all the plans: a range of services, open spaces, transport needs, employment centres, are all laid out to make access simple. Unlike British New Towns and urban estates, which were increasingly created for the motor car, in many communist (and formerly communist) countries car ownership remains low and commuting is on foot, by bicycle or by public transport. Therefore, housing is closely tied to workplaces and services (see case study 9.3, page 217 on commuting in Moscow).

Since the communists came to power in 1949, China has remained a command economy with a powerful planning system at all levels. As the most populous country in the world (population 1000 million), as well as one of the largest, China is a mainly rural society, but one which is urbanising rapidly. Between 1949 and 1983 the state sector built 21 million flats in urban settlements, to accommodate 85 million people. Remarkably, 47 per cent of these were completed between 1979 and 1983. This massive effort has helped to reduce overcrowding, although by western standards, Chinese accommodation remains cramped. For instance, the Chinese use a measure called a 'living area' which is the floor area of bedroom per person. (A bedroom frequently doubles as a living room.) In 1978 the average living area was 3.6 sq. metres, in 1985 it was 6.3 sq. metres. Yet 30 per cent of Chinese people have less than this average.

The examples in this case study illustrate the Chinese approach to planned housing provision and how it has evolved over time. Part I focuses on the capital city, Beijing, where population rose from 1.65 million in 1949 to 5 million in the mid-1980s. The state responded by providing a fourfold increase in housing space. Notice how the scale and character of the planning units change through time and compare them with British New Town shifts from earlier to later models. Part II is a study of the planned development of Hongshan Village, near the city of Hangzhou to include both agriculture and industry. It is useful to compare its design and functions with the planned settlements in the Dutch Yssel Meer project. Both parts are written by Chinese planning officials and illustrate clearly the communist belief in the virtues and achievements of centralised and local planning.

Key understandings

◆ Chinese housing needs are massive, and of a distinctive type, based upon their cultural heritage and way of life.

◆ The state is the sole provider of formal housing in a command economy such as China.

◆ Centralised planning leads to standardisation, but the ability to provide large numbers of dwellings.

◆ Many large-scale Chinese housing projects resemble British and European schemes of the 1960s in their planned layouts.

Part I: Beijing: housing and community development

Overall residential development

In terms of overall city planning, the following two major principles are underlined when selecting the sites of residential quarters:

● One is that they should be leeward from industrial districts and have a beautiful environment; and

● the other is that they should be as close as possible to work places, so as to save workers commuting time and ease urban traffic.

For more than 30 years now, the existing houses in the old city area have been repaired or equipped with public utilities, and residential quarters have been built in new suburban industrial districts, and in areas where research institutions, universities and government offices are concentrated. The number of residential units built in the suburbs after 1949 account for two-thirds of the total new houses in Beijing, and there are about 100 housing estates of varying sizes around the old city proper.

Organisation of urban life

How to organise urban life is an important question in city planning and city building. Residential quarters in old Beijing typically consist of row upon row of tidy, parallel houses with courtyards and a lane between every two rows. At the head of a lane of a 500 metre block, there are groceries, drugstores and breakfast bars, fairly complete commercial services on a one kilometre block and bigger commercial services every two kilometres away.

Most of the lanes – the local roads – or 'Hutongs' run from east to west, while commercial streets run vertical to the lanes in the south-north direction. This kind of layout not only affords residents easy access to transport and shopping centres but keeps residential areas away from noisy traffic.

- In the early 1950s, a group of housing estates in a large scale community were built, such as the districts at Zhenwu Temple outside the Fuxingmen Gate (resource 4.21). These estates, generally small in scale, occupy an area of about 9 to 15 hectares each. In addition to commercial service facilities, there are primary schools, nurseries and cultural establishments along with parklands and children's playgrounds. Attention is given to sufficient sun exposure and ventilation.
- In the mid-1950s, the idea of making the small estates a basic housing development unit was proposed, namely, that they should have access to several surrounding urban highways, and generally would cover somewhere from 30 to 60 hectares with an average population of 10 000 to 20 000. In these estates, public transport vehicles are not allowed to pass, and there is a rational distribution of primary and middle level schools, children's facilities, shops and other public services.

The expansion in scale of such housing development projects can save investment in urban construction, reduce the number of intersections, raise urban transport speed, create a quiet living environment and make the architectural layout more flexible. The residential areas at Baiwangzhuang in the west (resources 4.22 and 4.23) were all built on the basis of this idea.

However, years of practice have shown that a fairly complete network of services can hardly be arranged and such small estates can hardly become independent, complete residential units. It is hard to build several small districts in areas where commercial and cultural establishments – food stores, restaurants, post offices, bookstores, cinemas and hospitals – are often overlooked, causing the residents some inconvenience.

By the mid 1970s, the idea had developed to build larger residential areas – generally over 60 to 100 hectares and with a population of 30 000 to 40 000 people – in a unified planning effort. Each of these residential areas has administrative authorities and fairly complete commercial service facilities, including food and vegetable markets, restaurants, food shops, department stores, bathing houses, post offices, savings banks and bookstores, cinemas, cultural centres, youngsters' and children's houses, hospitals and outpatient departments.

Such a residential area itself is an independent social cell, exercising management functions to meet the demands of the residents in their livelihoods.

At the same time, it is a rule that every residential area must have parklands of more than two hectares and sports grounds. Patches of small lawns should be allocated in subordinate neighbourhoods. Local residents are asked to plant trees and flowers, take care of lawns and install benches in the openings between building blocks to beautify the environment (resource 4.23).

In order to provide the people with easy access to public transport, a residential area is generally divided into several small districts crossed with roads leading to the city's trunk highways; bus stations are set up at each outlet. This pattern is, of course, different from patterns familiar in those countries where transport mainly relies on private cars and where residential areas are not divided into smaller districts.

Building height and density

With the decrease of usable urban land and, at the same time, with the progress in building materials and construction techniques, the number of storeys of Beijing's residential buildings and their density have increased constantly over the last 30 years or more.

In the early 1950s, quite a few residential areas of one-storey houses were built in the vicinity of the old city and in the industrial districts of the suburbs; the gross density measured around 3000

4.21

Beijing – view of the residential quarters at Zhenwu Temple, outside the Fuxingmen Gate

Beijing – view of the residential quarters at Baiwangzhuang in the west

square metres of floor space per hectare.

Later on, some two and three-storey residential buildings were developed with a gross density – floor space per hectare – of about 6000 square metres.

When constructing one-storey or low-storey buildings, investment is relatively low, but land requirements are high and the total investment in public utilities increases if compared with high-rise buildings. Therefore, based on years of experience, city planners generally stipulate that residential building in the city proper cannot be built with less than four to five storeys. Subsequently, they demand buildings in downtown Beijing be four-eight storeys, and buildings along main streets and in important districts be eight-ten storeys and higher (resource 4.25). As a result, fairly big residential areas mainly with four or five-storey buildings were built all around the city.

Owing to limitations in urban facilities, building equipment and technology, tall buildings in the 1960s and early 1970s were fewer. The gross density in residential quarters with ordinary residential buildings was around 8000 to 9000 square metres.

High-rise buildings became possible following the improvement in building techniques and equipment, and the expansion of gas supply and central heating in 1976. So a number of new residential districts with 10, 12, some even 16, 18 and 20-storey buildings mixed with 6-storey ones, sprang up.

The proportion of high-rise buildings in the new residential districts such as Tuanjiehu (resource 4.24), has reached 30 per cent and the gross density has risen between 10 000 and 12 000 square metres per hectare.

In a large city like Beijing with such a dense population distribution and such an acute land shortage, the increase in residential density and height of residential buildings is unavoidable. On the other hand, higher residential buildings mean higher construction costs, higher energy consumption, bigger maintenance fees involved and complicated questions of fire control and inconvenience, particularly for the elderly. We are of the opinion that higher buildings should be intermingled with medium-high ones and that the latter should be introduced in the main.

House types

The traditional houses in Beijing are one-storey with courtyards around them – Si He Yuan. The large clusters of houses not refurbished, in the old city area, belong to this type. Si He Yuan, separated from the outside and with fairly quiet courtyards inside, is usually exclusively dwelled in by a single, quite often large, family. It indeed has many good points, yet occupies much land.

With progress in society and changes in the way of life, family structure changes and big families give way to smaller ones of three or four people.

As a consequence, the traditional Si He Yuan house types, formerly owned by single families, are now being shared by several households, and have been separated, divided and subdivided in such a 'messy' way that most of the urban residents dislike them.

Therefore, only a small proportion of well-preserved traditional Si He Yuan in the old city area are to be retained. The majority of them will be rebuilt.

Over the last 30 years or more, with regard to the designing of new houses, researches have been done in many aspects. In the 1950s,

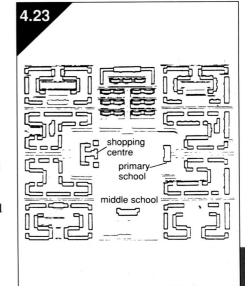

Beijing – general layout plan of the residential quarters of Baiwangzhuang in the west

Beijing – view of the residential quarters at Tuanjiehu

Beijing – layout plan of the residential quarters at Tuanjiehu

family traditional habit of living together with the elderly.

Special attention will be given to the development of satellite towns in the outlying counties. Along with new projects, industrial and others, residential quarters will be built in these satellite towns corresponding at an appropriate rate.

With the large-scale construction of satellite towns in outlying areas, the focus of housing development after 1990 will step by step move from the city proper to the remote outskirts.

(Source: Dong Guang-qi, 'Beijing: housing and community development', *Ekistics*, 322, January/February 1987, pp. 34–39)

Part II: Hongshan: a new village on the banks of the Qiantang River

Hongshan, a new village for workers on a farm in Xiaoshan County under the jurisdiction of the city of Hangzhou – 20 km east of Hangzhou – lies near the province's main artery, Hangzhou-Wenzhou Highway. One of the tributaries of the Shaoxing-Xiaoshan Canal, navigable by 60-ton ships, runs through the village (resource 4.26).

Hongshan is composed of seven hamlets and covers a land-area of 666 hectares. There are 845 households with a total population of 3413 of whom 2100 men and women engage in farming, as well as industry, and side-line occupations which include farm produce processing, building materials, farm machinery repair, tailoring, aquatic farming, livestock and poultry raising.

The village features an all-round development of agriculture, industry and side-line occupations and an integration of farming, industry and business. The main crops are cotton and paddy rice with a per-hectare yield of 15 tons for food grain and 1.53 tons for cotton. Industry plays a major role in the village's economy.

residential buildings with outside or inside corridors and apartment-type houses were designed. The apartment houses, with each family having two or three bedrooms (one of which serves concurrently as a sitting room), a kitchen and a toilet, are most welcome. Such a suite is suitable for a family of three or four.

With the rise in people's livelihood and living standards, this type of residential housing has also improved. Compared with the

1960s, those in the 1980s have greater balcony space, more built-in wardrobes and a living room – more living space and more comfort.

In accordance with China's current economic conditions and capacity, housing conditions will not be drastically improved in the next twelve years or so. Roughly speaking, each family will have two or three bedrooms and a small sitting-dining room. This structure is in conformity with the Chinese

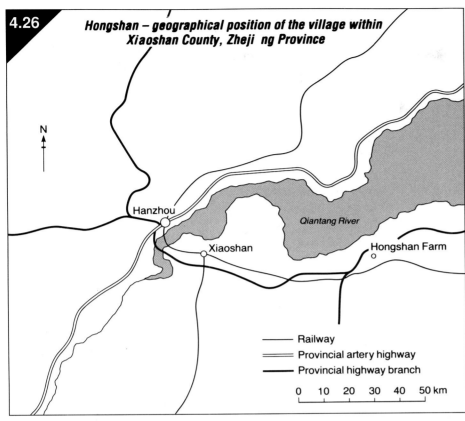

4.26 **Hongshan – geographical position of the village within Xiaoshan County, Zhejiang Province**

Hanzhou

Xiaoshan

Qiantang River

Hongshan Farm

—— Railway
══ Provincial artery highway
━━ Provincial highway branch

0 10 20 30 40 50 km

A self-supporting economic entity

The Hongshan Farm grew out of a wasteland on the bank of the Qiantang River. Work to build a farm began in 1969. Initially, the yields were low and the farm was in an economic fix. The farmers had to rely on the State for food grain supply, loans and relief. After five years of hard struggle, however, the farm managed to have a surplus of food grain. It has taken five more years of work on farmland capital formation and development of a diversified economy, for the farm to get rid of poverty.

In the ensuing five years beginning in 1979, while developing farming, the farm began to integrate agriculture and industry with business. The income in 1983 quadrupled the 1978 figure. However, the housing conditions were still very poor. About 700 straw-thatched huts were scattered over 6 sq. km.

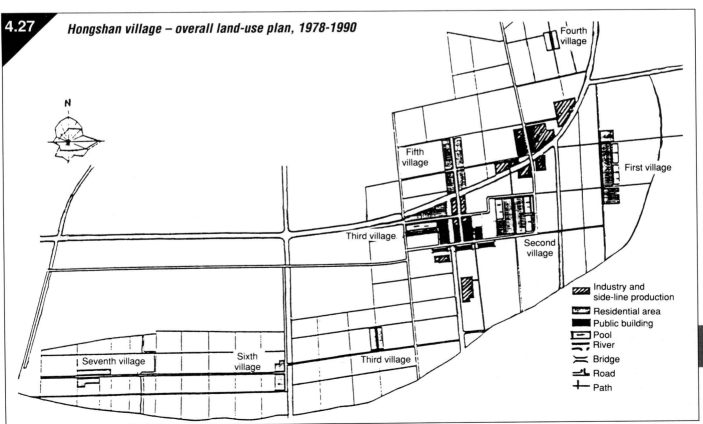

4.27 **Hongshan village – overall land-use plan, 1978-1990**

Fourth village

Fifth village

First village

Third village

Second village

Seventh village

Sixth village

Third village

▨ Industry and side-line production
▥ Residential area
■ Public building
⊡ Pool
〜 River
✕ Bridge
⊥ Road
+ Path

CASE STUDY 4.4 *Planned housing in a communist society –*

Land use								river
item	total	farming	industry & side-line	housing	public buildings	roads	aquatic farming	channels and wasteland
area	666.53	498.27	7.64	18.49	1.55	8.84	4.67	127.07
%	100	74.76	1.15	2.77	0.23	1.33	0.7	19.06

Hongshan's new village: balance sheet of land allocation by type of use (in hectares)

4.28

Building a new human settlement

In 1976 the keen desire to improve housing and environment for production and living, resulted in a plan for the construction of a new village.

Planning principles

The farmers worked out the following principles as guidelines for the development of the new village settlement:

- Farmland, irrigation, roads and housing should be planned in a coordinated 'unified' way and development should materialise in stages.
- The plans and the process of development should be convenient to both production and livelihood, and equal attention should constantly be given to both the improvement of production and the advancement of living conditions.
- Special emphasis should be given to the need for maximum protection, safeguarding farmland and minimum sacrifice of farmland for other uses.
- In formulating the plan and the program of development, both immediate and future needs should be taken into consideration.

A programme and plan

On the basis of these principles, the farm proceeded to the formulation of a general development programme and plan for the construction of the new central village (resource 4.27).

The programmed allocation of the farm's total territory by type of use is given in resource 4.28.

The most characteristic lines of the plan, deriving from the program, may be summarised as follows:

- Square or rectangular pieces divided into farmland, crossed by a water network consisting of one 'river' and a number of irrigation ditches making the farm look more like a garden.
- Drainage and pumping installations are displayed right by the farmland. Public buildings in close connection with each other form the public centre.
- Three residential hamlets (each housing a production bridge) in a 'radiating' pattern are distributed around the centre, on its east, west and north sides.
- An industrial complex for building materials (with factories for cement works, cement pre-fabricated parts, terrazzo works, and a marble plant) is located in the north-east with easy access to land water transportation and communication lines, etc. forming an independent industrial zone
- Much leeway is provided in the plan for future development of the central village and the industrial area.

Implementation

Construction work began in 1977 and proceeded in stages. In 1987, the Hongshan Village, virtually at a stage of completion, included the following:

- **Housing** The largest project foreseen in the whole program,

and the one that the farmers were most concerned with. In the seven years between 1978 and 1985, 85 000 sq.m (floor area) of two-storied cement-and-brick houses have been erected and 23 500 sq.m for auxiliary installations (warehouses, stables and toilets). Each farmer averages a living space of 25.2 sq.m and 7.5 sq.m for the auxiliary space – which amount to more than three times the 1977 figures.

Each housing unit consists of two dwellings and features front and back courtyards – the front yard for living and the back yard for other purposes. Most dwellings consist of two rooms, each about 3.6 metres wide, with a courtyard attached. The layout with rooms and other spaces in proper sizes is simple and rational. Finally, in terms of style, the houses maintain some of the traditional architectural features of southern China, such as the round gate to the courtyard, the small gate tower, and the tilted eaves (resource 4.29).

- **Public buildings** In the past, there was only one primary school and a dilapidated small shop. Farmers had to walk 5 km to a nearby town to buy daily necessities. The new public centre covering an area of 1.55 hectares – comparable to a rural market town's centre – includes, apart from the farm office building, a laboratory in the institute of Agricultural Sciences, an exhibition building of the 'Company of Agriculture, Industry and Commerce,' schools, a hospital, a cinema, an entertainment centre, an hotel, a restaurant, shops, a post office, a bank, a market place and a bus terminal. By the end of 1985, completed buildings were occupying a total area of 6890 sq.m, out of which 2552 sq.m were for the primary school and the middle-level school, 1180 sq.m for an hotel and a restaurant, 500 sq.m for shops and 484 sq.m for a meeting hall; more than 10 other buildings, including the farm office, the hospital and the bank had also been completed. A cinema with a seating capacity of 1100 was under construction.

The farm authorities consider the construction of the public buildings as a first priority and plan to have the centre built within five years, knowing the importance of this endeavour in enriching the life of the farmers and of all other peasants in the vicinity (resource 4.30).

- **Infrastructure** A network of roads already covers the farm area. Parts of the stretches already maintain sewage installation and lamp-posts already exist on the farm. Fresh water tanks are completed – one in each hamlet and most of the farmers are already connected with treated water.

- **Plantation** Special efforts made for the afforestation of the farm have achieved substantial results: Metasequoias and Chinese parasol trees already line the roads; weeping willows are planted next to the village ponds; the front of the office buildings and of the hotel are already enjoying the beauty of flower beds, snow pines and osmanthus trees; each household grows flowers and tends a lawn in front of the house; the village is simply a garden in itself.

(Source: Yang Binhui, 'Hongshan: a new village on the banks of the Qiantang River', *Ekistics*, 322, January/February, 1987)

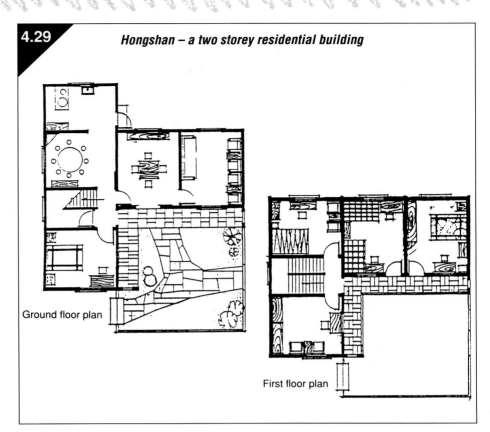

4.29   ***Hongshan – a two storey residential building***

Ground floor plan

First floor plan

Activities

1   Summarise the main changes in the approach to planning housing developments in Beijing. Compare these trends with those in British urban and New Town planning. (You will need to consult the relevant chapters in standard textbooks on urban geography.)

2   From the materials in these two examples, describe the main characteristics of housing in China and compare it with examples from other countries you have studied or which you can research.

3   What role do the local people of Hongshan play in decision-making about their living and working environments? To what have they given the highest priorities?

4   In small groups: discuss the advantages and disadvantages of the Chinese approach to housing and housing provision.

4.30

Hongshan – a road along a residential area

CHAPTER 5

Places for work – the changing geography of industry and work

Introduction

One of the main aims of geography is to describe and explain how space is organised on planet earth. In economic geography this often means understanding the 'what', 'where', 'how' and 'why' of industrial location.

As we are also interested in understanding changes over time, we must add the 'when' of industry (resource 5.1). Remember too, that as industries grow, decline and change location, they influence job opportunities and therefore the quality of people's lives. There is no more vivid example than the motor vehicle industry, where thousands of workers and their families are affected by decisions made by directors of a small number of multi-national companies such as Ford. For instance, the Ford company has dominated the town of Dagenham since the first cars rolled off the production line in 1931. At its peak in the mid-1950s, the complex was producing 1.4 million vehicles a year. Today, each time Ford introduces a new model or proposes a reorganisation, it has factories spread across the European Community to choose from – and Dagenham holds its breath (resource 5.2).

Theories and models of industrial location have been constructed to help us in our understanding of individual countries, regions, cities, industries or companies. These generalised approaches may be grouped into four main types each with its own strengths and weaknesses: (i) cost and profit, (ii) behaviouralist, (iii) structuralist, and (iv) dynamic. They are outlined below, but you should check your understanding of the main models and theories before studying the case studies in this chapter.

(i) Cost and profit theories

The traditional approach to location theory is to assume that industry will locate where costs are lowest. Differences in the cost of land, labour and capital

Ford Sierras from the Dagenham plant lined up at Tilbury Dock

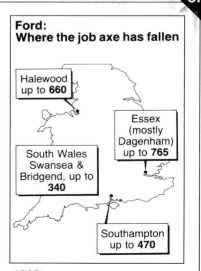

Ford axes 2100 jobs across UK

Ford yesterday announced huge job cuts across its UK plants. Ford admitted that 2100 jobs will be axed this year in a programme of cutbacks hitting all of its major UK plants as well as smaller sites.

The cuts follow the loss of 2000 jobs at Ford last year and will reduce the company's British workforce to around 38 000 compared with 72 000 in the early 1980s
(Source: *The Guardian*. 8 February, 1992)

Ford: Where the job axe has fallen

Halewood up to **660**

Essex (mostly Dagenham) up to **765**

South Wales Swansea & Bridgend, up to **340**

Southampton up to **470**

(called the **factors of production**) over space explain the chosen location, e.g. cheap labour regions or areas with low land costs will attract industry. Equally, one method of attracting industry is to alter these factors of production, e.g. by subsidising labour costs, or providing free land and infrastructure. Perhaps the best known cost-minimisation theory is that produced by Max Weber, which was later modified to account for the relationship between costs and revenues.

(ii) Behaviouralist approaches

Many industrial locations do not fit neatly into the cost and profit models, so attention has turned increasingly to the decision-making process and how decision-makers within individual companies perceive and interpret the production and marketing environment. At the simplest level, someone with capital and ambition is likely to locate near where s/he lives: 'Here I am, what shall I invest and produce here?' rather than 'I want to start a business – where is the best place to locate it?'

With multi-plant and multi-national companies, decisions may be made on the basis of existing factories in relation to the distribution of demand. For industries in the public sector – **nationalised** industries, locational decisions have been influenced by the policies of the government which owned them. This behavioural approach suggests that regional patterns of industry and industrial change are the outcome of numerous decisions taken by individual owners and managers.

Resource 5.4 illustrates how individualistic this locational decision-making may be. Anita Roddick's *Body Shop* was one of the most successful businesses of the 1980s. One of her key decisions has been the location of a factory on the sprawling Easterhouse Estate in Glasgow. This decision was not only economic (she believed it would be profitable), but was also driven by a desire to help improve the quality of life for a socially and economically struggling community.

(iii) Structuralist approaches

Here, location of industry is related to the structure and evolutionary development of society. For instance, the geographical patterns of jobs in a capitalist, western society will be different from those found in a centrally planned, 'command' economy, or from those of a fundamentalist Muslim society. The distribution of industries and jobs are explained in terms of the power structure of a country.

So, for example, capitalist entrepreneurs, (the power group of business owners), may close domestic components firms if they can buy more cheaply abroad. (This book has a UK publisher, but is printed in Hong Kong.) Or on the other hand, they may locate in an Enterprise Zone to take advantage of government incentives. In both cases, they will attempt to control costs and raise profits, illustrating the important understanding that all four types of locational theory or model interact and so help the explanation.

(iv) Dynamic models

These approaches are based on the concept of a product cycle (resource 5.3). Location in this instance, is related to the life cycle process of a product or industry. The most typical locational sequence is for gradual dispersal from the original area of innovation to occur. A classic example on the global scale is the motor vehicle industry (see case study 5.4). An alternative scenario to that where an industry thrives but changes in location, is that of the industry which simply comes to the end of its natural life and fades away, e.g. mining for specific raw materials (see case study 5.1).

Four outstanding features of the geography of work across the world over the past 40 years or so have been as follows:

1 The fundamental re-structuring of industry in advanced, industrialised countries.

5.3

Product cycle model showing changes in production and location over time

STAGE OF DEVELOPMENT	1. New product. Continual change to improve the product and production	2. Standardised product and production process	3. Alternatives and/or better products developed
OUTPUT			
LOCATION	Close to Company HQ and/or Research and Development Centre. Metropolitan region	Geography of the firm developed. Peripheral regions and countries and metropolitan regions	Only most efficient plants survive. Rationalisation. Periphery only?

Washes whiter

Can soap redeem Easterhouse in Glasgow? The Body Shop thinks so.

Easterhouse is apparently the largest, and one of the most socially disadvantaged, housing schemes in Europe. Over 55 000 people live in decaying, post-war council houses with very limited amenities. Houses are boarded up, pubs are few and far between, male unemployment runs at 60 per cent, debt is a major problem, and a shambling bus service is the only link between Easterhouse and the European City of Culture (Glasgow).

Yet it is in Easterhouse, that Anita Roddick has built her church. In 1988 Roddick, the ecological Madonna of the Body Shop Empire, arrived in Easterhouse. Depressed by the environment, but overwhelmed by the spirit of the community, Roddick decided that the Body Shop chain had 'to put something back'.

Within six months, the Body Shop had invested more than £1 million, converting 36 000 square feet of factory space into a highly-scented environment called Soapworks, a slightly implausible manufacturing centre for vegetable soap, on the Queenslie Industrial Estate.

If the unpopular imagination still saw Easterhouse as an urban desert, the local community saw itself as an enterprising housing scheme, ideally suited to export Jojoba Oil to the world.

In a new-age version of Worker's Playtime, the sound of the Beatles blasts out of the factory speakers. Radio 1 mingles with the smell of soap. Michelle MacIntyre works the 9 till 6 shift at the Soapworks. She is 20, but in white dungarees and a Body Shop bonnet she looks almost child-like as she checks bars of Moroccan mud soap and packs them into boxes.

Michelle was unemployed for six months before she joined Soapworks. She once worked on a YTS scheme at a factory miles from Easterhouse, but the atmosphere was claustrophobic, and, according to Michelle, 'there were 800 women; it was bitchy so I jacked it in'. For the first time in Michelle's life, work has become worthwhile. 'I don't hate getting up in the mornings', she says, 'work isn't that bad now'.

Although there is no union at Soapworks, all 50 workers attend regular meetings where they can air grievances and suggest improvements. The canteen sells health food and the management encourages an awareness of environmental issues – videos on whale hunting and Brazilian rainforests are available to the staff. But Michelle has not been enticed by the green environment or Body Shop products. She still has the Glaswegian's native suspicion about washing herself in Moroccan mud soap, and admits that 'It's just a job'.

The Body Shop's third-world production policies have the benefits of binding enterprise and new-age values into redeveloping disadvantaged areas, but they allow an older and more insensitive side of capitalism to thrive: luxury goods for the privileged are manufactured on the back of deprivation.

According to members of Soapworks staff, they used to be paid less than their English equivalents in Littlehampton. But mindful of the delicacy between the poor north and rich south, Body Shop regraded the pay rates. Nonetheless, the company extracts many financial benefits from being sited in a deprived area like Easterhouse.

(Source: S Barclay and S Cosgrove, 'Washes Whiter', *New Statesman and Society*, 20 April 1990)

2 The emergence of new industrial 'giants'.
3 The struggle of developing countries to industrialise.
4 The realisation of the environmental impacts of continued industrial growth and the implications of these impacts.

As the industrialisation process advances, societies enter the so-called post-industrial age. Service industries grow more rapidly than the manufacturing sector, leading, for example to the global explosion of tourism (see Chapter 8). Even in manufacturing, growth shifted from many of the traditional industries based on bulky raw materials and products. Many high growth industries are relatively footloose, attracted by high quality environments, prosperous regions, etc, which cause significant changes in first, the types of jobs available and second, where they are available. This leads, in turn, to regional and national differences in unemployment, prosperity and migration (see also Chapter 1).

CASE STUDY 5.1 *Jobs, lives and the product cycle – an example from the mining industry*

Background

One of the most popular generalisations in economic geography is the idea that it is unwise to rely only on one industry – it is more sensible to have a broader economic base. It is used when advising developing countries, specialised regions and one-industry towns. Within an industry, we warn against dependence on a single product or on a single company. The origins of such advice lie in the dynamics of demand, supply, technology, industrial processes and organisation, and especially in the idea of a **product cycle** (see resource 5.3 on page 93).

As a demand for a raw material or a product emerges, a supply is organised to satisfy this demand. Jobs are created, migrants move in, communities grow, and a 'knock-on' effect to service industries from construction work to hairdressers, occurs. However, unless investment from this prosperity is used to ensure jobs and income beyond the original product, then the community is at risk. Should the

product become obsolete, or too expensive, then the local industry is likely to fail, triggering a downward spiral of unemployment, poverty, progressive decline in the service industries which local people need, out-migration and environmental deterioration.

Nowhere is this 'boom-and-bust' cycle more closely illustrated than in the mining industry. Mining is a resource-based industry, supplying non-renewable raw materials which are in demand, from wherever they are found and are available for extraction. The finite supply of a mineral at a given location, the often inconvenient and remote location of the mineral, the specialised nature of the industry, the powerful environmental impact and changing demand for a particular mineral, combine to place mining settlements at risk in the long term. As the product cycle ends, so a 'ghost town' may emerge (resource 5.5). This case study, from the South Wales coal mining region, illustrates the product cycle process and its impact upon the lives of local people and the environment.

Key understandings

- Mining is a resource-based industry.
- The usefulness of and demand for individual resources fluctuates over time.
- Mining in a given location passes through a production cycle.
- Over-dependence upon a single product is likely to create long-term problems for communities and regions.

Maesteg and the passing of the coal industry

As coal mining extracts a finite and wasting resource, its evolution in a settlement or region will exhibit the economic and demographic dynamics of the product cycle as summarised in the model in resource 5.6. The extract in resource 5.8 gives an excellent resumé of what this cycle has meant to the town of Maesteg, and how it has endeavoured to adapt as the coal industry has faded.

The environmental impact of mining is intense and specialised, adding to the difficulties of revitalising such areas as mining declines. During the peak years of the product cycle, in the 1920s, there were well over 200 pits spread across South Wales. By 1990 there were only ten. The mining and associated metals industry, plus the physical environment of deeply cut valleys, created distinctive linear settlements with simple morphologies: a main street, railway and river forming the axis; one or more collieries with buildings and spoil heaps; perhaps an iron or steel works; rows of terraced houses lining the valley sides like a series of steps (resource 5.7).

5.5

Calico, an old Gold Rush town in California, once abandoned, has now been restored and reopened for tourism

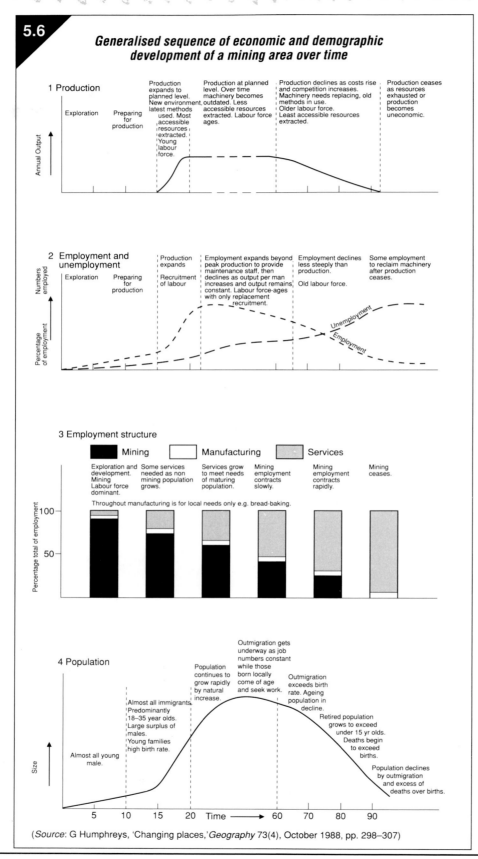

5.6

Generalised sequence of economic and demographic development of a mining area over time

1 Production

Annual Output

Exploration | Preparing for production | Production expands to planned level. New environment, latest methods used. Most accessible resources extracted. Young labour force. | Production at planned level. Over time machinery becomes outdated. Less accessible resources extracted. Labour force ages. | Production declines as costs rise and competition increases. Machinery needs replacing, old methods in use. Older labour force. Least accessible resources extracted. | Production ceases as resources exhausted or production becomes uneconomic.

2 Employment and unemployment

Numbers employed

Percentage of employment

Exploration | Preparing for production | Production expands. Recruitment of labour | Employment expands beyond peak production to provide maintenance staff, then declines as output per man increases and output remains constant. Labour force ages with only replacement recruitment. | Employment declines less steeply than production. Old labour force. | Some employment to reclaim machinery after production ceases.

Unemployment

Employment

3 Employment structure

■ Mining   □ Manufacturing   ▨ Services

Exploration and development. Mining Labour force dominant. | Some services needed as non mining population grows. | Services grow to meet needs of maturing population. | Mining employment contracts slowly. | Mining employment contracts rapidly. | Mining ceases.

Throughout manufacturing is for local needs only e.g. bread-baking.

Percentage total of employment
100
50

4 Population

Size

Almost all young male.

Almost all immigrants. Predominantly 18–35 year olds. Large surplus of males. Young families high birth rate.

Population continues to grow rapidly by natural increase.

Outmigration gets underway as job numbers constant while those born locally come of age and seek work.

Outmigration exceeds birth rate. Ageing population in decline.

Retired population grows to exceed under 15 yr olds. Deaths begin to exceed births.

Population declines by outmigration and excess of deaths over births.

Time →   5   10   15   20   60   70   80   90

(*Source*: G Humphreys, 'Changing places,' *Geography* 73(4), October 1988, pp. 298–307)

The skilled and arduous nature of mining, plus the lack of alternative occupations and the relative isolation of many traditional mining settlements, generated communities of great social strength. This sense of place and community pride has made the loss of mining in places like Maesteg, very hard for many inhabitants to endure.

Pride in the past is a key reason why mining has become an element in the tourism industry. Industrial heritage is today seen as an attractive resource, one which will generate new jobs and income, and help to restore local pride and community strength. For example, in the early 1980s, a research report set out the tourism potential of the South Wales valleys, using industrial sites as a central resource (resource 5.9). Perhaps the best-known attraction so far is Big Pit at Blaena, where groups are taken into a coal mine by retired miners. Another important element in the drive for community renewal and to attract new industries, is the upgrading of the environmental quality, for example by the removal of old mine buildings and equipment, and the landscaping of spoil heaps (resource 5.10).

5.7

Typical colliery town, Clydach Vale in the Rhondda, South Wales. Notice how the houses are built into the valley sides like a series of steps

5.8

The evolution of mining places

My long established interest in the geography of mining stems from my good fortune in having been born and brought up in the mining town of Maesteg in the centre of the South Wales Coalfield. It was and is a fascinating place for any geographer. Although founded in the 1820s as a new town to serve the iron works of the Lynfi valley, it soon became dominated by coal mining which continued to expand until the 1920s. The development was accompanied by a major influx of migrants. Sharp contraction of demand for coal after 1926 led to closure of local mines. By 1934 only three remained open and these survived for another forty years. The population declined slowly over this time, accompanied by considerable net out-migration as the birth rate exceeded the death rate. In the 1940s, an electricity generating station, a small industrial estate and a paper making works were built locally as a result of Government Distribution of Industry policy. In addition large numbers of local residents found work by travelling south every day to the Bridgend industrial estate and west to the steelworks at Port Talbot. All these developments helped stabilise the population though net out-migration continued. With the aid of government incentives, further new industries were attracted to the town after 1966, to try to offset further contraction of the coal and steel industries. The three local coal mines were closed between 1977 and 1984 and the Port Talbot steelworks reduced its labour force from 18 500 in 1967 to 12 500 in 1972 and then to 4500 by 1981. The accompanying loss of job opportunities for Maesteg workers resulted in unemployment rates (and youth unemployment rates in particular) rising to their highest levels for fifty years.

A wide variety of changes accompanied the evolution of the economic geography of Maesteg just described. These ranged from changes in the population, social structure, service provision and housing development, to dramatic landscape changes both in the urban fabric and along the valley sides where waste heaps and old mine areas were landscaped and the Forestry Commission planted conifers in places.

The changes in the human geography associated with coal mining which occurred in Maesteg were predictable. Mining exploits a wasting resource. This means that it will have a beginning and an end, at the latest when the mineral resource is exhausted. The sequence of accompanying geographical change can be modelled quite easily as shown in resource 5.6. Understanding of this kind means that where a mining development does occur, it is possible from the beginning to anticipate the changes and to plan ahead for acceptable geographical change rather than simply accepting as inevitable what would happen without such action.

The model described includes the simplifying assumption of a mining area being a closed local labour market. That Maesteg is not a closed system is illustrated by the major daily journey-to-work net outflows. As a result it has become a dormitory centre. This raises practical questions as to what are the characteristics of a successful dormitory town and how can these be encouraged and/or maintained to ensure continuing support from this source in future. Other former mining settlements in South Wales have been less successful in maintaining their local economic support so that net population loss has continued for over half a century. Here a different question arises. Given that in this case future change is relatively easy to chart, how do you plan for decline? How can you ensure a satisfactory service provision matching the particular needs of a poor and ageing population? Such services would include adequate public transport provision for a population with low car ownership and increased health care provision for the aged poor. Planning for growth is relatively easy and well documented. Planning for decline is a neglected art.

(Source: adapted from G Humphreys, 'Changing places', *Geography* 73(4) October 1988, pp. 298–307)

Activities

1 **Group discussion**:

   a Using the product cycle model as a basis (resource 5.6), identify ways of preventing a region entering the phases of decline and suggest how the various components of the model would be different.

   For example:

   the role of central government,
   the role of local authorities,
   the role of local people,
   the role of private businesses.

   b One alternative is to accept that the disappearance of mining means the end of the settlement. What strategies should be adopted to plan for this, and who should be making the decisions? What support would they need?

   c In what ways might the model and the strategies for modifying it be different if the mines are owned by (i) the State (nationalised industries) or (ii) private companies?

2 **Suggestion for a coursework project or essay**

   Test the usefulness of the product cycle model by applying it to other industries and other regions.

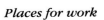

Ebbw Vale: transformation of spoil heaps for a garden festival

A redundant Ebbw Vale steel worker laughed at the absurdity of the whole idea. 'In all my life I never heard anyone say, "Let's go to Ebbw Vale for the day"'. Yet once the Garden Festival opens in May that is just what it is hoped that up to 40 000 people a day will be doing. It is a part of a scheme to transform the valley, provide hundreds of homes and over 1000 jobs, through a joint venture between the private sector, the Welsh Development Agency, and the local authorities. Local opinion is mixed about the 2 million cubic metres of earth moved, the 1.5 million trees and shrubs and the £60 million cost of greening a wasteland of spoil heaps and slag, from the coal mines and the huge steelworks. Over 12 000 jobs were buried in the ruins.

How green is my valley – the garden site emerges. On the facing valley side, the nearest row of houses are new and built on infilled industrial land. The upper terraces are renovated 18th century industrial workers' houses of the village of Cwm

How green is my valley, at last

Just 50 years after the publication of *How Green Was My Valley*, the nostalgic vision of that title will be fulfilled. An end is in sight to the Industrial Revolution's legacy of dereliction to the Welsh mining valleys.

Gwyn Griffiths, director of the Welsh Development Agency's land reclamation department, forecasts that if investment continues at current levels, the greening of the Rhondda and neighbouring valleys will be completed in 10 years.

Richard Llewellyn's best-selling novel about life in a Welsh mining community appeared in October 1939 and sold 50 000 copies in its first year. It was filmed by John Ford in Hollywood a year later.

Removal of the real-life slag heaps and the clean-up of the Welsh countryside had to wait 25 years after Llewellyn's attack on the exploitation of a community and its environment. It began in the wave of revulsion that followed the 1965 Aberfan disaster, in which 116 children and 28 adults died when a tip collapsed on the village school.

Since 1966, more than £160 million has been spent on reclaiming 15 000 acres of derelict land throughout Wales. According to Mr Griffiths, an area the size of four football pitches is currently being cleared each day. Part of the reclamation work is funded by the profits from sale of 250 000 tons of coal recovered each year from tips abandoned by the coal barons.

Despite occasional setbacks, such as the recent redundancies at the nearby Hoover plant, there are encouraging signs that the clean-up programme, allied with the introduction of improved road links, is attracting new industries.

As Mr Griffiths points out, reclamation should be seen as only the first stage in regeneration of the valleys. So far, 50 housing developments, 11 lakes and innumerable playing fields occupy land once annexed by industry. At Ynyscedwyn in the Swansea Valley, a housing estate, hospital and sheltered accommodation for the elderly now stand on a site once occupied by a noxious tin-plate works.

Even more dramatically, perhaps, Barratt has established an exclusive housing estate at Clydach Vale, in the Rhondda, overlooking the old Cambrian Colliery. The pit, where in 1965 more than 30 men died in an underground explosion, was closed exactly one month before the Aberfan tragedy.

Now, says Mr Griffiths, it is important that new developments should be of a high standard to avoid instigating a new cycle of dereliction. One happy outcome of the closure of more than 150 collieries since nationalisation, he observes, is that once inky waterways are now clean: 'Trout are to be seen again in the Taff and other South Wales rivers.'

It is difficult to measure environmental improvement, since a newly-greened landscape can take up to 15 years to mature, but Mr Griffiths is optimistic: 'The Industrial Revolution brought a huge mass of dereliction, which overwhelmed everybody, Now we're seeing off the last of the problem.'

Three decades to repair the ravages of centuries will not be a bad achievement, according to Mr Griffiths. The ultimate test, he feels, is when visitors don't realise a site has been reclaimed. He was in Gilfach Goch recently and was pleased with what he saw. 'Suddenly, the trees have stopped looking like planted trees.'

(Source: Alan Road, *The Observer*, 8 October, 1989)

CASE STUDY 5.2 *The rise of the Pacific Rim*

Background

By the next century Asia will be the undisputed workshop of the world, with a cluster of mini-Japans doing to the rest of the world what Japan is today.

(*The Guardian*, 24 November, 1989)

Despite outbreaks of political unrest and recurrent environmental disasters, most countries in east Asia are achieving rates of economic growth greater than Western nations (resource 5.11). This is particularly true of countries which form part of the 'Pacific Rim', where Japan has been joined by such nations as South Korea, Taiwan, Hong Kong, Singapore and Thailand. In some cases, this growth has been sudden and explosive. For instance, Thailand's rate of growth doubled in 1987 to 7 per cent, and has been running at above 9 per cent a year since. This makes it one of the most rapidly expanding economies in the world, although there is evidence that this new wealth is not yet finding its way to the poorer people. At the same time, property and land prices in Bangkok, the capital, more than doubled between 1988 and 1990. (See also case study 4.2, Chapter 4 on housing provision in Bangkok.)

These economies have often been helped in the early stages by Japanese capital and equipment investment, and by the business skills of their Chinese populations. While there are still fears of 'economic colonialism' – over-dependence upon Japanese companies who use the countries as sources of cheap labour, the proportion of home-financed and managed businesses is growing. The wealth created is transforming lifestyles and these newly industrialising countries (NICs) are becoming a major source of tourist and business travellers, and hence of spending power in other countries (resource 5.12).

Countries around the Pacific Rim have become fully aware of the potential – and dangers – of this economic expansion.

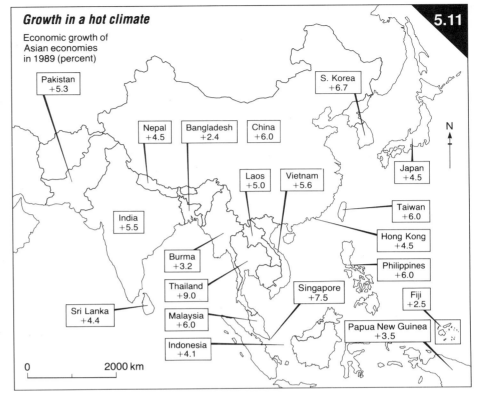

Growth in a hot climate

Economic growth of Asian economies in 1989 (percent)

5.11

Pakistan +5.3

Nepal +4.5

Bangladesh +2.4

China +6.0

S. Korea +6.7

Japan +4.5

Laos +5.0

Vietnam +5.6

India +5.5

Taiwan +6.0

Hong Kong +4.5

Burma +3.2

Philippines +6.0

Thailand +9.0

Singapore +7.5

Fiji +2.5

Sri Lanka +4.4

Malaysia +6.0

Papua New Guinea +3.5

Indonesia +4.1

0   2000 km

N

Australia and New Zealand are both increasing their exports to East Asian countries, for instance, the Japanese prefer grass-fed New Zealand beef with its lower fat content to American corn-fed beef. Conversely, both Australia and New Zealand are concerned with the scale of Asian investment and the potential pressures for immigration from the densely populated regions across the Pacific (resource 5.13). Even the United States is looking increasingly across the Pacific rather than towards Europe: since 1982, the total trade crossing the Pacific between the USA and East Asia nations has been greater in value than the US-Europe Atlantic trade. Apart from Canadians crossing into the USA, the Japanese ranked first in 1989 in foreign nationals entering the United States, mostly, of course, business visitors.

This case study examines four of the East Asia NICs – Hong Kong, Singapore, Taiwan, South Korea, and identifies the character of the industrial growth, and what has caused it. What is particularly impressive is first, the speed with which it is occurring and second, the relatively restricted resource base upon which it is built. Note too, the varying roles played by governments and private businesses in the industrialisation process.

Key understandings

- Countries in East Asia are achieving some of the highest rates of industrialisation in the world

- Within the next few decades the Pacific Rim may become the economic powerhouse of the world

- Some East Asian countries are achieving industrialisation from very modest resource bases, but with the aid of an ample, hard-working and skilled labour force.

- Key problems for the future are to sustain growth and to improve the re-distribution of the wealth through all strata of society.

5.12

Island of Greed

A wave of wild wealth washes over Taiwan

The big money being made on the Taiwan stock exchange is but one index of a wave of cash that is swamping the island and its 20 million people. Over the past five years, average income has more than doubled, the new Taiwan dollar has risen 58 per cent against the US dollar, and real estate prices have soared. During the years of huge trade surpluses, Taiwan accumulated $75 billion in foreign exchange – in contrast to $82 billion for Japan.

Conspicuous consumption is unmistakable on the clogged streets of Taipei, where imported cars from Europe and the US are popular despite 40 per cent import duties. Mercedes-Benz sales have nearly doubled in the past two years. At the brass-and-wood Tau Tau Restaurant, one of many that cater to ostentatious diners, a host can order a $1400 plate of bear's paw for the table, or two small pieces of elephant trunk in soup at $57 a serving.

Many of the newly rich have dumped excess cash into the real estate market and in just two years have driven prices up 250 per cent or more. An unassuming 1200-sq.-ft. apartment for a young family in a middle-class suburb has tripled to $350 000, while a spacious 2300-sq.-ft. executive's condo in the quiet suburb of Tienmou has quadrupled in value to $1.5 million.

The dark side of the money game has been a rise in crime, particularly robbery and extortion of the well-to-do. Kidnappings were up 53 per cent last year, and last Fall a crime scare sent Mercedes sales plummeting at least 20 per cent. Says Wang Lu-yen, 35, a successful entrepreneur: 'A few years ago, I never even locked my car, but now I have a driver with a black belt.' Small wonder that some auto-repair firms are doing a thriving business bulletproofing luxury cars.

To some Taiwanese, affluence is eroding the very virtues that made prosperity possible: hard work and savings. The average workweek has shrunk 8 per cent, the savings rate is expected to drop this year to a seven-year low.

(Source: *Time*, 19 March, 1990)

5.13

Iwasaki Resort Hotel, Queensland, built with Japanese money

cent. Industry has also diversified. In Taiwan in 1952, almost 70 per cent of exports were food processed goods, principally rice and sugar. By 1983, this had dropped to only 5 per cent (now dominated by luxury items like tinned asparagus) having been overtaken by electrical machinery and textiles which now occupy the top positions.

How has all this been achieved? Many factors affect a country's success in industrialisation: natural resources, size and position, skills of the population, government policies and political stability, and world economic conditions. By examining each of these it may be possible to understand more clearly why this group has been so successful.

Natural endowment

One factor common to all of these countries is their comparatively modest natural resource base. Most of the mineral wealth of the Korean peninsula is in the North and, on partition after the Korean War, the South found itself with few resources except zinc, coal and tungsten. Taiwan has small quantities of copper, oil and gas, but insufficient for domestic needs. Neither Singapore nor Hong Kong possess significant mineral reserves and their

Pacific sunrise – East Asia's newly industrialising countries

The phenomenon

During the period since the end of the Second World War, manufacturing has become more widely spread in the world. Most of the less developed countries now have a manufacturing sector and some, like India and Brazil, have established a powerful industrial base. Few, however, have emerged onto the world stage to challenge the existing industrial concentrations in Western Europe and North America. Japan is one, and now, shining ever more brightly in the light of the rising sun, are four of Japan's neighbours: Hong Kong, Singapore, Taiwan and South Korea. Together, they contribute to the increasing importance of the Pacific Basin as an economic region. Let us

look first at the scale of development in these four rapidly changing economies.

In the period between 1960 and 1980, only oil rich Oman and Saudi Arabia, together with mineral exporting Botswana, managed to exceed Singapore's rate of growth. The other three East Asian NICs were not far behind. These four East Asian economies have weathered economic storms better than most. They have also become more competitive with Japan. The most impressive contributor to this growth has been industry.

The significance of the growth in the industrial sector in South Korea and Taiwan is clearly demonstrated in resource 5.14. The figure also shows the decline in the relative importance of agriculture in these countries. In 1960, 86 per cent of Korea's exports were agricultural or other types of primary products, but, by 1982, this had fallen to 10 per

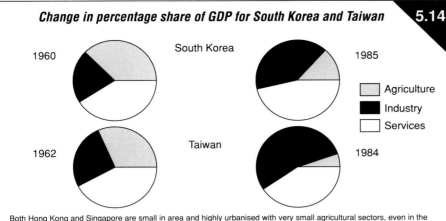

Change in percentage share of GDP for South Korea and Taiwan 5.14

South Korea

1960   1985

Taiwan

1962   1984

- Agriculture
- Industry
- Services

Both Hong Kong and Singapore are small in area and highly urbanised with very small agricultural sectors, even in the 1960s. Thus, their pie charts would not show the same shift from agriculture to industry as that shown above for Taiwan and South Korea.

agricultural resources are very limited because of their small size (around 1000 sq. km each).

South Korea and Taiwan are bigger but still relatively modest in size. A large proportion of their land is high and unsuitable for agriculture. This meant that, as population increased, there was little opportunity to sustain a surplus of agricultural produce for export. This is not to say that agriculture has been unimportant: progressive modernisation following postwar land reforms has enabled it to flourish.

The lack of a primary source of foreign exchange was arguably an advantage. None of these countries has become dependent on the export of one or two primary commodities. Many developing countries have frequently become overdependent on mineral or agricultural exports.

Historical perspective

Colonial status has had a significant bearing upon economic development. Hong Kong and Singapore both developed as part of the British Empire's world-wide network of supply stations and took advantage of the trading links which had grown up. Both are in superb geographical positions for trading (resource 5.15). Singapore guards the route from East to West through the Strait of Malacca, as well as being

centrally located for the entrepot trade from mainland South-east Asia and the islands of Indonesia and the Philippines. Hong Kong occupies a similar position in East Asia and has prospered from its role as China's 'back door'. Both also have magnificent natural harbours.

Taiwan and South Korea were under Japanese domination for the early part of this century. In both, a small industrial base was established during this colonial period. In order to assist trade with Japan, improvements were made in

transport and harbours, and agricultural production was encouraged, especially in Taiwan's sub-tropical climate. In both countries, Japan converted relatively backward and closed economies into countries in which industry and farming were developed and supported by a basic infrastructure.

Although devastated by the Second World War, all of these economies in different ways had begun to lay the foundations for industrial growth. But in the postwar period, each had its own crisis. Hong Kong received massive immigration from China at a time when trading links between the two were severed. Korea suffered a debilitating war which left the country divided. Taiwan's population was swelled by the flight from mainland China of huge numbers of refugees who brought an entirely new political and demographic situation to the island: Singapore seceded from the Federation of Malaysia. Out of this adversity each has built industrial and economic success.

Population

Population pressure has been a

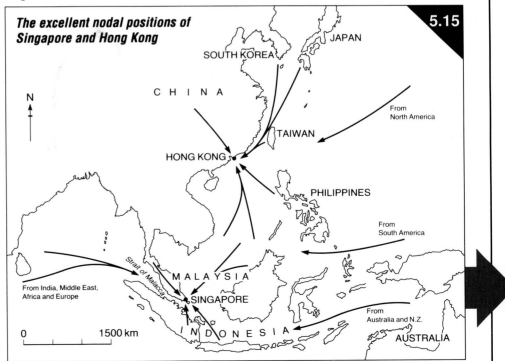

The excellent nodal positions of Singapore and Hong Kong 5.15

JAPAN
SOUTH KOREA
CHINA
TAIWAN
HONG KONG
PHILIPPINES
From North America
From South America
MALAYSIA
SINGAPORE
Strait of Malacca
From India, Middle East, Africa and Europe
INDONESIA
From Australia and N.Z.
AUSTRALIA

N

0   1500 km

factor in development. Hong Kong and Singapore, with very small areas, had both experienced large scale immigration from their larger neighbour. Taiwan had received over a million Nationalists from the Chinese mainland – today its population density is three times that of Japan and nine times that of the People's Republic of China. South Korea sustained extensive repatriation of nationals at the end of the war. Birth rates were also high, but all of these countries have succeeded in controlling and reducing them. However, the labour force continued to grow.

Population was the major resource which each country possessed. The peoples also had positive features in common. The level of education was relatively high. Japan, as the leader in the field, had introduced technology into both South Korea and Taiwan, while workers from both of these countries who had worked in Japan, or its other colonies, returned at the end of the war with new skills which a purely agricultural economy could not have generated. Many of the refugees fleeing from Communist China into Hong Kong and Taiwan were capitalist entrepreneurs who were eager to set up businesses in their new countries. In Singapore, too, the immigrants were largely Chinese from Malaysia who saw greater opportunities for prosperity in Singapore.

All these peoples, Japanese, Chinese and Koreans, share in the historical philosophy of the Confucius, who extolled the virtues of hard work, loyalty to superiors, social harmony and consensus of views. In addition Japan, Taiwan and South Korea each has a largely cultural and linguistic unity which is rare in many developing countries, and is a feature which has furthered the common purpose surrounding industrial growth.

The labour force, then, was blessed with both the motivation and the skills which laid the foundations of postwar industrial expansion. All these countries embarked upon labour intensive industry, and, while labour costs were held at rock bottom, the prices of their products were very competitive.

Government activity

Each NIC has many disadvantages compared with those countries where industry is already established. There is a lack of capital, skill and technology, not only in the sphere of production but also in marketing and management. Local markets are poorly established and foreign markets are already served by well known and trusted suppliers.

Textiles is often one of the first of the new industries (it was particularly important in Hong Kong). It uses cheap labour, simple skills and concentrates on goods which will sell in home markets where purchasing power is low. But technology still has to be bought, in the form of machinery, if industry is to expand. Infant industry has to be protected by tariff restrictions placed on imports. However, mere import substitution (making locally what had previously been imported) did not prove profitable enough for Taiwan or South Korea. Once home demand had been satisfied, growth slowed down. Clearly the size and prosperity of the home market plays a considerable part in determining the size and variety of import substitution industry. Japan had a large home market which was an important stimulus to the development of consumer electrical industries after the war. But home markets in the other East Asian countries, notably Hong Kong and Singapore, are small.

In each country, except Hong Kong where virtual free trade existed, government management of the economy has been decisive. By selecting key export growth industries and promoting them with financial incentives, governments played a crucial part in economic planning. It was the dramatic change in government policies towards export promotion which heralded the economic growth from 1961 in Taiwan and 1964 in South Korea. In the case of Hong Kong and Singapore, the absence of raw materials or fuel, the small home market and the heavy involvement in world trade by reason of their port functions made it inevitable that export promotion would be necessary to promote industry from the start. In the 1970s governments in both South Korea and Taiwan moved to establish heavy industries like petrochemicals, steel and shipbuilding. Now South Korea outsells Japan in world shipbuilding markets.

In each of these countries, including Japan, there was a strong and autocratic government in power for an extended period. Thus decisions which were made held, and in the long term, planning proceeded uninterrupted by changes of policy or administration.

Foreign investment and technology

The role of foreign aid in the recovery and survival of Taiwan and South Korea after the Second World War was not a permanent feature, and with the exception of Singapore, all of these states have expanded their industry with very substantial internal savings. Reliance upon foreign investment has been less than in Latin America. Foreign transnational companies are present, but frequently in association with local firms, and it is only in the microelectronics field that they tend to dominate production outside Singapore. Major investors in East Asia are Japan and the United States, and these have helped the spread of high technology industries: oil and petrochemicals in Singapore and microelectronics everywhere. Without transnational capital, it would be difficult for NICs to find the resources to enter these fields in which research and development require so much expenditure. At the same time, while less interest is shown in the more traditional and low technology areas such as textiles, both Japan and the USA use low cost factories in NICs to supply world markets. Assembly plants have been set up for watches, electronics and other labour intensive operations using cheap labour.

All of these activities in the business conscious atmosphere of East Asia, have quickly developed links with other areas of the economy. Petrochemicals produce synthetic fibres for textile industries, and therefore reduce imports; they also provide the basis for the manufacturing of fertilisers. Electronics assembly encourages the manufacture of sophisticated parts instead of importing them. These developments are also being supported by governments.

Markets

From the late 1950s until 1974, the world economy was expanding and market capacity was increasing rapidly, especially in prosperous Western Europe and North America. However cheap produce from Asia caused concern over redundancies in regions such as Lancashire.

In a sense, these NICs were in the right place at the right time. Countries like these are very dependent on world markets because, without export sales, income would collapse. Indeed, it is difficult to see how any of the four could sustain such large scale industry of the home market alone. Growth since 1974 has continued, although at a more erratic rate, and there has been a significant improvement in the standard of living of the people, especially in Singapore and Taiwan (resource 5.16).

But they have had to work hard. As trade has slowed, so markets have become more competitive in two ways. The rich countries, comprising the chief markets, witnessing large scale imports of manufactures from the NICs and the declining competitiveness of their own industries, began to resort to protectionism as labour, shed from industries like textiles and motor

cycles, failed to find work elsewhere. At the other end of the scale, there are other countries beginning to develop industry successfully who are employing cheaper labour, thereby threatening the positions formerly held by Hong Kong, South Korea, Taiwan and Singapore. This process is aided by transnational corporations which can easily transfer production in footloose industries like electronic assembly from Singapore, where wages are rising, to Thailand or Malaysia where they are not. Japan has always been one step ahead and has countered the problem by moving into higher technology and capitalising on the greater skills of its workforce. The NICs are beginning to do the same. Taiwan's economic development has reached a stage where further growth will depend upon its ability to raise the level of technology. Science parks, like that at Hsinchu, 70 km southwest of Taipei, which contained 82 hi-tech plants in 1988, are increasingly seeking to attract the finance and technology necessary to move upmarket.

Conclusion

It is possible to identify some parallel strands in the industrial development of the four East Asian NICs. But it would be wrong to attribute growth to identical factors. Each country is unique. Three of them had strong government guidance, but Hong Kong did not. Singapore leaned heavily on foreign investment, while the others did not. In Hong Kong and Taiwan small firms dominate the private sector of industry. There are some interesting similarities. Each country took advantage of favourable trading conditions by exploiting its position and its people to maximum effect. But each also has its uncertainties.

South Korea has existed in a state of armed hostility towards its northern neighbour since the end of the Korean War. The fortunes of both Hong Kong and Taiwan are closely linked with those of China: both are populated largely by Chinese and both were once part of China. In 1997, Hong Kong becomes part of the People's Republic of China and many are not hopeful that Hong Kong will continue to enjoy the freedom in world markets which has hitherto underpinned its success. Taiwan too, fiercely anti-communist, has viewed with concern the return to hard line policies on the mainland.

(Source: B Heppell, 'Pacific sunrise: East Asia's newly industrialising countries', *Geography Review*, March 1990, pp. 7-11)

Activities

1   For each of the four countries, make a list under these headings:

   a The resources and types of industry.

   b The rates of growth.

   c The roles of government and of private businesses (domestic and multinational companies).

   d The prospects and problems for the future.

2   Using reference sources, assemble further information about the four countries.

3   Using your lists and additional information, compare and contrast the countries in terms of their resource bases, their populations and the characteristics of their industrial growth.

Average annual percentage growth of GNP		5.16
Country	**1960–1980**	**1980–1985**
Republic of South Korea	9.5	7.9
Hong Kong	8.5	5.9
Singapore	10.2	6.5
Taiwan	9.1	6.6

CASE STUDY 5.3 *Regional shifts in the UK*

Background

In the United Kingdom, as in most industrialised countries, the balance of employment opportunities is shifting away from manufacturing into services, from primary and secondary industry into the tertiary and quaternary sectors. This trend affects not only the type of jobs available, but also their location as the following extract makes clear:

'In the changing industrial geography of the United Kingdom, there are two sets of changes occurring, both exciting. The first are the changes in the geographical patterns and landscapes in which people live. The second are the changes in the theories and explanations of what has been happening.

Three major changes occurred which provide the basis for understanding the geographical shifts. There was a dramatic decline in manufacturing employment in Britain from 8.3 million in 1970 to 6.7 million in 1980 and then more rapidly down to 5.3 million at the end of 1986. Whereas manufacturing employed 35 per cent of the employees in employment in 1970, this has fallen to only 25 per cent in 1988. British manufacturing also experienced major structural change. The industries which declined most were those which fuelled the industrial revolution in Britain 200 years ago, including iron and steel making, the textile industries, shipbuilding and clothing manufacture. The industries which declined least were mostly either those supplying home markets with consumer goods such as furniture, paper and printed matter, or more 'high tech' industries supplying both home and export markets such as electronic engineering, instrument making, and pharmaceuticals. Historically these two groups of industries had very different regional distributions. The former were heavily concentrated in the north and west, whilst the latter were less concentrated, but with a larger proportion in the south and east. It is not surprising, therefore, that there was a changing regional distribution of manufacturing employment with the regions suffering the highest proportions of manufacturing employment loss being those with concentrations of the more rapidly declining, older industries.

There were further changes at the sub-regional level as British industry became redistributed. The dominant trends were the loss of manufacturing from the major cities and conurbations, especially from inner cities, and a growth in the proportion of industry located around the edges of larger settlements and in smaller towns in more rural areas. At an even more local level, a high proportion of manufacturing became located on industrial estates rather than on independent factory sites. The most important exceptions to this were the largest factories such as cement works or car assembly plants.

A change also occurred in the geography of individual industries. The shifts in their regional distribution are well illustrated by the textiles industry. In 1970, cotton was still king in Lancashire. The textile industry had more employees in the north-west region than in any other region in Britain and it had been the largest manufacturing employer there since the last century. By 1986 this pattern had been replaced. In 1986 both the East Midlands and the Yorkshire and Humberside regions had more textile employees than the north-west.

After 1970 manufacturing production was increasingly concentrated within large enterprises. For many familiar products – motor cars, television sets, compact discs, bread or beer or fish fingers – the five largest companies produced well over 50 per cent of British output. In many cases, such as beer or fish fingers or cars, the figure was over 75 per cent. This has geographical significance because many large companies have a chain of production, with one of their factories making one component, which is passed on to another factory of the same company for sub-assembly and so on. Moreover, within large companies functions are frequently spatially separated. This has contributed to important changes in the industrial geography of Britain. Control functions have become increasingly concentrated, particularly into south-east England and in the larger cities of other regions. As a result, smaller settlements have become increasingly concerned simply with production. Average income and stability of jobs in these places is much lower than elsewhere. The reduced affluence is then reflected in many other aspects of society. For example, in areas dominated by production functions the job opportunities available are much different from those in areas where control functions are concentrated.'

The message of the above passage is the growth of the south and east at the expense of the north and west. This suggestion of a north/south divide is supported by regional unemployment levels (resources 5.17 and 5.19). Remember too, that high levels of employment and income tend to generate yet more jobs by increasing spending and investment. These regional differences persist despite a wide range of government policies since the 1940s, targeted at regional regeneration and the restriction of growth in south-east England, e.g. Assisted Area status, Urban Development Councils, Green Belts etc. Regions and cities too, have mounted campaigns to attract industries.

The materials in this case study indicate, however, that a counter-movement is gathering momentum, especially in the service industry sector (resources 5.21 and 5.22). As you read these resources, note particularly the regions being affected, and whether jobs are being directly created, or whether existing personnel are being moved to the new location. Remember that even in the latter case, the extra people and income will have a positive 'knock-on' (multiplier) effect in the host region (resource 5.18).

Key understandings

◆ The balance of industrial employment is shifting from the manufacturing to the service sector.

◆ The balance of regional job opportunities is constantly shifting.

◆ Moving business into a region creates jobs both directly (new jobs and relocated personnel) and indirectly) through the 'knock-on' or multiplier effect).

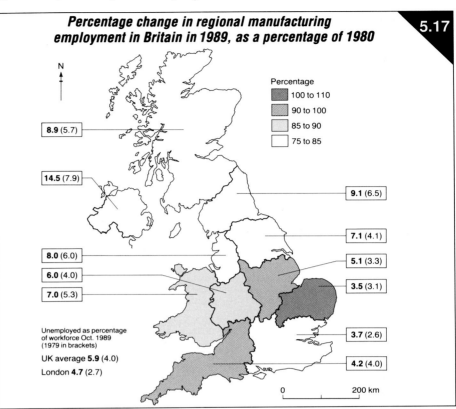

Percentage change in regional manufacturing employment in Britain in 1989, as a percentage of 1980

5.17

Percentage
- 100 to 110
- 90 to 100
- 85 to 90
- 75 to 85

8.9 (5.7)
14.5 (7.9)
9.1 (6.5)
7.1 (4.1)
8.0 (6.0)
5.1 (3.3)
6.0 (4.0)
3.5 (3.1)
7.0 (5.3)
3.7 (2.6)
4.2 (4.0)

Unemployed as percentage of workforce Oct. 1989 (1979 in brackets)
UK average **5.9** (4.0)
London **4.7** (2.7)

0   200 km

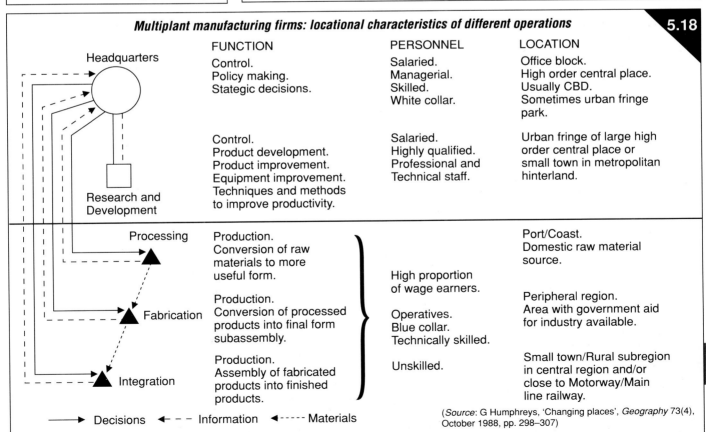

Multiplant manufacturing firms: locational characteristics of different operations

5.18

	FUNCTION	PERSONNEL	LOCATION
Headquarters	Control. Policy making. Stategic decisions.	Salaried. Managerial. Skilled. White collar.	Office block. High order central place. Usually CBD. Sometimes urban fringe park.
Research and Development	Control. Product development. Product improvement. Equipment improvement. Techniques and methods to improve productivity.	Salaried. Highly qualified. Professional and Technical staff.	Urban fringe of large high order central place or small town in metropolitan hinterland.
Processing	Production. Conversion of raw materials to more useful form.	High proportion of wage earners.	Port/Coast. Domestic raw material source.
Fabrication	Production. Conversion of processed products into final form subassembly.	Operatives. Blue collar. Technically skilled.	Peripheral region. Area with government aid for industry available.
Integration	Production. Assembly of fabricated products into finished products.	Unskilled.	Small town/Rural subregion in central region and/or close to Motorway/Main line railway.

→ Decisions   ◀ - - Information   ◀----- Materials

(*Source*: G Humphreys, 'Changing places', *Geography* 73(4), October 1988, pp. 298–307)

5.19

Regional contrasts

The notion that Britain does not have any regional problems because there are rich parts of Yorkshire has always seemed wide of the mark. Aggregations have to be made if there is to be any real understanding of the real world or it would merely become a succession of impossibly complex and random events. The figures which aggregate economic data on a regional basis show higher unemployment and lower incomes in the areas outside London and the South-east and sometimes reveal spectacular problems of local and regional decline. Moreover, there is little reason to believe that those problems will disappear of their own accord in any reasonable timescale. The regional problem is becoming one of the most spectacular blemishes on the Government's economic record.

Start with a look at incomes. The difference between the richest and the poorest region of Britain in terms of income per head is now the widest for ore than a decade. Almost all the poorer regions (with the exception of the North, which raised its relative standing for the first time in a decade in 1987) have grown more slowly than the richer ones. Income per head in the richest region – the South-east – is 42 per cent higher than in the poorest British region – Wales – and 53 per cent higher than in Northern Ireland. This compares with an equivalent difference a decade before of 35 per cent and 48 per cent.

There is, though, a caveat. The figures do not allow for regional price differences. Rents and land values are sharply lower outside the richer regions. It is also likely that the prices of many goods and services are lower. This particularly applies to services whose principal cost is labour (like hairdressing, restaurant meals, transport services) rather than goods which can be traded between regions and countries. The real gap will be far narrower, but there is no study to suggest by how much.

These differences in income per head are also less pronounced for those in work. Lower incomes in poor regions arise in part because more people are out of work. Unemployment remains very much higher outside southern England. Moreover, these figures if anything understate the gravity of the problem because unemployment is far from being a good measure for regional distress. It is the result of a whole series of adjustments – including migration from the poorer to the richer regions. Net migration from the relatively poor areas was not large – it amounted to 71 000 in 1986 – but it was enough to cancel out their natural population rise over the period 1981–86. Without migration, which is generally seen as a sigh of economic weakness in an economy, the unemployment rates in the poorer regions would be even higher in the sort term.

Another way of assessing regional dynamism is to look at the figures for employment. The results of the 1984 Census of Employment were finally released in 1987 and showed a far more dramatic skewing of job prospects in the regions than was suggested even by the unemployment figures. The calculations based on the census showed that only one region outside the southern three saw a rise in employment and that was the East Midlands with a modest 6000. If the self-employed are excluded, the figures showed that a mere 6 per cent of the job losses were in the three southern regions and 94 per cent in the Midlands and the North. The regional pattern appears to have been remarkably persistent in both downturn and upturn. Broadly, the regions which showed the sharpest job losses also experienced the slowest recovery of jobs.

Why do regions suffer such diverse fates? The Government's advisers argue that a contributory cause has been pay inflexibility, including in some industries the settlement of pay according to national rates regardless of local labour market conditions. It is certain true that pay differences are relatively small when similar jobs are compared, which means that there is little incentive to bring northern workers to southern jobs or vice versa. The differences in overall average pay rises because there are more lower paid *occupations* in the North.

Nevertheless, the regional differences in unemployment also arose because of the accident of differening industrial structures rather than pay inflexibility per se. The near-two million drop in manufacturing employment from the 1979 peak to the 1986 trough particularly hit the northerly regions, because more of their labour forces are involved in manufacturing. For example, manufacturing accounts for 35.8 per cent of jobs in the West Midlands compared with only 20.6 per cent in the South-east. Manufacturing was simply prices out of its markets. Southern England also benefits from a disproportionate share of the fastest growing industry – banking, insurance and finance.

Part of the answer to regional problems is, therefore, to pursue macro-economic policies (for interest rates, tax, public spending and the exchange rate) which do not bear particularly heavily on a single sector of the economy. At one point this was regarded as an advantage of monetary policy as against the apparently more discretionary effects of Government tax and public spending decisions. However, the uneven impact of the 1979–81 monetary squeeze highlighted the arguments for using macro-economic levers in a balanced way.

Regional problems are less than they would naturally be, thanks to national policy instruments which reduce regional inequalities automatically. A progressive tax system which raises more revenue from people with higher incomes and higher spending will clearly raise a disproportionate amount of money from the richer parts of the country, while the public spending side of the Government's accounts is meant to be equally shared around. In the case of unemployment benefit, there is a direct compensation to regions with high unemployment.

Thus, rich parts of the country run budget surpluses which fund budget deficits in poorer parts. The EC Commission's McDougall report found that public finance flows benefited Wales by 7.8 per cent of regional product; Scotland by 6.1 per cent and Northern Ireland by 16.1 per cent. The public finance outflow from the South-east was worth 4.8 per cent of regional product.

Nevertheless, most British governments since the war have also run a specific regional policy. An important economic justification is that regional policy can help to reduce inflationary pressures in booming regions is some of the slack is taken up in depressed ones. reducing the mismatch between regions should enable a higher level of output and employment in the country as a whole, without sparking off wage inflation. On some occasions, governments have encouraged labour to move to the growing regions, but this was often politically unpopular and may have had fewer effects than supposed. Most regional measures have been directed at encouraging people to stay in the depressed regions by providing more jobs. That also makes sense economically because of the sunk costs in providing a viable economy.

Under Mrs Thatcher, however, regional spending more than halved in real terms, in part because the Government argued with justice that previous regional policy measures proved to be costly failures. Assisted areas cover about 35 per cent of the working population. In so-called 'intermediate areas', the Government can make money available for specific projects and companies. in 'development areas'. there can also be selective assistance but there is a 15 per cent automatic grant towards new plant and buildings, up to a limit of £10 000 per job created. Both the new and the old systems continue to encourage relatively investment-intensive production.

Surely a more sensible approach to reducing regional inequalities would be to make labour more attractive to hire, since it specifically directs policy at what the Government is aiming to keep in the regions. One possibility would be employment subsidies paid on the additional members of a workforce in a given year, though such measures have in the past been criticised by the EC Commission as unfair competition within the Community. Another possibility is to reduce some part of the tax on labour. One proposal is for variable rates of income tax, with especially low rates in the most depressed regions. Part of the benefit would almost certainly be passed back to the employer, making it more willing to hire labour. Another alternative, with very similar effects, would be regional reductions in employer's National Insurance contributions. The effect would be to concentrate help on the local people rather than their machines.

(Source: Christopher Huhne, *The Guardian*, 10 January 1990)

NHS to quit London base

The headquarters of the National Health Service and the planned social security Benefits Agency are to move from London to Leeds.

Nearly 2000 civil servants are being offered inducements worth more than £12 000 per family, plus the trouble-free sale of their house, to leave behind what Whitehall calls the congested and miserable working conditions in the capital.

In a deal billed by the Treasury as Whitehall's most generous passport to the good life in the provinces, 1000 staff of the NHS management executive and 650 Department of Social Security employees are being urged to move to a new office complex in Leeds from 1991.

In addition, the 150 staff of the Chief Adjudication Officer are being pressed to move from Southampton to Leeds.

Mr Kenneth Clarke, the Health Secretary, said: 'In future the NHS will be managed from Leeds, and policy strategy will be laid down by ministers and their officials here in Whitehall.'

In the DSS, more than half the 1550 headquarters posts will stay in London. But, crucially, the arms-length agency which will administer the benefits system from 1992 is to be based in Leeds.

Mr Tony Newton, the Social Security Secretary, said: 'Moving to Leeds will help us carry out our tasks more efficiently and effectively and should make it easier to recruit and retain staff.'

The deal for staff involves a cash offer of between £1500 per individual and £3500 per family; a lump sum payment of £8750 to cover the lost London weighting allowance for five years; and a guaranteed price for their home even if it has to be sold below market value.

For those who wish to buy a second home in Leeds, the Treasury will pay legal costs and is considering other inducements.

Included in the deal is an allowance of up to £77 a night for the first 30 days in expenses for the civil servant, partner and children to have a look at Leeds; an advance of a half-year's salary which need not be paid back for a decade, and reimbursement of any public school fees lost by moving.
(David Hencke and David Brindle)

Immigration HQ may leave capital

A plan to move the Home Office's immigration and nationality department from Lunar House in Croydon, south London, to an unspecified site in the West Midlands is being considered by ministers.

The relocation would affect 1600 posts, although not all the southern-based civil servants would be expected to move. The proposal has been advanced to avoid recruitment difficulties in the south-east to find cheaper property and to establish a public inquiry office in a more central location.

The Joint Council for the Welfare of Immigrants fears that a move could disadvantage immigrants in the south and marginalise issues by separating officials and ministers.

Mr David Waddington, the Home Secretary, is expected to make a decision by the end of next month. One option is to put the new immigration headquarters into the same complex as a proposed national centre for the prison service.

The possible move for the Prison Department was mooted in August in a consultation paper than envisaged moving 1100 posts from its headquarters in Cleland House, Westminster, and 400 from its four regional centres.

If the two services were moved to the same site, it would create a centre with 3100 jobs.

Home Office sources say that the motive for moving the prisons headquarters lies in a reorganisation of the service being considered to eliminate the regional tier of administration and establish a structure of 14 area managers, each responsible for nine or 10 prisons.

The plan requires a headquarters in central England to smooth communication. Prison governors say the scheme is 'unworkable'.

The National Union of Civil and Public Servants does not oppose relocations in principle, but questions the value of moving so many posts to an area of relatively low unemployment.
(Source: John Carvel, *The Guardian*, 15 November, 1989)

Army of officials heads for provinces

Thirty-four thousand civil servants could join the 300 000 who already work in provincial towns and cities by the end of the century.

Whitehall officials say this number could be moved out of London without disrupting government business.

One hundred thousand of the 500 000 white collar civil servants are based in London, and a further 100 000 are distributed across the South-east.

Fewer than 20 000 civil servants, mainly policy advisers to ministers, the Cabinet and Parliament, could be left in London by the middle of the next century.

Developments in technology and communications are making it easier to base government departments outside the capital.

At the same time, London is becoming increasingly expensive and unattractive for Whitehall and private industry.

The exodus started in the 1960s and 1970s when governments built computer centres for ministries outside the capital.

They included the huge complex to handle benefits for the Department of Health and Social Security at Newcastle upon Tyne, moves out of London for the Inland Revenue and the location of the Customs and Excise computer centre in Southend in Essex.

Six hundred civil servants at the Overseas Development Administration and the Crown Agents relocated to East Kilbride in Scotland earlier this decade. The Health and Safety Executive went to Bootle, and the Manpower Services Commission (now the Training Commission) went to Sheffield. Bootle was unpopular, but Sheffield – which also became the headquarters for the Midland Bank – was seen as a big success by those who left the capital.

As well as the decision, announced yesterday, to move nearly 2000 health and social security civil servants to Leeds, thousands more are scheduled to leave London and the south-east.

At least 1100 civil servants at the Department of Employment will go to Runcorn and Sheffield; 2200 Inland Revenue staff will be moved to the north; and most of the remainder of the Patent Office in London will move to Cardiff. About 1200 Department of Social security staff will go to Lancashire and 150 Land Registry staff will move to Hull.

Most of the staff employed by the Office of Population, Censuses and Surveys in Holborn are to leave London.

The Stationary Office is based in Norwich; the Companies Registration Office is in Cardiff and the Driving and Vehicle Licensing Directorate is in Swansea. The new social security agency will be in Leeds.
(Source: David Hencke, *The Guardian*, 15 November, 1989)

Employment moving away from London

5.22

27 000 jobs on move to regions

Costs and labour shortages are forcing a growing number of companies to flee from London.

More than 7000 jobs were moved in 1989 and almost 20 000 more are due over the next two years with the government in the van, say researchers Jones Lang Wootton in a survey published yesterday.

Twenty companies moved this year, 49 are set to go by 1993 and another 23 are considering moving – and not just to the suburbs. Half are going to the regions, especially the south-west.

Office rents have soared in London over the past couple of years but political factors are also significant as government departments make up more than a quarter of moves. The Ministry of Defence is decamping staff to Newcastle while the Department of Social Security is sending 350 jobs to Belfast.

Among the private groups BP Exploration transferred 400 jobs to Glasgow this year. Next year Chase Manhattan is sending 480 to Bournemouth and Barclays 1000 to Coventry.

(Source: David Lawson, *The Guardian*, 13 December, 1989)

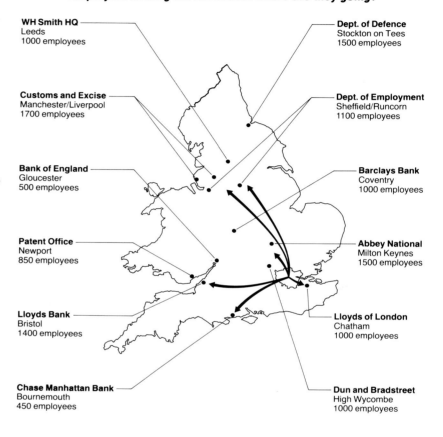

Employers moving out of London: where are they going?

WH Smith HQ
Leeds
1000 employees

Customs and Excise
Manchester/Liverpool
1700 employees

Bank of England
Gloucester
500 employees

Patent Office
Newport
850 employees

Lloyds Bank
Bristol
1400 employees

Chase Manhattan Bank
Bournemouth
450 employees

Dept. of Defence
Stockton on Tees
1500 employees

Dept. of Employment
Sheffield/Runcorn
1100 employees

Barclays Bank
Coventry
1000 employees

Abbey National
Milton Keynes
1500 employees

Lloyds of London
Chatham
1000 employees

Dun and Bradstreet
High Wycombe
1000 employees

Activities

1 From resources 5.17 to 5.22, construct a matrix using the following structure:

| Who is moving | Where from | Where to | How many jobs | | Reasons for move | Who makes the decision |
			(a) move to destination	(b) created at destination		

2 **Group discussion:**

Produce a second matrix and complete it for:

a one public sector organisation, and

b one private company, using the following structure:

(NB Use evidence from the resources in the case study and suggest other possible advantages and disadvantages.)

| Organisation | Advantages | | | | Disadvantages | | | |
	To the organisation	To the individual	To region of origin	To region of destination	(same four columns)			

CASE STUDY 5.4 The Japanese motor vehicle industry in North America

Background

One of the most important features of industrial change in the 1980s was global expansion by Japanese companies. This expansion ranged from financial investment in buildings, through the take-over of existing companies, to direct investment through the construction of offices and factories for Japanese companies. This growth affected even the wealthy, industrialised USA: by 1989, Japan had become 'the most important foreign investor in the United States'. World Tourism Organisation figures for 1989 ranked Japan first in international arrivals into the USA. These figures are predominantly business travellers, and indicate the scale of Japanese business interests in the United States.

In manufacturing industry this investment has raised considerable controversy. On the one hand, Japanese companies are seen as major providers of new jobs, and as innovators in technology and management styles. Others see these activities as part of a plan to expand Japan's trade and to dominate the US market. A 1986 survey showed

Key understandings

◆ The Japanese motor vehicle industry has developed a large-scale manufacturing capacity in North America and captured more than 25 per cent of the domestic market.

◆ Japanese investment includes both assembly plants and component suppliers and has followed a clear cycle of evolution.

◆ The locational decisions by Japanese companies have produced a regional reconcentration of the motor vehicle industry in North America, which includes the traditional 'auto' heartland.

◆ The Japanese motor vehicle industry is organised on a different basis from the US industry, and this helps to account for its distinctive locational pattern, and its success.

5.23

Japanese-owned plants by state, December 1986

State	Number of plants	Estimated number of employees	State	Number of plants	Estimated number of employees
New England	30	4491	S. Carolina	10	1750
Connecticut	7	809	Virginia	4	1440
Maine	1	50	W. Virginia	1	200
Massachusetts	12	1673	East South Central	53	19 022
New Hampshire	7	1714	Alabama	10	3551
Rhode Island	2	100	Kentucky	17	5806
Vermont	1	145	Mississippi	4	817
Mid-Atlantic	84	11 840	Tennessee	22	8848
New Jersey	33	2822	West South Central	45	9689
New York	30	6073	Arkansas	4	1528
Pennsylvania	21	2945	Louisiana	2	395
East North Central	130	36 684	Oklahoma	6	622
Illinois	46	13 216	Texas	33	7144
Indiana	16	6570	Mountain	14	1311
Michigan	33	10 373	Arizona	6	1064
Ohio	32	7430	Colorado	2	61
Wisconsin	3	1095	Idaho	0	0
West North Central	22	3159	Montana	0	0
Iowa	3	346	Nevada	4	130
Kansas	1	22	New Mexico	1	28
Minnesota	2	150	Utah	1	28
Missouri	9	1120	Wyoming	0	0
Nebraska	6	1466	Pacific	227	38 329
N. Dakota	0	0	Alaska	25	4956
S. Dakota	1	55	Calfornia	163	28 355
South Atlantic	81	13 818	Hawaii	10	535
Delaware	0	0	Oregon	7	1289
Florida	7	1380	Washington	22	3194
Georgia	34	5550			
Maryland	4	890	Total	686	140 343
N. Carolina	21	2608			

that Japanese companies owned factories in 45 States and employed over 140 000 people, – under 1 per cent of total manufacturing employees, but growing more rapidly than in US-owned companies (resource 5.23).

Foreign direct investment (FDI) in manufacturing by Japanese companies has focused upon products and countries where they have already established markets through exporting completed products, e.g. electronic equipment, motor vehicles. The opening of manufacturing plants in a foreign country by FDI is usually the final phase in what is known as the **product cycle**. (Note that this is a manufacturing product cycle, and is therefore different from the mining cycle we examined in case study 5.1, pages 95–98):

Phase 1
A company introduces a new product to the home market as a result of technological and management innovation.

Phase 2
Output expands to take advantage of the economies of scale, and so to keep prices down.

Phase 3
A market is identified in another country and the company begins to export the product.

Phase 4
The company sets up an assembly plant in the 'host' country. The product is then shipped in CKD form (completely-knocked-down) i.e. like a kit, to be assembled in the host country.

Phase 5
The company develops manufacturing capacity in the host country by organising a network of parts suppliers. Gradually, the proportion of parts imported from the home country decreases, and the proportion made in the host country increases. This allows the assembly plant to grow in size and efficiency.

Phase 6
The company invests in additional

5.24	North American assembly plants of Japanese automobile firms				
	Location	Parents	Production start date	Annual capacity	Employment
Honda	Marysville, Ohio	Honda (100%)	1982	360 000	5000
Nissan	Smyrna, Tennessee	Nissan (100%)	1983	240 000	3300
Nummi	Fremont, California	Toyota (50%) GM (50%)	1984	250 000	2600
Honda	Alliston, Ontario	Honda (100%)	1986	80 000	700
Mazda	Flat Rock, Michigan	Mazda (100%)	1987	240 000	3500
Toyota	Georgetown, Kentucky	Toyota (100%)	1988	200 000	3000
Toyota	Cambridge, Ontario	Toyota (100%)	1988	50 000	1000
Diamond-Star	Bloomington Normal. IL	Mitsubishi (50%) Chrysler (50%)	1988	240 000	2900
Cami	Ingersoll, Ontario	Suzuki (50%) GM (50%)	1989	200 000	2000
Subaru-Isuzi	Lafayette, Indiana	Fuji Heavy Indus. (51%) Isuzu (49%)	1989	120 000	1700
Honda	E. Liberty, Ohio	Honda (100%)	1990	150 000	1800
Nissan-Ford	Avon Lake, Ohio	Nissan (3%) Ford (3%)	1991	130 000	1300
Totals				2 260 000	28 800

plants, generating further supplier networks, while rival companies, in a process called **competitive reaction**, follow the lead firm into the host country, to create a new production cluster.

This case study demonstrates the product cycle by examining the spectacular penetration of the US market by the Japanese motor-vehicle industry. In particular, the materials show (i) that Japanese companies have gone beyond CKD 'kit' assembly to full manufacturing capacity, (ii) that while US vehicle manufacturers have been dispersing from their traditional Detroit hub, the Japanese 'transplants' are concentrating geographically, (iii) that the Japanese success in this highly competitive market is due in large part to the way they organise the production process.

Auto Alley, USA

The new wave
In the early 1990s there are at least 250 Japanese-owned vehicle assembly and components production factories in North America, the great majority in the United States, and almost all built since 1980 (resource 5.24). The reasons most frequently given for this rapid expansion during the 1980s are as follows:

1 To avoid the threats of tariff barriers and laws to protect US industries, e.g. the 1981 Voluntary Restraint Agreement, under which Japanese firms agreed to limit their exports to USA.
2 The rise in the value of Japanese currency, the yen, which increased the costs of exporting components and finished products from Japan to North America.

However, there are several other reasons: (i) the market for vehicles in Japan was becoming increasingly competitive and so companies sought out other markets; (ii) Japanese vehicle manufacturers were becoming more productive, while US manufacturers were stagnating; (iii) as the Japanese share of the US market grew (1970: 4 per cent; 1988: 15 per cent), so investment inside the US became more attractive.

The pioneer investors in transplants were Honda and Nissan, whose interest in the United States as early as 1970 was triggered by the dominance of Toyota in the home Japanese market and the obvious potential of the North American market. Both companies adopted similar strategies. They chose small towns in rural areas (Honda in Marysville, Ohio, 1977; Nissan in Smyrna, Tennessee, 1979), and opted for specific market niches as pilot schemes (the Honda plant would build motor-cycles, and Nissan pick-up trucks).

After this experimental period, both companies expanded their production to cars in the early 1980s.

This success led to a wave of FDI by eight of the nine Japanese motor vehicle manufacturers, with plans for twelve assembly plants by 1991, four in joint ventures with North American companies (resource 5.24). All but the NUMMI (New United Motor Manufacturing, Inc., a joint venture between General Motors and Toyota) plant in California are new factories. By the early 1990s, employment is set to reach 30 000 and annual output will exceed 2.25 million vehicles. The expansion did not end with the 1980s – Nissan is to double its capacity to 0.5 million vehicles a year; Honda and Subaru-Isuzu intend to double their output capacity, companies are expanding their product range into luxury cars and into US-based research and development. The impact on the 'Detroit Big Three' (Chrysler, Ford, General Motors) has been increasingly serious (resource 5.26).

A second wave of growth has been FDI in North America since 1982 by Japanese component supplier companies (resource 5.25). In 1991 there were up to 250 such plants, almost all new, and employing 30 000 people. Many such companies already have contracts with the vehicle assembly companies at home in Japan.

These transplant investments by both assembly and component supplier companies have been helped considerably by state and local governments competing vigorously to entice these investments and job opportunities. Resource 5.27 shows the range of inducements offered. Notice that the states tend to fall into two categories: first, those traditionally industrialised states, such as Ohio and Michigan, which are part of the 'Rust Belt' suffering decline, and second, states with a relatively low industrial base, e.g. Tennessee, and the non-coal mining areas of Kentucky.

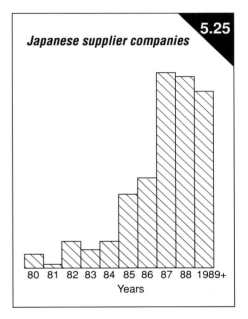

5.25

Japanese supplier companies

(bar chart showing Years: 80, 81, 82, 83, 84, 85, 86, 87, 88, 1989+)

5.26

Major overhaul

Pounded by the recession and international rivals, GM will close 25 plants and lay off 74 000 workers. Will the bloodletting end there?

The Christmas speech from the chairman of General Motors traditionally sounds like an address from a head of state. But this year's message from chairman Robert Stempel was like no other in the 83-year history of the giant corporation.

As of January 1, Stempel said, he company would embark on a three-year programme that would close 25 North American plants and reduce its current workforce by 74 000 or about 19 per cent. GM would abandon for the foreseeable future its hopes to regain its lost share of the US market, which has fallen in the past decade from 45 per cent to just over 35 per cent. GM would emerge by 1995 only half as large as it was a decade earlier.

Japanese automakers, whose success in the US has come largely at GM's expense, feared that the cutbacks would add fuel to the political backlash against Japan. Toyota, for one, took the remarkable step of publicly expressing sympathy for laid-off GM workers.

GM, even after shedding as many plants and people as there are in all of Chrysler, will still be the world's largest automaker – but no longer the richest. Toyota, Japan's leading carmaker, has $12.7 billion in cash reserves against GM's $3.5 billion. Toyota shows every indication of reinvesting its huge sums to improve both product and design. Unless GM can return to profitability and make similar investments, the current cutback won't be its last. (Source: adapted from William McWhirter, 'Major Overhaul', *Time*, 30 December, 1991)

Locational patterns

Resources 5.28 and 5.29 show the distinctive locational pattern of the Japanese companies. Eleven of the twelve assembly plants are located in a north-south zone from South Ontario (Canada), through Michigan, Illinois, Indiana, Ohio, Kentucky and Tennessee. This 'transplant corridor' or 'Auto Alley' is organised along several interstate highways (motorways). Only the NUMMI plant at Fremont, California is outside this corridor. This is surprising in view of the strong West Coast FDI by Japanese companies in other industries, e.g. in California there are 35 high-technology computer plants, focused in 'Silicon Valley', south of San Francisco, and in Los Angeles, while Oregon and Washington have emerging 'Silicon Forests'.

The supplier transplant locations are also concentrated in 'Auto Alley' (resource 5.29). By 1990 there were 52 Japanese supplier firms in Ohio, 33 in Kentucky, 32 in Michigan, 19 in Tennessee, plus 12 in California. Of the 250 or so suppliers, 80 per cent were in the transplant corridor. One outcome of this invasion, in addition to the use of American component suppliers, is that approximately 75 per cent of the finished product, i.e. the assembled 'Japanese' vehicle, is manufactured within the US. This is almost as high a proportion as for the 'domestic' products of Ford or General Motors. Indeed, certain Nissan and Mazda models are manufactured *only* in North America, and exported to Japan!

Careful study of resource 5.30 shows that the Japanese firms have created **integrated vehicle production complexes**. These complexes have three main characteristics: first, most supplier firms have followed the assembly plants in selecting sites adjacent to small towns in rural areas. Second, there is a tendency for supplier firms to cluster around the particular assembly plant they supply, or in locations accessible to several plants. Assembly companies

Japanese investor	State	Financial support ($ million)	
Toyota	Kentucky	Total support	125.0
		Site acquisition	15.0
		Site improvement	20.0
		Technology centre construction	10.0
		Worker training	33.0
		Road improvement	47.0
Diamond-Star	Illinois	Total support	83.3
		Road improvement	17.8
		Site acquisition	11.0
		Water system improvement	14.5
		Worker training	40.0
Mazda	Michigan	Total support	52.0
		Worker training	19.0
		Road improvement	4.0
		Low-interest loans for site and sewerage improvements	20.0
		Loans to small municipalities	0.3
		Federal subsidy	1.0
		Railway improvement	7.5
Nissan	Tennessee	Total support	19.0
		Worker training	7.0
		Road improvement	12.0
Honda	Ohio	Total support None announced, but some believe $22 million was provided in subsidies	

5.27 State government support for U.S. plants of Japanese assembly firms

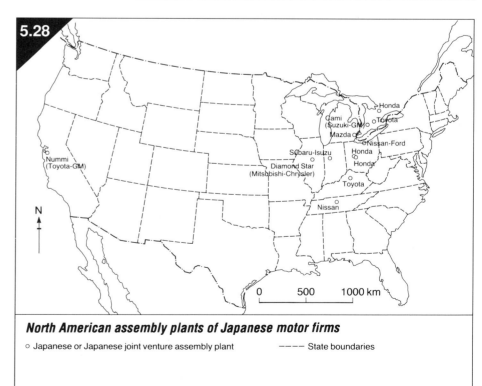

5.28

North American assembly plants of Japanese motor firms

○ Japanese or Japanese joint venture assembly plant   ---- State boundaries

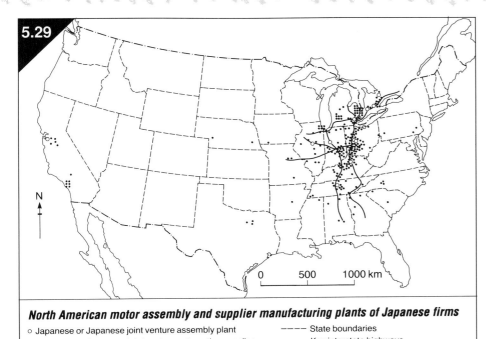

5.29

North American motor assembly and supplier manufacturing plants of Japanese firms

○ Japanese or Japanese joint venture assembly plant — — — State boundaries
· Japanese or Japanese joint venture automotive supplier ——— Key interstate highways

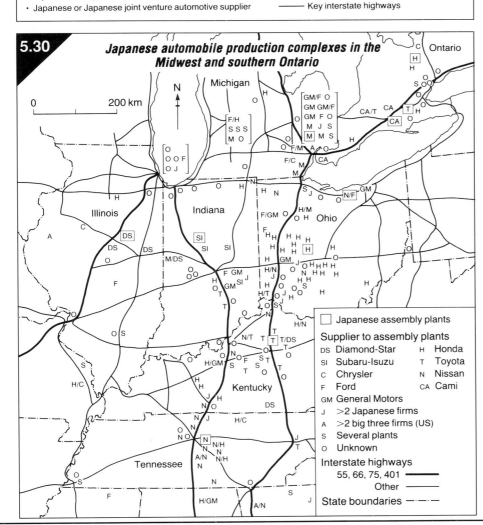

5.30

Japanese automobile production complexes in the Midwest and southern Ontario

	Japanese assembly plants

Supplier to assembly plants

DS	Diamond-Star	H	Honda
SI	Subaru-Isuzu	T	Toyota
C	Chrysler	N	Nissan
F	Ford	CA	Cami
GM	General Motors		
J	>2 Japanese firms		
A	>2 big three firms (US)		
S	Several plants		
O	Unknown		

Interstate highways

55, 66, 75, 401 ———
Other ———
State boundaries — · — · —

generally require the suppliers to locate not more than a two-hour drive from the main plant. Third, many of the suppliers are between 30 and 50 km apart. Resource 5.31 is a basic model of an integrated complex or cluster.

Explaining the patterns

At first impression, it may seem that the Japanese have simply joined the Americans in their vehicle heartland centred on Detroit, Michigan. However, this is only one part of the explanation. The key to understanding lies in the way Japanese manufacturers organise vehicle production, which is quite different from the approach of US companies. Since Henry Ford introduced the continuous assembly line more than 50 years ago, the American car industry has achieved economies and efficiency through reliance on highly specialised machinery, strict division of labour, long production runs of single models, and separate competitive contracting from diverse individual component suppliers. This 'Fordist' approach is known as the 'Just-in-case' (JIC) method, because it requires firms to carry large stocks (inventories) of components 'just in case' suppliers fail to deliver (resource 5.32).

In contrast, the Japanese have organised their production on the 'Just-in-time' (JIT) principle (resource 5.32). This is based on flexible machinery and working practices among the labour force, plus the close integration of a component supplier network into the system to ensure smooth production. This relationship between the assembly company, e.g. Nissan, and its suppliers, where interaction between managers is close and regular, helps to explain the integrated production complex model of resource 5.31.

The JIT system was developed in Japan with a non-unionised labour force and a distinctive company-worker relationship. Companies such as Nissan and Honda were

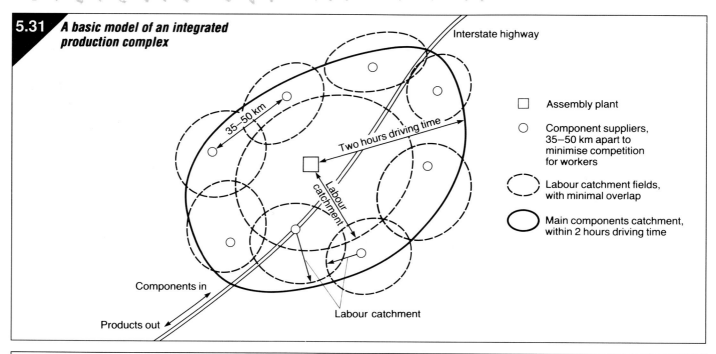

5.31   A basic model of an integrated production complex

- □ Assembly plant
- ○ Component suppliers, 35–50 km apart to minimise competition for workers
- ⬭ Labour catchment fields, with minimal overlap
- ⬭ Main components catchment, within 2 hours driving time

Interstate highway
35–50 km
Two hours driving time
Labour catchment
Components in
Products out
Labour catchment

Organisational alternatives   **5.32**

US system: 'Just-in-case' JIC	Japanese system: 'Just-in-time' JIT
1 Machinery designed to do a single task.	1 Flexible machinery quickly adaptable to different products.
2 Strict job demarcations for each worker. Strict division between white collar and blue collar jobs.	2 Teams of workers organised to rotate jobs, resolve minor problems and respond rapidly to changes.
3 High volume of single models.	3 Flexible machinery and labour allow short runs of individual products.
4 Individual parts suppliers dealt with separately. Large stocks (inventories) of parts kept 'just-in-case' needed because of failure by parts suppliers to meet deadlines.	4 Close relationships with whole supplier network reduces stocks (inventories) to a minimum and maintains the flow of production. Thus, parts are organised to arrive from the suppliers 'just-in-time'.

doubtful whether JIT could succeed in North America, with its strong Trades Union tradition. The decision to locate the early assembly plants in more rural areas, yet within the industrial heartland region, with existing components suppliers, e.g. Marysville, Ohio, was influenced by the availability of a suitable but less rigidly unionised labour force. Once flexible agreements on working practices were established, the Japanese companies could move nearer to the large cities, e.g. Mazda into metropolitan Detroit, where dispersal and stagnation of the US vehicle industry was creating

unemployment. When difficulties with US components suppliers were encountered, the Japanese companies encouraged suppliers from Japan to set up plants, and so develop the integrated production complexes e.g. Nissan in Tennessee, where land was cheap, but there were few established suppliers. As the scale and benefits of this FDI have become apparent, so more US states have come to woo the Japanese with ever improving deals (resource 5.27).

(Source: adapted from A Mair, R Florida and M Kenney, 'The new geography of automobile

production: Japanes transplants in North America', *Economic Geography*, 64(4), October 1988, pp. 352–373)

Activities

1 Use the information in this case study to illustrate the working of the manufacturing **product cycle** (page 93). Set out your answer in terms of the six phases.

2 In recent years, the US domestic vehicle industry has been

dispersing to the South and West regions, away from its traditional heartland. Explain how and why the Japanese FDI is producing a regional reconcentration of the motor vehicle industry.

3 What evidence does resource 5.33 give which indicates that motor vehicle manufacture is organised today on an international rather than national basis? What effect is this having in the UK, and why should the UK economy benefit from Japanese investment? Has the situation changed since the article was written in 1989?

4 **Group discussion**:

a Discuss the benefits and costs of the JIC and JIT systems.

b Japanese vehicle manufacturers are increasing their FDI in the UK. Is their strategy similar to the one they have used in North America? What are the reasons for their expansion? (You will need to investigate the background to the FDI in the UK, e.g. where, why, when and on what terms? How have they organised their component supply?)

5.33

Britain's multi-national car industry

Just because you snapped up a G-registered Ford car in the August sales spree doesn't mean you invested in the British motor industry.

More than 130 500 Ford cars passed through the showrooms last month, with demand for new number plates setting new records, but only 78 000 of these so-called 'British' cars were actually manufactured in the United Kingdom.

Top-of-the-range XR4 models, capable of more than 120 mph, are built in Genk, Belgium along with the Sierra-Cosworth. The Granada and Scorpio are put together in West Germany.

Even if you opted for a new Fiesta model – hailed as Britain's response to the invasion of Euro-hatchbacks – the car could just as well have been made in Valencia as Ford's works at Dagenham.

Such is the 'Europeanisation' of the motor industry that Britain is increasingly being used as just one more staging post in a continent-wide network of manufacturing plants.

Major companies such as Ford and General Motors, which between them account for around 40 per cent of the 2.2 million cars sold in the UK last year, shuttle production around the European markets according to the peaks and troughs in the order books.

Any shortfall in British production, and a sophisticated computer network ensures that there are imported vehicles to meet the gap. Orders can be met instantly from spare capacity elsewhere in the European network.

It is this tremendous industrial muscle wielded by Britain's two biggest suppliers which helps to explain the paradox: why is Britain running such a large deficit on motor sales when demand is increasing by more than 10 per cent a year?

The £3.42 billion shortfall between motor exports and imports accounts for nearly one third of Britain's total deficit on visible earnings.

It is one of the most important single reasons why the country is trading so deeply in the red.

And it is a compelling reason why the Government should continue to welcome in big Japanese conglomerates interested in investing in our domestic car industry. Building on its link-ups with the likes of Nissan, Honda and Toyota is the only practical option to help reverse this declining trend.

Britain is being forced to bring in more exports because its indigenous carmakers are unable to meet the demand. The Rover Group remains the country's biggest 'independent' car maker but supplies just under 14 per cent of total sales.

Even this time-honoured marque has been forced to bow to economic reality by announcing plans to sell a 20 per cent stake to Honda.

With Volkswagen Audi, Peugeot Talbot and other big European players gradually nibbling out bigger British market shares, the plight of the UK motor industry can only worsen after 1992.

Within this context then, Britain has no alternative but to fight the imports as a satellite of the biggest Japanese motor conglomerates.

By the second half of the 1990s Japanese car makers will account for at least one third of all UK car production, according to most projections.

The likes of Honda may be headquartered in Tokyo, but at least if its production is manufactured within the UK, this at least secures British jobs, and benefits the country's motor component sector, if its production is manufactured within the UK.

Japanese investment is fast gathering momentum.

● Honda, besides its plans for a Rover link-up, has committed itself to building 100 000 cars in the UK by 1994.

● Toyota is looking at rolling out at least 200 000 cars at its Derby plant by 1998 although this timetable is likely to be brought forward.

● Nissan is looking at a similar level of output from its Sunderland factory by 1994.

The key question bothering economists is whether extra Japanese-led production will be enough to offset the damage from European imports. The Society of Motor Manufacturers and Traders declines to hazard a guess.

The Society says that one domestically-produced car sale represents one less import, whoever owns the manufacturing plant.

Most projections suggest that it will take at least five years for the tangible benefits of Japanese investment to come through into the balance-of-trade figures.

Until then Britain's depressed motor industry will continue to be a victim of European cross-border trading in the run-up to 1992.

(Source: Patrick Donovan, *The Guardian*, 28 September, 1989)

CASE STUDY 5.5 *New industries need new cities –*

Background

From the mid 1980s, Japan has begun a fundamental restructuring of her industry with the intention of achieving 'the transformation from an industrial economy to a research and information network economy'. The intention is to stimulate investment and job creation especially in technology-intensive industries with a highly sophisticated research and development component.

Japan's manufacturing industry, based along the Tokyo-Osaka axis, has always relied on imported raw materials, and the export of an increasing proportion of the products. Today, the policy of the government and private companies is to develop this productive capacity abroad, nearer the resources and the markets. Hence the explosion of Japanese 'transplants' in Europe, North America and Asia. Case study 5.4, (pages 109–115) illustrates the process in the motor vehicle industry, but it is happening too in the massive electronic equipment industry, where all major companies are expanding their foreign manufacturing, e.g. NEC, Sony, Canon.

Employment within Japan will be increasingly reliant upon knowledge- and information-based industries (see page 106). These rapidly expanding high-technology industries are in many ways 'footloose', but they do require quite different arrangements of land uses and infrastructure from the traditional manufacturing industries. For example, a sophisticated telecommunication infrastructure is as important as a road and rail network, and their 'raw materials' and component parts may be ideas and research rather than oil, iron ore or rear axles.

Japan is using strong government policies of urban and regional planning to develop this industrial structure, and the examples in this case study illustrate three main aspects of their approaches:

(i) redevelopment in the major industrial metropolises such as Tokyo and Osaka, (ii) the designing and building of 'science cities' appropriate for the high-tech industries, (iii) the encouragement of regional networks of satellite cities whose main aim is to spread development beyond the traditional axis.

The 'intelligent business offices' mentioned are part of a programme by the Ministry of Construction. In this programme, buildings in major redevelopment schemes are fitted with advanced optic fibre networks as the basis of their communication systems. 'To be called 'intelligent', buildings must generally have advanced building management system – incorporating sophisticated security and air conditioning – and secure communications systems which are linked to outside information and communications networks'. Other East Asian cities, such as Singapore, are organising their economic and social operations according to these high-tech principles.

Key understandings

◆ High technology industries require distinctive land use and organisation structures.

◆ Japan is building living and working environments specifically for high technology industries.

◆ High technology industries need closer interactions between research, education and production.

Organising thinking cities in Japan

Part I: Metropolitan redevelopment

Anti-pollution laws and congestion problems have become a major barrier to further expansion of manufacturing in large metropolitan areas. This is especially true for

Tokyo and Osaka, both with coastal locations and considerable port facilities. Land pressures are so great that reclamation schemes have extended development into the coastal waters. As port needs change, and further reclamation schemes are planned, the new developments and redevelopments are focused on 'the management and research end of industrial and technological growth' with 'state-of-the-art infrastructure which supports white collar activities'. The projects, designed to upgrade communications and telecommunications, are called 'teleport programmes'.

Tokyo teleport

The Tokyo Metropolitan Government (TMG) is preparing to develop a reclaimed island (zone No. 13) in Tokyo Bay as a teleport-based sub-city centre of 100 hectares located some six km away from the downtown area (resource 5.34). While the eastern side of the reclaimed land will be retained for harbour uses, the heart of the district will be a high level telecommunications centre with information oriented business accommodation capable of twenty-four hour operation. The planned Tokyo Port Bridge will give direct access to the island from the mainland in 1992, and a new transportation system, such as a monorail and underground express highway, will be provided to service subsequent phases up to the year 2000. In conjunction with the teleport will be a complex of 'intelligent' office buildings and other facilities to serve a working population of about 10 000 persons. There will be 320 000 sq.m of housing space and 150 000 sq.m of commercial and cultural facilities. Waterside restaurants, shops, sports and recreation facilities will complement the technology-intensive infra-structure and will make for a multifunction urban area rather than just another commercial centre.

Yokohama Minato Mirai 21

Minato Mirai 21 (MM21) is translated from Japanese into English as 'the new port city for the 21st century' and comprises a large-scale coastal redevelopment plan scheduled to be completed by the year 2000 at the cost of about $20 billion (resource 5.35). It will be constructed on a 190 ha site along the bay area of Yokohama, 30 km, south of Tokyo. Sixty per cent of the site is old shipyard land acquired from Mitsubishi Heavy Industries Limited; the remainder will be reclaimed from the sea. At the core of the project will be an information centre linked to a teleport for international and local communication services,

intelligent business offices, cultural facilities and residential areas – a city within the city.

MM21 will contain modern shopping complexes equipped with TV shopping facilities and moving sidewalks, a new Yokohama City Art Museum, a five thousand seat convention hall, a private memorial park and other open space covering twenty-five per cent of the site. It is predicted that MM21 will support a daytime population of 190 000 while its residential area will house just 10 000 persons. The housing will

consist of modern apartments for single business people. Families are not expected as the project contains no schools. MM21 originally did not include any housing but as a '24-hour city' concept was promoted, the designers decided to include some residential space.

Osaka Technoport

Since the war, and a shift in Japan's trade patterns from contintental Asia to across the Pacific, which has favoured Tokyo, Osaka – Japan's second largest metropolis – has lost its share of commerce, finance and industrial strength to the capital. It is now planning to revitalise its economy and stem the flow of the key administrative and economic control functions which have gone out of the region to Tokyo. Osaka must become cosmopolitan and information intensive in order to reinforce its role as a trade, technology-based production and finance centre. Fortunately, a host of big projects – such as the nearby Kansai International Airport and Kansai Science City – promises to help the city attain these goals by boosting its infrastructure capacity to attract and retain knowledge-intensive industries. The biggest of these undertakings is the Osaka Technoport, based on three vast coastal reclamation areas totalling

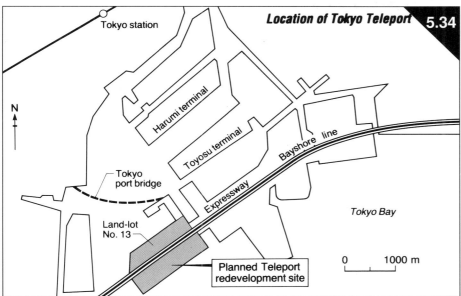

Location of Tokyo Teleport 5.34

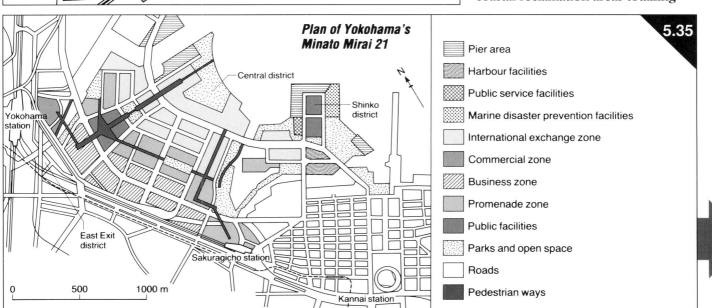

Plan of Yokohama's Minato Mirai 21 5.35

Pier area

Harbour facilities

Public service facilities

Marine disaster prevention facilities

International exchange zone

Commercial zone

Business zone

Promenade zone

Public facilities

Parks and open space

Roads

Pedestrian ways

seven hundred hectares. Together they will form a new type of town combining information, research and advanced technology development and international trade.

The reclaimed islands are 10 km from downtown Osaka, and are called Nanko (south port) and Hokko (north port, comprising two islands) (resource 5.36). Of these two areas, Nanko is available for development and already contains Osaka Port Town, a high density residential redevelopment project for forty thousand persons. As for the two islands at Hokko, one is ready from 1990 and the other by the year 2000. It is envisaged that the Osaka teleport will be located on Nanko Island, a Research Park on Hokko North and a World Trade Park on Hokko South (resource 5.36). An express road to these islands from the mainland was completed in 1989. In the next decade an underground rail link will be developed to bring the Technoport complex closer to downtown and the new Kansai International Airport. To extend the communications functions of its Technoport, Osaka plans to establish a public-private joint venture (the Osaka Media Port) to lay optic fibre cables from the teleport site to the downtown area, utilising the existing subway network.

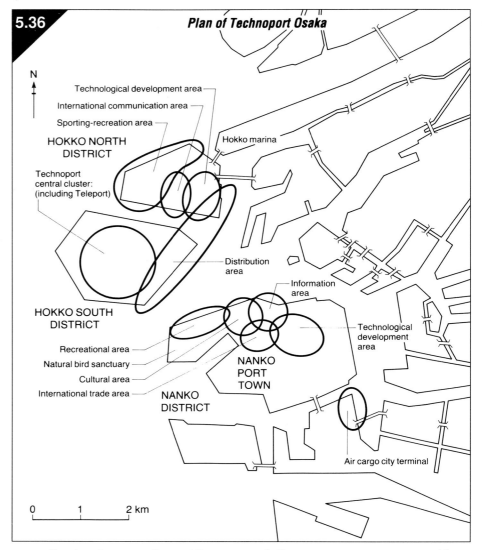

5.36   *Plan of Technoport Osaka*

N

Technological development area
International communication area
Sporting-recreation area
HOKKO NORTH DISTRICT
Hokko marina
Technoport central cluster: (including Teleport)
Distribution area
HOKKO SOUTH DISTRICT
Information area
Recreational area
Natural bird sanctuary
Cultural area
International trade area
NANKO DISTRICT
NANKO PORT TOWN
Technological development area
Air cargo city terminal

0   1   2 km

Part 2: Technopolis and Science Cities

One reason for Japan's phenomenal success in industrial innovation has been the emphasis placed by government and private companies on research, higher education, and their linkages with production. The best illustration of this approach is the 'technopolis programme', which aims to encourage a nationwide network of satellite cities of around 50 000 persons. More than twenty are now operating, and although they vary in form, each tends to be built around clusters of inter-linked establishments for Research and Development, higher education and production, and with a particular

type of technology as a focus. The primary aim, therefore, is to organise the land uses and communication networks in ways which allow this knowledge- and information-based type of industry to operate efficiently. A secondary aim is to spread regional development beyond the traditional Tokyo-Osaka axis, but this is proving difficult to achieve. The initiative for attracting the research institutes, industries etc. rests largely with the prefecture in which a technopolis is found. (A prefecture is an administrative district.)

Larger versions of these technology towns are the 'Science Cities'. The first, at Tsukuba, 60 km north of Tokyo, was begun in 1963, has been

in full operation since 1979, and by the late 1980s was reaching its target population of 100 000 (resource 5.38). It began essentially as an 'academic' city, with emphasis on universities and research institutes, and still has about 40 per cent of the national total of such institutes. By the 1980s however, there was a disappointing spin-off from the reseach into industry, so the city plan was enlarged and an extra 400 hectares zoned for industry. In addition, new road and rail communications via the Joban Expressway and Joban Line have brought central Tokyo within one hour's journey time. The integrated cluster outcome of this growth shows up clearly on resource 5.37.

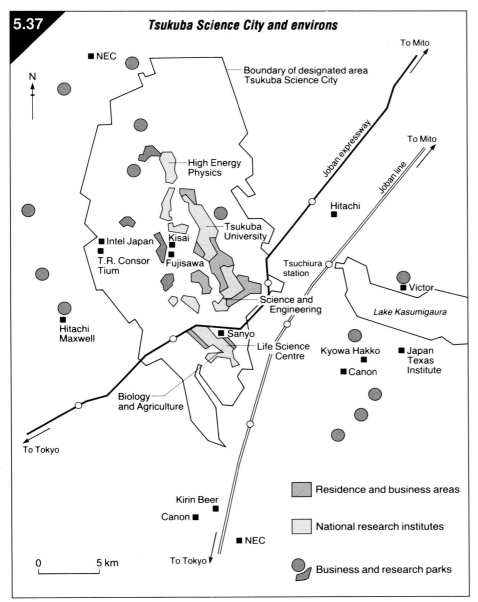

5.37

Tsukuba Science City and environs

To Mito

NEC

N

Boundary of designated area
Tsukuba Science City

Joban expressway

To Mito

Joban line

High Energy
Physics

Hitachi

Tsukuba
University

Intel Japan
Kisai

T.R. Consor
Tium

Fujisawa

Tsuchiura
station

Victor

Science and
Engineering

Lake Kasumigaura

Hitachi
Maxwell

Sanyo

Life Science
Centre

Kyowa Hakko

Japan
Texas
Institute

Canon

Biology
and Agriculture

To Tokyo

Kirin Beer

Canon

NEC

0   5 km

To Tokyo

Residence and business areas

National research institutes

Business and research parks

A second major science city is under development at Kansai, 30 km from Osaka and Kyoto. Planning on a 2500 hectare site began in 1978, and has become a joint venture between government and private industry.

Throughout all these types of scheme, three primary aims stand out:

(i) to assemble the different stages in the production process in an efficient manner;

(ii) to create efficient communication networks within and beyond the development;

(iii) to provide high quality living and working environments for employers and employees.

(Source: adapted from D W Edgington, 'New strategies for technology development in Japanese cities and regions; *Town Planning Review*, 60(1), 1989, pp. 1–26)

Activities

1 By the use of labelled and annotated diagrams, illustrate how the Japanese are achieving the three primary aims of the schemes outlined in the case study.

2 **With a partner:**

Much urban planning in Britain since 1945 has focused of the creation of *separate land use zones*, e.g. zones for industry, housing, and transport. In contrast, the Japanese schemes in this case study are *integrating land uses*. What are the advantages and disadvantages of each of these approaches, and particularly, why do you think the Japanese are adopting the integrated policy? (You may find it useful to compare the Docklands Scheme in London with these Japanese schemes.)

CHAPTER 6

Places to spend – the retailing revolution

Introduction

Retailing in British cities has been based upon a well established hierarchy, from the CBD or 'High Street' at the top, through major district centres, local suburban centres, to neighbourhood parades and the local corner shop. Using numbers of outlets, floor space, type and range of goods, for example, as measures of size or 'mass', Christaller's Central Place Theory and Gravity Models have been applied to this hierarchical structure, relating mass to spatial distribution of shopping centres and their spheres of influence. Over the past twenty years or so in Britain and other industrialised countries, this traditional structure has come under increasing pressure from the 'retail revolution'. The case studies in this chapter illustrate the five major dimensions to this revolution: (i) the location, grouping and spacing of retail outlets, (ii) the character of the shopping environment, (iii) the organisation of the retail industry, (iv) the shopping behaviour of consumers and (v) planning policies of local and central government.

Much attention has focused on the struggles of the traditional 'High Street' to survive competition from off-centre and out-of-town superstores, retail parks, and regional shopping centres (case studies 6.1 and 6.2). Yet equally strong forces have been at work within the lower levels of the hierarchy, causing fundamental changes among local parades and corner shops (case study 6.3).

Throughout much of the 1980s, the retail industry was one of the most profitable sectors of economic activity. As a result, there was massive investment, especially at the upper end of the scale by a small number of developers and retail corporations, e.g. ASDA, creating thousands of jobs. Yet worries are emerging that too many shopping centres are chasing a finite number of customers (resource 6.1).

The following extracts (resources 6.2 and 6.3), provide a useful background to the detailed case studies. As you read them, take care to identify evidence of the five dimensions of the 'revolution'.

Key questions

The key questions explored in this chapter are:

◆ What is the place of the High Street in the retailing hierarchy?

◆ Does the High Street compete with or complement out-of-town centres?

◆ What is the future role of district and local retail centres?

◆ Who should make the main decisions about retail location – planners or private developers?

6.1

Arcades of affluence turn into ghost towns

Modern shopping malls, one of the most visible signs of prosperity and confidence until now, are becoming half-empty monuments to a more optimistic era.

Developers all over Britain have been caught out by the change and are struggling to fill vacant floor space as business confidence wanes and interest rates remain high.

The symptoms of the problem are evident in south Hampshire. The £37m Swan centre in Eastleigh opened five months ago, but has struggled to fill its floor space after stores that would have provided the main attraction dropped out. It has filled only 29 of its 40 shop units and has failed to attract a big department store, the key to success for many similar schemes.

Down the coast at Portsmouth, Port Solent, an 84-acre marina complex of shops, offices and homes five miles from the city centre, is having trouble finding customers 15 months after being opened.

Ian Terry, senior development surveyor for the complex's developer, Arlington Retail Development, said his company was confident of attracting more businesses. But he admitted that only about half the 29 prestige shop units on the boardwalk had been let, in spite of a six-months rent-free offer.

In London, Tobacco Dock, the £50m 'Covent Garden of the East End' that opened this year in a Georgian warehouse in docklands, is a widely quoted example of the retail slump, with its handful of big name shops such as Next, Monsoon and Body Shop often virtually deserted.

Most retailers agree that a well-designed shopping centre in the right place at the right time should still succeed. Such centres include those planned for Dudley, Thurrock and Sheffield next year. It's the smaller district centres that are not in such good positions which may face problems.

The shopping centres that will suffer most are the older sites, such as the Greyfriars centre in Ipswich and the Coutts Bank development under Charing Cross in London, which have never been successful because they were badly designed or are in the wrong place.

George Adams, a director of the retail consultant Management Horizons, partly blames bad design for the malaise. 'Few shopping centres are as attractive to people as a conventional high street,' he said. 'Developers should perhaps think more about the high street and less about self-contained shopping centres.'

(Source: Richard Palmer and Hugh Pearman, *The Guardian*, 3 December 1989)

Quality going out of town

The retail boom has caused a rise in quality of shopping, both in terms of the external appearance of shopping schemes and in the design within the shop itself. There is also mounting evidence that the shopper is becoming more demanding and discriminating. Good design has been shown to pay dividends.

The rise in quality can be seen both in town centres and out-of-town. There is a growing awareness by local authorities, retailers and financial institutions owning property that town centres need to be made more attractive to withstand the out-of-town threat.

More remarkable than the improvements in town centres has been the rise in quality out of town, particularly in retail parks. Out-of-town shopping takes two basic forms. The first consisting of regional and district centres, seeks to reproduce the town centre, but without its disadvantages. Regional centres, such as Brent Cross and the MetroCentre in Gateshead, serve the same function as large city centres. By locating on freestanding sites, these centres gain the advantages of cheap land, easy site assembly, good parking and access.

District centres perform a similar role for the smaller town centre. These developments are anchored by a food superstore, but in addition contain the same type of unit shops as would be found in a medium size town. Example are Beaumont Leys outside Leicester, Cameron Toll in Edinburgh and Hempstead Valley near Gillingham.

We also now have a few speciality centres situated away from traditional retail cores. Examples are the shops in the Albert Dock refurbishment in Liverpool and Canutes Pavilion in the Southampton docks.

The early retail parks looked like conventional industrial estates. Some had been originally designed for warehouse users, and changed to retail parks during letting. Little attempt was made to appeal to the shopper's eye or to make it easy to move from one retail warehouse to another.

The change in the last few years has been dramatic both internally and externally. The main DIY operators such as B&Q are now building stores to a very high specification. In appearance they are often nearer to a town centre department store than the traditional warehouses of only a few years ago. The interiors, in particular, are as attractive as most equivalent town centre stores. The out-of-town operations of WH Smith – 'Do it All', and Boots' – Childrens World, are up to the standard of their high street parents.

The external form has changed as well. The retail park is now coming to resemble what its name implies. Many have been well landscaped. Car parks are often paved instead of being just asphalt, and walkways are more commonly provided with canopies.

We have also seen an improvement in the quality of freestanding superstores. Inside the emphasis is increasingly on better customer service and high quality provision of fresh fish, meat, fruit, vegetables, delicatessen and bakery. In-store cafes, toilets, and banking facilities are becoming standard. The new Asda at the former Odhams site near Watford is one of the most spectacular recent examples.

The term out-of-town is often used to describe retailing located outside existing centres, but in many ways it is misleading. Off centre would be a more accurate word, planning restrictions on development in the open countryside and the availability of derelict industrial land means that most off centre development takes place within existing urban areas. Many superstores and retail parks are in fringe city centre locations and claim to be part of the main shopping complex.

(Source: Russel Schiller, 'Quality going out of town', *Town and Country Planning*, June 1988)

The retail revolution in Britain

A defence of the town centre and its position at the top of the retail hierarchy has been central to British planning since the Second World War. Any retail innovation is seen as a threat of some kind to the existing order, rather than perhaps a valuable addition to it.

In the last 20 years two developments in particular have been seen as confrontational. First, the development of the superstore has resulted in an increasing proportion of grocery and other convenience expenditures moving out to existing or new district centres or green-field sites, to locations that are either closer to where people now live or more convenient for many of them to reach. A fatal situation arises, however, in those instances where a town centre loses all its major grocery outlets.

The second change is the growing trend towards off-centre retail warehouses and parks for a variety of non-convenience items. Both involve changes in retail organisation and consumer behaviour which if catered for would have seriously affected the urban fabric.

The high-order, out-of-town centre, on the other hand, has to be seen as a much greater threat. Its functions are the very ones that the town centre is expected to dispense: it is at the same level of the hierarchy, involving the same national retailers and has the locational advantages of the superstore.

It is as a result of its overprotected past that the town centre today faces such serious challenges. What we see is in large measure a retail environment better suited to conditions that prevailed 30 years ago, when car ownership was much lower, a higher proportion of the population lived within easy walking distance or a short bus ride of the town centre and consumer expectations were very different.

For an inner-city population and for those dependent on public transport the town centre undoubtedly remains the most convenient location, and there is the added advantage of a wide range of facilities, retail and non-retail, in that one location.

For a growing, decentralised, car-owning, middle-class population, either beyond the reach of good public transportation, or unwilling to use it, the town centre has become an increasingly frustrating experience, to be endured rather than enjoyed. At the times that consumers are able to shop, approach roads and car parks are clogged.

A pleasant, pedestrianised town centre is often ringed and cut off from its inner-city neighbourhoods by urban motorways, car parks, no-go subways, monster roundabouts plus the associated noise and pollution.

The need to increase and upgrade retail space has often had to take place in an area where space is limited and land costs are high. Yet already some of this post-1950s redevelopment is looking shabby as public expenditure declines, retailers and consumers needs change, developers move on to greener pastures and the elements take their toll.

While the development of the in-town, enclosed shopping centre has provided for a confortable, all-weather environment, this attempt to copy the American regional shopping centre has frequently given a part of the town centre a fortress-like appearance. In addition, the dominance of the multiple retailer has given the British high street or in-town centre a mundane, carbon-copy like appearance. The question then arises as to what improvements can be made internally and what can be better done by shifting some retail services to another location.

Taking some high-order, retail functions away from the town centre can provide for better shopping environments in-town as well as out-of-town.

Developing a greenfield site or taking over from some redundant commercial land use results in a spatially more extensive facility, often one-storey in height facing an enclosed mall, with plenty of public circulation space and surface car parking, and locations that tie into motorway and trunk-road routes and where a growing percentage of the population, and especially car owners, now live. These centres often perform roles that are barred from in-town centres, including recreational facilities, garden centres, car servicing and various retail warehouse functions.

(Source: Hugh Gayler, *Town and Country Planning*, October 1989)

Big retailers get bigger

Britain's biggest retail chains have further increased their share of total high street takings.

The 10 largest retailers accounted for more than one third of all retail sales in 1990/91, Their share of all sales was 34 per cent, compared with 31.9 per cent in 1989/90 and 29.4 per cent five years ago. The 10 include all the main supermarket chains.

Sainsbury and Tesco are Britain's biggest retailers, each with domestic sales of more than £6 billion. Marks & Spencer is in third place with just under £5 billion, followed by Asda and Argyll, which owns Safeway. The remaining members of the top 10 are Isosceles, the owner of Gateway, Kingfisher, Boots, John Lewis, which includes Waitrose, and Sears.

(Source: *The Guardian*, 23 March 1992)

CASE STUDY 6.1 *The future of the High Street as a shopping centre*

Background

The 'High Street' (resource 6.4) sits at the top of the traditional retailing hierarchy, but there has been growing concern about its future. Questions such as these are being asked: is it losing out to out-of-town shopping centres (resource 6.6)? Is it being strangled by traffic congestion? Is it losing its character and variety as a small number of major companies come to dominate the retailing scene? (See resource 6.5.) Are shoppers demanding more attractive environments?

There is no doubt that High Streets are changing rapidly, and there seem to be five main aspects to this change.

1 **Form and visual appearance** Large companies project standardised images and shop styles. Larger stores are broken into smaller units. A 'core and frame' structure is emerging, the edge of the core being definable as the point beyond which expensive refurbishment is not economically viable.

2 **Land use** Functions are becoming more varied, with increases in personal consumer services (hairdressers, 'keep fit' centres); financial services (banks, building societies); household services (estate agents, interior-design consultants); medical and health services (opticians); leisure services (restaurants, fast-food outlets, video-hire agents); business services (printing, computer-leasing agents); government services (job centres; local government offices) Resource 6.7 illustrates these trends in London's Oxford Street, a 'High Street of the highest order'.

3 **Land values** Land rental prices have been rising, making investment attractive and increasing competition between developers looking beyond

Is the traditional variety of the High Street (left) being overwhelmed by the larger retail groups (right)

retailing, e.g. office blocks rather than shops, to maximise profits.

4 **Social significance** The perception of the High Street as a focus for the community has become less strong in many towns and cities.

5 **Place in the urban structure** The position of the High Street in the retailing hierarchy of the urban structure is under threat as retailing diversifies in character and location.

When we ask why High Streets are changing, the answers come under four main headings.

1 The **cost structure** of retailing has changed. So, in order to benefit from the economies of scale, companies opt for **larger** stores (lower costs per sq.metre), **replicate** stores, – standardised stores in a range of locations, and alter the **scope** of their stores in terms of product mix, i.e. tending either to specialise through targetting (as with the 'Next' chain strategy) or to adopt a broad product range (e.g. Marks and Spencer).

2 The **financing** of retailing has changed as a result of

takeovers/mergers, causing rationalisation of outlets along a High Street, and an increased power of large scale investment, making extensive out-of-town sites attractive.

3 There have been marked shifts in **consumer demand and behaviour**. For instance, five types of shopping are identifiable, each of which has its own requirements in terms of location, atmosphere, product range and type: **essential** shopping, **purposive** shopping (i.e. shopping trips for specific, pre-determined items), **time-pressured** shopping, **fun** shopping, and **experimental** shopping. Remember, you may be a different type of shopper at different times of the week!

4 Changes in **planning regulations and policy** can constrain or accelerate change. For example, planners, in their efforts to sustain traditional shopping hierarchies may slow down change in the High Street, yet cause developers to press ahead elsewhere, leading to the development of, for example, out-of-town sites.

6.5

Hobson's choice at High Street plc

On today's high street, you can buy anything you want – as long as it is sold by Burton, Next or Marks & Spencer. In the decade of the retail boom, top store groups have sought to 'maximise their potential' by buying up rivals and complementary businesses. Few people realise that when they shop at Miss Selfridge, Warehouse or Wallis, they are in fact buying from Sears; when they buy from BHS and Mothercare, they are helping to boost Storehouse's profits.

By 1986 one-shop operations accounted for 89 per cent of all retail businesses in Britain, but only 2.88 per cent of the value of goods sold. In 1987, 105 businesses changed hands, at a cost of a staggering £3225 billion.

While it makes sense for retailers to use combined purchasing power and to streamline distribution costs, it is hard to see how some of the biggest acquisitions – Currys by Dixons, BHS by Habitat (now Storehouse), Debenhams by Burton and Fosters by Sears – has helped boost customer choice on the high street.

A Saturday afternoon spending spree could well take you into just one shop: Burton. The company's many fascias include Dorothy Perkins, Top Shop and department store group Debenhams; it sells more clothes than any of its rivals. Chairman Ralph Halpern is acknowledged to be a pioneer of retail targeting – devising chains to suit particular age and social groups.

But when he took over the Debenhams chain four years ago, one of the first things he did was to incorporate Burton Group shops as concessions within the department stores, despite their already rampant presence on the high street.

Nevertheless Burton does not have all that easy a ride in the fashion market. In the menswear sector, Sears (Fosters and Hornes) and Next provide competition, if only at the expense of smaller companies. The three businesses together have almost twice as many outlets as all the other chains put together.

When it comes to women's clothes, Burton is even more dominant, with nearly double the number of outlets of its nearest rival, the Next group.

So while retailers like to claim that they are striving to provide what the customer wants, shoppers have less and less choice about where they buy their skirts and suits, and finding the right pair of shoes could put them in an even more difficult situation.

Sears' subsidiary, the British Shoe Corporation, operates most of the best known high street chains, such as Dolcis, Saxone and Freeman Hardy & Willis, with over three times as many stores as its nearest rival, Clarks.

The company is admittedly trying to address this situation by giving each chain a more distinct image: it has been split into several divisions to reflect the markets it wants to aim at.

The search for a different pair of high street earrings will be equally difficult. Ratner's cheap and cheerful approach to selling jewellery now operates in over 1000 shops in Britain, all selling a remarkably similar range of products (under the Ratners, H.Samuel and Zales names, among others). His nearest rival has only 100 stores.

Store ownership on this scale has produced homogenised High Streets from Carlisle to Clacton. Smaller local retailers have less and less chance of survival as the big operators push up the price of occupying prime site property.

The problems of multiple owner-

A difficult decision. But are we getting as much choice as we think?

ship are not limited to the fashion business. Dixons, together with its subsidiary and erstwhile rival Currys, is the market leader in selling electrical goods. It has built up its strength by boosting sales of own-label goods – products made specifically for the company and sold under brand names such as Matsui and Saisho. In a retail sector like this, the limited number of players in the market gives consumers little choice about where they buy their television or hi-fi. By pushing own-label products at the expense of better-known branded ones, Dixons is cutting this choice even further.

And as grocery superstores force more and more smaller supermarkets into closure, the decision about where to take the weekly shopping list is more likely to be based on ease of access, rather than a positive choice between Sainsbury, Tesco or Asda.

(Source: Jane Sturges, *The Observer*, 29 October, 1989)

Key understandings

◆ The High Street is at the top of the traditional urban shopping hierarchy.

◆ Changes in financial, organisational and behavioural factors are changing the balance of attractiveness between High Street and out-of-town locations.

◆ Land uses and functions in High Streets are becoming more varied.

◆ People's shopping habits are changing, related to economic and lifestyle changes.

6.7

Land use in Oxford Street

| | Square metres of space | |
	1982	change 1971–82
Retail	490 749	−16 778
of which major stores	258 049	+4243
Hotels	131 805	+15 813
Offices	563 975	+5263
Residential	55 530	−4027
Transport	81 186	+5592
Warehouse/industry	80 648	−2326
Public building	45 033	+5329
Education	38 851	−4531
Other	47 467	+1912
Total	1 535 244	+6257

6.6

Asda quits city centre

A city centre supermarket is to close with the loss of 140 jobs, it was revealed today.

The Asda store in The Pallasades, near Birmingham's New Street station, will cease trading on January 27 after almost 20 years.

A company spokesman partly blamed The Pallasades Shopping Centre for the move. He said the site was inconvenient, with restricted access for customers and deliveries, compared to the firm's out-of-town super-stores.

(Source: *Birmingham Evening Mail*)

Is there a future for the High Street?

The forecast below was written in 1988. As you read it, ask yourself two questions:

(i) Does this forecast seem to be accurate, i.e. is this what is happening in the 1990s?

(ii) Are such suggestions for unified management feasible in a High Street with which you are familiar, and what are the key problems to be overcome?

'Product retailing will still be present in smaller, more mixed-use High Streets but it will be supplying less of the essential and purposive types of consumer needs. The High Street simply will no longer be convenient for this type of shopping. The fun, or leisure-orientated, type of shopping will be more typical of the High Street but this will have to be reflected in the whole of the marketing mix of the High Street retailers.

Most importantly, the mix of uses on the High Street will have to be **managed**. The leisure-service retailers will find locations alongside leisure-goods retailers. In some North American cities a lead has been given with the establishment of powerful Downtown Associations. In reality this move to 'leisure' retailing is less a radical change than a return to the idea of the town centre as a place for 'a day out at the shops'. This was largely the consumer use of central cities at the turn of the century.

What is now required is a willingness to change and to allow change in the High Street in accordance with a plan and with some overall vision of what the High Street should be providing. The idea of integrated management for the High Street is implicit in this view of a possible future. Just as the large shopping centres to be built out-of-town will be tightly managed, why not the High Street? High Street management exists in a few cases already. Certainly there are precedents from overseas, notably Japan and Denmark. Some British local authorities are actively considering how such a scheme could be implemented given the great variety of owners and participants in High Streets.

It seems certain the High Street will survive but it will change because consumers, retailers and society generally change. In order to facilitate change, intervention through land-use planning or High-Street management, is appropriate and necessary.'

(Source: J A Dawson, *Geographical Journal*, 154(1), March 1988, p. 11)

In the case study which follows, two 'professional' viewpoints are set out, both published in 1988. The first presents the case for the decentralisation of retailing, while the second argues that it is possible for High Street and out-of-town retail centres to co-exist.

Alternative scenarios for the future High Street

Part I: Retail decentralisation

The author of this report was a Professor of Land Economy, and approached the topic from a property value perspective.

Evidence of retailing change

There are three types of evidence for change: property evidence, retailers' behaviour, and evidence from the location of new shopping developments. The property evidence amounts to a fall in shop profits in many highly-valued town centre positions, and to rental growth in these shops at a lower level than would otherwise be expected.

The evidence of retailers' behaviour falls into three parts. Firstly, there has been a hedging of bets by established High Street durable retailers. W H Smith have opened an out-of-town DIY chain called Do-It-All. British Home Stores have joined with J. Sainsbury to invest in an out-of-town superstore called SavaCentre. F W Woolworth have invested heavily in the leading DIY chain, B&Q, and the electrical discounters, Comet. This hedging of bets is an attempt by retailers to reduce their risks in the face of decentralisation.

Secondly, there are a number of examples of mainly new chains of durable retailers who are locating for the most part outside high-rented town-centre areas. Examples are Toys R Us the American toy chain, Textile World, World of Leather, Allied Carpets and MFI furniture. These are all retailers of high-order durable goods which, according to central place theory, should be located in town centres.

The most significant evidence from retailers' behaviour comes from those champions of the High Street who have had a public change of heart. By far the most spectacular of these are Marks and Spencer who

announced in 1984 that they were to develop out-of-town stores. More recently we have had the case of Boots who announced the development of a series of 30 000 sq. ft retail warehouses. Another significant example is John Lewis Partnership which announced in 1986 that it was to develop its first out-of-town department store on the M40 near High Wycombe. This evidence of the change in retailers' behaviour is supported by the evidence of new shopping-centre proposals. In 1987, out-of-town schemes made up 80 per cent of all proposals.

Decentralised retailing has powerful advantages for both consumer and retailer. The retailer benefits because he is freed from congestion, has lower costs and a more efficient and spacious layout, to offer a wider range. The shopper benefits through easier car access and parking and often cheaper goods with a wider choice. There have been two obvious catalysts. The first was the decision of Marks and Spencer, that bellwether of the retail flock, to decentralise in 1984, and the second was the success of retail developers in taking advantage of Enterprise Zones. In fact the first decentralised Marks and Spencer opened in October 1986 in the MetroCentre which is situated in the Gateshead Enterprise Zone.

Form of decentralisation

Retail decentralisation can be seen as a series of three waves. The first wave of decentralisation involved food. During the 1970s, the supermarket companies began opening large, new stores outside town centres often paid for by the sale of their old town-centre shops. This wave is now largely spent although superstores are continuing to grow. Many planners now welcome the loss of food because it relieves congestion and car-parking pressure.

The second wave involves retail warehouses. It arrived 5 to 10 years after the first wave. It includes bulky

goods such as furniture and carpets, and larger branded goods such as white electricals. These two categories have been joined by DIY, a largely new form of retailing. When retail warehouses began to appear it was argued that they were necessary because the town centre could not offer adequate floorspace to display bulky goods. As with food shops, the sheer size of the merchandise made easy car parking essential. A move to a cheap and spacious decentralised location was the logical answer.

The larger town centres certainly rode the first wave without difficulty, and it is claimed that they can survive the second wave too. Their strength lay in comparison shopping, with its heart in clothing. In 1983 in Oxford Street, for example, out of 226 retail shops, 153 sold clothing and footwear. Clothing, particularly fashion, appears not to be threatened by the second wave.

The third wave of decentralisation involves clothing, quality comparison goods, and some supporting services traditionally found in the town centre. Apart from Marks and Spencer it includes names such as Habitat, Laura Ashley, Toys R Us and World of Leather. All these traders sell comparison high-order goods, including some which are expensive and of high quality. The third wave, therefore, competes directly with the town centre.

The third-wave developments which are currently being proposed fall into two main types. First, there are regional centres such as Brent Cross. In many countries the decentralisation of comparison shopping is accommodated in regional shopping centres. The one and only example of the free-standing regional centre in Britain is Brent Cross. With over half a million sq. ft of retailing, the regional centre re-creates the shopping facilities of a town centre but without congestion. The second form of decentralised development is the retail park. These are usually converted industrial estates designed to hold 4 or 5 retail warehouses. This is a peculiarly British invention. It has arisen because of a combination of lack of sites and absence of demand for industrial estates by the users for which they were originally intended. Most retail parks are under 200 000 sq. ft in size and contain stores selling DIY, furniture and discount electricals. Their impact on the town centre is therefore marginal. (See case study 6.2 on pages 130–135.)

Impact on town centres

The opportunities for new regional centres are limited. They need a catchment population of over a quarter of a million and a large site area. Although they will clearly take sales from existing centres, they can often mesh into the existing retail hierarchy as have Brent Cross and Milton Keynes.

Retail parks of up to 200 000 sq. ft have limited impact, and those which grow above 500 000 sq. ft turn themselves into regional centres, as happened with the MetroCentre in Gateshead. The problem comes with the intermediate size between 200 000 and 500 000 sq. ft. Hybrid centres of this size can accommodate Marks and Spencer, a superstore and some of the more specialist third-wave retailers like Ikea or Textile World. It is possible to imagine a centre, situated on the edge of a town of 100 000 population, consisting of Marks and Spencer, Tesco, Toys R Us, Habitat, Allied Carpets, MFI, Comet, a multi-screen cinema, fast-food restaurants and bank. Such a centre would total less than 500 000 sq. ft gross and would not provide a concentration of fashion to match the town centre. Nevertheless such a grouping would offer formidable competition. It would for example offer greater choice of furniture, carpets, electrical goods and toys than was available in the town centres. It would also probably contain a bigger Marks and Spencer than in the town centre, all combined with free parking and easy car access.

As this type of centre could easily exist on the edge of a town of 100 000 population there could be more of them than regional centres, and they could affect one single free-standing centre more directly. This type of centre creates a dilemma for many town-centre retailers. The market is often too small for them to have branches both in- and out-of-town, which is their option with regional centres. Even if they wish to move out, there may not be the opportunity. It can be difficult to accommodate a unit shop on a retail park.

Some consultants see speciality retailing as the town centres' answer to decentralisation. There has undoubtedly been an expansion of speciality retailing appealing to a leisure-oriented semi-tourist market in Britain in the last few years. Covent Garden is the best known example. It is unlikely, however, that the growth of this type of retailing will match the decline of main-stream retailing following decentralisation.

The town centre will survive because it will still offer an unrivalled variety of shops and, more importantly, services. But it could become increasingly difficult to attract investment.

(Source: R Schiller, 'Retail decentralisation. A property view', *Geographical Journal*, 154(1), March 1988, pp. 17–19)

Part II: The co-existence of High Street and out-of-town retailing

The author of this article was a Property Development Director of ASDA, and therefore approached the topic from a specific viewpoint.

Planning, like retailing, has to change to meet the changing aspirations of society, its 'customers'. Customers' demands have changed because of increasing affluence, increasing mobility, increasing sophistication, a change in lifestyle, all of which comes down to one fundamental concept, that of choice. The customer is seeking choice. If one store does not provide what he or she wants, the next shopping trip will be made elsewhere, similarly, if the parade, town or conurbation does not provide that choice within it, the next level of choice is to shop in an adjoining town or county. High Streets, as well as shops, compete with one another.

There has been both qualitative and quantitative change in demand. In qualitative terms, the consumer is demanding a better choice, involving a wider range of products, and also a better environment, with an atmosphere and an individuality in a store or a shopping area. Shopping experience has to be pleasurable. Retailing is becoming more leisure-orientated, it has to be acceptable and convenient, and it has to be special, specialised and individual, relating to a lifestyle.

Demand for convenience and pleasure means more space. The cramped over-trading supermarket is no longer acceptable; if there is a better alternative the shopper will go there. The additional services and the rising ratio of staff to customers, the customers' service facilities, changing rooms, delicatessens, crèches and all of the other facilities that the consumer is seeking mean more space. The accessibility and convenience demanded by the customer means large customer circulation areas, large car parks and bus turnround facilities. Again it means space. The combination of specialisation to provide choice and space to provide the quality and quantity has meant retailing has had to change. Retailing is no longer concentrated into one type of shop, it is a series of services housed in a variety of store types in a variety of locations targeted at a variety of needs in the community.

No longer do the simple geographic models for retail location hold good. The hierarchical structure, so popular with planning authorities, which was derived from geographical research, is now out of touch with the demands and habits of the modern shopper. It ignores the fragmentation of shopping into different functional sectors, each providing a different product range within a different space and having different operational and locational requirements, but with complementary functions. These broad categories are:

1 Off-centre food-based superstores

These cater for the high-bulk 'chore' trip for the necessities of life. Increasingly, consumers demand not only the simple facility of buying the majority of their convenience items under one roof, but higher standards of service and environmental amenity.

Large sites are required to accommodate sales and warehousing floor space, customer facilities, car parking and landscape areas. Such store locations can assist with easing of town centre congestion by the removal of car-based shopping trips. The imposition of a food-based superstore on a town centre can often result in severe congestion and yet provide little spillover shopping into the adjacent non-food shops.

Obviously superstores should have good access by both private car and public transport but unless the road system is of a high calibre, town centre superstores can cause more problems than they are perceived to have solved.

2 Non-food superstores

These also seek large sites which are rarely available or accessible in the centre and such is the range of the bulky products that a shopping trip to this type of scheme is rarely related to any other form of shopping trip. As a consequence their imposition on the town centre or the High Street makes no sense whatsoever. They are best located in accessible off-centre sites and preferably congregated together for the convenience of the customer and for environmental considerations.

3 The corner shop or local parade or District Centre

These provide an important and social community focus. There is a belief within the planning profession that the opening of a food superstore will immediately cause the closure of all such shops over a widespread area. The closure of such shops began a long time before the opening of the first superstore in Britain, but we are now beginning to see a resurgence of interest in these stores. This type of corner-shop operation is complementary to superstores in so far as the bulk purchasing at a superstore on a weekly or monthly basis creates a need for regular topping-up shopping for perishable items such as fresh meats, dairy products, salads, vegetables and fruit as well as a broad range of items which run out.

The small independent sector can also provide greater flexibility in opening hours, and also clearly satisfies that market demand which requires personal service. (See case study 6.3.)

4 The quality High Street of the late 20th century

Many plans and planners aspire to a healthy High Street. We must, however, look at the purpose it serves for the community. It is often an historic focus of the road system, and this often means that it is congested. It is therefore an unsuitable location for high-bulk shopping trips either for food or non-food bulk items. Nevertheless, the often historic environment provided by the urban fabric provides a wonderful backdrop for modern quality retailing, services and leisure-orientated operations. The removal of the large-bulk stores and their trips from the town centre is the first prerequisite. There are then three steps to be taken by the local planning authorities. Firstly, there is a need for pedestrianisation and traffic management schemes. The nature of the comparison trip for high-value, low-bulk items is dependent on pedestrian movement around the centre, although arrival in that centre may be by car or bus. High levels of vehicle penetration

into the centre are both unnecessary and environmentally undesirable, particularly in areas where the historic fabric of the centre forms an important backdrop to shopping.

Secondly, there is a need to be much more sympathetic in the treatment of planning applications within the High Street. The purpose of the town centre is not solely retailing; there are three parts to its future base, firstly retailing, secondly servicing and thirdly leisure-orientated operations, whether these be the market area such as Covent Garden, Albert Dock, Liverpool or Waverley Market, Edinburgh or the food courts so common, popular and attractive in North America. Planners should seek to relax the Use Classes Order in order to encourage the wide range of services and facilities that the consumer is now seeking in the High Street.

The third element is the appointment of a High Street Manager or Town Centre Manager to co-ordinate and run that location as if it were one entity. It is on this basis that the High Street is capable of coexisting with out-of-town retailing.

Where proposed Mega Schemes out-of-town concentrate on a very small number of very large units, sometimes including a food-based superstore, e.g. M & S, C & A, Boots and John Lewis, then conflict with the High Street will be minimal because those operators will retain a presence in the High Street. However, where the Mega Schemes include a very high proportion of small units and leisure and entertainment facilities they will be competing directly for operators who cannot afford to run an in-centre and out-of-centre operation simultaneously. Out-of-town schemes of that type will be competing and threatening the very future of the High Street.

(Source: D Gransby, 'The coexistence of High Street and out-of-town retailing from a retailing perspective', *Geographical Journal*, 154(1), March 1988, pp. 13–16)

Out-of-town shopping centres and the family man

Just after Christmas, I had an experience which did a little more to teach me about the differences between out-of-town and town centre retailing.

My family (that is, my wife, four-year-old daughter and ten-month-old son) and I drove into Bristol city centre with the intention of plundering the January sales.

Out first obstacle came at the city centre end of the M32 motorway, wich was completely clogged with stationary traffic. Police were doing their best to keep the traffic flowing, but this seemed to involve directing drivers away from the city centre (which was presumably full). We left the motorway early at a minor junction and drove around the St. Pauls area for several minutes until we found an on-street parking space. The children were bundled into coats, hats, scarfs and buggies in preparation for the walk to the shopping centre.

On arrival there, we found that many, many others had the same idea: the pavements were overcrowded, the shops stifling and the streets full of stationary cars. Cigarette smoke hung like a pall over the pedestrian precinct. The few restaurants that exist were full; nowhere was there a place to sit down or change a baby's nappy. Escalators represented almost insurmountable hazards to a buggy-carrying family

The children were bored within about 20 minutes; my wife and I felt flustered, rushed and not a little threatened. We returned to our car empty handed, glad to be out of the hustle and bustle.

On the way home, we drove off the motorway at the next junction (the Eastville Business Park) to pay a visit to a children's goods retailer. We parked the car virtually adjacent to the door on the large free car park. The store was warm, but not oppressive, with plenty of space to wander among goods displayed in a pleasing, low-density arrangement. A lift (wide enough to take a pram) was provided for access to the upper floor.

My daughter instantly discarded her coat and shoes for some fun with the large bouncy shapes in the children's play area. I put my son down for a crawl here while I sat on the sidelines, watching the Muppet Babies on the children's video, and my wife went to spend our money. I even got chatting to other fathers.

Finally managing to tear our daughter away from the helter-skelter slide we retired to the store's cafe for a snack. The staff kindly provided some heated baby food (at the same cost as a jar from a supermarket) and, of course, a high chair for my son.

Nappy-changing followed: changing mats, baby wipes, cotton wool and cream were provided both in a specifically dedicated 'mother and baby room' and in each set of toilets. While I was performing the honours, my wife and daughter had trims at the store's hair salon.

Were we enjoying the new concept of shopping as a leisure experience? No, I do not think so. We were just partaking of a facility where all of the basic comforts were provided. In itself, this was enough to make shopping with children an immensely more pleasurable experience out of town than in the city centre. As to the range of experiences, I would have said that my children enjoyed the playing, sliding, video-watching, eating (and, of course, nappy-changing) provided by the store considerably more than being pushed through a forest of legs in the crowded, stifling and dangerous city centre.

I drove home remembering the days when (as a planner and a single man) I used to think that out-of-town shopping facilities competed with those in the town centre. Now (as a family man) I think they are in a different league.

Perhaps I hardly need to add that the town centre has a long way to go in terms of providing basic comforts and facilities before it attracts my family on another shopping trip.

(Source: John Allinson, *Town and Country Planning*, February 1989)

Activity

Group discussion:

Read resource 6.8, and then (a) evaluate the viewpoints and proposals presented in the case study in the light of this personal comment, and (b) list the changes which would be necessary before this family is likely to be attracted back to town centre shopping. What proposals given in the case study would help create such changes?

NB The materials in this case study provide an excellent basis for group or individual projects on retailing topics. Issues and hypotheses can be identified; categories and classifications can be the basis of data collection; comparative studies can be set up, etc.

CASE STUDY 6.2 *Layout and land usage in retail*

Background

Case study 6.1 has identified three waves of retail decentralisation in Britain in the last 25 years (page 126). The third, and most recent, wave consists of two types of development: the regional centre (resource 6.9), and the retail park. A retail park is defined as having at least three separate units, one of which must be a superstore/hypermarket, and a minimum of 50 000 sq. ft of retail sales area. There are two basic types – those where individual units have grown independently on the same general site, and those which have been planned as a entity. A key characteristic is the increasing functional range of such parks. This case study illustrates two retail parks in Swansea, neither of which was planned as an integrated unit, but which have been extending their functions. The materials examine (i) the layout and functional character of the parks, (ii) the ways people use them and (iii) the relationship between layout/character and usage.

6.9

The regional shopping centre

This form of shopping centre has been developed most fully in North America and has a number of characteristic features. Firstly, such centres are large. A regional centre is usually defined in the UK as one with more than 400 000 sq. ft of sales floorspace. Put another way, that is roughly 13 times larger than the average size of a Sainsbury's store in 1987. These centres are also designed principally for shoppers travelling by car. As such, a large number of car parking spaces are required. (The exact ratio is debated, but 10 000 spaces per million sq. ft of sales floorspace is often quoted.) The preferred option of developers and retailers is for all parking to be at ground level rather than multi-storey. This increases the typical area required for a regional shopping centre site to perhaps 120 acres.

Internally, the centre is normally structured around a limited number of 'anchor' tenants. The anchor tenant is a well-known name in high-street retailing, usually a variety or department store, occupying the largest shop unit in the centre. It generates customer traffic to and through the centre and is typically located at the ends of the shopping malls. Between the anchor tenants, the malls have rows of smaller units occupied by specialist retailers. The centre may also have additional special features, such as a cinema or leisure park, to further attract visitors. The entire shopping centre, with the exception of the car parking areas, is totally enclosed and air-conditioned to provide a stable shopping environment throughout the year. Great care is taken in the internal design of the centre. For example, much attention is given to signposting and the position of different types of shops to prevent any one mall becoming a 'dead' zone with few shoppers.

This form of shopping centre is obviously very difficult to accommodate in existing town centres. An entire centre would require the removal of an extensive area of existing buildings. Car parking, if it could be accommodated at all, would almost certainly have to be multi-storey rather than street level. There would also be problems of congestion on roads leading to the centre and difficulties in making deliveries to retailers in the centre. For these reasons, developing a large-scale shopping centre on a 'green field' site away from an existing town centre is the preferred option of most retail property developers.

(Source: A Treadgold and E Howard, 'The MetroCentre: a new type of shopping', *Geography Review*, 2(4), March 1989, pp. 26–27)

The Metrocentre at Gateshead

Key understandings

◆ Retail parks are an important new component of the retailing system.

◆ Retail parks occur in planned and unplanned forms, which influence their layout, character and efficiency.

◆ Retail parks rely on car-borne customers.

◆ Stores and retail warehouses vary in the linkages they have with outlets.

◆ Linkages between outlets vary according to the function, product type and location of the store or warehouse.

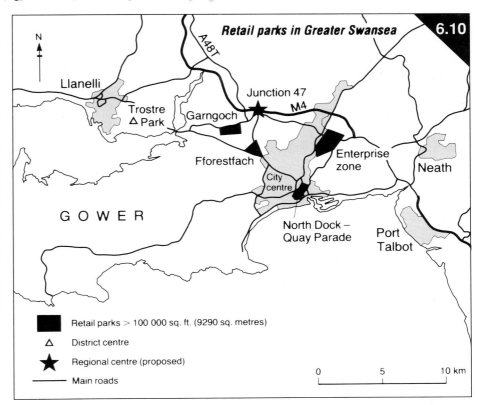

Retail parks in Greater Swansea 6.10

- ■ Retail parks > 100 000 sq. ft. (9290 sq. metres)
- △ District centre
- ★ Regional centre (proposed)
- — Main roads

0   5   10 km

How people use retail parks in Swansea

The two retail parks studied, the Swansea Enterprise Zone park and the Fforestfach park, are located on resource 6.10. Both offer easy access and parking, and are supported largely by a car-owning clientele. Once inside the parks, however, how do the shoppers behave? In particular, do they 'one-stop shop' or do they use several stores; what factors influence the use of more than one store; how do the shoppers move around the parks?

In order to answer these questions, on-site surveys were carried out in October 1986 (Fforestfach) and October 1987 (Enterprise Zone), each over a Friday–Saturday period. At particular locations, shoppers were asked which of the stores they had already visited or firmly intended to visit during their shopping trip. The results are summarised in resources 6.11 and 6.12, and detail the linkages between stores.

The tables need careful study, and can be interpreted by columns and by rows. For example, take *column 2* on *resource 6.11*: this represents the shopping linkages between the Tesco superstore and all other

stores, expressed as a percentage of the shoppers visiting Tesco (total = 375 people). Thus, of the 375 shoppers at Tesco, 19 per cent visited or intended to visit Norman's superstore, and 21 per cent B&Q. To illustrate how the *rows* of percentages can be used, let us take the Tesco – MFI linkage. Our *column 2* tells us that 12 per cent of Tesco's shoppers also visit MFI. This is 43 people ($12/100 \times 375$). By using *row b*, we find that these 43 people represent 24 per cent of MFI's 177 shoppers ($43/177 \times 100$). The figures tell us that the linkage is more important for MFI than for Tesco, i.e. The higher the percentage, the more significant the linkage.

Other questions in the survey reveal that shoppers are attracted by the convenience of the shopping environment offered by the car-parking facilities and long shopping hours, and by the perceived competitiveness and quality of goods offered. However, neither park functions as a strongly integrated shopping centre, e.g. the low levels

of linkage revealed in resources 6.11 and 6.12. In particular, there is a distinct difference in patterns of usage between superstores and retail warehouses. Superstores have more restricted trading areas than retail warehouses. On the other hand 'customer loyalty to the superstores is relatively high for the regular purchase of convenience goods. The retail warehouses appeal to the more occasional shopper, who might also use the superstores'. The parks tend not to be used for multi-store visits, the average number of stores visited per trip being 2.3 for the Enterprise Zone and 2.1 for Fforestfach (resource 6.13). These figures are much lower than surveys have found in traditional 'High Streets' and district shopping centres. The shopping linkages for the two parks may be analysed by **functional characteristics** and by **spatial dimensions**. Use the maps in resources 6.14 and 6.15 and resources 6.11 to 6.13 to help your understanding as you follow these functional and spatial relationships.

6.11 Swansea Enterprise Zone Park: Linkages between stores as a percentage

		Floor space ('000m²)	1 Normans	2 Tesco	3 B&Q	4 Handiland	5 Poundstretcher	6 Halfords	7 Currys	8 Comet	9 Shoe City	10 Second City	11 Textile World/ Bensons Beds	12 Allied Carpets	13 Queensway	14 MFI	15 Mammoth	
a	Normans	3.8	–	19	9	12	38	20	12	16	20	17	13	15	13	6	9	Superstores
b	Tesco	4.2	31	–	28	29	22	21	18	24	26	23	17	13	17	24	17	
c	B&Q	2.9	11	21	–	38	12	19	15	15	17	20	17	25	47	41	24	D.I.Y., variety
d	Handiland	1.9	4	7	12	–	6	5	4	8	3	6	4	4	9	9	7	
e	Poundstretcher	1.1	18	6	5	7	–	13	13	9	19	22	27	18	9	6	9	
f	Halfords	0.9	9	6	7	6	13	–	20	9	14	9	8	6	12	9	4	Auto parts, Electrical
g	Currys	0.9	7	6	7	6	16	25	–	50	9	11	4	7	9	11	11	
h	Comet	1.2	8	7	6	11	9	10	45	–	4	4	7	9	12	10	20	
i	Shoe City	0.5	10	8	7	4	20	14	8	4	–	45	13	1	3	6	5	Clothing Shoes
j	Second City	1.0	12	10	12	11	32	14	14	6	66	–	23	8	12	12	4	
k	Textile World Bensons Beds	1.1	4	4	5	4	18	6	2	4	9	11	–	32	13	11	9	
l	Allied Carpets	1.4	6	3	8	4	14	5	5	7	1	4	36	–	36	18	26	Furniture Furnishings
m	Queensway	4.0	4	4	13	8	6	9	6	8	2	6	13	32	–	29	33	
n	MFI	3.2	4	12	26	19	10	14	15	16	10	14	25	38	69	–	36	
o	Mammoth	2.3	1	4	7	6	6	3	6	13	4	2	9	24	33	15	–	
A	Nos. visiting store		228	375	275	85	109	105	128	113	110	162	75	85	75	177	76	
B	Nos. of visits to other stores		363	521	508	157	280	219	283	263	283	378	207	252	278	470	202	

Fforestfach retail park: linkages between stores as a percentage   **6.12**

	Store name and type (gross floorspace m² × 2)	Floor space ('000m² × 2)	1 Tesco	2 Ultimate	3 Carpetland	4 Do It All	5 Texas	6 MFI
a	Tesco Superstore	5.6	—	50	58	42	39	51
b	Ultimate, Electricals	0.5	8	—	38	12	10	16
c	Carpetland	0.5	6	23	—	9	9	12
d	Do It All, DIY	3.3	25	43	56	—	78	62
e	Texas, DIY	3.4	19	29	44	63	—	45
f	MFI, Furniture	4.6	22	41	53	44	39	—
A	Number of respondents visiting store	548	91	55	332	268	235	
B	Number of visits to other stores	619	293	219	641	522	498	

6.13

Numbers of stores visited and intended visits

| Number of stores | Enterprise Zone | | | | Fforestfach | |
	All respondents %	Superstore main store visited %	Retail warehouse main store visited %	All respondents %	Superstore main store visited %	Fforestfach Retail warehouse main store visited %
1	37.2	49.8	30.1	41.0	58.9	22.8
2	27.4	25.9	28.3	29.0	21.0	37.1
3	17.4	12.6	20.1	17.2	11.1	23.5
4	9.8	9.0	10.3	7.5	5.9	9.2
5	4.2	1.8	5.6	3.4	2.1	4.6
Over 5	4.0	1.0	5.6	1.8	0.9	2.7
	n = 1090	n = 390	n = 700	n = 835	n = 423	n = 412

Functional characteristics

1 Free-standing status

The low number of stores visited per trip suggests that stores are relatively independent of each other. The figures show that this is especially true for superstores, which tend to generate proportionally fewer visits to other stores than do the retail warehouses. Many shoppers use the superstores as one-stop convenience shopping centres for bulk purchasing. Look at the bottom row of resource 6.14 which expresses the number of visits to other stores as a percentage of the respondents visiting a store: thus 100 visitors to Tesco generate only 139 visits to other stores, whereas 100 retail warehouse visits generate 200 or more other visits. In Fforestfach, a similar but less marked pattern occurs (resource 6.15).

2 Diffuse spin-off

Despite the relatively free-standing status of superstores, because the numbers visiting them are much higher than visitor numbers to retail warehouses, superstore visitors form significant proportions of the visitors to other stores. The survey found that 'the superstores generate important linkages to other stores throughout both retail parks, while being less dependent upon linkages in the opposite direction'. This linkage between functionally different outlets, i.e. between outlets with different product types, is called diffuse spin-off. The diffuse spin-off is unbalanced: retail warehouses benefit more from the presence of superstores than vice versa, e.g. the Tesco–MFI linkage at Fforestfach.

3 Comparison shopping

Some of the strongest linkages are between stores with similar product ranges, produced by purposeful shopping trips where shoppers like to compare prices, styles etc. before buying. For example, note the Curry's–Comet, and the MFI–B&Q linkages in the Enterprise Zone park. The strongest comparison linkages are between furniture and furnishings outlets.

4 Complementary shopping

Linkages are generated by visits to stores selling related but not identical product types, e.g. a visit to a clothing store may generate a visit to a shoe outlet, and vice versa. Thus, 66 per cent of those shopping at Shoe City also visit the Second City clothing store, and 44 per cent vice versa. This complementarity may be difficult to distinguish from 'comparison' shopping where outlets overlap in their produce range, e.g. shoppers at Fforestfach may visit MFI for furniture and then Carpetland for carpets (complementary shopping), or may visit both outlets for carpets (comparison shopping).

5 Market segmentation

This aspect of shopping behaviour brings out linkages between outlets targetted at specific types of customer. This is seen most clearly in the 'price conscious' segment of the market where shoppers visit apparently unrelated stores because of their pricing policy, e.g. Norman's superstore and Poundstretcher clothing outlet both operate a 'discount' price policy and have significant linkage – 18 per cent of Norman's shoppers visit Poundstretcher and 38 per cent vice versa. At the other extreme, World of Leisure specialises in high cost leather furniture and has low linkages with other stores or warehouses because there are no other stores in this 'high price' niche on the Enterprise Zone park.

(Source: adapted from R D F Bromley and C J Thomas, 'The impact of shop type and spatial structure on shopping linkages in retail parks', *Town Planning Review*, 60(1), January 1989, pp. 45–70)

The Swansea Enterprise Zone Retail Park and shopping linkages between the stores

6.14

Unplanned, and spatially diffuse, with a sales area of 39 200 sq. m sales area, it lies 5 km to the north of Swansea city centre, close to an M4 junction. Total of 27 units, including two superstores, 2 DIY warehouses, 11 furniture and furnishing stores, plus clothing and footwear outlets

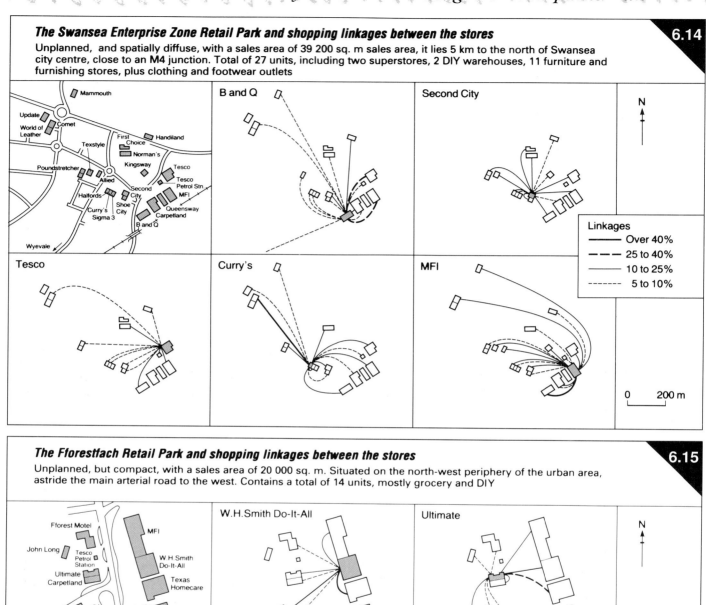

Linkages

——	Over 40%
– – –	25 to 40%
———	10 to 25%
- - - -	5 to 10%

0   200 m

The Fforestfach Retail Park and shopping linkages between the stores

6.15

Unplanned, but compact, with a sales area of 20 000 sq. m. Situated on the north-west periphery of the urban area, astride the main arterial road to the west. Contains a total of 14 units, mostly grocery and DIY

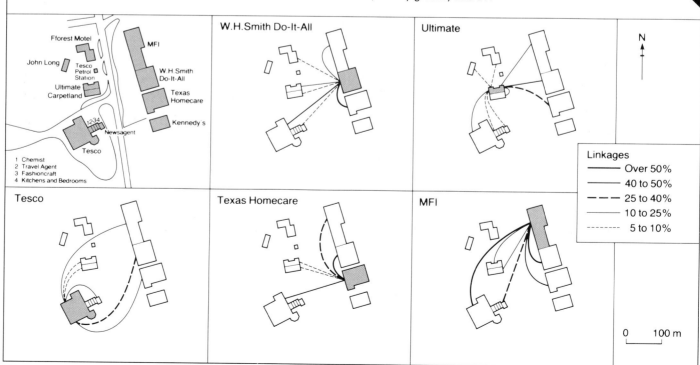

Linkages

——	Over 50%
——	40 to 50%
– – –	25 to 40%
———	10 to 25%
- - - -	5 to 10%

0   100 m

Activities

1 With a partner:

Use the resources in this case study to evaluate these statements (Identify specific examples supporting or dismissing the statement):

a Spatially adjacent stores generate significant linkages, even when offering dissimilar goods.

b Particularly strong linkages occur when proximity is combined with functional similarity (comparison) and complementarity.

c Shoppers visiting more centrally located stores are more likely to visit nearby outlets in relatively large numbers, than those visiting peripheral stores.

d A compact layout generates relatively high levels of linkages.

e Linkages at Fforestfach are adversely affected by the main road running through the park.

2 By the use of resources 6.16 and 6.17 describe and explain the pattern and movement within the two parks.

3 Group decision-making exercise

The Swansea Enterprise Zone retail park is essentially unplanned. Take the 27 units and plan a layout for the park, using the results of the case study survey as guidelines for your decisions.

a Use the existing site and road system as your 'base map'.

b Draw out a large plan of the site on card. Use coloured cut-outs, Lego blocks, Monopoly buildings etc, for the individual outlets, to assist your discussion of layout, relative positioning of stores etc.

6.16

Mode of travel between stores: Swansea Enterprise Zone retail park and the Fforestfach retail park

Mode of travel	Respondents visiting more than one store	
	Swansea EZ %	Fforestfach %
Walked between stores	18	58
Drove between stores	74	33
Walked between some, drove between others	8	10
	n = 725	n = 468

6.17

The relationship between attitudes to distance between stores, numbers of stores visited, and mode of travel between stores

Attitude to distance	Enterprise Zone					Fforestfach			
	Number of Stores visited (%)								
	All over 1	2	3	4	over 4	All over 1	2	3	over 3
Very convenient	22	21	22	24	26	23	28	19	18
Convenient	55	56	56	58	48	54	55	60	44
Inconvenient	14	12	18	10	16	14	10	15	22
Very inconvenient	5	5	4	4	6	6	3	5	12
Do not know	4	6	0	4	4	3	4	2	4

	Walk and Drive	Walk	Drive	Walk and Drive	Walk	Drive
Very convenient	27	20	30	29	14	19
Convenient	53	60	53	59	54	38
Inconvenient	12	13	12	6	22	28
Very convenient	2	4	3	2	7	13
Do not know	5	3	2	3	3	2

CASE STUDY 6.3   *Do we need a new breed of*

Background

It is perhaps surprising, but as recently as 1950, most town planners were predicting that the majority of families would never have access to a car. So, residential areas were planned to enable routine shopping for household necessities to be carried out locally, on foot. Particularly for housewives and others remaining at home during the day, local shops provided convenience, encouraged social contacts and awareness of social facilities and events.

The role of local shopping centres such as these can be seen in the planning of early New Towns such as Hemel Hempstead. These towns were designed around 'neighbourhoods' of some 5000 people, and each neighbourhood was seen as large enough to support a 'parade' of convenience shops. Networks of footpaths linked the homes to the shops. Even in 'Mark II' New Towns of the 1960s, such as Runcorn, the viability of the neighbourhood shopping centre in terms of catchment area and walking distance (0.45 km in a straight line was the assumed maximum distance), was a key factor influencing density and layout of residential areas.

By the early 1970s, things were changing: retail developers began to follow the American trend of building larger convenience shopping centres. These required a larger catchment area, assumed that a high proportion of customers would shop by car, and so provided ample car parking space. One outcome was a decline in the prospects for small centres in new residential areas; the 'corner shop' and small 'parades' came under threat. By 1980, large new housing developments were served only by 'district centres' based around superstores. They usually give easy car access and parking, but may be unfriendly for pedestrians.

During the 1980s, despite the growth of mega-centres, illustrated in case studies 6.1 and 6.2 there has been a revival of interest in developing small stores. These 'convenience stores' of 100–300 sq.m sales area serve the secondary needs of those who carry out most of their grocery shopping at superstores, and also the primary needs of a local clientele. Developers, including several multiple firms and voluntary trading groups see these stores as having a local catchment with a high proportion of visits being on foot. Yet concern is still expressed that the shopping opportunities for the less mobile members of our society are declining.

This case study examines this issue in two parts. Part I reviews the ways in which the retail industry is responding to the continuing demand for convenience shopping, in terms of location, organisation and product range. Part II summarises a research project in Cardiff, which revealed the persistent significance of shopping on foot, and its characteristics. The results are set out in some detail as they provide a very useful exemplar of how to analyse your data in a project on shopping patterns. The materials of both parts I and II provide a valuable resource for constructing an individual or group project with a retailing focus.

Key understandings

◆ There is still a need for shops located within local communities.

◆ Accessibility is a crucial factor in a local shop's success.

◆ 'Convenience' has several meanings or traits, which combine to enable local shops to compete with superstores.

◆ To survive, when catchment areas are limited, local stores must adapt and reorganise.

Part I: Convenience stores for the future

Large new superstores built both within town and district centres and on out-of-town sites have become increasingly common features in many urban areas in Britain but there is now growing interest in the development of a new generation of 'convenience stores' within residential areas. These stores are loosely defined as occupying between 50 and 300 sq.m of retail floorspace and their concept of convenience is expressed in a variety of ways. Stores have long trading hours (opening for at least 16 hours a day, 7 days a week), they have a clearly laid out self-service style to allow quick shopping and they carry a wide range of convenience foods. Ideally the product range will be geared to meeting the emergency and impulse needs of the local population and it might typically include groceries, fresh fruit and vegetables, frozen goods, confectionery, newspapers, books and small toys, toiletries, beers, wines and spirits, cigarettes and tobacco, small everyday household goods and fast food as well as photographic printing, dry cleaning and video hire services. Location is important: store operators try to be close to the central or focal point of a residential area and hence be convenient for pedestrian shoppers while at the same time offering adjacent car parking to attract passing motorists.

The concept of the convenience store seems to have originated in the USA in the 1920s but rapid development has only occurred since the early 1960s. Within North America the number of convenience stores had risen from 2500 in 1960 to some 58 000 by the mid 1980s and a number of large chains, each with its own unique store layout and design, were the market leaders. The largest operator – The Southlands Corporation – which trades at 7-Eleven and Quick Mart, have some 8000 stores ranging across 41 states of the USA and 5 provinces in

Canada. Franchising forms a significant element in the organisation of some of the major chains and in recent years the development of joint stores and petrol stations has become an increasingly common feature of convenience store operations in the USA.

A number of retail innovations originating in the USA have spread to Britain and there is growing evidence to suggest that convenience stores will become a flourishing new element in the retail sector of the British economy. Two sets of factors are put forward to help explain the growth of convenience trading. Firstly, the trend towards one-stop weekly or fortnightly shopping trips to large superstores is said to lead to an increasing need to 'top up' supplies at local convenience stores. Secondly, the growth in the number of two-income families is putting a higher value on convenient and time-saving shopping outside normal working hours. However, convenience trading is not new to Britain. Traditional corner shops whose owners have been compelled to open long hours in an attempt to retain their commercial viability have been fulfilling a convenience function for many years. The major element in this traditional pattern of convenience trading involves individual and independent shopkeepers and while an increasing number of traders have expanded their product range and their opening hours, multiple groups seem best placed to exploit the convenience niche in the market.

A small group of specialist companies have embarked on convenience store development programmes. This group includes three major companies (Sperrings, Misselbrook and Weston and 7-Eleven) all of which concentrated their initial development programmes in Greater London and the south of England. Sperrings first developed the modern convenience store concept in Britain in Southampton in the early 1970s. By

1986 the company had a network of 60 stores across 9 counties of southern England, but half of their outlets were in Hampshire centred on their original base in Southampton. Almost all of Misselbrook and Weston's stores are within either local or neighbourhood shopping centres serving residential areas of between 3500 and 8000 people. Sites close to hairdressers, sub-post offices, chemists, public houses, youth clubs, schools and health centres are favoured and the availability of car parking facilities is also an important locational factor. The majority of the early 7-Eleven stores have been opened in Greater London but wider future expansion is planned. The first 7-Eleven store was opened at Hendon in north London in 1984 and the company favour busy suburban shopping areas. Their stores carry a very wide product range and amusement arcades and video machines are used in an attempt to attract young customers.

The second major form of convenience store development involves the conversion of existing shops to a new trading format. Voluntary groups (partnerships of independent retailers and wholesalers who provide bulk purchasing and marketing services for the members) such as Spar ('Eight Till Late'), Mace ('Convenience Express') and VG ('Late Stop') are playing the leading role. Spar, for example, first launched their 'Eight Till Late' conversion programme in 1981. Within this programme the accent has been on retaining the group's traditional packaged grocery trade in combination with a new emphasis on cigarettes, beers, wines and spirits and other emergency and impulse lines. By 1986, 1000 of Spar's 2700 outlets had been converted to the 'Eight Till Late' format and those converted stores were spread throughout Britain. Spar claim that conversion can double a store's customers and increase its turnover by 60 per cent: total annual turnover from the new

format stores reached £300 million in 1986. Mace launched their 'Convenience Express' style in 1985 and they suggest that existing neighbourhood stores with a catchment area of at least 1000 households and which are visible to car borne and pedestrian shoppers are particularly well suited to the new format. A variety of other types of retail companies have also embarked on conversion programmes. Cullens have converted 30 of their chain of small and increasingly unprofitable supermarkets into what they describe as 'up-market' convenience stores with a large delicatessen in addition to the usual convenience product range. Their locational requirements are for 150 sq.m of floorspace in small shopping areas within densely populated residential areas.

A third focus of development centres on a diversification into convenience stores by some of the major petroleum companies who are aware that 20 million cars are driven onto petrol station forecourts each week. Texaco ('Star Food Shops') and Murco ('Shopstop') have made the largest early commitment to convenience trading and nationally based chains of joint petrol stations – convenience stores: but BP ('Foodplus'), Ultramar ('Ultraspar') and Total ('Petropolis') also have experimental development schemes on restricted regional bases. Many operators argue that petrol and conveince stores are a good mix. Petrol fits into the convenience store product range, the expansion of existing buildings requires limited capital investment, many petrol stations already open 16 hours a day. Nevertheless, forecourt convenience stores may need to attract pedestrian customers as well as motorists if they are to be successful.

All the major convenience store operators stress that they are not in direct competition with the large supermarket and superstore groups who specialise in meeting bulk shopping needs and they argue that they can fulfil a distinct and growing niche in the market.

However, the adoption of aggressive marketing strategies and competitive pricing policies by the convenience chains may well further reduce the economic viability of small supermarkets and independent local shopkeepers and thus add to the growing number of shop closures. At the same time the growth of a network of convenience stores within some residential areas may provide a valuable improvement in the level of retail provision for some sections of the population.

Looking to the future, trade estimates suggest that between 4000 and 6000 convenience stores may be trading in Britain by the mid 1990s. The specialist convenience store operators have concentrated their initial development programmes in the south of England where disposable income is at its highest (resource 6.18). It remains to be seen whether other parts of Britain can generate the convenience trade necessary to justify property acquisition and development costs and to generate a profitable return on this capital investment. The voluntary groups, a number of existing retail chains who are interested in convenience trading and the petroleum companies already have national networks of outlets and, for them, conversion to convenience store format clearly involves much lower capital costs.

(Source: P Jones, 'The geographical development of convenience stores in Britain', *Geography*, 73(2), April 1988, pp. 146–148)

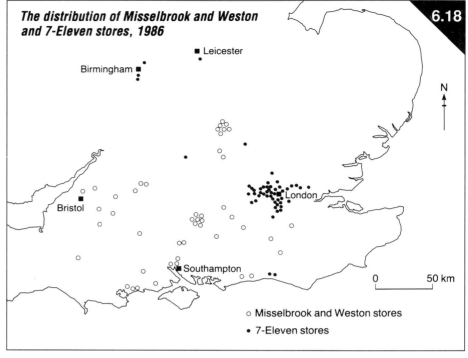

The distribution of Misselbrook and Weston and 7-Eleven stores, 1986

6.18

○ Misselbrook and Weston stores
● 7-Eleven stores

0   50 km

Part II: Many people still walk to the shops

The information in Part II of this case study is based upon the results of the Cardiff Consumer Panel survey of 1982, believed to be the most comprehensive survey of urban shopping behaviour ever carried out in Britain involved the collection of continuous daily records of the food

and grocery shopping of 454 households in the city over a period of 24 weeks (January to July). The basic unit for these records was the store visit. For each visit made to an individual store by a panellist or other household member, information was obtained about the name and location of the store, the mode of transport to the store, the origin and subsequent destinations of the trip, the products purchased at the store, and the total expenditure on food and grocery items. In addition, a wide range of socio-economic, demographic and attitudinal information was obtained describing each panellist and his/her household.

Walking to the shops in Cardiff

The overall importance of walking trips

The first question was whether walking trips were characteristic of most groups of shoppers rather than being confined simply to an immobile minority. Resource 6.19 shows that walking trips formed over half of all trips made for food and groceries by panellists, over 90 per cent of whom were women. The young (aged under 35) and old (aged over 54) panellists shopped on foot more often than the middle-aged, although differences between age-groups were not great. Panellists without full- or part-time

---

Key understandings

◆ The shopping trip on foot remains common in most age and socio-economic groups.

◆ Shops in accessible locations remain important within local communities, i.e. convenience stores.

◆ Communities vary widely in the location and character of shops they can support.

◆ Shopping trips on foot are generally less than 1 km in each direction, and made relatively frequently, but involve low spending per trip.

employment, with pre-school age children, and without the use of cars, tended to rely more on walking trips – this last factor is particularly important. There were also considerable differences in behaviour between the subgroups of the panel living in eight sample areas of Cardiff (resource 6.20). The main influence on the percentage rate of walking trips was the availability of a car for shopping followed by a measure of the accessibility of local shops.

The most important conclusion must be that walking trips formed a major component of shopping behaviour for all types of household in virtually all types of urban location. While as expected, these trips are particularly important for those without cars and/or with young children, there is clear evidence also that many shoppers carry out walking trips even when they have full car availability.

Length of walking trips

The second question posed related to the length of typical walking trips for food and grocery purchases. This might have some bearing upon the catchment areas of local shops, and hence planning standards for retail provision and residential density.

The length of a shopping trip was defined as the straight-line distance between the panellist's home and the first shop visited during the trip. This means that the distances reported below should be multiplied by a factor of perhaps 1.2–1.5 to represent true road or footpath distance. Trips made from workplaces were ignored, as were reported trips made on foot to the city centre or to outlying superstores.

The distribution of mean distances travelled in panellists' walking trips is shown in resource 6.21 and related to some panellist characteristics in resource 6.22. This shows that over the whole panel the mean straight-line distance covered in walking trips was 0.68 km. This

Panellist or household characteristic	Sample size	Mean number of walking trips per week	Walking trips as % of all trips
6.19 Mean frequencies and relative importance of walking trips, related to panellist and household characteristics			
Age of panellist.			
16–24	(17)	2.90	67.0
25–34	(134)	3.32	64.8
35–44	(82)	2.58	50.9
45–54	(89)	2.66	50.1
55–64	(82)	3.35	62.6
65+	(47)	3.14	59.4
Working status of panellist:			
Full-time job	(69)	2.36	50.4
Part-time job or student	(136)	2.94	55.0
Retired or not working	(246)	3.26	62.4
Car availability for shopping:			
All the time	(134)	1.59	32.1
Sometimes	(151)	3.16	60.4
Never/No car owned	(166)	4.06	76.3
Number of children aged 0–4:			
None	(364)	2.89	56.4
1 or 2	(87)	3.64	67.4
Area of residence:			
Rhiwbina	(88)	1.57	31.0
Whitchurch	(44)	2.72	53.8
Cathays	(73)	4.03	75.3
Roath	(27)	5.06	79.7
Rumney	(60)	3.61	67.9
Llanrumney	(66)	3.23	61.6
Llanederyn	(54)	3.63	71.5
Heath	(39)	1.29	30.4
Panel mean	(451)	3.02	58.3

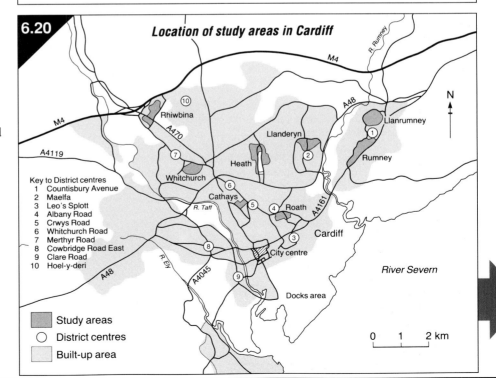

6.20 Location of study areas in Cardiff

Key to District centres
1 Countisbury Avenue
2 Maelfa
3 Leo's Splott
4 Albany Road
5 Crwys Road
6 Whitchurch Road
7 Merthyr Road
8 Cowbridge Road East
9 Clare Road
10 Hoel-y-deri

Study areas
District centres
Built-up area

0 1 2 km

estimate is somewhat affected by a small number of excessively long trips, and the median distance travelled (0.55 km) gives a more reasonable 'average' distance travelled. There was some variation in this distance according to car availability, with households with full car availability walking further on average. There was no tendency for older panellists to travel shorter distances. The greatest amount of variation existed with respect to area of residence. In resource 6.22, results are aggregated into three categories of residential area. Firstly, 'outer Cardiff private housing' (the Rhiwbina, Whitchurch and Heath areas) with quality housing, high levels of car ownership and sparse local shopping opportunities, Secondly, 'outer Cardiff public housing' (the Rumney, Llanrumney and Llanedeyrn areas), areas of mainly local authority housing at low density and with few small local shops, but good access to district shopping centres. Thirdly, 'Inner Cardiff private housing' (the Cathays and Roath areas), areas of late nineteenth century terraced housing with numerous local shopping opportunities. Resource 6.22 shows clearly that residents in the areas with fewer local shops tended to walk further on average.

Overall, some 57 per cent of the total amount of money spent on walking trips for food and groceries was spent within 0.5 km (straight-line distance) of the home, and 90 per cent within 1 km. This suggests that most local shops have a strictly local walk-in catchment, although this is not to say that walking shoppers necessarily use their nearest store. Trips of over 1 km were most common in outer residential areas with a lack of adequate local shopping facilities.

Expenditure made on walking trips

The average household was found to spend £8.64, or about one-third of its total food and grocery expenditure per week, on trips made by foot. However, households without cars spent more on walking trips – usually over half of their total food and grocery expenditure. For most households, walking trips were relatively frequent but relatively unimportant in their contribution towards the week's shopping expenditure.

These results confirm the importance of walking trips to small suburban food stores. These trips tend individually to generate small amounts of expenditure, but are so frequent that together they account for about two-thirds of expenditure on food and groceries. Patterns of shopping in suburban centres are thus very different from trips to the city centre or outlying superstores, which are associated with much larger volumes of expenditure and are carried out mainly by car (resource 6.23).

Testing the nearest-centre hypothesis

The hypothesis that shoppers visit the nearest shopping centre offering the goods required has often been examined in geographical studies. It would seem particularly appropriate to walking trips, as the effort put into such trips is immediately apparent to the shopper, who might therefore want especially to minimise effort.

6.22

Panellist Group	Sample size	Mean trip length (km)	Mean amount spent (£) per trip on food and groceries
Mean distance travelled and amount spent on walking trips			
Age of panellist:			
16–34	(145)	0.64	3.04
35–44	(70)	0.72	3.23
45–54	(74)	0.82	3.33
55–64	(78)	0.56	3.03
65+	(41)	0.69	2.53
Car availability for shopping:			
All the time	(101)	0.78	2.70
Sometimes	(145)	0.66	3.13
Never/No car owned	(162)	0.63	3.25
Area of residence:			
Outer private	(140)	0.87	2.82
Outer public	(170)	0.65	3.57
Inner private	(98)	0.44	2.55
Panel mean		0.68	3.07

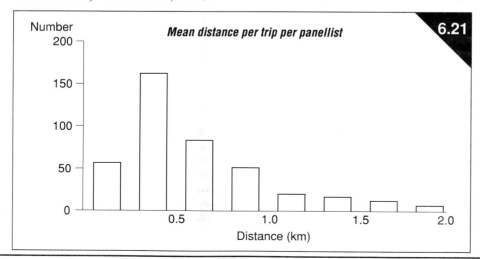

6.21 Mean distance per trip per panellist

Number — Distance (km)

Food and grocery shopping visits and expenditure in suburban stores in Cardiff

| | Visits made by | | All shoppers |
	Foot	Other mode	
Proportion of visits (%)	68	32	
– district centres	68	32	
– local centres	68	32	
– multiple grocers	56	44	
– other grocers	73	27	
– other shops	70	31	
Proportion of expenditure (%)	66	34	
– district centres	65	35	
– local centres	66	34	
– multiple grocers	53	47	
– other grocers	71	29	
– other shops	67	34	
Mean expenditure per visit (£)	1.51	2.42	1.88
– district centres	1.47	2.26	1.76
– local centres	1.56	2.64	2.04
– multiple grocers	2.55	4.12	3.50
– other grocers	1.42	2.34	1.82
– other shops	1.30	1.96	1.54

The amount spent on walking trips to each suburban shopping centre in Cardiff by each panellist was measured. Distances from each panellist's home address to the nearest six shopping centres were calculated. Resource 6.24 shows the proportions of total walking-trip expenditure made at local centres.

Some 43 per cent of this expenditure was in fact made in the nearest centre, 63 per cent within the nearest two centres. On average, the nearest centre lay one-third of a kilometre (straight-line distance) from the home and the nearest five within one kilometre. The aggregate results suggest that minimisation of

effort is by no means the only criterion in shoppers' choices of destination, even when travelling on foot.

In order to control for variation in accessibility, a smaller sample of 118 living in the 'Rumney' and 'Llanrumney' areas of Cardiff was analysed further. These areas share a district shopping centre (Countisbury Avenue), and are close to a smaller local centre (either at Burnham Avenue or Llanrumney Avenue (see resource 6.26). The characteristics of these centres are described in resource 6.25 and reaffirm the observation made above, that shoppers do not necessarily patronise their nearest centre while making walking trips. Only 17 per cent of the walk trip expenditure made by those panellists living closest to the smallest centre (Burnham Avenue) actually took place in this centre, most shoppers preferred to walk further to the much larger Countisbury Avenue centre with its multiple grocery stores and greater range of fresh food shops. The Llanrumney Avenue centre was more successful in retaining expenditure from its local area. The Countisbury Avenue centre clearly dominated walking-trip expenditure from the Rumney-Llanrumney area as a whole. Panellists have clearly shown greater regard for the price-savings and range of goods available in larger multiple-owned stores than for the accessibility of small local stores. At the time of the panel survey, savings of up to 20 per cent could be made in multiple or cooperative stores in Cardiff compared with independent grocers, for a standardised 'shopping basket' of branded groceries.

(Source: C M Guy and N Wrigley, 'Walking trips to shops in British Cities', *Town Planning Review*, 58(1), 1987, pp. 63–79)

Expenditure related to nearness of centre to home 6.24

Order of centre (by distance from home)

Cumulative percentage of walking trip expenditure

CASE STUDY 6.3   *Do we need a new breed of convenience shops?*

Expenditure patterns of Rumney-Llanrumney panellists for walking trips

	Percentage of walking-trip expenditure in:			
	Burnham Avenue	Llanrumney Avenue	Countisbury Avenue	Other centres
Panellist location				
Closest to Burnham Ave.	17	0	80	3
Closest to Llanrumney Ave.	0	43	45	12
Closest to Countisbury Ave.	0	5	91	4
All Rumney-Llanrumney Panellists	6	18	70	7

Notes
(1) These percentages are averaged out across all households concerned and should be interpreted as 'The average household living closest to the Burnham Avenue centre spent 17.0 per cent of its food and grocery expenditure (made in trips on foot) at that centre', and so on.
(2) Characteristics of the shopping centres. Burnham Avenue included one small independent grocery store, and three other shops where food or groceries were available. Llanrumney Avenue included two affiliated grocery stores, and two other shops where food or groceries were available. Countisbury Avenue included three small supermarkets (two owned by multiple firms and one Cooperative), and 14 other shops where food or groceries were available.

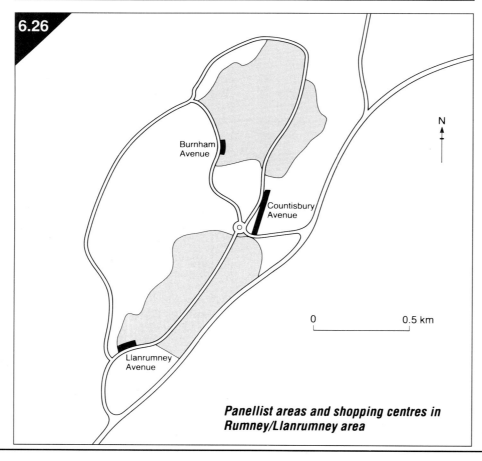

6.26

Panellist areas and shopping centres in Rumney/Llanrumney area

Activities

1 **Group project**: Select a residential area accessible to you which contains 'corner shops' and/or a local shopping 'parade' (define the areal boundaries). Design a research programme to investigate one or more of these questions:

a What is the retail provision within the study area and how do the residents use it?

b Is there a location, and a niche in the market, for one of the new breed of convenience stores described in this case study?

c Is there evidence that the retailing system in the study area is responding to the 'retail revolution' illustrated in case studies 6.1 and 6.2?

2 **Group discussion:**

a The results of the Cardiff research led the survey team to suggest the policy implications set out in resource 6.27. Read these suggestions carefully, then discuss (i) their advantages and (ii) the problems likely in establishing such retail patterns. NB Include the various 'interested parties' in your discussion, e.g. customers, planners, local councils, private developers, shop owners, large retail companies.

b To what extent are the various patterns of retail provision evident in your local district?

3 **Suggestion for a project**

This case study provides a number of further opportunities for a class or individual project in a local district, on shopping behaviour, provision and needs. Clearly, you need to scale down your survey and select carefully, specific issues, hypotheses, objectives, methodology, e.g. you might concentrate on consumer behaviour, on needs, or on spatial distributions.

Implications for policy

The policy implications of the findings may be considered in relation, firstly, to new shopping development and, secondly, older shopping areas.

In areas of rapid residential growth, a continuing problem lies in finding the right mix of convenience shopping provision. In the last ten years or so a common solution has been to provide a superstore-based 'district centre', located for easy access by car, supplemented if necessary by small 'corner shop' grocers located among residential areas. This type of system makes sense commercially, but in terms of consumer welfare may be inferior in some respects to the system of larger shopping parades common in the 1950s and 60s. The latter system provided a greater choice for the walking trip consumer today's superstore-based centre may be too far from home, and/or difficult of access by foot because of its car parking and servicing requirements.

Although it would be unrealistic to propose a return to the more generous standards of retail provision typical of the 1950s and 60s, there may be two ways in which current standards can be improved for the foot shopper. Firstly, access on foot to district centres could be improved by their better integration into pedestrian systems as research has shown that the distance people are prepared to walk depends partly upon the ease of the journey.

Secondly, the size and nature of purely local shops could be reconsidered instead of providing two or three very small 'corner shops', within a large residential development, one medium-sized 'convenience store' might be more appropriate. These stores, which have become a major focus of retail growth in North America, are now being developed in parts of England by specialist multiples, voluntary groups and petroleum companies. These stores may offer services such as photographic printing, dry cleaning, and video hire as well as selling food, newspapers and other items. In the future, these shops might also take on an extra role of remote ordering and delivery points for customers who wish to use superstores but cannot reach them. Such convenience stores would be a desirable destination for foot trips, as they would provide a wide range of goods at fairly competitive prices, although they would still be unlikely to dominate residents' expenditure patterns.

Since the 'convenience store' is actively being promoted by a number of private sector agencies, implementing their development should be less problematic than attempting to provide very small stores or small groups of shops, which in the past has often been the responsibility of the local authority. The authority's role should now be to identify sites for convenience stores which would combine the requirements of accessibility for local shoppers travelling on foot, with visibility to passing motorists. The importance of the latter requirement should not, however, be overemphasised. Convenience store developers need to be made aware that, in contrast to the North American experience, much of their trade would be derived from walking trip consumers.

In older residential areas, with their less well organised patterns of convenience shopping, market forces and the initiative of individual shopkeepers tend to have more influence than statements of intent by local planning authorities. So far as the walking trip consumer is concerned, loss of isolated corner shops may not be a problem if other shops can provide a more adequate range of goods at more competitive prices. However, planners might again seek to improve foot access to, and within, the larger shopping centres through traffic management measures. Rationalisation of these centres to reduce distances between complementary shops would be a useful longer-term policy, although this may be difficult to implement. Finally, planners and local councillors should perhaps put more pressure on retailers to maintain the choice of multiple- or cooperative-owned supermarkets in urban shopping centres walking trip consumers are particularly vulnerable to closures of these stores, which unfortunately have been occurring at rapid rates.

A modern convenience store (part of the 'Circle K' group). Accessible to housing and schools, on a main road, open long hours, sells food, newspapers, drinks and has videos available for rent

A small 1950s local parade with living areas above

CHAPTER 7

Places to work and live – farming and the countryside

Introduction

Farming of some kind is still the primary land use of at least 75 per cent of Britain's surface area, yet agriculture employs only 2.5 per cent of our working population. A second agricultural revolution has taken place since 1945 with a declining labour force producing ever-increasing outputs (resource 7.1) from a slowly shrinking hectarage (resource 7.2).

The result in Britain and the rest of the EC had been the achievement of self-sufficiency and indeed, surplus production in a number of major products (resource 7.3). This has given us the well-known butter, beef and grain 'mountains'. These are huge quantities of surplus produce bought up and stored by EC governments or sold cheaply to developing countries (resource 7.4).

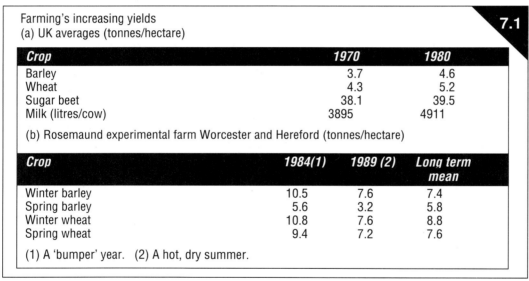

Farming's increasing yields
(a) UK averages (tonnes/hectare)

7.1

Crop	1970	1980
Barley	3.7	4.6
Wheat	4.3	5.2
Sugar beet	38.1	39.5
Milk (litres/cow)	3895	4911

(b) Rosemaund experimental farm Worcester and Hereford (tonnes/hectare)

Crop	1984(1)	1989 (2)	Long term mean
Winter barley	10.5	7.6	7.4
Spring barley	5.6	3.2	5.8
Winter wheat	10.8	7.6	8.8
Spring wheat	9.4	7.2	7.6

(1) A 'bumper' year.   (2) A hot, dry summer.

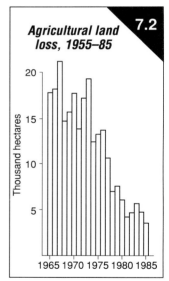

7.2

Agricultural land loss, 1955–85

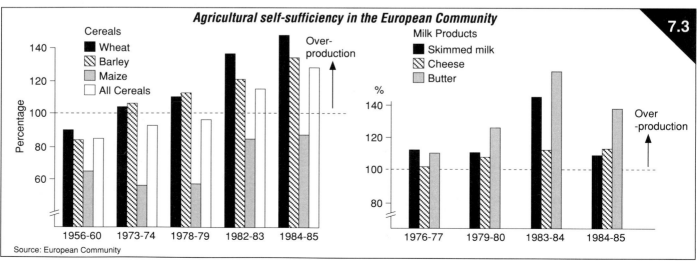

7.3

Agricultural self-sufficiency in the European Community

Source: European Community

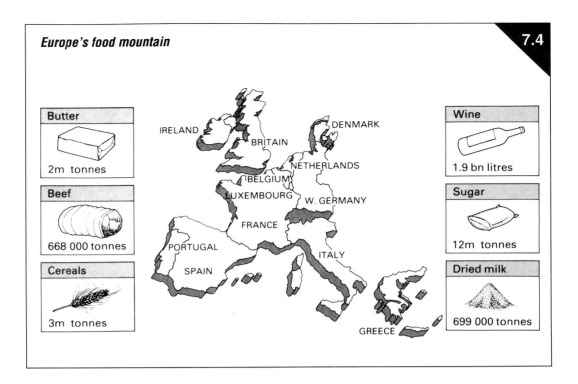

Butter — 2m tonnes

Beef — 668 000 tonnes

Cereals — 3m tonnes

Wine — 1.9 bn litres

Sugar — 12m tonnes

Dried milk — 699 000 tonnes

IRELAND, BRITAIN, DENMARK, NETHERLANDS, BELGIUM, LUXEMBOURG, W. GERMANY, FRANCE, PORTUGAL, SPAIN, ITALY, GREECE

In terms of productivity this has been a resounding success story, but as had become evident by the late 1980s, at considerable economic, social and environmental costs. Two-thirds of the EC budget is poured into the Common Agricultural Policy (CAP). The social structure of rural communities has changed fundamentally, with remote areas depopulating, accessible locations attracting commuters and beautiful regions becoming swamped by retirees or 'weekenders'. Modern technology creates a new environment of large fields, expensive machinery, a wide range of chemicals and specialised buildings, producing new farming landscapes and closely controlled ecosystems. Nowhere have the landscape changes been greater than in regions of intensive arable and animal rearing enterprises (resource 7.5). Criticisms of this 'new agriculture' have been mounting on all three fronts – economic, social, environmental – until in the early 1990s, a fundamental review of what we desire and expect from our rural landscapes is under way (resource 7.6).

One significant government response has been to establish Environmentally Sensitive Areas (ESAs), areas within which farmers are encouraged and required to sustain traditional farming methods and landscapes. By 1992, there were 31 ESAs located in contrasting environments.

The case studies in this chapter take up a number of the key issues in the agriculture and landscape debate. Case study 7.1 places the question of over-production in a global context, and suggests that it is the **distribution** of the production rather than the quantity which lies at the heart of the debate. Case study 7.2 returns to the British scale and focuses particularly upon the changing patterns of arable production. It shows clearly that British agriculture is still a mixture of old and new. Case study 7.3 draws our attention to some of the unintentional outputs from modern intensive farming systems, in particular the water pollution caused by heavy applications of nitrogenous fertiliser and by silage slurry leakage. Case study 7.4 highlights one important response to the mounting evidence of the impact of intensive techniques: organic farming, in the search for long-term sustained yield and environmental quality.

Before working through these case studies, it will be useful for you to review your understanding of the CAP and British government (MAFF) support policies, e.g. intervention prices, levies, subsidies, grants, quotas and so on.

Between 1945 and 1990, approximately 200 000 km of hedgerows have been removed in the UK (more than 20 per cent of the total). They are a valuable aesthetic and ecological resource in our landscape, helping to maintain its richness and diversity. Even where they remain, they are mostly changed in character. Photo (a), left, shows a traditional hedge laid by hand: it provides a thick base, makes a strong stock barrier and supports a wide range of wildlife. Photo (b), right, shows a hedge cut by a mechanical slasher: it lacks 'body', gives little protection and is a poor habitat for birds and animals.

7.6

EC policy blamed for rural damage

The countryside is still being destroyed at an alarming rate by the subsidy system of the Common Agricultural Policy, which encourages ripping up hedgerows, destroying woods, and using too much fertiliser and pesticide, according to the Council for the Protection of Rural England.

Its report, Paradise Destruction, showing how agricultural policies damage the countryside, says policies are dominated by those representing the interests of farming communities.

The aim of the report is to 'shatter the insulated world in which these decisions are taken, exposing the process which allows huge quantities of money to be spent on environmentally destructive practices'.

In the past two years some of the giant surpluses in the European Community had disappeared. The visible signs of excess which had caused public criticism had not been got rid of by reform but by dumping large unwanted surpluses on export markets.

The council argues that artificially high prices maintained in the community by subsidies to farmers damages the British environment. High prices encourage farmers to produce more by increasing the area farmed and boosting crop yield.

In order to increase the area under cultivation farmers drained wetlands, took out hedges, ploughed up moorland, and razed woodlands. This scarred the landscape, threatened wildlife, and increased soil erosion.

Boosting crop yield meant increasing use of fertilisers and pesticides. If prices were reduced the use of these products would become less economic.

The effects of increasing crop yield by artificial means meant a decrease in wildlife, increased nitrate leaching into water supplies and a general fall in diversity of landscape and wildlife.

The report suggests that the emphasis of CAP should switch to paying farmers for producing what society wants: the upkeep of the countryside, and production of food at lower cost to the environment with an emphasis on food quality and hygiene. The council wants farms to remain viable to save land being lost to urban development, mineral extraction, and coniferous forests.

It also wants food prices to be cut and says this can be done by paying direct income aid for farmers, conditional on environmentally good practice. It would cut out unnecessary surpluses and cost less both in cash and in countryside loss.

(Source: Paul Brown, *The Guardian*, 26 March 1990)

CASE STUDY 7.1 *Food and the global dimension*

Background

On the one hand we are bombarded by shock/horror images and headlines of starving families across the world. On the other hand we are told that the EC, USA and Canada in particular are producing too much food, and should be reducing yields and taking land out of cultivation. In personal terms, health and fitness magazines tell us how to 'diet' and exercise to improve our health, while charities and aid agencies plead for our money to help millions of people to achieve a minimum food intake. The message, therefore, seems to be more one of improving the distribution of food, rather than worrying about the amount produced in the world. The following article indicates that reality is far more complex. It shows clearly that there is undoubtedly gross mal-distribution of available food production, due for example, to government policies, the structure of international trade and varying technologies. Yet it also warns that the globe may be rapidly approaching its productive limits, and that overall, population is growing more rapidly than food production (resource 7.7).

The author of the article, René Dumont is a world-renowned French agronomist and economist who was adviser to the United Nations and the Food and Agriculture Organisation. Here, he warns of a potentially catastrophic food crisis, following a fall in food output due to environmental factors, deteriorating soil, water and climatic conditions.

Key understandings

◆ There are serious inequalities in the availability of food across the world.

◆ Production and productivity increases of food are finite.

◆ There is evidence that production and productivity are slowing more rapidly than world population growth.

Freshly planted intensive rice paddies at Sabah, Malaysia

World food crisis – a forgotten threat

'In 1966, Bernard Rosier and I wrote 'Nous Allons à la Famine', in which we voiced our fears that the world would shortly be hit by severe food shortages and even famine. We were not far off the mark: the Sahel and Ethiopia, in particular, were stricken by famine in 1973–74 and 1983–84.

Much more widespread than famine is chronic malnutrition. Although under-estimated by many, it now affects an increasing number of developing countries, from Africa south of the Sahara to the Indian subcontinent and large areas of Central and South America.

Lester Brown, in 'The Changing World Food Prospect' (Worldwatch Institute, October 1988), expressed alarm about grain production, which accounts for over half the world's food. From 1950 to 1984 it would seem that grain production rose 2.6 times, from 624 to 1645 million tonnes. That rate of increase was far greater even than the world's population explosion: the amount of grain available per capita rose by an extraordinary 40 per cent during those 34 years. But those living in the poorer countries mostly had no more to eat than before, and all too often less. The greatest beneficiaries of the increase were the wealthy countries and their armies of habitual overeaters.

Since 1984, there has been a complete reversal of the situation. Little attention has been drawn to the fact that world grain production per capita has fallen by 14 per cent over the last four years.

Just before the 1987 harvest, world grain stocks were 459 million tonnes, or enough to meet world requirements for 101 days. By harvest time 1988, only 295 million tonnes, or 54 days' requirements, remained.

From 1978 to 1984 China recorded an equally unprecedented increase in agricultural production as a result of decollectivisation and the increased use of fertilisers (which more than doubled between 1976 to 1981). But from 1985 to 1988 it never succeeded in equalling its 1984 production, whereas its population continued to rise by 1.4 per cent – or 15 million people – a year.

India did not succeed in matching its record 1983 production until 1988, by which time it had 800 million mouths to feed. And since the disastrously late monsoon of 1987, its reserve stocks have been exhausted and it has had to start importing grain once more.

As for the United States, after a record grain harvest of 345 million tonnes in 1985, it could manage only 277 million in 1987 and 190 million in 1988. Maize production plummeted from 212 million in 1985 to 116 million in 1988.

With a grain production of 195 million tonnes, the former Soviet Union was forced in 1989 to import a further 40 million tonnes.

Lester Brown suggests that we have been ploughing up too much land that is vulnerable to erosion. Under the United States Conservation Reserve Programme, 11 per cent of cropland will be returned to grass and forest cover by order of the Department of Agriculture.

India estimates that 129 million hectares of its land have been damaged by erosion: that works out at 39 per cent of the country's total area, but represents a far greater proportion of its arable land. Whereas topsoil loss in the United States is put at 3 billion tonnes, in India it is thought to be over 5 billion tonnes. In the much smaller Ethiopia, topsoil erosion in 1978 was reportedly 1 billion tonnes. Not only in many regions of Africa, but elsewhere in the world, the desert continues its inexorable march forward, engulfing 6 million more hectares of land each year.

The deterioration of nature, pastures and forests is helping greatly to reduce the world's agricultural potential. There has also been a considerable waste of water resources for irrigation purposes. What is more, excessively high urban water requirements mean that water for irrigation is increasingly hard to come by.

Groundwater levels beneath over a quarter of irrigated land in the US are falling by between 0.15 and 1.2 metres a year, and 'fossil' water deposits, which cannot be replenished, are now being tapped.

The area of irrigated land in the United States, which peaked in 1978, has since fallen by 7 per cent. The corresponding level in China has dropped by 11 per cent over the same period, because the situation there has been aggravated by neglect of irrigation systems, one of the negative consequences of decollectivisation.

Problems with irrigation

Although irrigated land worldwide rose from 40 million hectares at the turn of the century to 94 million in 1950 and 249 million in 1980, the upward trend has since levelled off or, as in the two cases just mentioned, been reversed. In poorly-designed irrigation systems, where there is often insufficient drainage, the tapping of groundwater asphyxiates the subsoil. Much land becomes unfit for cultivation as a result of excess salts and alkalis, i.e. salinisation.

In theory there are many ways in which the area of arable land world-wide could be extended. The trouble is that many regard the felling of tropical forests as an ideal solution, despite the fact that it is now generally accepted that the disappearance of such forests – now occurring at a rate of 11 million hectares a year – will have catastrophic repercussions. Low-grade pasture land, which becomes virtually barren after a few years, is replacing the magnificent Amazonian forests, which lost 4 per cent of their total area in 1987 alone.

Steep terrain in Central and South America, and especially in the Andes, is difficult to farm as it requires terracing, which is immensely labour intensive. Such farmland is quickly damaged by erosion when no longer terraced (resource 7.8).

There are limits to the benefits of irrigation. Many a fertile valley has been unnecessarily flooded by huge dams and thus lost to farming. Less damage would have been done by a series of mini-dams spaced out at regular intervals. This technique is now widely accepted as a solution.

One way of countering the constraints of poor soil and insufficient irrigation is intensive farming, which often relies on a heavy use of chemical fertilisers. In 1950, 14 million tonnes of them were used in the world; the figure in 1984 was 125 million tonnes, which works out at an increase of over 11 per cent a year.

It has consequently proved possible to more than double world average grain yields per hectare (from 1.1 to 2.3 tonnes). But from 1984 to 1988 the manufacture of such fertilisers increased by only 10 million tonnes, or less than 2 per cent a year, and grain yields no longer increased appreciably. World consumption of chemical fertilisers rose from five kg a year per capita in 1950 to 26 kg in 1980 and then remained stable until 1988.

Overuse of fertilisers in the developed countries, particularly in Britain and the Netherlands, has often resulted in groundwater pollution. It was once believed in some quarters that the kind of increases in grain yields which were achieved in the past could be repeated indefinitely; but that was not true. Rice now has a maximum yield of four tonnes per hectare, and wheat between six and seven, while maize can manage only slightly over seven.

Threat of climatic changes

Now an even more formidable threat has appeared on the horizon. Until recently, all forecasts of food production were based on the virtually certain knowledge that the world's various climates were invulnerable to major meteorological upheavals. In a word, they could be relied upon. That certainty has now collapsed.

It has now been established beyond doubt that increased carbon dioxide levels in the air as a result of an excessively rapid increase in the use of fossil fuels, among other things, has caused the world's climate to warm up since the beginning of the 70s.

Of the six years with the warmest world average temperature since the beginning of the century, five were recorded in the 80s (1980, 1981, 1983, 1987 and 1988).

The temperature increases caused droughts in the United States which reduced maize production by 17 per cent in 1980, 28 per cent in 1983, and as much as 35 per cent in 1988.

The warming-up process will raise the level of the sea – and threaten the existence of all the great river deltas, especially those in Asia, which, from Pakistan to northern China, provide a habitat for some 200 million people.

Since the last Ice Age 18 000 years ago, the world temperature has risen by only four degrees. It is now feared that by the year 2050, the temperature increase could be between two and six degrees.

The damaged ozone layer increases exposure to ultraviolet rays. That not only results in reduced photosynthesis – and thereby less production of carbohydrates – but means that irrigation is less effective.

Until 1986, the International Rice Research Institute (IRRI), the body responsible for developing the dwarf varieties of rice essential for the 'green revolution', put out justifiably optimistic bulletins on the rice-growing situation.

In September 1987, it began to express alarm about the lateness of the monsoon and the floods in the Indian subcontinent. In October 1988 it noted that Asia had produced 19 million tonnes less rice in 1987 – a fall of 4.3 per cent – and had been forced to increase its imports by 15 per cent.

The champions of economic liberalism are in favour of subjecting poor agricultures to international competition. Former US President Ronald Reagan talked of abolishing all forms of farm subsidies. But in any case such subsidies hardly exist outside the developed countries, where they encourage a form of intensive agriculture that has often harmed the environment.

In Canada, for example, subsidies to the grain-producers of the West financed the destruction of the soil by encouraging farmers to grow only

7.8

Intensive hill agriculture in montane rainforests, Sabah, Malaysia

wheat, without fallowing their fields or growing fodder plants. This had the effect of speeding up erosion.

If the decline of the less favoured nations were to continue, it would make their rural populations poorer and incite them to drift into shanty towns. This in turn would only increase the world's food shortage: and the first to suffer would be the Third World countries.

In 'The Changing World Food Prospect', Brown concludes that in view of the present situation, responsibility for the world's food security in the 1990s should be shifted from farmers to those responsible for energy and family planning policies.

If it turns out to be possible to reduce the waste of fossil energy relatively fast, then climatic deterioration could at least be slowed down.

But the future of the world hinges above all on whether or not we can curb, and the stop, the world's terrifying population explosion. The population explosion is ruining any chances there might have been of raising living standards in the great majority of the poorer countries. But when the education of girls became general in Sri Lanka, in Kerala and in Thailand, it became possible to halve

the growth rate of the population.

It now seems to me quite out of the question that agriculture will ever succeed in meeting the demands of a long-term population explosion. It is not always remembered that an annual population growth rate of, say, 3 per cent (which is quite common in African countries) would, were it to continue for a century, result in a 19-fold population increase.

(Source: R Dumont, 'World food crisis – a forgotten threat', *Development and Co-operation*, No. 5, 1989, pp. 15–17)

Activities

1 Summarise the evidence presented which suggests that we are threatened by a global food shortage.

2 **Pair discussion**:

  a Why is food production growth likely to slow down?

  b Why is it suggested that policies adopted by the developed countries may make the situation worse for developing countries?

Background

Changes in British agriculture over the past 40 years have been so profound that they have been called a 'second agricultural revolution'. Yet overall, the pattern remains a mixture of traditional features and recent innovations, as resource 7.10 shows, for England and Wales. Equally, the fundamental landscape changes brought about especially by changes in arable farming, cannot be denied.

Britain's arable crop farmers have been at the centre of some of the most intense debates concerning the future of the countryside. They have been at the forefront of improved productivity and profitability, encouraged by both MAFF and EC support policies, and the term 'agribusiness' applies clearly to the so-called 'cereal barons' of England's eastern counties. The extract in resource 7.9 illustrates this 'high tech' approach. But note when it was written – 1982. Since then, attitudes have begun to change. For instance, such farmers are accused of creating devastating changes in the countryside, with new, prairie-like landscapes replacing the visual and ecological richness of the traditional scene.

The article used in this case study plots the way British arable farmers have been responding (a) to market trends, (b) to new crops and varieties, and (c) to EC policies, especially the financial support systems, e.g. subsidies, intervention prices, levies. There is no doubt that arable crops have been the basis of prosperity for many farmers in all regions of Britain, either directly or as feed for animals. What is equally clear is that these 'good' years may be over, and farmers are being required to think much more carefully about the role of arable cropping in their enterprise.

7.9

The agribusiness approach

At Sutton-on-Trent in Nottinghamshire, Steve Dakin farms 3000 acres with an efficiency that would be the envy of many a manufacturer.

His 15 tractors and five combines can cut 200 acres of corn in a day. That means having almost £1m tied up in capital equipment that is used for a few days every year. But it also means that he needs only eight regular workers (with two casuals and five students at harvest) and that he can clear the land quickly for the next sowing. Dakin reckons to gain a hundred-weight of wheat per acre for every week that he saves in starting the autumn sowing.

The drive to cut waste and maximise profit is relentless. Every year Dakin buys up to 2000 store cattle which he fattens, largely on potatoes which he has grown and which are too small or too badly damaged to sell.

(Source: *The Sunday Times*, 29 August 1982)

Intensive cattle farm near Skegness. Notice how the requirements of the farm have affected the landscape.

Key understandings

◆ Arable cropping remains the predominant enterprise in the eastern counties of England but a range of crops are grown in all regions.

◆ There has been a change of balance between major crops in recent years, and new crops are being introduced.

◆ EC policy is a major factor in determining the location and character of arable farming.

Trends in arable farming in England and Wales

Since the UK joined the Common Market there have been fundamental changes in agricultural production. Some structural changes were underway before 1973, e.g. a decline in both the number of farms and farm workers and an increase in the average farm size and the capital invested in agriculture. But, undoubtedly, membership of the European Community has accelerated certain changes and arable farmers, stimulated by the CAP, have greatly increased production and adopted a range of 'alternative crops'. In 1986 the cereal harvest reached 24.4 million tonnes – second only to the record harvest of 26.5 million tonnes produced in 1984 – and oilseed rape was firmly established as the major alternative crop with an area of 271 604 hectares Over the past decade the development of a variety of alternative crops including oilseed rape, linseed, lupins, protein peas and beans, evening primrose and even sunflowers have coloured the English landscape and provided the farmer with viable break-crops in intensive arable systems. In arable farming there has been a trend to increased specialisation; crop yields have improved due to the advances made by plant scientists and the

---

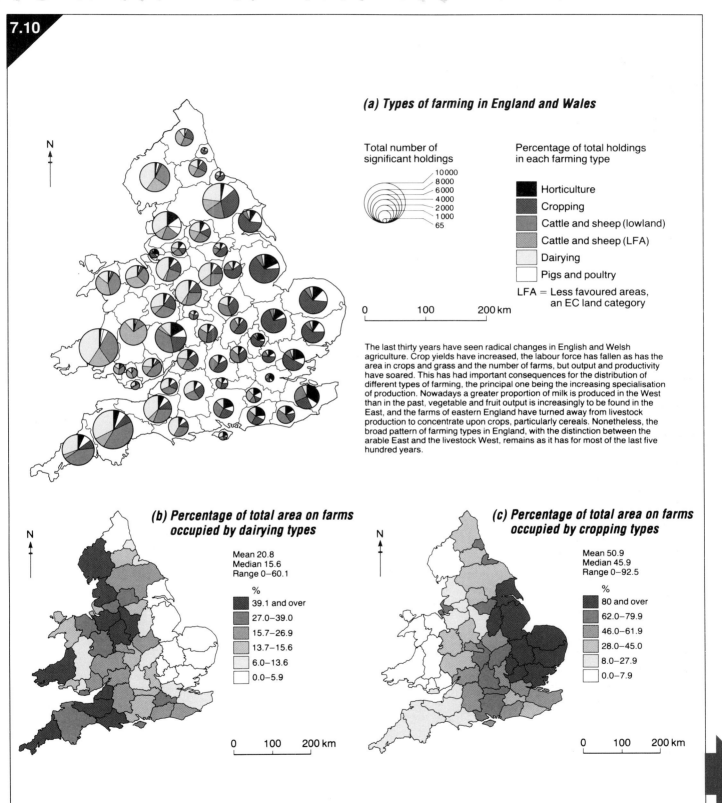

7.10

(a) Types of farming in England and Wales

Total number of
significant holdings

- 10 000
- 8 000
- 6 000
- 4 000
- 2 000
- 1 000
- 65

Percentage of total holdings
in each farming type

- Horticulture
- Cropping
- Cattle and sheep (lowland)
- Cattle and sheep (LFA)
- Dairying
- Pigs and poultry

LFA = Less favoured areas,
an EC land category

0   100   200 km

The last thirty years have seen radical changes in English and Welsh
agriculture. Crop yields have increased, the labour force has fallen as has the
area in crops and grass and the number of farms, but output and productivity
have soared. This has had important consequences for the distribution of
different types of farming, the principal one being the increasing specialisation
of production. Nowadays a greater proportion of milk is produced in the West
than in the past, vegetable and fruit output is increasingly to be found in the
East, and the farms of eastern England have turned away from livestock
production to concentrate upon crops, particularly cereals. Nonetheless, the
broad pattern of farming types in England, with the distinction between the
arable East and the livestock West, remains as it has for most of the last five
hundred years.

**(b) Percentage of total area on farms
occupied by dairying types**

Mean 20.8
Median 15.6
Range 0–60.1

%
- 39.1 and over
- 27.0–39.0
- 15.7–26.9
- 13.7–15.6
- 6.0–13.6
- 0.0–5.9

0   100   200 km

**(c) Percentage of total area on farms
occupied by cropping types**

Mean 50.9
Median 45.9
Range 0–92.5

%
- 80 and over
- 62.0–79.9
- 46.0–61.9
- 28.0–45.0
- 8.0–27.9
- 0.0–7.9

0   100   200 km

greater use made of artificial fertilisers, pesticides and fungicides; and mechanisation has increased. As a result UK farmers now produce 80 per cent of all the indigenous-type food consumed in the UK and production in several sectors exceeds domestic consumption thereby creating surpluses.

Patterns of cereal production

The improved output of cereals in England and Wales is partly a result of increased specialisation and since 1980 the average size of cereal enterprise has risen by 17.8 per cent to 43.6 hectares and the number of holdings growing cereals declined by 13 per cent. Almost three-quarters of the total cereal area in the UK occurs on holdings with 50 hectares and over of cereals. As resource 7.11 illustrates, the main change in cereal production has been the considerable increase in the wheat area at the expense of barley and oats.

One important factor in this change is the influence of the CAP. The support system for cereals was the first to be created and the initial support prices were high. This reflected the importance attached to cereals both for direct human consumption and as an essential livestock feedstuff, and the fact that almost 60 per cent of the total arable area of the Community is devoted to cereal production. As wheat is the most important cereal, higher threshold and target prices were provided for wheat than for barley and oats.

Plant scientists have also contributed to the recent dominance of wheat. Over the last decade it is estimated that improved varieties have contributed yield increases of 3 per cent per annum for winter wheat but only about 1 per cent for barley and oats. Thus winter-sown varieties of wheat have a potentially higher gross return per hectare than that for the other cereals. Consequently autumn-sown wheat now accounts for 95 per cent of the total crop and in 1986 the wheat acreage exceeded that for

barley by some 455 359 hectares (resource 7.11).

The distribution of wheat growing has not changed greatly since 1973. A core area of production is found in the central and east Midlands with a spur extending south-west into Wiltshire, where wheat takes up 50–58 per cent of the area of total tillage (resource 7.12). Lincolnshire heads the county list with 207 801 hectares in 1986 compared with 125 625 hectares in 1973.

Despite the decline in barley area there was an increase in production from 7.3 million tonnes in 1973 to 10.0 million tonnes in 1986, mainly as a result of improved husbandry and the introduction of higher yielding varieties. A major change has been the swing to autumn-sown varieties with potentially higher yields at the expense of spring sown. The distribution for barley has changed (resource 7.13) mainly as a result of the decline in acreage

associated with the larger barley growing counties. The barley acreage as a percentage of total tillage in 1986 was only 19.4 per cent in Lincolnshire and 17.6 per cent in Cambridgeshire, whereas in the south-west, west and north Wales and Cumbria the relative importance of barley has increased. In Cumbria the figure reached 76 per cent in 1986. Clearly, feed-quality barley is a crop which can flourish in the cooler and wetter parts of the country, although the largest acreages and the better quality grain are still associated with the eastern half of England.

Most of the wheat and barley produced in England and Wales is of feed quality, rather than bread-making or malting quality, and consequently the home market for feed grains is overloaded. Thus by November 1986 the intervention stores nationwide held nearly 3.8 million tonnes, i.e. the 'grain mountain'.

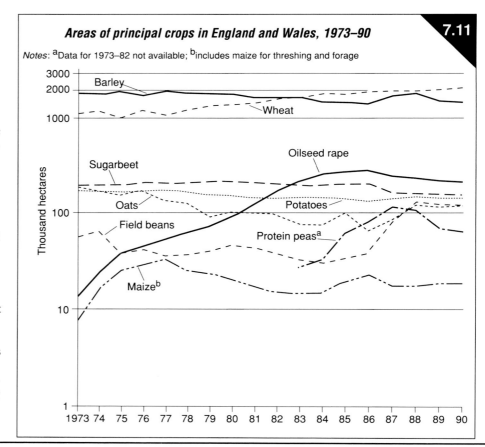

7.11

Areas of principal crops in England and Wales, 1973–90

Notes: [a]Data for 1973–82 not available; [b]includes maize for threshing and forage

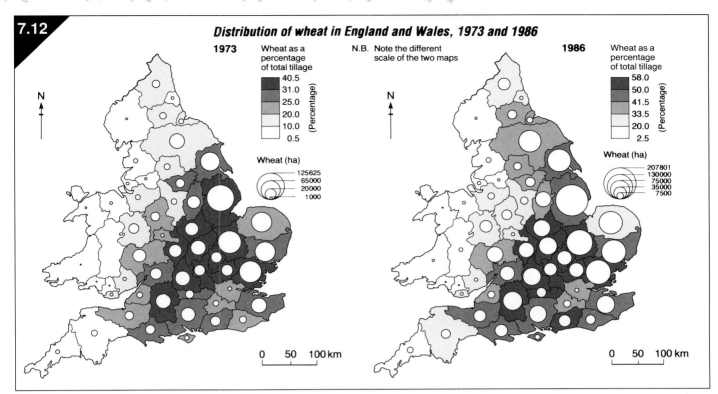

7.12

Distribution of wheat in England and Wales, 1973 and 1986

1973

Wheat as a percentage of total tillage

40.5
31.0
25.0
20.0
10.0
0.5

(Percentage)

N.B. Note the different scale of the two maps

Wheat (ha)

125625
65000
20000
1000

1986

Wheat as a percentage of total tillage

58.0
50.0
41.5
33.5
20.0
2.5

(Percentage)

Wheat (ha)

207801
130000
75000
35000
7500

0   50   100 km

The cereal support system under the CAP has tended to benefit the large cereal grower, thus leading to more specialisation. It has made high-cost farming on unsuitable land marginally profitable so that Grade III land can be used for cereals. Agronomists are divided on the effects of the virtual monoculture of cereals in some areas in eastern England and the possible long-term environmental effects of the heavy use of nitrogen fertiliser and pesticides. There are indications that soil structure is deteriorating and soil erosion increasing, and environmentalists are concerned about the wider effects on animal and bird life and on the visual appearance of the landscape.

The economic and financial problems created by the overproduction of cereals (and other farm products in surplus) are difficult to solve. However, in the case of wheat, there is still a need for more home-grown grain of milling quality. The inclusion of home-grown wheat in the millers' grist has increased steadily from 43 per cent in 1975/76 to 82 per cent in 1984/85,

but dropped back to an estimated 62 per cent in 1985/86. The remainder of the grist, about 1000 million tonnes, is imported, largely from North America.

Alternative cereals

Partly because of the difficulties of marketing feed-quality wheat and barley and the need to counteract the undesirable effects of a continuous grain cycle, farmers have sought 'alternative crops', some of which could act as 'break crops' in the intensive cereal system. Within the cereal sector, oats and durum wheat are crops which have offered direct alternatives to wheat and barley, with maize a more speculative crop.

Oats provide a low-cost substitute for the main grains, but the crop has had a rather chequered history. Between 1973 and 1984 the area under oats decreased 60 per cent in a steady fall from 194 00 hectares to 77 500 hectares, but due to increased yields per hectare overall production fell only 48 per cent. Then in 1985 the area jumped 31

per cent but there was a decrease of 34 per cent in 1986 to only 67 078 hectares. Millers currently import up to 40 000 tonnes of higher quality grain and this is a market than UK farmers could fill with new varieties, both winter sown and spring sown.

There is some scope for cereal growers to grow more durum wheat which is used for breakfast cereals (puffed wheat), semolina and various pasta products. Pasta consumption in the UK is increasing at 7 per cent a year and home-grown durum content could be raised to 40–50 per cent provided the growers can meet the quality requirements of the millers. About 6400 hectares were grown in 1984 compared with 200 hectares in 1980. So far yields have been rather variable, ranging from 2.5–6.0 tonnes/hectare and the results are therefore disappointing.

The fluctuations in the popularity of maize as a versatile crop for grain or forage purposes show that a post-war revival of interest began in the late 1950s for forage maize and the late 1960s for grain maize, which together occupied 34 588 hectares in

CASE STUDY 7.2 *Trends in arable farming in England and Wales*

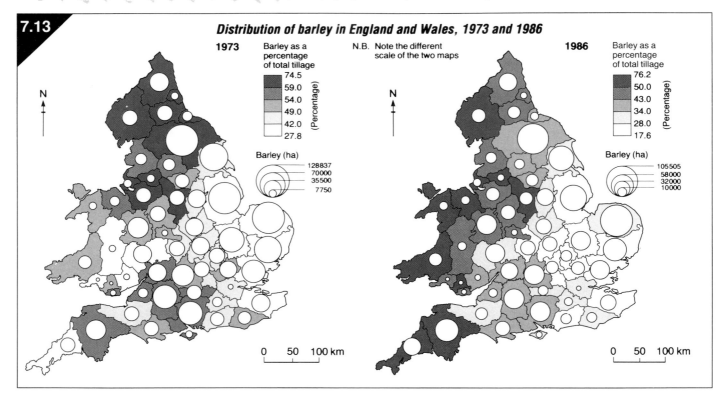

Distribution of barley in England and Wales, 1973 and 1986

1973 Barley as a percentage of total tillage

| 74.5 |
| 59.0 |
| 54.0 |
| 49.0 |
| 42.0 |
| 27.8 |

Barley (ha)
128837
70000
35500
7750

N.B. Note the different scale of the two maps

1986 Barley as a percentage of total tillage

| 76.2 |
| 50.0 |
| 43.0 |
| 34.0 |
| 28.0 |
| 17.6 |

Barley (ha)
105505
58000
32000
10000

0   50   100 km

1977. Grain maize acreage, in fact, peaked in the early 1970s whereas forage maize acreage increased steadily until 1977 when the pattern of development and spread was curtailed by poor harvests. Maize for forage or silage, in which the considerable vegetable growth is cut and chopped for preservation, does not require the cobs to fully form or ripen. Consequently the crop can be grown in lowland England and Wales from Devon to Yorkshire, whereas grain maize is largely restricted to areas south and east of a line drawn from the Severn to the Wash. Since 1978 when forage maize occupied 25 805 hectares and grain maize only 653 hectares, the maize crop has not been differentiated in the MAFF June statistics, which show that the combined crop declined to 15 118 hectares in 1983. It has shown signs of recovery and the acreage increased to 23 419 hectares in 1986 due to the advent of early maturing varieties mainly for forage.

Potatoes and sugar beet

Potatoes and sugar beet are two important crops which have their own special control systems to overview their growing area and production, i.e. quotas. Potatoes are not subject to direct EC regulations or intervention and in the UK production is supervised by the Potato Marketing Board. Since 1973, however, the area under potatoes and the number of growers have declined. In 1973 there were 38 753 registered producers in the UK, 211 000 hectares were planted and production was 6.5 million tonnes. In 1986 the returns indicated 22 565 registered producers, 167 000 hectares and 6.1 million tonnes. Again the production figure indicates the greater yield per hectare from improved varieties and husbandry.

The potato marketing scheme was revised in 1984/85 and new regulations for support buying by the Board cover the next five years. One major worry of the Board is that of overplanting, with growers exceeding their allocations. However, in 1986 the target area for UK registered producers was set by the government at 161 000 hectares but only 150 090 hectares were planted.

With the admission of Spain and Portugal to the European Community increased market competition might be anticipated, especially in relation to the sale of early potatoes.

The pattern of distribution of potato growing in England and Wales has not changed a great deal since 1973. The most notable feature is the reduction of area planted in Lincolnshire, Cambridgeshire and Norfolk, although these counties grow the largest acreages. Potatoes are a significant crop in the western half of the country with two roughly parallel producing areas, one in north-west and west Wales and Cornwall, and the other extending from Lancashire through Cheshire into Staffordshire and Shropshire.

Sugar beet has its own special system of control and subsidy under the CAP. The sugar regime normally runs for five years at a time and under it each country is allocated an overall quota. The UK is currently (1988) permitted to produce a total of 1 144 000 tonnes of sugar from the home-grown beet crop. The overall quota is separated into an 'A' quota of 1 040 000 tonnes and a 'B' quota of 104 000 tonnes with the latter subject to an increased levy on production. The quotas are based on production over the previous five-year period. In 1982 and 1984, the quotas were exceeded and the surplus had to be exported without EC financial aid, or carried forward to the next year. Unlike other member countries whose production quotas range from 102–230 per cent of consumption, the UK quota only covers half the country's sugar requirement, because special access to the UK market by mainly Caribbean cane sugar growers was permitted by the EC at the Lomé Convention.

All sugar beet is grown under contract with the British Sugar Corporation and in 1986 some 11 400 holdings grew on average 18.0 hectares of beet. In 1986 the total crop area in England and Wales was 204 591 hectares. The distribution of the crop has remained stable, reflecting to a large extent the location of the 13 processing plants (reduced from 17 in the early 1980s due to the reduced quota and the modernisation of factories). The main producing areas are in eastern England from the Yorkshire Wolds to the Thames estuary and in the west Midlands.

Alternative crops

The general conditions which a potential new crop must meet include: (1) the suitability of the crop for given climatic and soil conditions; (2) the compatibility of the crop with existing farming systems or its potential as a base for a new system; (3) its market potential must be such that it meets an existing need or has appropriate characteristics to ensure acceptance as a viable alternative; (4) the contribution of the crop to the farming system must represent an appropriate return to the farmer.

Over the past two decades UK farmers have been experimenting with a range of crops to see if they meet these general conditions, and one crop which has proved very successful is *oilseed rape*. This crop has also benefited from the fact that the European Community is generally deficient in vegetable oils and fats, producing less than half of total requirements. The Community has to rely heavily on imported oils such as soyabean, cottonseed, sunflower and groundnut. Under the CAP, therefore, encouragement has been provided for the growers of oilseed rape through attractive support prices and to the oilseed crushers in the form of a subsidy to encourage them to use home-produced rapeseed rather than imported oilseeds. As a result the area under oilseed rape in England and Wales has dramatically increased at an average annual rate of almost 37 per cent, from 13 674 hectares in 1973 to 276 362 hectares in 1986. Now over 13 000 growers plant an average of 23.0 hectares of rape with yields averaging 3.25 tonnes/hectare and production reaching 971 000 tonnes in 1986. Oilseed rape is now more important in terms of acreage than potatoes or sugar beet. The success of oilseed rape is partly due to its value as a break crop in intensive cereal systems and because the profit margins per hectare are generally higher than for feed-quality grains. As a break crop rapeseed provides a good entry for winter cereals, especially winter wheat, and standard cereal equipment can be used for cultivation and harvesting. Rapeseed now accounts for 30 per cent of UK edible oil needs compared with 2 per cent in 1973.

In the early 1970s oilseed rape was largely restricted to a semicircle of counties in the south and south midlands, with Hampshire (2621 hectares) as the major producer. Over the decade the main production area has moved north-eastwards, with Lincolnshire as the largest producer (35 203 hectares in 1986) and the arable areas of eastern Scotland growing some 22 099 hectares. The northerly shift is in response to several factors, one of which was the emergence of pest and disease problems associated with the increased acreage in southern England. The development of higher-yielding, disease-resistant varieties, with increased oil content (40 per cent) has provided farmers with a choice of varieties – some more suitable for northern areas and most of them for autumn sowing. The residue from the crushing of rapeseed is also valuable as a protein-rich meal for use in compound animal feeding stuffs.

A second alternative as a source of vegetable oil is *linseed* or flax, which depending upon the variety, produces an oil from the seeds or fibre from the stem. Flax fibre was introduced into the UK by the Romans and it was a valuable crop in the medieval period. In recent years, however, its importance has fluctuated widely. Wartime demand for fibre and oil and compulsory planting produced a record acreage of linseed of 34 697 hectares, but by the mid-1950s it had almost disappeared because of cultivation difficulties and the competition from synthetic fibres. Flax fibre has seen a minor revival over the past few years in Northern Ireland (400 hectares in 1985) and in Scotland on Tayside (290 hectares in 1985) where attempts have been made to re-establish a scutching mill to process the fibres.

Linseed for oil extraction received a boost in the mid-1970s with the introduction of new varieties. Again there was a peak of over 3000 hectares in 1976 followed by a trough of 326 by 1980. The trend since then has been steadily upwards with 6915 hectares in 1986.

Linseed has considerable potential as a temperate oil crop, which provides a low-cost, spring-sown alternative to cereals. The oil has a firm market, which is currently met by importing over 50 000 tonnes of linseed, mainly from Canada. The development of new, higher yielding varieties and the added incentive of direct acreage subsidy under the CAP are encouraging farmers to grow more linseed. The crop is mainly grown in eastern England from the Humber to the Thames.

Protein crops

A second sector in which the European Community is presently deficient is that of protein feed. Some 80 per cent of protein requirements are imported, mainly in the form of soyabeans from the USA. The unreliability of overseas protein sources stimulated the Commissioners to provide support for home-produced protein in 1978. Since then guaranteed support for protein crops has increased 60 per cent in six years and, as a result, peas and to a lesser extent field beans have become attractive and profitable break crops in the UK.

Field beans, traditionally a heavy land crop in East Anglia, are renowned for variability of yield and have therefore lost ground in recent years to oilseed rape and cereals. In 1973, 59 707 hectares were grown in England and Wales compared with only 32 234 hectares in 1984. However, the development of higher-yielding, disease- and pest-resistant varieties, together with the EC subsidy, have revived interest in field beans and the acreage increased to 59 546 hectares in 1986. The crop has the added advantage that it can be winter or spring sown to fit into different cropping systems.

Peas are the main combinable crop after oilseed rape in England and Wales. Encouraged by the EC protein subsidy the area under peas had increased rapidly since 1980 and in 1986 over 80 800 hectares were grown. Peas fit well into the cereal rotation and provide a bonus in the form of residual nitrogen which benefits the following crop.

It is estimated that the UK protein market is around one million tonnes, which allows a five to sixfold expansion over the current acreage. From the EC point of view attracting cereal farmers to grow pulses means a financial saving in support expenditure, a reduction in cereal surpluses, a greater self-sufficiency and less dependency on imported proteins and a saving of currency on imports.

Conclusion

The CAP, along with advances in farming techniques and improvements in crop varieties, has enabled farmers to intensify, concentrate and specialise to such an extent that the costs of purchasing, storing and disposing of agricultural surpluses threaten to exhaust the financial resources available and the Community faces a recurrent financial crisis. Overproduction has also created problems in the world market as EC countries have attempted to dispose of their intervention stocks, and to reduce access to the Community market by non-member countries. As a result other world grain producers, particularly the USA and Australia, have threatened retaliatory action.

The EC ministers must decide which of the numerous proposed measures – including raising the intervention standards, establishing quotas, introducing 'set-aside' or land-diversification schemes, or cutting prices – are going to be required to tackle the problem effectively (resoucre 7.14).

(Source: J E Wrathall, 'Recent changes in arable crop production in England and Wales', *Land Use Policy*, April 1988, pp. 219–231)

Activities

1   From resource 7.11 and the text, describe and explain the changes in the balance between wheat, barley and oats production since 1973.

2   From resource 7.12 summarise the changes in the pattern of wheat production, 1973–86.

3   Make a list of the reasons for the introduction and location of 'alternative crops'.

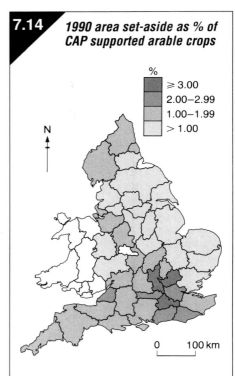

7.14 *1990 area set-aside as % of CAP supported arable crops*

%
≥ 3.00
2.00–2.99
1.00–1.99
> 1.00

N

0   100 km

1   The farmer must take on an obligation to set aside 20 per cent or more of 'supported arable crops' for five years, although he/she can opt out after three years. (Supported arable crops include all cereals, peas and beans harvested in dried form for human or animal consumption, sugar beet, hops, oilseed rape, linseed and fresh vegetables.

2   The land set aside must be maintained as fallow with a green cover crop, put to woodland or used for non-agricultural purposes (eg. farm-based accommodation, farm shops, provision of educational facilities and livery; but excluding residential, industrial, retail or similar land uses).

3   The rates of compensation vary according to the different uses the set aside land is put and whether or not it is located within a Less Favoured Area (LFA).

4   Farmers wishing to adopt the woodland option for a period of longer than five years (eg. up to 40 years) can take advantage of the MAFF's Farm Woodland Scheme.

5   The application of pesticides and fertilisers on land set aside is, in general, prohibited.

CASE STUDY 7.3 *A critical look at the nitrate issue*

Background

Nitrate levels in groundwater, streams and lakes have been rising in countries which have adopted advanced agricultural practices. Both intensive arable and animal rearing enterprises generate increased inputs of nitrate into the ground and surface hydrology. To boost crop yields arable farmers have applied increasing quantities of nitrogen (N) fertilisers to their land. For example, in Britain in the mid-1950s, a typical winter wheat field would receive at most 75 kg/hectare; by the 1970s, 100 kg was common, and by the late 1980s, totals were approaching 200 kg/hectare. Nitrate is an important plant nutrient and occurs naturally in soils so, by adding nitrogen-fertiliser, the farmer encourages that growth by invigorating the nitrogen cycle. Resource 7.15 summarises how this works. Intensive animal rearing inputs nitrogen into the soil and water systems via leakage from silage clamps and the spreading or leakage of slurry manure (Part II of this case study).

Key understandings

◆ Applications of nitrate fertilisers to soils by farmers have increased, and have helped to raise yields.

◆ Scientific evidence casts doubt on whether the increased nitrate levels of many streams and lakes are directly the result of 'surplus' nitrate added by farmers.

◆ Nitrate enrichment of water creates ecological changes and health hazards.

◆ Any policy to reduce nitrate levels in water will take a long time to have an effect.

◆ Intensive animal rearing produces water pollution via silage liquid and slurry leakage.

7.15

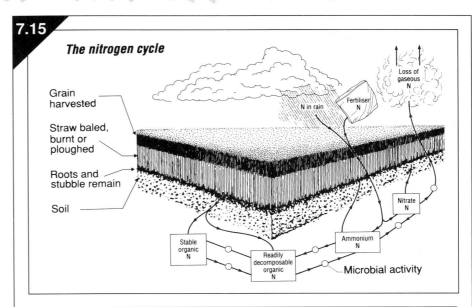

The nitrogen cycle

Nitrogen and the nitrogen cycle

The nitrate ion (NO_3) represents just one part of the complex nitrogen cycle which involves many phases

Nitrogen (N) is *fixed* from the atmosphere by bacteria. These can be associated with plant root nodules in legumes or they can be elsewhere in the soil. Nitrogen taken up by plants is said to be *immobilised* in plants where it forms the basis of plant proteins.

This nitrogen is returned to the soil in leaf litter and in animal dung from herbivores. Nitrogen is present in the soil organic matter as organic nitrogen. This is then *mineralised* by soil bacteria into ammonium (NH_4^+). This may be used directly as a nutrient by some plants. Ammonium can also be oxidised to nitrite (NO_2^-) and then nitrate (NO_3^-); this oxidation is termed *nitrification*. Nitrate may also be used as a plant nutrient or it may be leached from the soil.

Nitrate can thus be formed naturally in unfertilised situations, from successive steps of nitrogen fixation – immobilisation in organic matter – the mineralisation of organic nitrogen to ammonium – the oxidation of ammonium to nitrate during nitrification.

The reverse of this situation is termed *denitrification*. Nitrate losses occur when nitrate is reduced to nitrite (NO_2^-). This denitrification process occurs especially under wet, anaerobic conditions.

The cycle is completed by the further fixation of the gaseous N produced by denitrification.

Nitrogen may thus be present in the soil in three main forms:

(1) organic nitrogen
(2) ammonium
(3) nitrate

In agriculture, nitrogenous fertiliser is added to increase crop growth, promoting leaf growth and high grain yields. Nitrogen is often seen as one of the most important elements to add, frequently representing the limiting factor on crop growth and one to which crops are the most responsive. Commonly used fertilisers are:

Ammonium nitrate: NH_4NO_3.
Compound: N.P.K. fertilisers (mixtures of nitrogen, phosphate and potassium).
Nitrochalk: $Ca(NO_3)_2$.
Urea: NH_4COOH.

A key point in the leaching of nitrate is that nitrate is an anion, NO_3^- and, as such, is not held in the soil. Positive cations such as NH_4^+ are adsorbed, or held by an electrical charge, on clay surfaces which are negatively charged. Anions, however, are repelled by the like charge of clay surfaces and so are not held in the soil. Instead, they are present in the soil solution where they can be easily washed out or *leached*. Nitrate is, however, such a good growth promoter that it is still well worth using.

(Source: S Trudgill, 'The nitrate issue', *Geography Review*, May 1989, p. 30)

7.16

Tampering with mother nature

Michael East of the Adriatic Information Service is disingenuous when he says that the problems on the beaches of Italy (and also Yugoslavia) are 'caused by a very natural substance, algae' (Letters, August 21).

The problem is algae, growing in unnatural profusion, and the algal problem is caused by an excess of nutrients in the water.

These nutrients come mainly from sewage and artificial fertilisers. Algal blooms on this scale cause enormous problems to marine life, by using up oxygen in the water when they die and start to rot.

Britain is not free of this problem. We already have algal blooms in some estuaries, and contributed to the huge Scandinavian blooms last summer, where algal slicks measuring 10–30 metres deep 10 kilometres wide affected coastal areas. Britain daily releases 4000 tonnes of agricultural nitrate into the sea, along with nitrates from other sources, including sewage.

Current plans to reduce this through a few Nitrate Sensitive Areas will go nowhere near solving the problem. Organic farming methods have been shown to substantially reduce nitrate leaching, yet are not included in current plans for NSAs. We can expect more algal blooms in European seas as long as we fail to tackle the problem of nitrate pollution with the seriousness that it deserves.

Nigel Dudley, Director, Soil Association.

(Source: *The Guardian*, 26 August 1989)

7.17

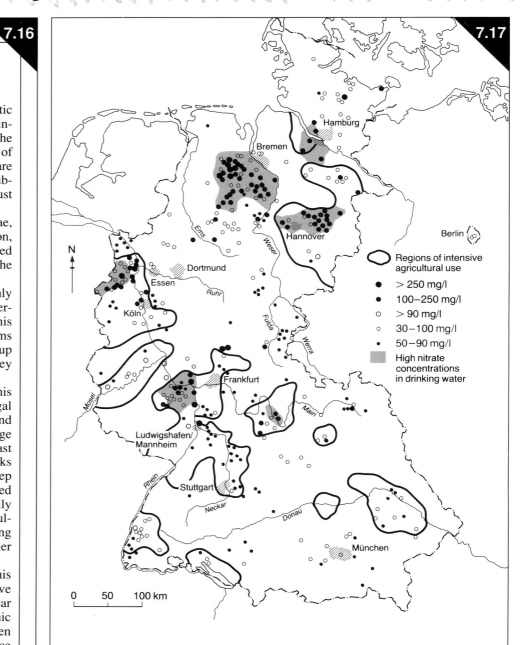

Regions of intensive agricultural use
● > 250 mg/l
● 100–250 mg/l
○ > 90 mg/l
○ 30–100 mg/l
• 50–90 mg/l
High nitrate concentrations in drinking water

Excessive nitrate concentrations in drinking water in West Germany, 1985

Investigations into nitrate levels have continued since the 1950s. By 1980, the maximum West German government and EC regulations were requiring a nitrogen maximum of 50 mg/litre in drinking water, but as the map showsd, levels well exceed this, especially in areas of intensive agriculture. The nitrogen debate centres on four lines of conflict between agriculturalists, fertiliser manufacturers, water authorities, environmental groups, and government agencies:–
1 Whether drinking water with nitrate content greater than 50 mg/litre is a health risk
2 Whether fertiliser application and spreading of liquid manure by farmers are the main causes of rising nitrate levels in groundwater, streams and lakes
3 Whether policies should be adopted to reduce nitrate levels, and if so which
4 Whether the costs of reducing nitrogen levels should be met by farmers ('the polluter pays' principle), the water suppliers and consumers ('the injured party pays' principle), or by society as a whole ('the taxpayer pays' principle).

In all countries in the European Community and in North America, there is increasing criticism of this nitrate-led, high-yield, intensive farming or 'agribusiness', which is leading to a fundamental review of the Common Agricultural Policy (CAP). Criticisms focus upon, first, economic problems caused by overproduction, e.g. grain, butter and beef 'mountains' and the impacts on water (resource 7.15). Part I of this case study explores this latter issue, where added nitrate is blamed for, (a) eutrophication (nutrient enrichment) of streams and lakes, causing algal blooms and oxygen deficiency (resource 7.16) and (b) creating health hazards for humans, e.g. stomach cancer and the 'blue baby' syndrome (methaemoglobimaemia or oxygen starvation in the blood). The issue is being taken seriously throughout the EC (resource 7.17).

In Britain, it has become a high-profile issue. For example, in 1988, the Department of the Environment (DoE) published a paper called, 'The Nitrate Issue', in which they related increased farming inputs to rising nitrogen levels in water, and hence to pollution. One of their recommendations for improving water quality was to change agricultural policy. However, the reasoning behind this relationship has been challenged by a number of agricultural researchers: they agree that nitrate levels in many streams and lakes are dangerously high, but suggest that the recently increased application of nitrate fertilisers may not be to blame. Part I of this case study, takes us through a critical review of the evidence. Remember, this is one viewpoint, so try to find others for comparative analysis:

'There are many vested interests in the nitrate issue. Fertiliser manufacturers and farmers are concerned to enhance their environmental image but remain unconvinced by the medical evidence. Environmentalists point to this doubt and say that we should act before it is too late, as well as stressing the ecological aspects of nitrate in water … What is clear is that the nitrate issue is a complex one where the evidence has to be carefully examined.' (Srudgill, *Geography Review*, May 1989)

Part II illustrates the farm silage and slurry aspect of pollution and how difficult it is to control.

Part I: Where does the nitrate come from?

Nitrate pollution is both wasteful and dangerous. Farmers are often blamed, because, in their drive to increase yields, they have used too much nitrogen fertiliser and their excess has percolated into our lakes rivers and water supplies. Therefore, it is claimed, if we stop using them so much, then the grain mountains will shrink and water pollution will be reduced. But is the argument really as simple as this?

It is true that nitrate-rich water can make babies ill, and in lakes and rivers, too much nitrate encourages the spread of water plants and algal blooms. The water plants can clog channels and the algae form an ugly surface scum. When the algae die, the decomposition process uses so much of the available oxygen that many other aquatic organisms die.

There is however, another side to the nitrate argument. For instance, consider the famous grain mountain: in 1988, about 1.7 mt were stored in Britain as intervention stocks, i.e. unsold grain bought under the CAP. An article, written after the 1988 harvest period claimed:

'[if] that harvest had failed; our stocks would have lasted about a month. Is this a mountain or a rather low reserve? Our balance of payments is bad enough without massive grain imports. What about the excess nitrate left by overuse of nitrogen fertiliser? Is this truly the root of the nitrate problem.'

Nitrogen is essential for crops as it is a component of the amino acids and proteins which plants need for growth. Plants take in the nitrogen they need as either ammonium or as nitrate. The nitrate is easily soluble in soil water and so is vulnerable to leaching (removal by percolating rainwater). The ammonium is less easily removed as it is strongly attracted to the surface of soil particles. But one task of soil microbes is to convert ammonium to nitrate, which is then susceptible to leaching. Thus, whether nitrate comes from chemical fertiliser, farm manure or the breakdown of organic matter in the soil, if it is not taken up by a crop, it is likely to be leached by percolating water.

It is at this stage that the depth of the water table becomes critical. If the water table is near the surface, e.g. where there is a thin soil profile overlying impervious strata, much of the water will move laterally to enter the surface drainage network of ditches, streams, rivers and lakes. Where the rocks beneath the soil are porous, e.g. chalk, limestone, the water table may be deeper, perhaps 50 m below the surface. In this case the nitrate is carried downwards and enters the aquifers (water-bearing strata). The significance of this becomes apparent when we recall that at least 60 per cent of our water supplies are drawn from these groundwater aquifers, or stores. Furthermore, as water and its dissolved nitrate may percolate downwards very slowly, e.g. less than 1m a year through chalk, there may be a time lag of perhaps 50 years between the introduction of the nitrate to the soil and its arrival in our water supply.

The next key question is whether nitrogen from unused fertiliser is to blame. This leads to another question: why is some nitrogen unused by plants? First, rainwater may wash it from the soil before it can be taken up by the crop, e.g. in a wet spring in southern England, around 15 per cent of the fertiliser nitrogen may be removed, although some of this remains within reach of the plant roots. Second, the plant may not need it at all. Research has shown that the major leakages occur during the cooler, wetter winter months. Precipitation exceeds evaporation so there is vigorous downward percolation during a period when there is little nitrogen take-up by plants – arable fields are either bare or covered by young, autumn-sown crops. So nitrogen fertiliser present in the soil at this time could become a problem. Yet experiments at Rothamsted Agricultural Research Institute showed that little does remain: winter wheat was given a typical nitrogen application of 190kg per hectare, yet only between 1 and 5 kg of nitrogen were left after harvest. Any other remnant nitrate was locked up in soil organic matter.

Yet substantial amounts of nitrate *do* leak from soils during the post-harvest months. So where does it come from? The answer is – from the soil itself. Arable soils contain abundant organic matter and organisms, which can contain 5000 kg of nitrogen in a hectare, but is 'locked up' and unavailable to plants or for leaching. It is the millions of microbes which break down the organic matter and release the nitrogen. They do this most vigorously in the autumn when the soil is still warm, is becoming moister and has minimal demands from crops. Thus, the researchers at Rothamsted claim that these nitrates are the biggest cause of nitrate pollution – responsible for a far greater concentration of nitrates in the water than direct losses from chemical fertilisers. Their recent findings support the results of much earlier experiments at Rothamsted. Between 1870 and 1915, they measured the water draining from the same 4 sq metre plots of soil. These plots received no fertilisers and were not cropped. After 15 years, the soil was still leaking an average of 45 kg of nitrogen as nitrate per hectare each year. As rainfall was supplying only 3 to 5 kg of nitrogen per year, almost all of the rest must have come from the organic store. Even after 40 years,

the leakage was over 20 kg per hectare.

The conclusion is therefore, that there is a large store of decomposable nitrogen in the soil which is released gradually over time. Thus, if we were to reduce the amount of fertiliser we apply, what would be the effect? The following calculations for winter wheat illustrate first, the impacts of a decade of **increasing** fertiliser application and second, the likely effects of **reducing** inputs. Between 1976 and 1985, farmers increased their applications from 100 to 190 kg per hectare. Taking 100 kg of fertiliser as the baseline, each hectare of winter wheat received an extra 1450 kg of fertiliser nitrogen during this decade. Much must have been taken up by the crop, as yields increased markedly, but inputs were consistently above the nitrogen uptake of the crops. The cumulative excess of nitrogen over the decade was about 300 kg per hectare, mostly entering the organic matter store. Thus, if the soil in 1976 contained the typical 5000 kg per hectare of organic nitrogen, then the increasing applications of nitrogen over the ten years added only about 6 per cent to the amount of organic nitrogen in the soil. Suppose now, that the farmers over the next ten years apply only 95 kg per hectare, i.e. a reduction of 50 per cent. The projected increase in organic nitrogen in ten years would be around 4 per cent – hardly a dramatic shift!

It is clear then, that any solution to the nitrate problem is long-term and may emerge through the changing nature of agriculture under EC policy. One option already in operation is **set-aside** (see resource 7.14 on page 156), whereby farmers take land out of production and so, hopefully reduce surpluses. However, the land must have some form of crop cover because of the risk of nitrate leakage as the microbes continue their work of breaking down organic matter. A grass cover would help, as grass

roots take up nitrate vigorously, holding the nitrate in the organic store and thereby reducing leakage. But if the farmer at any time did plough the land then there would be a surge of nitrate release as the organic matter was broken down.

Forestry is another option, as mature woodland leaks little nitrate. The danger periods here are after felling, when soils may be exposed, causing leakage to accelerate.

A third option is **organic farming**. Organic manures are seen as more environmentally friendly, but they are a distinct pollution risk. Fields fed regularly with farmyard manure contain up to 100 kg more nitrate per hectare in the critical autumn months than chemically fertilised fields, because there is more organic nitrogen for the microbes to break down. Furthermore, organic systems include more legumes, e.g. clovers, that 'fix' nitrogen from the air through their root bacteria. Legumes, usually in combination with grass, cause nitrogen to accumulate, and so, when ploughing does take place, there is a surge of nitrogen release and accelerated leakage.

A fourth option is to **use less nitrogen fertiliser**, but as we have shown, this is not the real cause of the pollution. As the Rothamsted researchers have stated, halving the nitrogen supplied to winter wheat would cut the yield by only about 10 per cent but farmers make all their profit on that last 10 per cent.

The key to the problem lies therefore, in the amount of nitrate still stored in the soil during the autumn and winter months, most being released from organic nitrogen. This may seem strange, because only 20 years ago the main concern was for the decreases in organic matter, for grassland contains more than arable land, and arable systems were gaining over much of Britain. This concern, alongside the pressure to increase yields, led to the huge growth of chemical fertiliser inputs.

Farmers have now learned that they have been inefficient in their use of nitrate fertilisers. During the 1980s they halved their inputs, mainly by reducing applications during autumn. Also, winter crops are sown as early in autumn as possible and quick growing varieties are used, in order to leave little bare soil during winter. Stricter regulations on the burning of straw and stubble have meant that more organic matter is ploughed back into the soil than 20 years ago. Results seem encouraging: data collected by Anglian Water from boreholes in Lincolnshire suggest that groundwater nitrate levels, after steady increases in several decades, have begun to decline. Significantly, this is an area where many farmers have shifted from spring to autumn sowing, thereby reducing the expanses of bare soil during the winter.

Part II: Pollution from farmyard wastes

Intensive animal rearing creates two main types of pollutant: animal slurry (liquid and solid body wastes, especially from cattle and pigs) and silage liquor. Slurry can be 100 times, and liquids leaking from silage clamps 200 times, as polluting as untreated domestic sewage. By 1979, approximately 1500 such pollution

incidents were reported. By 1985 this figure had risen to 3500, and by 1989 has exceeded 4000. Resource 7.18 gives the figures for 1985 and 1986, issued by the Water Authorities Association. Notice that the slight fall in total figures was caused by a 41 per cent increase in pollution by silage effluents.

Because silage can be made without the cut grass being dry, it has been replacing hay as animal fodder, and its production tripled, 1976–86 (resource 7.19). It is made mainly in May-June and the Nature Conservancy Council claims that heavy rains at this time can increase leakages from the silage clamps. Resource 7.20 when compared with the figures of resource 7.19 seems to support this claim: 1985 was a wet summer while 1986 received, in most regions, below average rainfall, hence the fall in silage pollution incidents in 1986.

The farmyard slurry issue is discussed in resource 7.21 which was published in March 1989. It illustrates the various individuals, interest groups and agencies involved, and the problems associated with controlling the pollution. Clearly, a shift of agricultural practice and policy to less intensive and more traditional methods would help.

Activities

1 Explain how the nitrogen cycle works.

2 What do we mean by eutrophication and what are its effects?

3 **With a partner:** produce two lists of evidence headed:

   (i) Farm-added nitrate causes water pollution

   (ii) Farm-added nitrate is not a significant cause of water pollution

4 The following suggestions have been made for reducing nitrogen application levels, while maintaining yields. With your partner explain how and why these suggestions might work:

a Avoid using nitrogen fertilisers between mid-September and mid-February.

b Give preference to autumn sown crops and sow as early as possible (Look at case study 7.2 and suggest what *adverse* effects this might have).

c Apply the nitrogen in several doses, when need is greatest.

d Do not apply nitrogen in fields near streams.

e Do not apply nitrogen before heavy rain.

f Use less nitrogen if last year was a dry year.

g Do not plough up grassland.

h Plough in chopped up straw, do not burn it.

i Reduce the cultivation (i.e. working over) of the soil as much as possible.

j Adopt sensible land uses – concentrate arable fields on flatter areas above slopes, introduce temporary grass rotations etc.

7.18 Total farm pollution incidents 1985 and 1986

Type of waste/pollutant or cause of pollution	1985 no	%	1986 no	%	change %
slurry stores	881	25	864	25	–2
run-off from slurry stores	185	5	143	4	–23
silage effluent	1006	29	592	17	–14
land run-off	237	7	313	0	+32
yard water	738	21	954	28	+29
treatment system failure	123	3	198	6	+61
sheep dip/pesticides	63	2	65	2	+3
mineral fertiliser	8	–	25	1	+212
vegetable washings	22	1	36	1	+64
oil spillage	126	4	102	3	–19
other	121	3	135	4	+12
total	3510	100	3427	100	–2

5 From the materials in Part II of the case study, summarise the factors which cause slurry pollution, and suggest ways of reducing it.

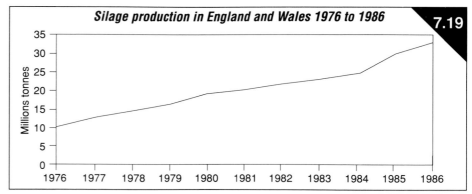

Silage production in England and Wales 1976 to 1986

7.19

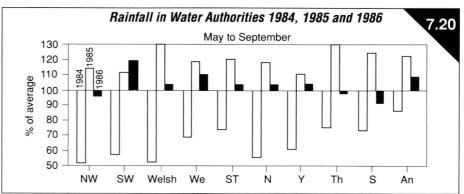

Rainfall in Water Authorities 1984, 1985 and 1986

7.20

May to September

7.21

Muck spreaders

When the first dead carp floated to the top of the moat at Stogursey Castle, local people knew immediately what had happened: a farmer, once again, had poisoned their stream.

First one Chinese grass carp broke the surface and lay belly-up, then another 12. Now the castle workers think pollution has killed all 45 of the fish they keep to eat underwater weeds, poisoning eels and the moat's only bream.

The experience of Stogursey, a medieval village in Somerset's Quantock Hills, is part of the hidden pollution toll of rural Britain. According to unpublished government figures, farms are spoiling rivers at a record rate. The 4000 farm pollution reports received by water authorities last year is a 10 per cent increase on the year before, and almost three times the figure for 1979. This is Britain's fastest-growing form of water pollution.

The slurry that slid into Stogursey brook came from and farmed by Metford Jeanes, a genial, grandfatherly figure whose family has worked the land for four centuries. He is open about his business and co-operates when the authorities call, but offences against the countryside land him in court almost every year.

In 1987 Cricket Malherbie Farms, the company of which Jeanes is chairman, was fined £4000 for three offences, including seriously polluting a stream when a temporary irrigation system broke down. Jeanes was also fined £500 after another case during drainage improvement works.

In 1986 there were fines for two offences caused by poor irrigation; the year before, two fines of £100 for inefficient irrigation; three pollution cases in 1984, another two in 1983.

Despite these warnings, it was badly-timed irrigation, feeding animal slurry to the fields, that caused the latest incident six weeks ago, killing the castle carp.

Jeanes, a former president of

Somerset National Farmers' Union, has a pollution problem because his herds have grown faster than the facilities to cope. Once there were 360 cows on his three farms, which occupy 800 acres of Stogursey and Nether Stowey; today 320 cows are split between two of the farms, and the third features a unit for 3000 pigs.

These animals generate so much waste, and the waste is so powerful, that it would take the human sewage of Swansea and Cardiff combined to equal his animals' potential to damage the environment.

A generation ago, when cows spent winters outside, their slurry fell on land as a natural fertiliser, now, penned in sheds, it must be scraped from the ground and put in slurry 'lagoons', sometimes holding millions of gallons of animal faeces and urine, used later to irrigate fields.

Another change is that, instead of using hay to feed cattle in winter, many dairy farms have a silage tower holding hundreds of tons of cut grass. The juices that drain from the silage are particularly destructive in rivers, where they deplete the oxygen needed by aquatic life.

If Jeanes had been a motorist with this number of prosecutions, he might have had his licence taken away by now; as a farmer he is unworried. 'Look, it's cheap money,' he said. 'When you have a problem that could take £200 000 to solve, a £2000 fine is nothing. Don't write that down.'

The authorities are alarmed. Particularly galling is that much of Britain's farm pollution goes into water that was clean, sometimes after a great deal of pollution control work. Lionel Beck, river quality manager for Yorkshire Water, said: 'As we make strenuous efforts to clean up rivers like the (industrially polluted) Aire and the Don, we see those improvements wiped out by the farmers.'

Formerly clean rivers such as the Tamar and the Torridge in Devon and Cornwall, and the streams that feed them, have become so contaminated with farm waste that it will take years to restore them to their former quality, even if the pollution stops.

In the south-west – which, with the north-west, has the worst farms pollution figures in the country – 14 per cent (230 miles) of the highest-quality rivers have been officially downgraded in one year.

Although some pollution is by accident, much is through neglect. For example, 40 per cent of cases involving silage are the result of keeping grass in a container that leaks; another 40 per cent because of inadequate facilities for storing the putrid green liquid that drains out, so strong it eats into concrete.

The effect on rivers is devastating: silage is 200 times more potent than raw sewage. Micro-organisms that feed on it rapidly remove oxygen from the water, killing fish and other life. Last year more than 3000 fish died when one farmer's silage effluent leaked into Colton Beck, near Kendal in Cumbria.

Almost as destructive is slurry, the animal waste. After heavy rain the lagoons can overflow, pouring into ditches or streams. Slurry is also sprayed on farmland to fertilise the soil. If too much is used or the land is waterlogged it runs off, contaminating lakes, ponds and watercourses.

This is what happened to Jeanes: his 2m-gallon slurry pool was full, he started pumping on to wet fields, and a system of Victorian drains carried it efficiently into ditch, stream and sea.

But the prosecution risk is low: after last year's 4000 reports there were fewer than 200 prosecutions, a rate of under 5 per cent. Even when in the south-west there have been several cases of fines as low as £25, or where polluters were conditionally discharged.

The saga of pollution that starts on West Country farms follows animals to market. Stockyards and slaughterhouses are among Britain's most persistent offenders. The wastes from holding pens, abattoirs and carcass rendering plants are some of the most polluting known.

An example is Hillsdown Holdings, one of Britain's largest farming and food groups, with interests in poultry, eggs, fresh meat and prepacked meals. Its subsidiaries include Buxted Poultry, one of the country's leading chicken producers, with more than 200 farms.

The company was convicted in 1986 for polluting a tributary of the River Waveney with poultry waste from its factory farm at Flixton, Suffolk, which processes 200 000 birds a week. But the plant went on discharging above legal limits and, in the 12 months until last January, was found to have polluted the river on 17 occasions.

At Bernard Matthews, Britain's biggest turkey processor, they handle 9m birds a year in two factory farms. At the Witchingham plant in Norfolk, where employees pluck, stuff and pack close to 100 000 turkeys a week, the company last year exceeded its pollution limits on five occasions. The Holton factory, 30 miles south in Suffolk, failed 21 of Anglian Water's tests. The water authority sent a letter of warning.

In Switzerland, the storage capacity for slurry and silage liquors has to be of sufficient size for the number of animals. But in Britain farmers are merely asked to observe a code of practice, which includes planning for the maximum amount of effluent likely to arise in wet weather.

The government's hope for stopping farm pollution is a £50m package of grants announced by the agriculture minister, last November. Farmers can claim up to half the cost of building or improving facilities for the storage, treatment and disposal of slurry and silage effluent.

This incentive is unique: no other section of the community has been offered money to stop breaking pollution laws.

Jeanes has come up with his own innovation: £160 000 of equipment to turn his slurry into methane, which is used to generate electricity he can sell to the national grid each night. He went ahead with this scheme partly because it would save him £22 000 a year in sewage charges. But his new methane digester is still not big enough to stop the slurry lagoon filling up.

According to the water authorities, the grants ignore some of the most important causes of pollution. There is no cash for protecting silage and slurry stores from rainwater.

On a 100-cow dairy farm, a farmer will typically have storage space for 150 000 gallons of slurry. But rainfall will increase that to anything up to 1m gallons, as Jeanes has discovered to the community's cost.

Some say that without stronger action in the courts nothing will change. 'Our policy of not prosecuting is wrong,' says Les Jolly, a pollution control officer in the northwest. 'We're all being too lenient.'

(Source: *The Sunday Times*, 5 March 1989)

CASE STUDY 7.4   *Organic farming and the*

Background

All forms of land use cause modifications to the soil. These may be immediate or gradual, slight or catastrophic, beneficial or detrimental. By far the most widespread agent of soil disturbance is agriculture: the removal or modification of the natural vegetation, often accompanied by the 'working' of the upper soil horizons. In the drive to feed and to improve the dietry intake of the world's growing populations, more land is being farmed and increasing proportions of farmland are being worked more intensively. This generalisation applies to shifting cultivators in, for example, Amazonia, where the fallow periods which 'rest' the soil are being shortened, as well as to the 'agribusiness' industry in USA, which calls on the high technology of chemicals and machinery.

Claims of increased total production and productivity (yields/hectare) cannot be denied, but from all parts of the world there is evidence that excessive demands are being made upon soil resources: fertility levels are falling and soil erosion is accelerating. For example, in the UK, the national Soil Map for England and Wales, published in 1986 by the Soil Survey, shows 44 per cent of arable soils to be at risk from erosion by wind and water (resources 7.22 and 7.23). In the USA, a 1982 report gave a similar figure for that country. The desertification of Africa's Sahel region is due in part at least to human causes.

Perhaps the most important reaction to this accumulating evidence is the growing acceptance of the merits of what is generally called 'organic farming'. A number of claims are made for organic farming. These are:

> 'Organic food preserves the fertility of the soil and maintains wildlife habitats and humane standards for livestock welfare; it also protects the environment and the natural balance of the countryside of mixed farming.

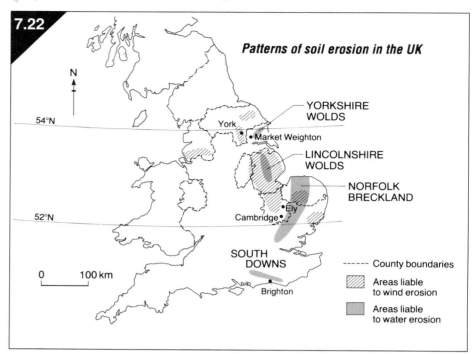

7.22

Patterns of soil erosion in the UK

N

54°N

York
• Market Weighton

52°N

Cambridge • • Ely

SOUTH
DOWNS

Brighton

0   100 km

YORKSHIRE WOLDS

LINCOLNSHIRE WOLDS

NORFOLK BRECKLAND

- - - - - County boundaries

Areas liable to wind erosion

Areas liable to water erosion

Organic food has obviously advantages for the consumer: it tends to have a higher concentration of nutrients and is largely without chemical residues ... Food writers have complained of the tasteless and watery quality of mass-produced vegetables for years; the reason is that nitrate-fed plants try to minimise the effects by taking up more water. Organic food costs more but ... when more farmers convert to organic systems, prices will fall.'

(Source: Colin Spencer, *The Guardian*, 23 July 1988)

There are signs that both in the UK and in the USA, organic farming is beginning to move from the 'green fringe' into mainstream thinking, e.g. the high sales profile given by major supermarket chains to their stocking of organically grown foods. The materials in this case study assess the situation at the beginning of the 1990s. Part I illustrates the efforts in Britain while Part II shows that a combination of market forces and scientific evidence seems to be energising an organic bandwagon (resource 7.24).

Key understandings

◆ The importance of organic matter and micro-organisms in maintaining soil fertility.

◆ Farming techniques based upon intensive inputs of chemicals are likely to reduce the level of organic matter and increase rates of erosion.

◆ Organic farming techniques can sustain soil fertility *and* be economically viable.

◆ A soil can tolerate a certain rate of annual loss because the soil formation processes can make up this loss.

◆ An organic approach to farming requires a fresh perception of the environment and of the quality of life associated with farming.

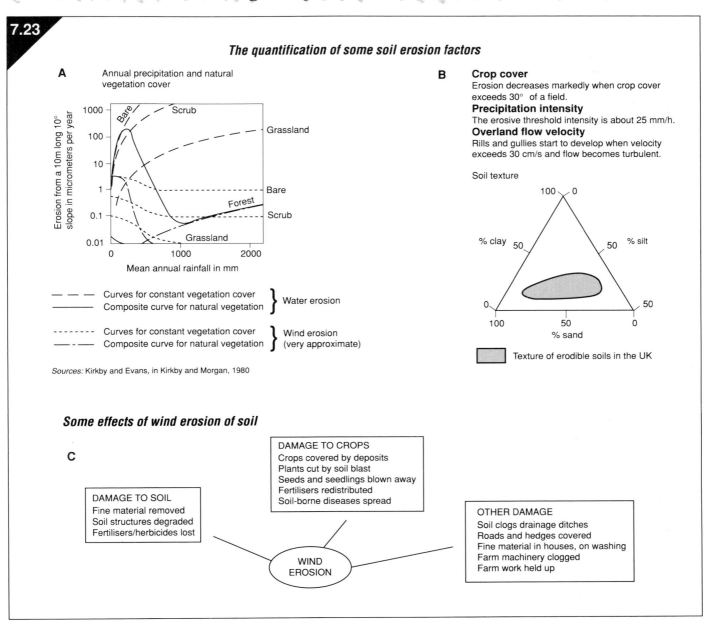

7.23

The quantification of some soil erosion factors

A Annual precipitation and natural vegetation cover

Erosion from a 10m long 10° slope in micrometers per year (y-axis)

Mean annual rainfall in mm (x-axis)

— — — Curves for constant vegetation cover
————— Composite curve for natural vegetation } Water erosion

- - - - - Curves for constant vegetation cover
— · — · Composite curve for natural vegetation } Wind erosion (very approximate)

Sources: Kirkby and Evans, in Kirkby and Morgan, 1980

B **Crop cover**
Erosion decreases markedly when crop cover exceeds 30° of a field.
Precipitation intensity
The erosive threshold intensity is about 25 mm/h.
Overland flow velocity
Rills and gullies start to develop when velocity exceeds 30 cm/s and flow becomes turbulent.

Soil texture

% clay / % silt / % sand

Texture of erodible soils in the UK

Some effects of wind erosion of soil

C

DAMAGE TO SOIL
Fine material removed
Soil structures degraded
Fertilisers/herbicides lost

DAMAGE TO CROPS
Crops covered by deposits
Plants cut by soil blast
Seeds and seedlings blown away
Fertilisers redistributed
Soil-borne diseases spread

OTHER DAMAGE
Soil clogs drainage ditches
Roads and hedges covered
Fine material in houses, on washing
Farm machinery clogged
Farm work held up

WIND EROSION

Part II, which gives examples from some of the naturally most fertile regions of USA, outlines how soils work to maintain their fertility, how maintaining fertility reduces the likelihood of erosion, and how the impact of agriculture upon this fertility-erosion equation varies significantly according to the techniques used.

Part I: Organic farming at the grassroots level – England

The following resources illustrate that there *is* a viable alternative to agribusiness. Organic farming at the scale described here, involves hard work, and a moderate income, but is clearly connected to quality of life and a deep concern for the environment (resources 7.25 and 7.26).

Activities

Read the extracts in resources 7.25 and 7.26 carefully then discuss, in a group or as a class, the economic, social and environmental benefits and costs of this approach to living and working on the land. Would you like to try and how would you go about getting started? What are likely to be the principal constraints upon organic farming becoming a component of mainstream British farming?

7.24

Americans embrace organic farming

The ecological revolution has reached the US government's farm support programme: a report from the National Academy of Sciences shows that chemical fertilisers and insecticides do not necessarily result in better crop yields than organic methods.

The report is a rousing endorsement of the high productivity of organic farming.

An agriculture department official, said the department would seek to 'put US farming on an ecosensitive basis'.

'Our goal is to develop techniques to maintain high agricultural output, without damaging the environment.' Much of the original doubt about organic farming was based on fears that it would cut farm produce and send food prices soaring.

At present, the subsidy structure actively discourages farmers from rotating their crops, because it cuts the acreage devoted to particular products on which the subsidies are calculated.

'Well-managed alternative farms use less synthetic chemicals, fertilisers, pesticides and antibiotics, without necessarily decreasing – and in some cases increasing – per-acre crop yields and the productivity of livestock systems,' the report says.

Fewer than 5 per cent of America's 2.1 million farmers use organic methods, but they are being urged to consider the potential savings in production costs – through not buying chemicals – as well as the environmental benefits.

The report, Alternative Agriculture, argues that organic methods can reduce pollution in two ways: they cut the pollution of ground water through the run-off of chemical fertilisers and avoid insecticides.

Organic farming is a misleadingly simple word for a complex process which includes crop rotation, careful soil analysis, and the planned interaction of crops and livestock.

It is likely to require greater management skills, longer working hours and more varied work from the farmers.

Those reluctant to change will find a powerful ally in the Fertiliser Institute, voice of the $8 billion-a-year industry, which condemned the report yesterday as 'an insult to American agriculture and to the consumer'.

The report had looked only at successful organic farms, not at those who had tried alternative methods and failed.

The five-year study of 14 organic farms included one farm in Ohio which has used no chemicals for 15 years and achieved corn yields 32 per cent higher than the local average and soya bean yields 40 per cent higher.

(Source: Martin Walker, *The Guardian*, 9 September 1989)

7.25

Finding new methods to farm the old way

Guy Ballard has been accustomed to the idea of nurturing the environment since childhood.

His father, who raised pigs and cattle and grew apples on a farm in Hampshire, was also an enthusiastic bird and butterfly watcher. This made him so sparing with pesticides that he won prizes for his economy in crop-spraying.

Now his son is one of a growing number who believe that specialised farming with chemical fertilisers, pesticides and herbicides, widespread in Britain since the second world war, must stop. Farming should use new techniques to adapt the traditional 'organic' methods of rotating crops, spreading muck and weeding by mechanical means, which kept the land fertile for centuries.

There are still only 1000 organic farms in Britain, accounting for less than 1 per cent of the arable land. But public demand for their products, inspired by concern over health and the environment, is increasing.

It was after discovering organic methods in America in the late 1970s that Ballard took a course at the Cirencester Agricultural College and found that the subject was scarcely mentioned. What he did know was that the land on the old farm needed to be regenerated – a task best begun by planting grass, clover and some deep-rooting crops.

The fine roots of the grass grow quite deep if left in for four years and can then be ploughed in to create an enormous amount of vegetable matter which improves the soil structure. It gives better drainage and better water-holding capacity during the dry season, and makes the soil much less liable to erosion or hardening. It also breaks down into humus and provides food for earthworms and micro-organisms, vital for long-term fertility.

Clover is used because it extracts nitrogen from the atmosphere via nodules on its roots. Deep-rooted crops such as alfalfa, chicory and rib grass bring up trace elements from the subsoil.

But fields of grass don't make money. Grazing does. Ballard chose to raise sheep – 140 ewes with lambs.

'Sheep are more difficult to farm

organically than most other animals because they are much more prone to parasites such as fly, scab and worm. In order to minimise or avoid the use of routine or chemical wormers, the sheep farmer has to be extremely good at managing grazing and moving the animals round to fresh fields.'

Conventional farmers counteract scab by using chemical dips, but these are shunned by the organic farmers. Instead, Ballard uses a compound derived from the pyrethrum plant which contains natural insecticide.

For worms he uses garlic. He finds zinc sulphate effective for foot-rot. For mastitis he uses the herbal homeopathic remedy belladonna with bryonia.

'Organic farming means avoiding antibiotics, but if they were needed to prevent suffering or death we would have no hesitation.'

Like sheep, crops are subject to pests and disease. Organic farming aims to discourage these by rotating crops among different fields. Avoidance of fertilisers also makes crops less vulnerable.

'What really causes severe disease problems in crops is excessive use of nitrogen fertilisers,' says Ballard. 'In making the plant grow well it become fleshier, more succulent, and more attractive to insects. It also makes the cell walls thinner so that they are more easily penetrated by fungus or aphids. If you keep a plant on a sensible natural amount of nitrogen it will grow tougher.'

The other main weapons that organic farmers have against weeds are mechanical devices such as the steerage hoe and the flame weeder.

The flame weeder can be used to burn off weed seedlings before the crop shoots appear. Once the rows of crops appear, the steerage hoe can be guided between them to rip out the weeds.

Cereals, cattle and mixed farming are all relatively straightforward to do organically. The more specialised the greater the problems. If a farm has no animals then the cost of the fertility building phase has to come off the profits made by selling crops. So every organic farm needs either a viable livestock unit or a niche market such as a farm shop, bakery or dairy producing yoghurt or cream.

Ballard reckons he just about breaks even selling his lamb at around £1.50 a pound, but prefers to do so at the farm gate or in Guildford market, rather than in supermarkets which cream off a hefty chunk of the profits. He would consider offers from wholesalers if the base price for lamb rose.

Organic products are still a tiny proportion of Britains annual £33 billion grocery spend. This year they will account for less than £50m – Britons spend more on pot noodles. But the Soil Association says that with the right incentives 20 per cent of the UK's 200 000 farmers could be growing crops organically within a decade.
(Source: Jane Bird, *The Sunday Times*, 26 November, 1989))

7.26

Getting down to the business

Organic growers all over Herefordshire have formed themselves into a co-operative to ease the difficulties of wheeling and dealing in the market-place. The kind of people who go in for growing vegetables in an environment-friendly way are not necessarily so hot when it comes to business: but then that is where Green Growers come in, only the fourth organic group to be formed in the country. Geoff Mutton has been chosen as co-ordinator for the growers' co-operative. Organic produce is big business and is keenly sought by the large supermarket chains. The Herefordshire vegetables are taken to a local collection point, and then to Lampeter, where Green Growers' marketing agent arranges their distribution.

Geoff Mutton has been growing his produce 'au naturelle' since 1976 and he would be the first to admit that the enterprise can be tough in the early stages. But he and his wife Pat have seen their business come through, and rise on the crest of the conservation-conscious wave. Geoff, who has a six-acre holding, has just won a prize for the best presented organic produce in an award scheme run by the Soil Association. He entered five varieties of fresh cut herbs in his own Thornbury Herbs retail packaging to win the special Food from Britain award.

Geoff sees a striking contrast between the optimistic outlook for organic growers and the current depressed climate for the rest of the agricultural and horticultural industries. A founder member of the Organic Growers Association, and a member of its management committee, Geoff has four acres sown to field-scale herb production. And when he's not busy working at all this, then he has his co-ordinating duties to do for the co-operative. But whatever the extent of his output, it obviously suits him. 'All the organic growers I know are happy people,' says Geoff. 'It's a philosophy of life that makes us want to be organic anyway. It's a caring about the environment. There are no short cuts and no large profits. You have to be of a certain disposition. I find it immensely satisfying to feel I can pass on my land and that I'm doing something to help my little patch of the environment,' he says.

The Muttons have quadrupled production of their fresh herbs at Lower House Farm and have been very busy with container-grown herbs and shrubs which have done very well indeed. At Thornbury they have two full-time employees, and up to eight part-timers during the summer months. The growing awareness of the environment, and the effect modern farming is having upon it, means that organic production is increasingly sought after by consumers. 'Most farmers would have regarded us as cranks seven years ago,' Geoff points out. 'Now they say we know it isn't right to put chemicals on the land, but what else can we do.'
(Source: Sally Boyce, *The Hereford Times*, September 1989)

Part II: A new American revolution?

Farming's organic future

Among the rolling hills of the Palouse region of eastern Washington State lie two neighbouring farms. The two have much in common: they lie on the same type of land and share the same soil; both have been worked since the early years of the century. But there is a crucial difference. One is an organic farm: it has relied on green manure crops, crop rotation and the natural fertility of the soil since first ploughed in 1909. The adjoining farm, slightly larger and cultivated a year earlier, became a 'conventional farm', nourished by fertilisers from 1948 and protected by pesticides since the early 1950s.

With the appearance of cheap fertilisers at the end of the Second World War and pesticides in the early 1950s, advanced countries quickly abandoned traditional or organic methods of farming and became heavily dependent on both agrochemicals and labour-saving machinery.

The US Department of Agriculture considers organic farming to be a system that avoids or excludes the use of synthetic fertilisers and pesticides and relies upon practices; such as crop rotation, the use of animal and green manures and some forms of biological pest control. Most organic farmers use modern machinery, recommended varieties of crops, certified seed, sound methods of livestock management, prescribed practices for conserving soil and water, and innovative methods of managing crop residues.

The 80-year-old organic farm has been managed without inorganic fertilisers and only limited use of pesticides. The farm grew winter wheat, spring pea and a green manure crop (for one or two years) in a three to four-year rotation. The conventional farm had a two-year crop rotation of winter wheat and

7.27

The Palouse terrain of eastern Washington State

spring pea, with pesticides applied to both. The organic farmer grew a green manure of either Austrian winter pea for one year (in a three-year cycle) or a mixture of alfalfa and grass for two years (in a four-year cycle). The green manure was always completely turned under in the soil. A green manure crop is usually a legume, such as alfalfa, sweet clover or Austrian winter pea; legumes enrich the soil with nitrogen compounds and with organic matter.

The study area (roughly 100 metres by 50 metres) lies on a 4-degree slope at the juncture of the two farms. The research is based on the assumption that all environmental conditions and soil properties at the site were similar until 1948. Any differences today can be attributed to the fact that after 1948 one farm was managed organically and the other conventionally.

Soil microorganisms enrich the soil as they live and die and are indispensable in their influence on crop production. They are a kind of hidden workforce that provides many key benefits. The most important of these are the breakdown of organic matter in the soil to humus and the release of nutrients held in organic combinations, which plants can then use. Microbes also help to stabilise

soil aggregates, fix nitrogen and break down some pesticides. In 1983, a survey found that the soil on the organic farm contained a much higher mass of microbes and showed much more enzyme activity than the soil on the conventional farm. Soil enzymes are derived primarily from microorganisms in the soil. These results indicated that the organic farm had larger and much more active populations of microbes in its soil.

There was almost 60 per cent more organic matter on the surface of the soil on the organic farm. These results support the findings of other researchers that organic farmers can, and generally do, achieve higher concentrations of organic matter in their soils than conventional farmers.

Organic matter has a profound impact on the quality of the soil; it encourages mineral particles to clump together to form granules, improving the structure of the soil: it increases the amount of water the soil will hold and the supply of nutrients: and the organisms in the soil are more active. On the experimental plots, the soil on the organic farm was well-granulated, the best structure for most ordinary crop plants; the other soil was not. The organically farmed soil also contained much more moisture: its cation exchange capacity (a measure of the soil's capacity to store nutrients) was greater; the total amount of nitrogen and available potassium were also much larger.

The combination of these factors gives the organically farmed soil better tilth than the soil on the conventional farm. The better the tilth, or physical condition of the soil, the easier it is to till and the easier it is for plants to germinate and push out shoots and roots.

The study area where we sampled the soil was made up of one type of soil called Naff silt loam. A typical Naff soil has two distinct layers: the dark-coloured surface layer called an 'A' horizon, has a texture of silt loam and is between 20 and 70 centimetres thick. The 'A' horizon makes up the topsoil, the richest and most easily tilled layer of the soil. The subsoil is a strong, silty clay loam 'Bt horizon' extending to a depth of up to 150 centimetres. Clay accumulates in the Bt horizon making it dense, sometimes to the extent that it cramps roots. The subsoil is less fertile than the topsoil.

The layer of crop-nourishing topsoil on the organic farm was about 16 centimetres thicker than on the conventional farm. This difference was not because of a build-up of topsoil but because the soil on the conventional farm was eroding much more quickly. Erosion not only continuously thins the topsoil, it also brings the subsoil nearer to the surface.

Water erosion was studied when both farms were growing winter wheat. The results were impressive: water erosion removed 32.4 tonnes per hectare on the conventional field, but only 8.3 tonnes per hectare on the organic field.

The scale of soil erosion is hard to grasp when described in terms of tonnes per hectare. But a little over 1 tonne of soil distributed over a hectare of land would form a layer of soil the thickness of a sheet of paper. The loss of a few tonnes of soil is the equivalent of peeling off a few pieces

of paper. Loss of 20 tonnes per hectare is almost invisible, but over the years the cumulative effect can be dramatic. Soil takes so long to form, yet it can be destroyed so quickly.

The US Department of Agriculture's Soil Conservation Service has developed a concept of 'soil loss tolerance'. The so-called 'T' value is the maximum rate of erosion that can occur without reducing the productivity of crops in the long term or the environmental quality of a specific soil. T values commonly range between 4.5 and 11.2 tonnes per hectare. The two estimates of erosion made for the conventional farm are either two or three times the maximum T value of 11.2 tonnes per hectare for Naff soils. The findings suggest that Naff soil on the organic farm will maintain its productivity in the long term whereas the soil on the conventional farm is becoming less productive as a result of erosion.

The Palouse region, covering an area of 0.7 million hectares, is a distinctive geological terrain of rolling hills and deep loess (formed from materials blown in by the winds over the past million years). It is one of the world's most productive regions for growing wheat and peas without irrigation. It is also one of the most rapidly eroding landscapes in the US because of the combination of farming practices and steeply rolling hills. Since the land was first cultivated more than a century ago, between a quarter and three-quarters of the original topsoil has disappeared from a further 60 per cent of the region's arable land.

Though the two fields in this study have the same type of soil and were probably virtually identical 40 years ago, the topsoil is now eroding more rapidly on the conventional field. At this rate, all the topsoil on typical Nafff and similar soils under conventional farming systems will be lost in another 50 to 100 years. When this happens, wheat yields from these soils could fall by one-

third or more. The organic farmers should be able to maintain the topsoil for generations to come.

Technological advances in the form of new fertilisers, pesticides, and plant varieties mask the decline in productivity as a result of erosion. Intensive farming has produced record-breaking yields year after year, but if erosion continues at its present rate, the topsoil will finally become so thin that fertilisers will fail to increase yields, and then they will begin to decline.

The average yields of winter wheat between 1982 and 1986 were 8 per cent lower on the organic farm than on the conventional farm nearby. The ability of the organic farmer to produce yields similar to neighbouring conventional farmers, even after almost 80 years of farming without fertiliser, may be attributed in part to a reduction in soil erosion.

The difference in the rate of erosion between the two farms can be credited mostly to different systems of crop rotation. The organic farmer uses a legume as a green manure, whereas the conventional farmer does not. By ploughing in a green manure, the farmer increases the amount of organic matter in the soil, which improves infiltration of the soil water and reduces runoff that washes away soil. While the green manure crop is growing, it also protects the soil from being broken up by rain.

As the organic farmer removes his land from production of either wheat or peas every third year, his overall output is smaller than the conventional farmer's by another one-third for the same amount of land. But, in the long run, it is the conventional farmer who loses – both his soil and his productivity.

(Source: John Reganold, *New Scientist*, 10 June 1989)

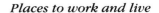

7.28

It's Ugly, but It's Working

As this year's planting season gets under way, an increasing number of growers are 'farming ugly' – gunning their tractors over fields ajumble with great clods of dirt and raggedy stalks left over from last year's harvest.

That untidiness is symbolic of a major shift in farming methods that is working its way across America's breadbasket. Reason: an emerging consensus that agriculture as it has long been practiced in the US is a threat to the land and its future productivity.

The clean swathes that farmers have plowed across the prairie are well suited to the efficient use of farm machinery. But they encourage erosion, which has allowed vast amounts of topsoil to be blown away by wind or washed into the rivers and lakes. Chemical fertilisers, insecticides and weed killers have contributed to harvests that make US agriculture the most productive in the world. Yet they have also leached into groundwater, contaminating wells in rural communities across the nation.

Nowhere are farmers more primed for change than in Iowa, proud producer of 20 per cent of the nation's corn. In 1988 and 1989, the state's natural resources department sampled groundwater quality in 686 rural wells. Nearly 15 per cent of them were contaminated with one or more pesticides. Weed biologist Jack Dekker is one of a growing corps of experts urging farmers to adopt a new approach called sustainable agriculture. But sustainable agriculture has blossomed into an effort to curb erosion by modifying plowing techniques and to protect water supplies by minimising, if not eliminating, artificial fertilisers and pest controls.

Not surprisingly, the most persuasive supporters of sustainable agriculture are those who have profited by it. Since 1981, Wilbert Blumhardt and his son Glenn have been fighting erosion on their 1200-hectare spread near Bowdle, S.Dak. by planting wheat, sunflowers, soy-beans and corn in fields littered by the debris from earlier harvests. 'That trash,' says Wilbert, 'serves an important purpose. It helps feed the soil, and it allows the water to soak in and not wash off into lakes and streams.' Last year the Blumhardts' fields produced 30 per cent more wheat than conventional farms in the area.

Besides new planting methods, farmers are experimenting with novel ways of fighting pests without resorting to chemical weapons. Joe and Dalton Maddox, a father-son team in Colorado City, Texas, once tried to eliminate mesquite (a non-edible scrub bush) on their 8900-hectare sheep and cattle ranch by dousing it with herbicides. Now they let the mesquite grow, relying on a cover of luxuriant pasture to control its spreading. 'We used to spray for cockleburs, (like sticky burrs) which were a big problem for our sheep,' says Joe Maddox. 'They would get into the wool and damage it. Then we got to thinking of what the herbicide might be doing to Lake Spence, which is a source of drinking water for a number of people.' Instead of spraying, the Maddoxes now bait cocklebur stands with salt to attract cattle. The cattle mill around the salt, crushing the cockleburs underfoot.

One of the most effective ways to reduce chemical use is also one of the simplest: crop rotation. Dick and Sharon Thomspon of Boone, Iowa, do not merely rotate corn and soybeans, as many of their neighbors do. They also include in their scheme legumes such as alfalfa and red clover, taking advantage of those plants nitrogen-fixing ability to reduce the need for fertiliser when they plant corn. To control weeds, the Thompsons rely on mechanical cultivation, restricting their use of herbicides to hand-spraying the recalcitrant thistles that grow along fencerows. Hogs and cattle round out the operation, providing a reliable source of manure that takes the place of chemical fertiliser.

Abutting the Thompson place is land farmed by neighbor Dave Synder. Like many larger growers, Snyder has judiciously reduced his use of chemicals over the years. But he finds the idea of replacing herbicides with mechanical cultivation on 730 hectares wildly impractical. Last fall the US Department of Agriculture began a study of two fields farmed by Snyder and Dick Thompson. Snyder's field produced 5 per cent more corn. But Thompson's field was riddled with soil-enriching earth-worms, while Snyder's boasted none.

Despite its benefits, sustainable agriculture is not a cure-all. Attempts to prevent soil erosion, for example, could enhance the ease with which water seeps into the soil, and might actually speed the passage of chemicals into underlying aquifers. Manure is organic, but if carelessly applied, it can pollute drinking water with nitrates as easily as artificial fertilisers do.

(Source: J Madeleine Nash, 'It's Ugly but It's Working', *Time*, May 28, 1990)

Activities

1 From resource 7.28.

 a List the main reasons why the farmers quoted are changing to organic farming.

 b What changes in farming practices are identified?

2 From part II of the case study:

 a Outline the role of micro-organisms in maintaining soil fertility.

 b Why is it important to maintain levels of organic matter in soils?

3 List the main differences between the techniques on the organic and the conventional farm.

4 How is soil fertility maintained on each farm?

5 Why is soil erosion more rapid on the conventional farm?

6 What is meant by 'soil loss tolerance', why does it vary and why could it be a useful piece of information in assisting soil conservation?

7 **Group discussion**

 Read the last paragraph of the main text again carefully, then base a discussion around these questions:

 a What is the 'message' and do you agree with it?

 b Are its suggestions practical and achievable? If so, how?

 c What is likely to happen if we do not change our approach?

CHAPTER 8

Places for play – impacts of the recreation and tourism explosion

Introduction

Leisure and tourism may be studied as a separate topic, or as an aspect of several topics. Thus, you may find the materials in this chapter useful also for combination with Chapters 2, (Making spaces for places), 5 (Industry and work), and 10 (Aspects of development), or as part of a topic on the environmental impacts of human activity. Finally, you may find a number of the ideas developed in these materials, valuable bases for individual or group projects.

Leisure has been defined in many ways, but stated generally, it embraces *activities we engage in or experiences we enjoy voluntarily, in time we perceive as being free from work demands or other obligations*.

Leisure opportunities and participation have an important influence on how we perceive our quality of life. While we must never forget that many millions of people throughout the world still lack opportunities for satisfying leisure, one of the outstanding features of the past three decades has been the world-wide leisure explosion. Based on increasing time availability, disposable income, personal mobility, interest and awareness, participation in leisure involves more people of all ages in more activities, in more places than ever before (resource 8.1)

At-home leisure grows as households acquire the widening range of electronic equipment. Outside of the home, 'opportunity fields' for recreation have been revolutionised by the spread of motor car ownership and both the public (central and local government) and private commercial sectors in many countries have responded by providing better and better facilities (resource 8.2) Increases in paid holiday entitlements as part of the job contract, linked to the coming of wide-bodied jet aircraft and package holidays, have enabled the 'pleasure periphery' of tourism to penetrate all corners of the globe (resource 8.3). All of this adds to a genuine 'leisure revolution'.

Leisure has become the world's second largest industry in terms of money generated, and from 1970 until the late 1980s was growing at between 5 per cent and 10 per cent a year, one of the fastest growth rates of any industrial sector. It is hardly surprising, then, that so many countries, companies and individuals have 'jumped on the bandwagon', and that the massive

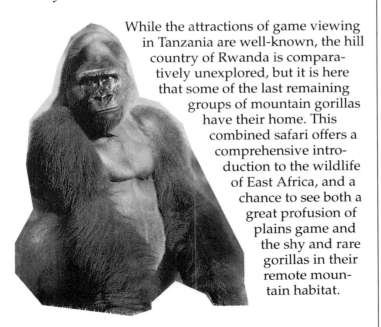

8.1

Gorilla Safari

Plains game and mountain gorillas: a safari to northern Tanzania and Rwanda

While the attractions of game viewing in Tanzania are well-known, the hill country of Rwanda is comparatively unexplored, but it is here that some of the last remaining groups of mountain gorillas have their home. This combined safari offers a comprehensive introduction to the wildlife of East Africa, and a chance to see both a great profusion of plains game and the shy and rare gorillas in their remote mountain habitat.

Domebusters

'We first opened the Domebusters to the general public on 11th February 1987, two years after work first started on the project.

As expected during the honeymoon period in the first two months, new daily attendance records were set. The old record of 2380 paying swimmers in one day, was soon broken, and attendances of over 3000 were commonplace. One crazy day in February saw 3929 paying swimmers of which 2686 rode the Domebusters.

A year on we expect around 2500 to 2800 swimmers per day in school holidays. In the 12 months to 10th February 1988 we had 501 194 swimmers (an increase on the previous year of 54 per cent) of which 297 372 people rode the Domebusters. (Making 3 166 266 descents).'

(Source: Peter Mills, *The Leisure Manager*, 6(9), September 1988, pp. 16–17)

Husky-sledging in Greenland

Our trip is based in Sisimiut, an isolated settlement in the western part of Greenland, which is much less well-known than the more accessible east coast. Here we meet up with our dog-team and guides, and get to grips with the tricky art of controlling the sleds and the dogs. The Arctic scenery here is strikingly impressive; we start with leisurely excursions over frozen lakes and small mountain passes, visiting villages that still live by fishing and by seal and polar bear hunting. A longer journey takes us further afield towards the glaciers, where there are magnificent panoramic views of the mountains and icefields, and we spend a night in the magnificent setting of the Arctic wilderness before returning to Sisimiut and home again via Iceland.
(Source: *Exodus*, 1990)

environmental demands and impacts of the leisure revolution are today becoming a major issue.

When studying leisure activities, we need to ask a set of fundamental questions.

- How much **time** do I need?
- How much **space** does it take and what type of space?
- What **facilities** are needed?
- What **equipment** and **skill** do I need, and can I afford it?
- Why would I do it and what **satisfactions** do I expect to get?
- **Who provides** the opportunities for the leisure activities and who **owns** the resources?
- Are the leisure activities **accessible** to me, and what do I mean by 'accessible'?
- What **environmental impact** do the leisure activities make, and how do they affect other people who live in the area?

It is clear that leisure varies enormously in the time, location, space and resources it demands, the impacts it makes, and who provides and has access to it.

Furthermore although leisure is all about 'freedom' and 'choice', it does need to be organised. In economic terms, we create a demand which is met by a range of suppliers. The nature of this supply depends upon our motivation and needs (why we go and what satisfactions we expect). Case study 8.1 illustrates the demand-supply relationship through the management of a US National Park to provide for 'the wilderness experience'. Case study 8.2 develops this theme by examining the competition for space and resources between different users, and the responses by the 'suppliers' or managers of the leisure opportunities in National Parks. Case studies 8.3, and 8.4 focus on world tourism, particularly the 'sun, sea, sand and sex' type of beach-based holidays.

All over the world, countries seeking economic growth have welcomed the rapidly expanding tourism market as a way of earning foreign currency, creating local employment and income and generating regional development. In recent years however, it has become increasingly clear that there are social and environmental costs to be set alongside the economic benefits. Furthermore, countries from Spain to the Seychelles are becoming acutely aware that tourism is a 'fashion' industry, where new places and new types of experience rapidly overtake earlier models. The nightmare of any tourism-based village, town, region or country is that the tourists will stop coming and go somewhere else! (Resource 8.4).

8.4

Holiday companies hide menace of foreign crime

The first day of his Florida holiday left David Creasey with a memory that will last a lifetime: two youths held him against a wall while a third shot him.

He had just returned to his hotel from a trip to Seaworld, Orlando, with his wife Marian and was about to unlock the door of his room. His attackers were lurking in the corridor.

'My wallet fell from my hand when the three jumped me but they shot me at point-blank range anyway. It was hellishly painful,' said Creasey, 49, a company director. The bullet passed through his left arm, and he is recovering at his home in Newark-on-Trent, Nottinghamshire.

The glossy holiday brochures had given him no warning of the level of security needed to protect himself from attack. Nor did his hotel provide it.

Creasey is one of thousands of British victims of holiday muggings and theft who are never aware of the true risks in their chosen resort until it is too late.

People staying in plush hotels in Third World countries do not appreciate the problems caused by the poverty around them. They are surprised when they are confronted with it. Many holiday companies gloss over the problems. For example, the Horizon brochure says of The Gambia: 'Little children will make lifelong friends with you for a cheap Biro or a packet of sweets from England.' It fails to mention that security guards are posted at the hotel, police patrol the beach and that it is dangerous to walk outside at night because there is no street lighting. New arrivals learn the facts in a two-hour briefing.

The Gambian tourist board insists that Banjul belly, a stomach complaint named after the country's capital, is a greater hazard than theft. Last year's police figures show that only 16 of the 112 000 tourists were attacked or had property stolen. Sally Cairns, communications manager for Horizon, said: 'I think most people are sophisticated enough to know what Africa is all about. I do not believe The Gambia is any more dangerous than any European capital.'

Theft, crowded beaches, pollution and poor service have led to thousands of holidaymakers rejecting Spain this year in favour of more sophisticated destinations, or staying at home. This summer British package holiday bookings for Majorca have fallen 40 per cent, the worst downturn in the history of the island's tourist industry.

East Germans are now being wooed as a new generation of package tourists to fill the gap left by the British. More than 10 000 will be given free holidays in Majorca over the next two years, courtesy of the Balearic Islands tourist board.

One of the first is Paul Ignatzi, a retired East German steel-worker, who with his wife Magdalena enjoyed his first holiday abroad last week. 'I'm so surprised how nice the people are and how clean and tidy the place is,' he said.

(Source: Richard Caseby and Edward Welsh, *The Sunday Times*, 27 May 1990)

Background

Leisure activities vary in the space and facilities they require, and in the numbers who can take part at one time and feel satisfied. Whether or not you enjoy a leisure experience depends upon a complex set of factors. Your level of satisfaction may be determined by the relationship between why you went (your motives), hence your expectations, and what actually happened when you were there. Ask yourself why you want to take part and what you hope to get from the activity and responses like the following may come to mind: meeting people, fitness, relaxation, excitement, solitude, privacy, improving or learning new skills, to 'get away from it all', to have fun, to feel good, and so on. Clearly the character and quality of the space and facilities you use are important in the satisfaction you get, but there is another crucial variable – how many other people are there at the same time. For instance, a poorly-attended open-air rock concert may be a bore, but a crowded picnic site may be irritating.

Two central concepts in this aspect of leisure analysis are **density** and **crowding**. Density is a measure of the number of people present at a recreational site at a given moment, and is easily quantified, e.g. 500 people on a beach 1 sq. km in size gives a density of 500 persons/sq. km. Crowding is an indicator of the perceptions of the people present, i.e. whether they *feel* crowded, and is thus a qualitative and less easily measurable concept. Density and crowding are related by (a) the type of leisure activity and (b) the reasons people came. Thus, apart from the music, you may go to an open-air rock concert for motives such as excitement and to meet people, whereas you might go on a picnic to relax. As a result, for many people, densities at a rock concert can be much higher than on a picnic site before most participants begin to feel 'crowded'.

The complexity of the relationship is illustrated by considering the same activity, using the same resource – spending a day at the beach (resource 8.5). Depending on who you are and why you came, the number of people present before you begin to feel crowded, varies greatly. Once you do begin to feel crowded, then your level of satisfaction, i.e. having your expectations met, starts to fall. In consequence, one of the factors you take into account when choosing a place to go and what to do, is how many others are likely to be there.

This introduces a third central concept, that of **recreation carrying capacity**, which itself has three components: physical, ecological and perceptual capacity. Physical capacity is how many people are physically able to participate at a site, e.g. the number of picnic tables. Ecological capacity is the amount of usage a site can withstand before the environment begins to deteriorate, e.g. footpath erosion. Perceptual capacity refers to the numbers which can be present on a site, i.e. the density, before individuals begin to feel 'crowded'.

Providers and managers of leisure resources and facilities have an increasing understanding of the density-crowding relationships of different activities and different people. Their management planning – how they design and organise leisure space with varying carrying capacities, reflects this understanding. This case study illustrates planned recreational opportunities, for the 'wilderness experience' with a designed carrying capacity which aims to facilitate a high quality leisure experience for a certain range of interests and motivations.

Key understandings

- Leisure competes for space with other resource uses, and hence needs planning.

- Leisure activities vary in their space, resource and facility demands.

- How leisure space is organised and managed influences, and is influenced by, the character of leisure activity and experience involved.

- Recreation carrying capacity, density and crowding are essential elements in explaining leisure behaviour and leisure management.

8.5

Enjoying the beach at Carmel, California. Though there are a large number of people, the beach doesn't seem crowded

Protecting the wilderness in a crowded world – the Yosemite approach

By 'wilderness' we mean wild and natural places, free from the impacts of human settlement and development. Such environments are valued by growing numbers of people, seeking the 'wilderness experience', e.g. backpacking, climbing, canoeing, independent camping, and also a number of psychological needs: solitude, privacy, independence, challenge, communion with nature, space, beauty and self-fulfilment (resource 8.6). Environments which can satisfy these needs usually have high conservation value too, and are frequently given protected status, e.g. Conservation Reserves and Wilderness Areas within National Parks. Thus, in our increasingly crowded world, this brings management for conservation and wilderness recreation very close together (resource 8.8).

Management strategy must be based upon low carrying capacity. If conservation objectives are to be achieved, human impacts must remain minimal, and equally, recreationists seeking the wilderness

8.6

Glacier Point in Yosemite National Park

experience are sensitive to crowding and will tolerate only low density use. Studies in North American wilderness areas show that while few users travel alone, most groups contain two to four people. If they encounter more than one other group during the day, and are aware of more than a couple of others when camping at night, then they begin to perceive the area as 'crowded'. Furthermore, the most desired characteristic of an environment is its 'naturalness', which is why places where conservation values are given high priority are so attractive.

As the competition for space and resources intensifies, so it becomes more difficult to obtain large blocks of suitable land, to give them protected status and to control their usage at very low densities. In North America it is at present easy to manage the great Parks and Reserves of Alaska for wilderness values for the following reasons: first, the federal government owns vast tracts, and second because of their remoteness and inaccessibility. In California the problem is much greater. Approximately 15 million people, many of them affluent and mobile, live within a half-day drive of Yosemite National Park (resource 8.7). Seventy-five per cent of the visits are made by California residents.

Yosemite is one of America's oldest and most popular National Parks, attracting approximately 2.5 million visitors a year. Although it covers a huge area (309 000 hectares), the bulk of the pressure focuses upon the 'honeypot' of the Yosemite Valley, a spectacular glacial trough. Approximately 90 per cent of the Park is designated as 'wilderness'. This designation means that the area will be managed with the following objectives:

'Natural systems and processes will be permitted to follow their courses with minimum intrusion by man. Visitor numbers will be limited to levels which do not significantly impact natural

environments. Uses relate to recreation under natural conditions, requiring self-sufficiency where development is virtually absent and conditions for solitude prevail.

(Yosemite National Park *Management Plan*, 1980)

By the early 1970s the Park managers were aware that increasing numbers were using the wilderness, or 'backcountry'. Field surveys during the summer of 1972 found trampled vegetation in the most popular areas, eroded and multiple trails throughout the backcountry, and up to 200 people camped at some of the mountain lakes at weekends. As a result, an entry permit system was introduced. An individual or group was required to purchase an entrance permit from the Ranger Service and to indicate their intended route. From this information, from 1973, the Wilderness Area was divided into a series of travel zones, each with its own carrying capacity. The capacity was based on the site of the zone, the length of trails it contained, and its ecological fragility.

'The acres and miles of trails were multiplied by desired campsite and trail usage densities to determine the maximum number of people to be permitted in each zone at one time, i.e. its 'at-one-time' capacity. These values were then adjusted downward by an assessment of the ecological carrying capacity. Zones with fragile, rare or vulnerable ecosystems, without a good potential for recovery, had capacities reduced. Zones with ecosystems that were common and easily repaired were given higher capacities'.

(Source: Wagtendonk, *Leisure Sciences* 4(3), 1981, p. 312)

This method produced a backcountry capacity of 4200 people at one time. Once a travel zone had reached its capacity, no additional use permits were issued and parties were rerouted to other zones. By

CASE STUDY 8.1   *Organising space for recreation*

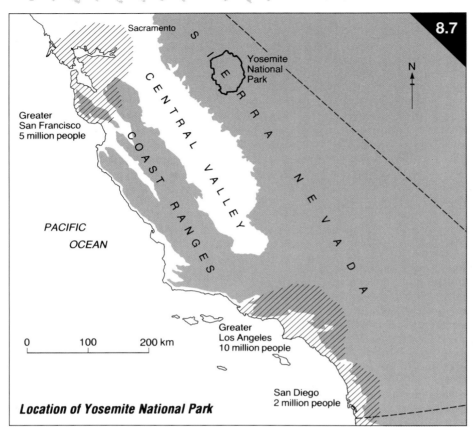

8.7

Location of Yosemite National Park

experience. It requires a delicate balance, for wilderness users need to feel free and independent, yet here they are, being controlled and managed! A further problem for the managers is the uneven spread of usage over time and space. Because of heavy snowfalls, winter use is restricted to low density cross-country skiing and snowshowing. (No developed ski facilities are

8.9

Bear scavenging in a trash can. Managing the 'wilderness experience' involves managing people, animals and places

1977, monitoring of how people were using the wilderness allowed the Ranger Service to introduce the 'trailhead quota' system of capacity management. A trailhead is the entry point to the Wilderness Area, e.g. a campsite, car park or other accessible point (resource 8.10). There are 103 trailheads giving access to the Yosemite backcountry (resource 8.13). The quota for a trailhead was worked out 'from data from wilderness permits that related travel zone use to trailhead use. The quotas for trailheads that contributed significantly to the zone's use were then adjusted up or down depending on whether the zone was being under- or over-utilised according to its given capacity'. The trailhead system adopted allows a maximum of 1485 per people per day to enter the backcountry if all the trailhead quotas are filled.

The purpose of this management system of carrying capacity controlled by permits, trailhead

quotas and travel zones is to control the numbers and distribution of backcountry users while preserving the qualities of the wilderness

8.8

US National Parks: visitor numbers

No of visitors	Forecasts
1980 : 220 million	2000 : 350–375 million
1981 : 239 million	2010 : 450–500 million
1982 : 245 million	2020 : 575–675 million
1983 : 244 million	
1984 : 249 million	
1985 : 263 million	
1986 : 281 million	
1987 : 292 million	
1990 : 317 million	

Park usage	1980	1990
Total visits	300 million	365 million
Overnight stops	16.5 million	16.3 million
Visits in hours	1134 million	1388 million
Visits – days	95 million	116 million

8.10

The Yosemite model of wilderness management

Wilderness area boundary

Travel zone A

Paths

Each trail has its permit quota

Carrying capacity of each travel zone is controlled by permit and trailhead quotas

Travel zone B has a common and resilient ecosystem so has a relatively high quota

Travel zone B

Travel zone C

50% of users are likely to be within a day's walk of the trailhead (shaded area)

Travel zone C is ecologically precious and fragile, therefore quota is kept very low

TH

Trails to wilderness

Ranger HQ

Road

Permits issued

Campsite; off-road vehicle parking

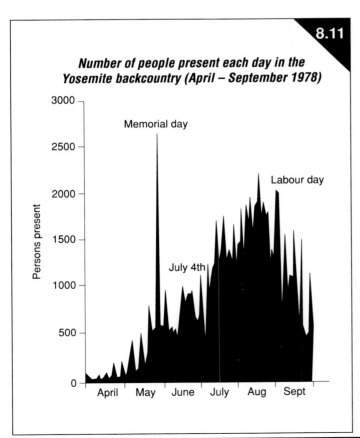

8.11

Number of people present each day in the Yosemite backcountry (April – September 1978)

Memorial day

Labour day

July 4th

Persons present

3000
2500
2000
1500
1000
500
0

April | May | June | July | Aug | Sept

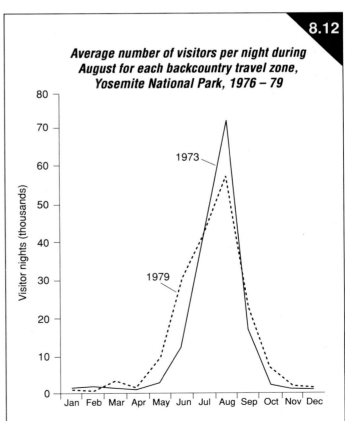

8.12

Average number of visitors per night during August for each backcountry travel zone, Yosemite National Park, 1976 – 79

Visitor nights (thousands)

1973

1979

80
70
60
50
40
30
20
10
0

Jan Feb Mar Apr May Jun Jul Aug Sep Oct Nov Dec

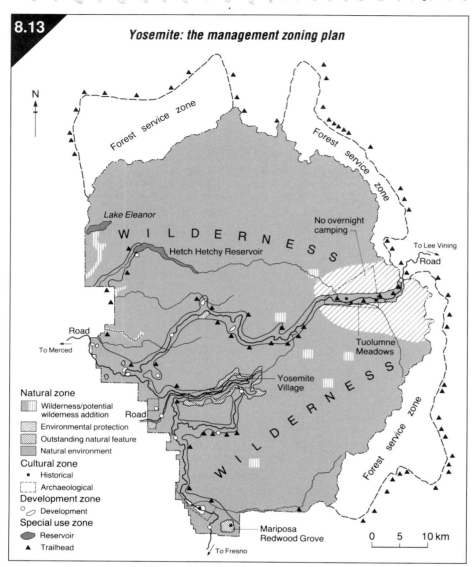

8.13

Yosemite: the management zoning plan

N

Forest service zone

Forest service zone

Lake Eleanor

W I L D E R N E S S

Hetch Hetchy Reservoir

No overnight camping

To Lee Vining
Road

Road
To Merced

Tuolumne Meadows

Yosemite Village

W I L D E R N E S S

Road

Forest service zone

W I L D E R N E S S

Natural zone

Wilderness/potential wilderness addition

Environmental protection

Outstanding natural feature

Natural environment

Cultural zone

▪ Historical

Archaeological

Development zone

○ Development

Special use zone

Reservoir

▲ Trailhead

Mariposa Redwood Grove

0   5   10 km

To Fresno

permitted within the National Park). Thus, use is concentrated into the May–September period, with severe peaking at weekends (resource 8.11). Yet the policy does appear to be spreading the load across the season more evenly (resource 8.12). Persuading the users to spread out more evenly is an equally difficult problem, for 60 per cent of all backcountry use is through only four trailheads (resource 8.14) and over 50 per cent of the use is within eight of 108 travel zones. Thus, during the summer, a small number of trailheads and travel zones consistently have their full quota, while other areas remain under-used. Again there is a dilemma for the managers: to increase the use of the under-used areas they must make them more accessible, yet by doing so they may threaten the wilderness values by putting in roads, trails and campsites.

Activities

1   Use the Yosemite case study to illustrate the importance of the 'density' and 'crowding' concepts in determining the carrying capacity for an environment.

2   **Group discussion**: Great Britain has no designated 'Wilderness Areas'. Which area would you propose for designation, and why?

8.14

Percentage use of the four most heavily used trailheads in the Yosemite backcountry in 1973 and in 1979.

Trailhead	Year	
	1973	1979
Tuolumne Meadows	36.8	32.1
Happy Isles	19.7	16.9
Cathedral Lakes	7.0	6.9
Hetch Hetchy	4.4	4.0
Total	67.9	59.9
All Others	32.1	40.1

CASE STUDY 8.2 *Playing space invaders – an example from the Lake District*

Background

The British countryside is one of the most valuable and popular resources we have for recreation, sport and tourism. The 1984 Countryside Commission 'Countryside Recreation Survey' found that on a typical summer weekend, up to 18 million leisure trips were made into the countryside (resource 8.15(a)). The great variety of activities engaged in, means that demands are made on a wide range of resources, both natural and human-made (resource 8.15(b)). These demands can place stress upon an environment, and nowhere are the pressures felt more intensely than in the eleven National Parks.

One of the most popular, the Lake District National Park, attracts over 14 million visitors a year, and offers opportunities for a whole range of activities and experiences. This diversity makes demands upon many types of resources and facilities, each form of activity imposing its distinctive impact. However, both the activities and the impacts are unevenly distributed. Localities which prove attractive to large numbers of people are known as 'honeypots'. In such places, competition for space and the use of resources is particularly acute, especially where sites are limited in size and contrasting activities are involved. The best-known Lake District honeypot is along the north-east stretch of Lake Windermere, between Bowness and Ambleside, where users of the lake surface 'compete' with people who come to stroll or picnic near the water, shop, and park their cars.

This case study focuses upon the smaller but intense conflict which has emerged along the eastern side of Derwent Water, south of Keswick, between the Kettlewell car park (GR 267195) and Shepherds Crag climbing face (GR 263185) (resource 8.16). In addition to illustrating the competition and conflicts typical of a restricted-site honeypot, the materials explore the concepts of carrying capacity, accessibility and compatibility. They also suggest techniques for carrying out a site assessment and include a resource management exercise.

Key understandings

- Locations especially attractive to recreationists are known as 'honeypots'.

- Competition for space and resources increases with the attractiveness of a location.

- Land ownership and physical site characteristics combine to create difficult management problems.

- Different recreation activities require different resources and facilities.

- Management policies should be based upon careful site and resource analysis.

The Kettlewell car park issue

Borrowdale is a broad U-shaped glacial trough whose floor in its lower, northern section is covered by the beautiful lake, Derwent Water. The narrow B5289 road runs the length of Borrowdale, squeezed between the lake and the fells. Running south from Keswick, it is intensively used by local and visitor

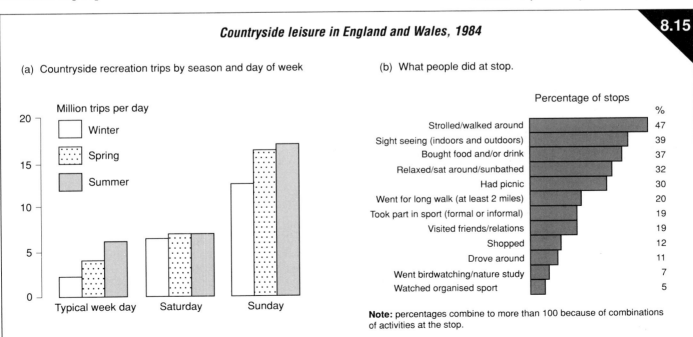

Countryside leisure in England and Wales, 1984 8.15

(a) Countryside recreation trips by season and day of week

Million trips per day
- □ Winter
- ▨ Spring
- ▨ Summer

(b) What people did at stop.

Percentage of stops

	%
Strolled/walked around	47
Sight seeing (indoors and outdoors)	39
Bought food and/or drink	37
Relaxed/sat around/sunbathed	32
Had picnic	30
Went for long walk (at least 2 miles)	20
Took part in sport (formal or informal)	19
Visited friends/relations	19
Shopped	12
Drove around	11
Went birdwatching/nature study	7
Watched organised sport	5

Note: percentages combine to more than 100 because of combinations of activities at the stop.

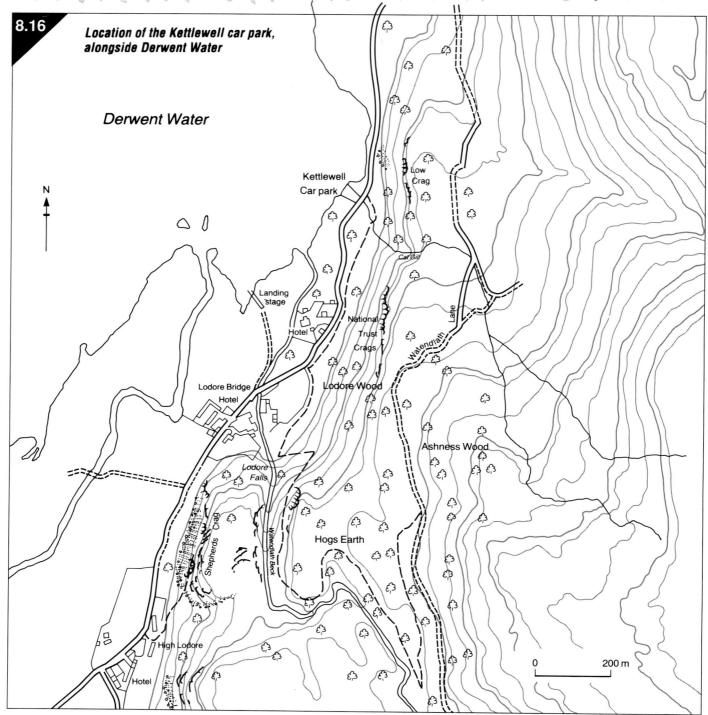

8.16 *Location of the Kettlewell car park, alongside Derwent Water*

traffic. It is the artery which connects the various scenic and recreational attractions of this part of the Lake District.

The pressures become particularly intense where (a) the road is tightly constricted by physical and land ownership factors, and (b) a range of attractive resources are clustered. One such site lies at the south-east corner of Derwent Water (resource 8.17).

1 The Kettlewell car park is one of the few lake-front and lake-surface public access points with boat-launching facilities.

2 Some of the precious natural deciduous woodlands clad the steep fellside and are accessible to the public.

3 The Lodore Cascade is one of the finest and most easily accessible waterfalls in the Lake District.

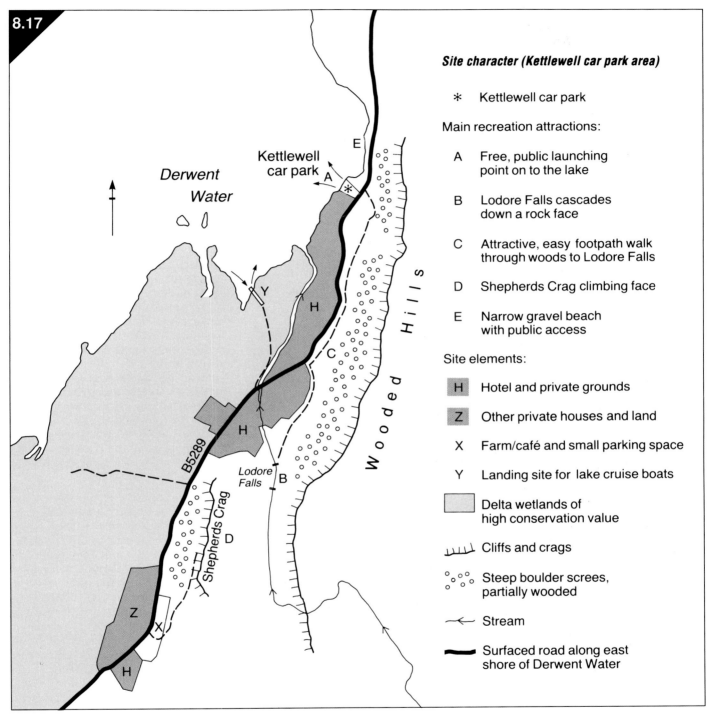

8.17

Derwent
Water

Kettlewell
car park

Site character (Kettlewell car park area)

✳ Kettlewell car park

Main recreation attractions:

A Free, public launching
point on to the lake

B Lodore Falls cascades
down a rock face

C Attractive, easy footpath walk
through woods to Lodore Falls

D Shepherds Crag climbing face

E Narrow gravel beach
with public access

Site elements:

H Hotel and private grounds

Z Other private houses and land

X Farm/café and small parking space

Y Landing site for lake cruise boats

Delta wetlands of
high conservation value

Cliffs and crags

Steep boulder screes,
partially wooded

Stream

Surfaced road along east
shore of Derwent Water

Wooded Hills

B5289

Lodore
Falls

Shepherds Crag

4 Shepherds Crag is a popular
climbing site.
5 The post-glacial delta which is
slowly infilling the southern end
of Derwent Water has created an
ecologically rich expanse of
wetland.

Public parking is permitted only at
Kettlewell and there is no roadside
footpath. There is recurrent tension
between various interest groups over
use of the car park, between vehicles
wishing to stop at the site and traffic
which is passing through and
between vehicles and pedestrians.

Site assessment

As almost all visitors arrive by motor
vehicle, the key issue is parking. The
National Park provided the car park
and launching point at Kettlewell (A)
with a capacity of approximately 30
vehicles (resource 8.18), primarily
for people wishing to use the lake

8.18

Kettlewell car park. View to the lake and boat launching beach from the road. Note the constricted entrance and space and the tree screen

8.19

Kettlewell car park. Boat launching beach. Note the cramped space and different uses – canoeists and picnickers

bird watchers who explore the delta wetlands, or serious walkers who use the footpath network across the fells.

It is clear, therefore, that during the summer half of the year at least, the capacity of the Kettlewell car park is inadequate to meet the demand, and there are pressures upon the National Park managers to provide more parking spaces. Before we consider the problems and the options, we need to appreciate the function of the car park. As almost all the visitors arrive in a vehicle of some kind, the Kettlewell car park acts as a vital control upon the numbers using the several attractions. Thus, one alternative is *not* to increase the car park capacity and so protect the environment from over-use and visitors from feelings of crowding. Already, there is considerable vegetation loss and erosion around the base of the Lodore Falls, and at times there are queues for the climbing routes on Shepherds Crag. Furthermore, increasing the parking capacity would mean more pedestrians crossing or using the narrow, winding road which is for the most part lined by walls.

The parking problem stems not only from the size of the car park but also from the different types of use. The 'at-one-time' capacity at Kettlewell is approximately 30 cars, but climbing groups may arrive in mini-buses and water-sport enthusiasts often tow trailers. Such vehicles considerably reduce the 'at-one-time' capacity. A second important aspect of capacity is the 'throughput' capacity, i.e. how many vehicles can use the car park in a given time, such as a day. For instance, the water-sports and climbing vehicles take up space for long periods. If such users dominate, the car park has a low throughput capacity. Beach-users and picnickers tend to stay for less than two hours, visitors to Lodore Falls stay perhaps an hour, while the 'stop-and-snap' visitors linger for perhaps 15 minutes. The shorter the stay, the greater the throughput capacity of

for canoes, sailboards and dinghies (resource 8.19). However, rock climbing has long been popular at Shepherds Crag, for which the only parking has been at the farm/cafe at X, where the owners allow a few vehicles to pull in. As a result, climbers now leave their vehicles at Kettlewell. A third group of visitors who have welcomed the Kettlewell car park are those who want to take the gentle stroll through the woods (C) to enjoy the Lodore Falls (B) without having to pay the fee

charged by the Swiss Lodore Hotel. A fourth group relax and picnic along the narrow stretch of gravel beach (E) and so leave their cars at Kettlewell. A fifth group use the car park as a pull-in from which to gaze over the lake, perhaps having a snack, before moving on. (Even coach tours use the car park as a 'photo opportunity' for the lake, spilling up to 50 tourists on to the car park for a few minutes!) In addition, there are smaller numbers of 'special interest' visitors such as the car park, i.e. the more vehicles and hence visitors who can enjoy the site in a day. One answer, therefore, might be to segregate visitor types by providing 'short-stay' and 'long-stay' parking areas, and to operate progressive pricing structures. (At present (mid-1991) parking is free.)

If the decision is to attempt to increase parking capacity, then we must search for locations. As resource 8.17 shows, the locality imposes severe physical limitations, with only a narrow strip of flat land between the lake and the steep, rocky crags of the trough wall. Equally important is the environmental quality of the area and the visual impact made by car park surfaces and parked vehicles. The current car park is small and carefully screened within trees. Enlargement could make it more visually intrusive. This would be particularly so if car parking was developed on part of the one extensive flat area, the open, delta wetlands. It would be possible to provide well-screened parking spaces in the woods on the opposite side of the road to the present car park. This would be convenient for access to Lodore Falls but would require removal of some of the deciduous woodland and increase traffic hazards along this winding stretch of the road.

Land ownership imposes equally strong constraints upon extending car parking and footpath capacities. The quality hotels (H) and other private owners (Z) are reluctant to lose some of their woodland and mature landscaped grounds for something from which they gain no benefit. The National Trust, which owns the woods leading to the Lodore Falls (C), gives priority to the conservation values rather than further development. It is already concerned about the environmental impact of visitors around the falls. One possibility is to support the farm/cafe (X) to extend the parking alongside the buildings. However, this is a rocky site, a working farm and a difficult entrance to the road.

If some extra capacity could be achieved here it would cater conveniently for the climbers and perhaps remove their long-stay vehicles from the Kettlewell car park.

Activities

Fieldwork and decision-making exercise (individual or group)

Selecting hypotheses

Although the Kettlewell issue contains a typical set of factors and variables, sites very widely and so we must be cautious about making generalised statements. Yet hypotheses upon which to base your study may be constructed out of the following: the greater the usage of the resources at a particular site, the more intense is likely to be the competition for their use, the more likely is conflict between different user groups, the more serious the impact upon the attractive resources, and the more complex will be the decision-making process to resolve the issue.

Procedures

How you carry out the investigation will depend upon:

    a how much time you have,

    b how many of you are undertaking the project,

    c the purpose of the exercise,

    d how much experience you have, and

    e the nature of the issue or problem.

Therefore the following are guidelines only, and may be adapted to suit your needs.

1   Familiarise yourself with the site and identify the key issues upon which you can construct your hypothesis, or set out the problem to be solved.

2   Produce the following field maps for the chosen site:

    a land use (use an established classification or devise an appropriate one),

    b land character (devise a classification based on resource 8.17),

    c key attractive resources and facilities for recreation.

3   On a base map, plot the distribution of ecological impacts. Devise your own scale – from 'none' to 'extreme', for example.

4   On a base map, plot the distribution of conflict levels – between recreation and other users and between different recreationists.

5   On a base map, plot the distribution and character of existing management inputs, e.g. toilets, information boards, car parks, fences, signposts, footpaths etc. Devise your own symbol system.

6   Analyse site usage. Collect information on variables such as numbers, length of stay, activities engaged in, mode of transport, resources and facilities used, distribution around the site, (e.g. plot 'at-a-moment-in-time' distributions at, say, five minute intervals over a selected period), those who stay on the site and those who use the site as a base for activities at a distance, reasons for coming and expectations from the visit, perceptions of satisfaction, crowding, conflict etc.

7   Identify the most urgent priorities for your site.

8   Use your field data to explore your selected hypotheses or to suggest solutions to the problems. (You may find that information on your site is available from the site owners, managers, interest groups, for example, which may be valuable in enriching your own field information.)

CASE STUDY 8.3   *Impacts of tourism development –*

Background

As the tidal wave of tourism has surged across the world, more and more countries, regions and communities have come to realise that the packaging and marketing of sun, sea and sand does not necessarily bring lasting wealth or happiness. There are economic, social and environmental costs as well as benefits to the host communities. Such impacts are felt especially strongly where tourism is superimposed upon a traditional rural society.

Tourists are notoriously fashion-conscious, choosing holiday destinations which are perceived as the 'in' places to visit, e.g. Nice and Monte Carlo in the 1920s and 1930s, Spain in the 1950s, the Caribbean in the 1960s, parts of Africa in the 1970s, the Pacific Islands in the 1980s. Elites and trend-setters 'discover' a place, whose image is then marketed by the tourism industry, attracting progressively more tourists, often triggering the process summarised by the model in resource 8.20. As this process gains momentum, so the impacts at the destination become stronger. Where

the tourist development is in an unpopulated area, the impacts may be primarily environmental. This is called 'enclave tourism'. More commonly however, locations attractive to tourists have already proved attractive for settlement. Indeed part of the attraction for the tourists are exotic cultures. However, a labour force is required for the development and running of the resort facilities, and local populations may simply be displaced as international tourism development companies settle contracts with governments for their lands, e.g. Turkey. More frequently, the tourism grows organically within the existing settlement system, with varying degrees of control by the local inhabitants, i.e. 'penetrative tourism'. Inevitably, however, a critical threshold is reached, when the tourism comes to dominate and the local economy, society and culture are rapidly distorted and even wiped out.

Small scale societies are particularly vulnerable to being overwhelmed by the tourism process. This case study, from the island of Bali, details how the progressive process of the tourism model of resource 8.20

transforms the morphology and function of a village, and is capable of causing environmental deterioration in a remarkably short period of time.

Bali is a classic example of the explosion of tourism into an island society, yet it is often quoted as an illustration of where cultural strength has been able to resist and absorb tourism without becoming degraded. Perhaps the primary tourist attraction of Bali has been not its sun-sea-sand resource but the beauty of its traditional dances and spectacular ceremonies (resource 8.21). Evidence does suggest that the dances have retained much genuine cultural meaning and that the tourists have to adjust to the patterns of the culture rather than vice versa. Yet this case study shows another side to tourism – the inevitable erosion of cultural values as tourism grows.

8.20

A model of tourism progression

Type	Numbers	Impact	Who, me?
Explorer	Very few	Accepts local conditions	David Bellamy
Offbeat	Small numbers	Revels in local conditions	'Across the Sahara by bus'
Elite	Limited numbers	Demands Western amenities	The international Hilton' set
Early mass tourism	Steady flow of numbers	Looks for Western amenities	Professional middle classes
Mass package	Massive arrivals	Expects Western amenities	Everybody and their mothers!

Increasing impact →

NB This model can be applied to an individual location through time, or to classify different places at a given moment in time.

Bali Panorama   8.21

Day 6 Tue to Day 10 Sat Bali
Five heavenly days of swimming, sunbathing, and enjoying the tranquil peace and beauty of this enchanting island and her charming people.

Key understandings

◆ In a specific location, the process of tourism development passes through a series of identifiable phases.

◆ Penetrative tourism progressively transforms existing settlements, societies and environments.

◆ The coming of tourism to a community fundamentally alters the economic basis of local life.

◆ Benefits and costs associated with the growth of tourism are unevenly distributed.

Tourism comes to a Balinese village

Kuta, on the Indonesian island of Bali, was a small, traditional agricultural and fishing village in 1970. By 1984 the village had been transformed into one of the most important tourism centres on the island. Located 2 km north of the international airport, Kuta is situated adjacent to the Indian Ocean on the narrow isthmus separating the arid Bukit peninsula from the rest of Bali (resource 8.22). The village covers 12.93 sq. km and encompasses two traditional villages, Legian and Seminyak. The whole area is subdivided into twelve traditional neighbourhoods (banjar) that are territorial, social, and cultural units.

Before the onset of tourism development, Kuta had a population of 9000. The cultural landscape of the village shared features common to most Balinese villages. The core of the village was at its centre, in the area defined by the crossroads of two main streets, Jalan Pantai and Legian-Buni Sari (resource 8.23). A banyan tree housing a shrine grew in the middle of the crossroads. In the premotorised-traffic era, the area around and under the banyan tree was the site of a periodic market and was used as a backdrop for dramas and dances. Additionally this area contained the village temple, which

is the most important public place in the village. To the east of the centre were the permanent covered market that served the entire district as well as various administrative offices. Surrounding the main intersection were most of the meetinghouses for the village, which were significant social, political, and religious foci for their respective neighbourhoods. Lying south of the residential zone were the death temple and graveyards. To the north were Legian and Seminyak, rural areas with no important public structures except the neighborhood meetinghouses.

Throughout Bali, the typical dwelling is a compound, sheltering a family or more likely an extended family, on an enclosed square or oblong plot of land. The compound is surrounded by a wall or fence four to five feet high with a single, gated entrance composed of two pillars supporting a roof that faces a street or alley. Inside a compound, pavilions are placed around a yard of hardened earth, and most of them contain areas for rice threshing, pig raising, and gardening. In Kuta the main residential zone consisted of a solid core of family compounds surrounding the principal intersection and extending to the alleys that connected the two

east–west roads. In 1970 this zone was exclusively residential; the walls enclosing each compound formed a continuous barrier along the main roads. Furthermore, the road-facing walls painted rose, blue, or white and the elaborately carved gates added to a distinctive character for Kuta as a village. Surrounding the core were other compounds located along streets in front of fields; additional compounds were scattered along the dirt paths that crisscross the many open fields in and around Kuta. A dominant feature of the landscape, these fields with dry, scrubby undergrowth, dotted with palm trees, were used for dry farming.

In 1970 most residents of Kuta derived their income from farming and fishing. Agriculture consisted of dry-crop farming, mainly of coconuts, groundnuts, soybeans, and cassava; cattle grazing on the surrounding fields; and pig raising in family compounds. The land in Kuta was unirrigated and productivity was low; furthermore, income from fishing was irregular until the establishment of a fish-processing plant in a neighboring village and the introduction of outboard motors in 1976. Hence the majority of villagers were poor.

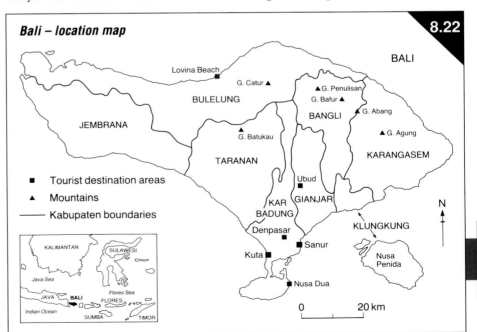

Bali – location map   8.22

■ Tourist destination areas
▲ Mountains
— Kabupaten boundaries

CASE STUDY 8.3 *Impacts of tourism development – an example*

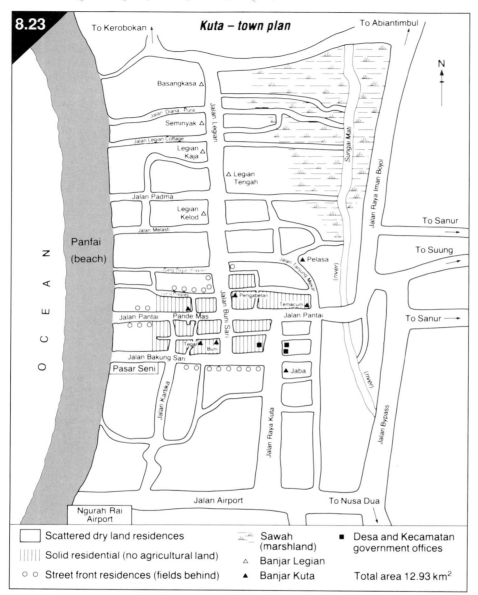

8.23

Kuta – town plan

To Kerobokan

To Abiantimbul

N

Basangkasa △

Jalan Diana Pura

Seminyak △

Jalan Legian Cottage

Legian
Kaja △

Jalan Legian

△ Legian
Tengah

Sungai Mati

Jalan Raya Iman Bojol

Jalan Padma

Legian
Kelod △

To Sanur

Jalan Melasti

To Suung

**Panfai
(beach)**

O
C
E
A
N

(river)

▲ Pelasa

Jalan Tanjung Mekar

Gang Rayur Poppies

Jalan Buni Sari

▲ Pengabetan

Jalan Pantai

Temacum ▲

To Sanur →

Jalan Pantai **Pande Mas**

Tegal ▲ ▲ Buni

■

Jalan Bakung Sari

Pasar Seni

▲ Jaba

Jalan Kartika

Jalan Raya Kuta

Jalan Bypass

(river)

Jalan Airport

To Nusa Dua

**Ngurah Rai
Airport**

☐	Scattered dry land residences	⩘	Sawah (marshland)	■	Desa and Kecamatan government offices
▥	Solid residential (no agricultural land)	△	Banjar Legian		
○ ○	Street front residences (fields behind)	▲	Banjar Kuta		Total area 12.93 km²

Governmental promotion of tourism as a means of economic advancement on Bali dates from 1969, when the first five-year plan upgraded the airport at Tuban for modern jet traffic and rehabilitated and widened the road system connecting the airport to Denpasar and Sanur. Assisted by funds from the International Bank for Reconstruction and Development, the Indonesian government hired a consulting firm to prepare a master plan for tourism on Bali. Adopting a top-down approach the plan advocated catering to tour groups from Australia, western Europe, North America, and Japan by providing international-standard hotels and a generally improved infrastructure. Two sites were selected for development: Sanur, located on the south-eastern coast six kilometres from Denpasar, and Nusa Dua on the Bukit penisula (resource 8.22). Kuta was not selected as a promising site for major development in spite of its accessibility and good beach.

The proximity of Bali to Australia proved to be advantageous for Indonesian tourism and for Kuta. Because flights are relatively inexpensive and short – Sydney is only five hours away – Australia has become the primary tourist-originating country for Bali. Australian tourists can visit Bali for less than they can a comparable Australian resort. The airfare is only slightly higher than the cost for a similar distance within Australia, and budget prices on Bali more than compensate for the fare differential.

A beachfront location offering easy ocean access, proximity to an international airport, a relatively close pool of tourists, and economical airfares were all factors that combined to favour Kuta. However, these factors were not sufficient to generate a tourism industry; what was needed was a business response from the residents of the area. Local residents at Kuta neither were aware of the tourism potential nor sought to promote it.

In addition to those activities, Kuta contained four small shops and each of the twelve neighbourhoods had its own coffee and eating stall. Several families also sold food, coffee, and sweets from carts along the main streets or near the fishing huts at the southern end of the beach. The village contained no restaurant, but two small hotels were located on the outskirts.

Pretourism Kuta was an ordinary farming-fishing village of little economic or cultural importance on Bali. It did possess one unique potential resource – the beach.

Balinese held beachfront property, the shoreline, and the sea in low esteem. Beach land not only was agriculturally unproductive but also was considered spiritually impure. However, to foreigners the wide, sandy beach at Kuta had the attraction of beauty and excellent surfing and bathing (resource 8.24).

Tourism and Kuta

Although foreign exchange is the most important reason for encouraging tourism, the central government also views this activity as a means to develop regions with few resources or little growth potential.

Kuta's beautiful beach was one of its primary attractions

Travellers came to Kuta to exploit the recreational possibilities of the beach, and the villagers simply responded to the new opportunities by providing them with basic necessities. The predominantly young, budget-oriented travellers were willing to accept, with minor modifications, local standards in food and lodging. Thus the demand for facilities generated by the tourists could be satisfied by using traditional resources – land, gold, agrarian products and animals, and by securing loans from family members. Such a response is typical in agrarian societies.

The start of tourism, 1970–1976

The early years of tourism development in Kuta saw increasing numbers of tourist arrivals matched by dramatic expansion of facilities as local entrepreneurs responded to the new opportunities. Only 6095 visitors stayed in Kuta in 1972. The next year the figure had risen to 14 522 and it was 18 010 for 1974, but then dropped to 14 852 in 1976. Before 1970 there were two hotels, one privately owned, the other government owned; by 1975 the area contained more than 100 locally owned accommodations and 27 restaurants.

The preferred investment among village-based entrepreneurs was a *losmen*, a one-story lodging with rooms constructed in a row. Investing in a losmen was relatively risk free, because the demand for rooms was high and investment costs were low. For example, the owner of a losmen business who made an initial investment of $800 to $1200 could expect to receive a profit within a year or, at a maximum, a year and a half, even with an occupancy rate of only 40 per cent. Occupancy rates typically were well above this level: in 1974 in the core area of Kuta they averaged 70 to 80 per cent. This activity stimulated a building boom in Kuta. Not only were new businesses being opened, but also established entrepreneurs were reinvesting their profits in expansion of existent facilities as well as opening new tourism businesses. By 1974, owning land in the core area of Kuta was less important, because the growing demand for rooms resulted in the spread of losmen businesses towards the beach (resource 8.25). Businesses were being established along the main streets in the Legian section and at sites between Jalan Padma and Jalan Dayan Poppies.

Local residents also invested in restaurants, but those enterprises never became as popular as losmen. In 1975, 27 restaurants operated in Kuta, 18 of which were Balinese

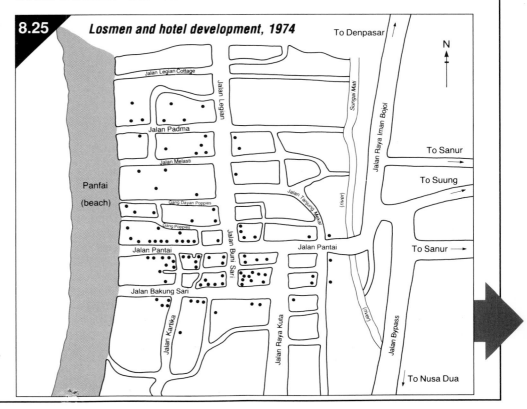

Losmen and hotel development, 1974

owned – 10 by local villagers and eight by Balinese from elsewhere on the island. Unlike losmen, restaurants generally required streetfront sites. Thus local entrepreneurs, if faced with the additional cost of securing such a location, preferred to invest in a losmen. Restaurants were more difficult to run than losmen, because the business required at least some skill in food services and management. Furthermore, in the early 1970s, food storage capacity was limited by the lack of electricity, which meant that owners had to shop daily.

Tourism growth 1977–1984

Tourism development in Kuta resulted in increasing land prices, which in turn led to a class of land-rich smallholders. Rice land, long the most highly valued property, soon became less important as land prices in other parts of the village soared. Between 1970 and 1984, the price of one *are* (one hundred square metres) of prime land in the core area of Kuta increased from $17 to $8000, and for beachfront property from $12 to $10 000. In contrast, the price of an *are* of rice land increased from $150 to only $400. Residents now assessed land for its commercial, not agricultural, potential and began converting street-front properties to commercial use, mainly as art shops selling clothing and textiles. These shops were developed in the late 1970s by established entrepreneurs who were seeking a new way to utilise their profits or by street-front property owners as an alternative to losmen or restaurants. Also shops utilised spaces along a street too small for an accommodation or restaurant. Owning a shop was advantageous because construction was inexpensive, and rent from a series of shops could provide an income. However, by 1980 these shops had changed the village atmosphere by hiding family compounds and concealing any visual evidence of noncommercial activity.

Entrepreneurial activity in Kuta was not confined to local villagers. Nonlocal Balinese participated in resort enterprises. Kuta offered entrepreneurs from other regions an opportunity to set up a tourism business in a fast-growing resort where investment costs, compared with those of other resorts on the island, were low. In the early years of tourism development, approximately 17 per cent of the investment in accommodations came from nonlocal Balinese. Between 1977 and 1980, nonlocals supplied more than 40 per cent of new investments. Most of the food stalls that opened to supply shop operators were run by women from neighbouring villages and, to a lesser extent, by migrants from Java.

Opportunities in Kuta also attracted business people from Java and even foreigners, who mainly invested in bars and restaurants. They were an ideal investment for foreigners, because they required less space than other activities. By 1983 approximately 44 per cent of the bars and restaurants in Kuta were foreign owned.

By 1977 the composition of the labour force in Kuta began to change. As local villagers left employment to open their own businesses, migrants filled the vacancies. Thus the demography of the village was altered. By 1982 the alteration was substantial. Kuta became the destination for migrants from other Indonesian regions. The migrants included hotel workers, business people, peddlers and job seekers. Migrants at Kuta usually rented a room in a family compound or in a losmen built especially for rental or converted from tourism use. The migrant labour force at Kuta thus gave a new business opportunity for local residents – room renting. Some families simply rented a spare room or two, but others constructed losmen solely for migrant rental.

The beachfront and the Legian section were two areas of Kuta where expansion of tourism facilities was significant after 1980. Unlike many other resorts where hotel construction occurred almost exclusively along the beach, development of the oceanfront zone proceeded slowly at Kuta. Facilities were initially located in the village and inside family compounds rather than along the beach. This preference reflected both the involvement of local villagers and their low social and economic esteem for oceanfront property. However, by 1984 hotel development was almost continuous from Jalan Diana Pura to Gang Dayan Poppies (resource 8.26). Development did not create a dense appearance because hotels were set back from the beach and were predominantly bungalow style. Additionally, existent vegetation was retained, and new plantings disguised to some extent the string of hotels along the coast.

By 1980, the main areas of Kuta, from Gang Dayan Poppies southward to Jalan Raya, had been developed. Hence the primary zone of subsequent development shifted to the Legian section because of greater availability of land and its lower price. Between 1980 and 1984, approximately 83 per cent of all new losmen, hotels, restaurants, and bars were located in Legian. The main street, Jalan Legian, underwent a dramatic transformation. Formerly the scenery consisted of fields and palms, and the roadside was bordered by a dense profusion of flowering shrubs. By 1984 this landscape had been replaced by a continuous series of roadside businesses that extended into Krobokan, a rice-farming village adjoining Legian.

At Legian, owners of street-front property especially benefitted from the spread of tourism as shops filled the space between restaurants, bars, losmen, and hotels. However, this development generated considerable traffic. By 1984, the main intersection at Jalan Legian and Jalan Pantai had become the traffic hub of Kuta. Traffic density became so

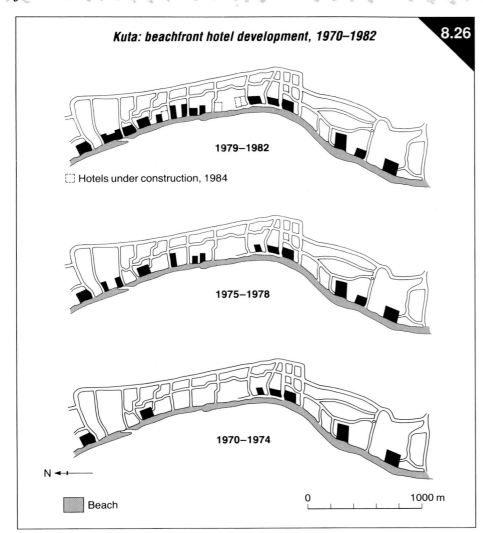

Kuta: beachfront hotel development, 1970–1982 8.26

1979–1982

☐ Hotels under construction, 1984

1975–1978

1970–1974

N

▨ Beach

0   1000 m

heavy that police officers were needed to keep order. The noise from motorcycles, automobiles, delivery trucks, buses, and vans forced 19 of the 23 losmen owners to convert to migrant-room rentals, because tourists would no longer stay in the area. Furthermore, the noise and the congestion severely affect the abilities of the villagers to make offerings at the shrine located there.

The environmental effect of tourism

The pressure of tourism development spoiled the beach at Kuta. Because of the ecological and social conditions created by tourism, a once beautiful beach became polluted, unpleasant, and diminished. The coral bed at the southern end of the beach was an early casualty. Coral, which was sold to lime kilns to be used for runway construction at the airport and for the new road system to the resort at Nusa Dua, began to be mined in 1968, and its destruction continued through the mid-1970s. Besides losing a valuable natural resource, removal of the bed resulted in severe beach erosion and, during high seas, loss of beachfront property. The entire length of the beach has been affected, with erosion now claiming approximately two centimetres a year.

Rubbish is another problem along the beach, where almost all of the plastic bags used by peddlers to package fruit, food, and assorted trinkets accumulated (resource 8.27). The most startling feature of the beach was the density of plastic straws, which after a decade significantly detracted from the aesthetic quality of the beach. At low tide, the wet sand is now a slick morass of rubbish and plastic bags and straws bob on the surface of the murky waters. The village authorities are aware of the rubbish problem and pay a clean-up gang to rake the sand and bury the debris every morning. Nevertheless, the effort is futile, because most of the rubbish buried each morning reappears after the next high tide and throughout the day a new layer of rubbish accumulates.

The social effects of tourism

Developments in Kuta have brought many changes. Firstly, the input of tourism money has allowed some individuals to become quite wealthy. One individual who owned a fourteen-room losmen made a profit of approximately $10 000 in 1977 and by 1984 was clearing $75 000 a year. Profits of this magnitude were typical of the more aggressive entrepreneurs in Kuta, who bought considerable plots of land on Bali and who now themselves take international vacations. The prosperity has attracted migrants who form a stable population

8.27

Rubbish along the beach at Kuta has become a serious environmental problem

employed either in the formal or informal sector of the economy. However, some came to Kuta to engage in illegal activities associated with resorts – thievery, prostitution, and drug dealing.

Violent crime was unknown until 1979. The victims were usually tourists, but by the latter half of the 1970s crime was affecting local residents. Robbery, which previously had been confined to losmen and hotels, was occurring in family compounds. Moreover, walking in the evening became uncomfortable for both tourists and local residents as certain streets were lined with prostitutes and drug dealers.

By 1980 Kuta accommodated more than 60 000 tourists, and the composition by nationality had become seasonal. As a result the names for the season used by villagers switched from the traditional wet, dry, cool, or hot to ones that identified the main tourist groups. December through February became known as *musim Jepan* (Japanese season); March as *musim perempuan Jepan* (Japanese women season); April through June as *musim Australi* (Australian season); July and August as *musim Perancis* (French season); and September through November as *musim bermacam-macam* (variety season). Furthermore, business owners in Kuta acquired a vocabulary of English, French, and Japanese words and phrases. Restaurant owners change their sign boards and menus according to the season: winter-month displays are in Japanese, but English dominates in spring, to be replaced by French in summer.

From village to town

Change in the landscape of Kuta to accommodate tourism has been an ongoing process for several decades, but since 1980 Kuta has had a new character. Between 1979 and 1980, tourist arrivals to Kuta increased from 36 000 to 60 000, a 67 per cent rise. By 1980, 33 per cent of the

tourists visiting Bali stayed at the village. Thus Kuta was firmly established as a tourist resort.

The governmental authorities on Bali recognised the importance of Kuta to the island's economy. In 1980 they officially recognised Kuta as a priority tourism area and changed its status from village to town. With town status, residents paid higher land taxes, but Kuta became eligible to receive certain types of governmental assistance like street paving.

Various services and businesses catering to the newer needs of residents began locating in Kuta after 1980. For example, a branch office of the electrical company opened in 1982 after power lines were installed throughout the village in 1981. Banks providing door-to-door deposit service for the shop operators are now available. Construction, plumbing, and electrical supply stores have opened in Kuta so the need to travel to Denpasar for equipment has been eliminated. Also tourists and residents can take advantage of twenty-four-hour photograph-developing outlets, xerox machines, money changers, a telegraph office, crating and shipping firms, shoe stores, and beauty parlours. Kuta has become an urban centre with businesses that provide services not only for the tourist industry but also for residents. By the mid-1980s tourist arrivals averaged more than 64 000 annually, some five times the resident population of Kuta. By 1990, arrivals exceeded 90 000

Conclusions

Tourism development at Kuta has had both positive and negative results. On the one hand, numerous individuals have become wealthy, and non-traditional employment is available not only to locals, but also to migrants from other parts of Bali and Indonesia. The infrastructure in Kuta has improved, and additional services are available. The government derives increased tax and foreign-exchange revenues, and many tourists enjoy a beach that otherwise would not be accessible to them. On the other hand, a traditional Balinese village is now a crowded, noisy, polluted, crime-ridden town at the mercy of a fickle international tourist market.

The development that emerged at Kuta provides important lessons. Firstly, it shows that individuals in a 'backward' village can easily embrace an entrepreneurial spirit and can quickly develop considerable economic activity without external intervention. Secondly, Kuta demonstrates the importance of budget-category travellers and the need for tourism planners to incorporate them into small-scale developmental projects. Thirdly, the conditions at Kuta illustrate the speed with which development can occur, the many problems that can arise, and the dangers of uncontrolled development to the very resources that led to its occurrence in the first place.

(Source: A Hussey, 'Tourism in a Balinese Village', *The Geographical Review*, 79(3), July 1989, pp. 311–325)

Activities

1 Analyse the Kuta case study by completing a matrix with the following structure.

	Economic	Social	Environmental
Benefits			
Costs			

2 How has the morphology of the settlement been changed by the coming of tourism?

CASE STUDY 8.4 *Is the party over? The example of Spain*

Background

The nightmare of every country, region, island and community that has encouraged tourism as the basis of economic growth and development, is that the tourists will cease to arrive and will choose to spend their money elsewhere. The massive international tourism industry tempts the holidaymakers with an ever-changing array of new destinations. The holidaymakers are fickle followers of fashion, and yield to these new temptations. This may not affect existing resort areas while overall demand is growing at least as rapidly as the supply. However, as developers in these older resorts cash in on the popularity by building more and more hotels, apartment blocks and villas, there may come a point at which the local infrastructure and environment becomes overwhelmed by the scale of the developments (resource 8.28). The quality of the holiday experience begins to fall, forcing resorts and tour operators to move 'down market' in attempts to fill the huge number of 'bed-spaces'. Remember, too, that even without excessive growth, a resort may lose its attractiveness, simply because it no

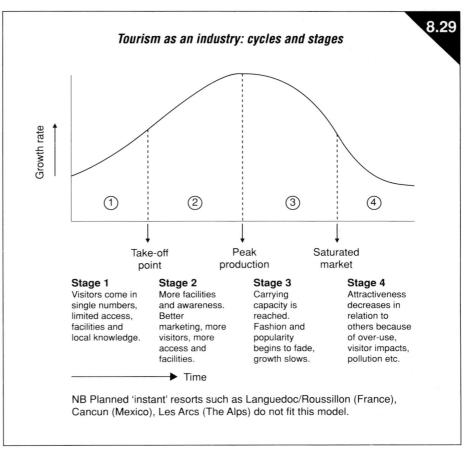

Tourism as an industry: cycles and stages

8.29

Growth rate →

① ② ③ ④

Take-off point · Peak production · Saturated market

Stage 1
Visitors come in single numbers, limited access, facilities and local knowledge.

Stage 2
More facilities and awareness. Better marketing, more visitors, more access and facilities.

Stage 3
Carrying capacity is reached. Fashion and popularity begins to fade, growth slows.

Stage 4
Attractiveness decreases in relation to others because of over-use, visitor impacts, pollution etc.

→ Time

NB Planned 'instant' resorts such as Languedoc/Roussillon (France), Cancun (Mexico), Les Arcs (The Alps) do not fit this model.

8.28

Overdevelopment along the Costa del Sol at Malaga and Torremolinos

longer offers what the tourist wants, e.g. the decline of many traditional British 'bucket-and-spade' seaside resorts.

We can suggest, therefore, that a typical holiday destination passes through a life-cycle of emergence-growth-prosperity-decline, as summarised in model form in resource 8.29. In this sense it is comparable to other single product towns such as mining settlements which prosper only while their key resource is highly valued (see case study 5.1). If stagnation is to be avoided, a resort has several alternatives:

1 Seek out a new market and type of tourist.
2 Provide new attractions.
3 Change function away from tourism.

Strategies range from targeting specific markets such as business conferences or long-stay packages for retired people, through conversion of hotels to self-catering apartments, to encouraging the

Key understandings

◆ A holiday resort is a form of single-product settlement which passes through a life-cycle of distinct phases.

◆ Continued resort success depends heavily upon fashion and 'image'.

◆ The continued success of a holiday destination depends upon its ability to offer an experience which satisfies the customer.

◆ The tourism industry has, in the past, paid too little attention to the environmental impacts of large scale development.

CASE STUDY 8.4   *Is the party over? The example of Spain*

retirement and second-home markets.

Nowhere does the life-cycle hypothesis seem more likely to be supported than in Spain. The long-continued tourism boom, based on Mediterranean sun-sea-sand, has produced a semi-continuous strip of resort development for 1000 km from the French border to beyond Gibraltar and on into Portugal (resources 8.30, and 8.31). Tourism has become Spain's leading industry. Today, the negative impacts are becoming all too apparent – many poorly designed, badly finished and over-large developments, too little investment in infrastructure (roads, water supply, sewage disposal facilities), and creeping environmental deterioration, seen most strongly in beach and ocean pollution (resource 8.32).

The first of the two main articles used in this case study (resource 8.33) was published from a conference held in London in January 1990 'to consider the impact of tourism on the environment'. It identifies first, the problem: tourist numbers are beginning to fall as a result of growing dissatisfaction with

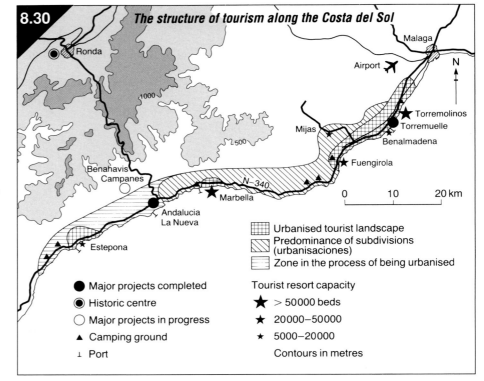

8.30 The structure of tourism along the Costa del Sol

the 'product' on offer (see also resource 8.34). Second, it suggests some causes of the problems, and third, it discusses strategies for combatting them. Finally, it raises the vital questions of which aspects

of environmental quality most concern holidaymakers, and how much they are prepared to pay for higher environmental standards (see also resource 8.36). The second main article details the massive economic implications of a fall-off in tourist numbers (resource 8.35).

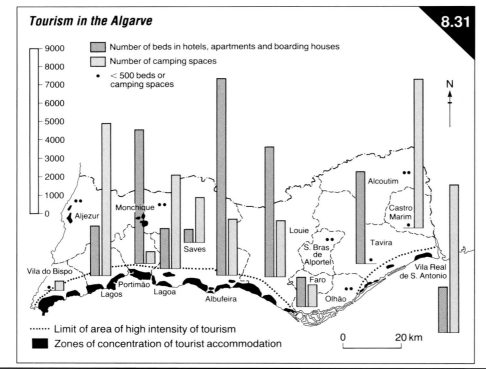

8.31 Tourism in the Algarve

8.32

Severe beach pollution on the Spanish coast

Activities

1 List the scale of Spanish tourism and the principal origins of the tourists.

2 What are the causes of the decline in popularity?

3 What are the major economic, social and environmental impacts of the tourism explosion?

4 What problem-solving strategies are being adopted and who is making the decisions?

5 **Group discussion:**

a (i) Does the history of tourism along the 'Costas' support the life-cycle model of resource 8.29? Produce a summary statement of the Spanish situation in terms of the four phases.

(ii) Suggest and evaluate strategies for taking a resort such as Benidorm into a new growth phase.

8.33

Crisis on the crumbling costas

The growth of tourism in Spain over just three decades has transformed some of Europe's most beautiful beaches from poor fishing villages to money-spinning pleasure domes.

Spain attracts over 50 million holidaymakers a year and most of them stay within conga dancing distance of a Spanish Mediterranean beach. In return for an indispensable contribution to their growing wealth, the Spanish have sold their sunshine and their sand – and, in many places, their culture.

But the number of paying guests is now dropping. And the drop is fast becoming a crisis. It has come about because the Spanish coastal resorts were built to please an undiscriminating market that for the first time was able to buy holidays abroad. These holiday factories were built in a haphazard, unsound, unplanned way to satisfy what seemed to be an unstoppable demand from foreigners. The inevitable results were pollution; destruction of the natural beauty and scenery that brought visitors there in the first place; litter and the tourists themselves cause; bottlenecks of traffic in the sky and on the roads that again the tourists cause.

The number of foreign visitors to Spain, from 1988 to 1989 dropped only by 0.2 per cent. But the number of visitors from Britain dropped by nearly 4 per cent and Spain's share of its important British package holiday market has dropped 6 per cent in four years.

This is not just a dip in sales because of Britain's high interest rates and last year's hot summer. West Germany's biggest tour operator Neckerman reports that the demand in the Federal Republic for holidays in Spain has stagnated too.

This slow-down in bookings is the first serious warning that if radical steps are not taken to clean up the pollution and improve the ambience along the Spanish coast, then Spain will be left with little more than obsolete urbanisations on a ruined coastline.

To start at the beginning you have to go back 30 years. Of course Benidorm, Lloret, Torremolinos and everywhere else that sells straw donkeys and sombreros were once picturesque but poor fishing villages.

In 1960 fewer than half a million Britons visited Spain. By 1971 this number had risen to more than three million – not far short of half the number of Britons who were then going abroad. By 1988 the number reached over 7.5 million. The majority of these were climbing down the steps of their charter planes and heading straight for a Spanish Mediterranean beach. And of course the British were not the only ones heading there. In 1988 the number of total visits to Spain was 54 million.

In those days, small rooms, thin walls and any basic design for exteriors were fine. After all, for most guests it was their very first experience of a hotel. To help put up the hotels, tour operators offered would-be hoteliers loans repayable against bookings. They advised on Anglicising or Germanising the food and the entertainment.

Economically, tourism has been very good for Spain. It accounts for nearly 10 per cent of the country's gross national product. In Majorca tourism accounts for 60 per cent of the gross national product – 85 per cent if you count the construction industry. A swing to self-catering is most noticeable in Majorca where now 57 per cent of the beds on the island are for self-catering holidaymakers.

Think back to the headlines of last summer. This year's Costas Crisis was last summer's Costa Sewage, Costa Stench and Costa Nightmare. The papers screamed lager louts in Lloret; a murdered waiter in Ibiza; turds in the sea and poisoned water in Salou.

The Spanish are not blind to the trends and are looking to other markets: to the smaller European countries like Holland that could not compete with the buying power of the giant British and German tour operators. And then there's Eastern Europe – a market that only six months ago was untouchable. Already the Balearic islands have invited 10 000 Eastern Europeans over for a free expenses-paid holiday. This enormous potential market will not fuss over standard of accommodation.

The holiday aspirations of Western Europeans are becoming more sophisticated. Those who can afford holidays enjoy a higher standard of living at home than in the early days of package hotel holidays and people want accommodation at least as good as at home.

The Spanish tourist industry is promising to refurbish. The government is offering low interest loans to upgrade rooms and improve facilities. Planning regulations and their enforcement are now on the agenda. Last year saw a new law, a fuller version of an earlier 1969 Law of Coastal Areas banning any new building nearer than 100 metres from the shore.

The Balearic Government as well has announced a budget of £65 million to improve public and tourist amenities such as waste disposal, street lighting and road, beach and park maintenance. It will also enforce planning regulations that ban the development of new one, two and three-star hotels or self-catering accommodation. Only four and five-star developments will get the go ahead, part of the aim to go upmarket.

Benidorm has the most to lose. The town has pledged £317 million to be spread over five years to create golf courses and parks, improve beach cleanliness and safety and clamp down on litter and noise. Benidorm is already judged to have a clean beach and clean sea, worthy of three blue flags. Benidorm is planning on-the-spot £50 fines for littering. The Benidorm authorities have also calculated that 400 tons of sand a year are lost from their beaches, taken away on the soles of sunbathers' feet and so they're installing footbaths.

Some hoteliers will manage to convert their bedrooms to apartments, perhaps to be sold to the Spanish. But what will happen to the places that are forced to close? Will they just stay boarded up until they fall down and contribute to the changing feel of the place? Will trading-up therefore have a negative effect on some resorts?

Think back to what happened to Italy. For 20 years it was the number one destination of tourists from northern Europe. It was hot, pretty and cheap. Brochure writers used to wax lyrical about the joys of a pleasant swim in the Bay of Naples before enjoying your cheap pasta and chianti.

Most holidays to Italy now are at the upper end of the market. People visit Italy for art and for expensive holidays in the countryside. And that's Spain's other plan. To spread the load and to introduce the cultural face of the country. Cut out low-yield tourism, and then spread the visitors around the whole of the country showing them the cities, the countryside and the quieter beaches.

This policy makes some disturbing assumptions. Surely in the established resorts, once the infrastructure is corrected to cope properly with the great numbers of holidaymakers, their transport and their sewage, little more harm can be done to the environment there? The habitat is no longer vulnerable. It is already ruined. What about the habitat of the interior and the undeveloped stretches of coastline? What happens to them if you develop them?

About 53 per cent of the species of mammals found in Spain are classified as under threat. the Cota Doñana, Spain's premier national park and one of Europe's most important wildlife sanctuaries is in danger of drying up because water is being extracted first for irrigation and now for tourist developments (resource 8.36).

The policy can also smack of elitism and assumes that people no longer want to go on holiday en masse.

Perhaps the success of Spain's purpose-built holiday factories is only faltering because little thought was given to the design and the upkeep of the places. But does that necessarily mean that the concept of purpose-built pleasure domes is outdated?

For evidence that holiday makers are still happy to pay to holiday with like-minded souls not indigenous culture, look at the success of the American theme parks. Disneyland and Disney World are the most prosaic of fun factories. And they work. Americans flock to them and Europeans dream of going there.

I like the suggestion an enterprising builder once made of building a wall round places like Benidorm and then charging people to enter it. Keep the beach clean, tart up the older rooms, green up the area with trees and parks.

What evidence is there that holidaymakers are at all interested in the environment? West German surveys show that when it comes to making holiday choices, the environment, clean beaches, clean water, attractive surroundings are more important than they have ever been in the past. Neckerman report that 60 per cent of their clients vote cleanliness and clean beaches above all other desirable facilities.

When a National Opinion Poll in 1986 asked people to name their most pressing concern, the environment polled just 8 per cent. On specific issues, 79 per cent were worried about dirty beaches and bathing water.

A survey in May 1989 found that the number of people concerned about the environment was then 40 per cent.

Last November in Benidorm a little research was carried out among British holidaymakers – mainly older people. The majority – 80 per cent – said they were fairly or strongly concerned about green issues.

When asked if they would pay more for an environment friendly package holiday 66 per cent said yes. And how much extra would they be prepared to pay? £5.

I have singled Spain out because of its success. The size of its tourist industry is the envy of many other countries.

Firstly, the damage that can be undone has to be undone. The weak infrastructure has to be tackled, then that hard-to-quantify aesthetic pollution needs to be faced.

The public might not want to act or to pay to improve the environment but as soon as the damage has a noticeably negative effect on their holidays they vote with their feet.

But stopping the rot and righting the situation also costs money. And who's going to pay? Remember those Brits who are only prepared to pay £5 to save the environment? If you multiply Spain's 54 million visitors by £5 you've got £270 million a year. Perhaps a tourist tax, a sort of Caring Costas tax levied to improve the environment would be seen as a good deed with the publicity value of being seen to be green.

(Source: Alison Rice, *The Observer*, 4 February, 1990)

Costa ditched as Spanish sun fades

Drug hauls, muggers and lager louts on the Spanish Costa del Sol have added an unpleasant flavour to the sangria and hamburgers of the package holiday market, and well-heeled tourists are taking their money elsewhere.

Sovereign Holidays said yesterday that it was dropping the Costa del Sol from its winter programme. This may be the beginning of the end of an era in which Torrelmolinos and Benilmadena became as familiar as Torquay and Blackpool.

The Costa del Sol still welcomes well over a million Britions a year with its combination of English pubs and Mediterranean sun. But the older, wealthier tourists have lost interest, and they now account for an increasing share of a market hit by high interest rates.

Keith Waller, marketing director of Sovereign said: 'Bookings are significantly down, particularly for Sovereign Holidays which is aimed at the over 35s with more money and experience.

'There has been some bad publicity over the murder of the British train robber Charlie Wilson, but it had a tired image anyway.'

Mr Wilson was shot dead by the swimming pool of his villa in Marbella last month, together with his dog.

Bored with the Costa, one in 10 holidaymakers now head for Florida, the Caribbean, and the Far East on new, cheaper charter flights.

The Costa del Sol's image has been dented by reports of attacks and drugs hauls.

Arturo Claver, director of the Spanish Tourist Office, defends the Costa, saying the Spanish government is trying to improve standards in an increasingly competitive market. Laws have been passed to prevent overdevelopment of the coast and all new buildings must now meet stringent regulations. but he admits: 'Supply does exceed demand in some areas of the Costa del Sol.'

He is vociferous on the subject of lager louts. 'I have never seen one. Lager louts are like migratory birds, only seen at certain times of the year in some places.'

Spain is still the most popular destination for package holidays: 65 per cent of Thomson holidays are in Spain, and it attracts a loyal following with high return rates. The Costa del Sol is holding up better than more down-market resorts on the Costa Brava says Peter Bothwell, marketing director of Lunn Poly.

Bookings are down, especially from southern England. Northerners with smaller mortgages are still getting their holidays.

He said: 'Bookings in the package holiday market may drop by as much as 10 per cent this year. But the average price has gone up. It is the lower end of the market which has been worst hit.'

(Source: Madeleine Bunting, *The Guardian*, 24 May 1990)

Tourism threatens Spanish wildlife sanctuary

A blaze last week at a garage in Spain's Cota Doñana National Park has intensified a political battle over the fate of the park – Europe's biggest sanctuary for birds. Conservationists are locked in a battle with financiers who want to expand tourism in the park.

Police investigating the fire have not ruled out arson. The blaze caused damage worth 50 million pesetas, about £281 000, and occurred nine days after environmentalists rallied against proposed developments in tourism. The wetland region, in south-western Spain, supports a wide range of flora and fauna, that includes several endangered species such as the lynx. It is also a key staging post for thousands of birds migrating between Europe and Africa.

The Matalascañas tourist complex and several agricultural developments sit around the 49 225-hectare park. These operations deplete water resources within the park to satisfy the demand for irrigation and tourism. Proposals to build a second tourist complex and golf course, the Costa Doñana, have aggravated the controversy. These facilities will demand still more water from the park, leading to the possible desiccation of large areas of the Doñana.

A recent report by three independent specialists contracted by the Spanish branch of the World Wide Fund for Nature, ADENA, and the World Conservation Union argued that increased extraction of water from the aquifers, coupled with the intrusion of brine as the water table drops, would severely alter local ecology.

Despite local and international opposition to the Costa Doñana project, notably from the Royal Society for the Protection of Birds, the proprietors of the holiday complex and the local authorities of the economically depressed Almonte town remain undeterred.

Salvador Echevarria, one of the principal shareholders in the project, said that building would start on the complex, designed to accommodate 32 000 people, as soon as the municipal authorities gave the go-ahead. A decision is imminent.

'Doñana has given work to only seven people from this town,' Echevarria said, 'and the park has acted as a constant brake on the agricultural development of this area. It would be unfair to deny it touristic development, especially if the pressure against development comes from outside Spain.'

Any move to allow the scheme to go ahead could harm Madrid's chances of hosting the new European Environmental Agency. A decision on the siting of the agency is due this month. Miguel Valladares of ADENA says: 'If Spain really wants the agency, and it does, it's going to have to mind its environmental Ps and Qs from now until the decision is made.'

(Source: *New Scientist*, 7 April 1990)

8.36

Hotspot turns blackspot

The sun may be beating down on Europe, but there is a dark cloud hanging over Spain. In what has been called European Tourism Year, the country that led the continent's Mediterranean beach boom for 30 years is experiencing its first crisis. Hotel bookings in the Costa del Sol are down by up to 30 per cent. And the national balance of payments showed a drop in tourist revenue of Pts 40 000 million ($405 million) for June alone, a 22.5 per cent decrease on last year.

The Spanish Government has been saying that it is wrong to talk of a crisis, that the trend may yet change and that the shortfall in foreign visitors is compensated by buoyant domestic tourism. Yet it is spending a record Pts9750 million ($97.7 million) on its 1990 tourism publicity campaigns. The official defensive line only highlights the crucial part that tourist revenue plays in Spain's economy, where it accounts for about 10 per cent of the GNP and 11 per cent of jobs. The drop in tourist revenue has increased the foreign deficit by 39 per cent, to Pts170 100 million ($1723 million).

The warning signs were there last year: a 400 000 drop in visitors to 50.9 million compared with 1988. There is some truth in ministers' remarks that the downturn may not be conclusive. August is the month that traditionally makes or breaks the Spanish tourist industry and last year – following the first July fall in tourist numbers in 30 years – it just managed to save it.

The healthy peseta has risen 11.5 per cent in real terms since 1988. This, and Spain's entry into the EMS last year with a subsequent rise in interest rates and foreign investment, has fuelled inflation.

All this makes it less of a bargain for visitors – and a positive deterrent for the British, by far the largest group of customers. But the problem is not a straightforward financial one. Value for money is now a more important factor than simple economy for many travellers. In the mid to late Eighties, prices were rock-bottom and expectations low. Now both have risen.

'People are buying better holidays in Spain this year, or not at all,' says a spokesman for Thomson Holidays, which has put up its prices by about 15 per cent since last year. In the midst of intense competition for customers in 1988, Thomson was forced to accept profits as low as £1 ($1.8) per customer; since the price war subsided (Thomson bought out one of its main rivals, Horizon), it now makes £5 to £7 ($9 to $12.6).

Where the package operators can readjust their stragegy, however, the hotelier can only sit and wait. José Ortega, who runs the Hotel Bavaria in Marbella, knows how that feels. 'This year has been deadly,' he says. Tourists come for a rest and spend their holiday in a traffic jam. Until our infrastructure is improved, they won't come.'

In an apparent, if overdue, acknowledgement of this problem, the Ministry of Tourism has established new objectives in tourist construction. Chief among these is the creation of high-quality supply in touristically underdeveloped areas – mainly inland and in places of historical and cultural interest. Particular emphasis is placed upon environmental concerns in the construction of new buildings, and the hotel grading system is to be made more stringent. Teaching by example, the Ministry has invested Pts2460 million ($25 million) in the upmarket state-owned Parador hotel network.

To tempt constructors and hoteliers to upgrade and relocate supply away from the coast, the tourism ministry has also drawn up new facilities for tourist credit, including the extension to 15 years of the maximum period for borrowing. Supporting this project is a Pts50 million ($507 000) 'Green Spain' promotion campaign, designed to convince tourists that there is more to the Iberian peninsula than high-rise hotels and saturated seasides.

Indications are that the tourists are already making this transition. The Spanish National Tourist office in London reports a 60 to 70 per cent increase in enquiries about inland Spain, to the deficit of the traditional coastal areas. 'It is a positive change since these tourists eat out more, buy more and provide more income to Spain. They also demand higher standards and encourage the upgrading of facilities,' said a spokesman. Keytel, the agent for Parador bookings, also reports a big increase, despite prices about 150 per cent higher than on package holidays. At the lower end of the market, the Balearic Islands, which employed 12 000 fewer workers this year, are slicing 30 000 to 50 000 hotel places and putting $200 million into higher quality developments.

It is not only foreign tourists who determine domestic tourist revenue. Thirty per cent more Spaniards are holidaying abroad this year than last, spending $3000 million.

The Spanish tourist trade associations are having to take a pragmatic view. Looking at an overall drop of 20 per cent in hotel revenue, they have announced the introduction of new employment regulations and partial closures, in an attempt to stabilise the market for next year. The Costa del Sol association has appointed its first marketing director, who in turn has taken on a public relations firm and is looking for an advertising agency.

After being rescued by August last year, the Spanish tourist industry resolved to attract more tourists from countries with strong economies, such as Germany. The most encouraging increase this year must be in the Japanese visitors, whose numbers are up by a third. Perhaps the answer to Spain's seasonal dilemma will come from the land of the rising sun.

(Source: Tessa Thomas, *The European*, August 3–5, 1990)

CHAPTER 9

Ways to move – transport policy issues

Introduction

Transport is a fundamental theme of geo graphy because it is all about the way space is organised by humans. In transport geography, we are concerned with (i) the linkages and flows that make up a transportation network, (ii) the centres, or nodes, connected by these linkages, (ii) the system of hinterlands and hierarchical relationships associated with the networks, and (iv) the environmental impacts of this network of nodes and links. It is not an easy topic, because although the description of a network may be straightforward, explaining its patterns or attempting decision-making exercises quickly takes us into the fields of politics, economics, and engineering, amongst others.

For instance, major airlines operate a 'hub-and-feeder' network, focusing the majority of their flights on a small number of routes in and out of a few major cities (resource 9.1). The rest of the destinations are fed via these hubs. Therefore, when an airline advertises that 'We fly you to more cities in the US than any other airline', it does not mean 'We fly you direct'! The hubs, or gateway cities, act as focal access points to a region. Before reading on, think of reasons why airlines operate this network structure, and whether it applies to other transportation modes.

The most common approach to the geography of transport in textbooks has generally been via a series of theoretical or generalised models based around either the time-cost-distance relationships, or hierarchical spheres of influence, or the evolution of connectivity in a network over time. On to this formal, numbers-based framework have been added increasingly in recent years, issues connected with the

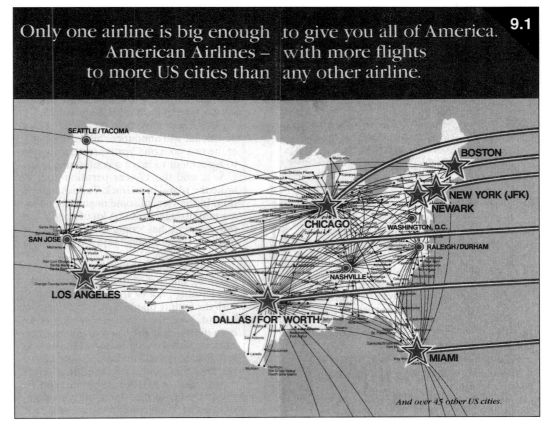

9.1

Only one airline is big enough to give you all of America.
American Airlines – with more flights to more US cities than any other airline.

And over 45 other US cities.

environmental impacts and the effect of transport upon quality of life (resource 9.2). Several case studies in this chapter focus particularly upon this latter dimension, raising issues, illustrating impacts, suggesting options and thereby encouraging you to clarify your thinking on where you stand on questions of transport.

As modern economies and societies have evolved, there has been an increasing separation of the three main elements in our lives: home, work and play (resource 9.3(a)). Equally, industrial processes have become more specialised, with more stages of fabrication (resource 9.3(b)). Thus, the movement of people, materials and products has continued to increase. There are signs that the advance of information communications systems may in the future reduce the need for movements and meetings, e.g. the coming of 'intelligent cities' such as those in Japan see case study 5.5, pages 116-119. For the present, however, the harsh truth is that our transport systems seem inadequate to support our way of life, either socially or economically. The two central concepts are **mobility** and **accessibility**. Our constantly increasing demand for mobility (the movement from one place to another) is outstripping the carrying capacity of the existing transport infrastructure, and so accessibility, the *ease* by which places can be reached, is decreasing (resource 9.4). The key issues focus upon: (i) the balance between different modes of transport, (ii) who should provide and pay for the transport infrastructure – the private or public sector, or some form of partnership, (iii) the extent to which an individual's freedom to travel should be controlled, and by whom, (iv) the degree to which the full economic costs of a transport network should be met by the users, and (v) the location and form of the transport infrastructure (where the roads, railways, car parks, stations and airports should be, and in what form).

9.2

On the road to ruin

The greatest single contributor to today's global environmental crisis is still one of man's best friends. The car burns up vital resources, pumps an array of poisons into the air, and bulldozes its way through unspoilt countryside and irreplaceable wildlife sites. But modern man remains in love with the freedom, convenience and status it bestows. During the last five years the amount of traffic on Britain's roads has increased by 27 per cent.

The car consumes oil, a precious, finite and diminishing resource. It accounts for nearly two thirds of the oil burned in the United States each year and almost half of the total consumed in Western Europe.

Burning petrol creates pollution. Lead, added to petrol to stop engines 'knocking', damages children's brains and reduces their intelligence. Nitrogen oxides emitted by cars are one of the main pollutants killing lakes in Scandinavia and North America and devastating forests all over Europe. And burning oil in the internal combustion engine is one of the main sources of carbon dioxide, the most important cause of the greenhouse effect.

In all, the car is responsible for one fifth of Britain's carbon dioxide emissions, about two fifths of its contribution to the acid rain cocktail, and almost all its airborne lead. At last lead is slowly being removed from petrol: about a quarter of all drivers now use unleaded fuel. At the insistence of the European Parliament all new cars sold from 1993 onwards will have to be fitted with catalytic converters, which reduce emissions of nitrogen oxides, carbon monoxide and hydrocarbons.

But Britain's carbon dioxide emissions continue to rise. Cutting fuel consumption is the only way to reduce them, yet between 1971 and 1985 Britain achieved a mere 7 per cent reduction, compared with 15 per cent in gas-guzzling America, 25 per cent in France and 40 per cent in Italy.

Pollution from cars kills up to 30 000 people a year in the United States alone, according to research at the University of California. Children who grow up in the most polluted areas in the Golden State suffer 10 to 15 per cent reduction in lung capacity for life. Ozone, one of the main ingredients both of the acid rain cocktail and of the photochemical smogs that plague Los Angeles and many cities, can aggravate heart disease, bronchitis and emphysema. And cars emit benzene, which causes cancer, and other poisons.

Some two thirds of the area of Los Angeles is devoted to motorways, roads and car parks, and still the average speed is expected to drop to 15 mph by the year 2000. Worldwide, about one third of all land area in cities is given over to the car.

Roads are increasingly damaging the countryside and wildlife habitats. A survey by Friends of the Earth in 1986 showed that road-building was harming no less than 110 officially designated Sites of Special Scientific Interest (SSSIs). New roads actively seek out SSSIs and other protected sites: they are cheap because they cannot be developed for housing, so road-builders use them to keep down their costs.

(Source: Geoffrey Lean, *The Observer Magazine*, 15 April 1990)

Transport generators

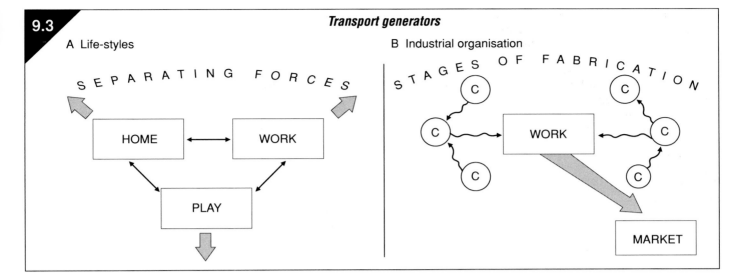

A Life-styles

SEPARATING FORCES

HOME ⟷ WORK

PLAY

B Industrial organisation

STAGES OF FABRICATION

C C C C

WORK

C C

MARKET

Roads lobby wants four M-ways costing £4.5bn

Roads lobby groups are seeking firm commitments from the two main parties to expand the motorway network, with at least four key new roads, at a cost of £4.5 billion. The roads lobby has been encouraged by the Department of Transport's announcement that the M25 is to be widened to four lanes, to which a circle of two-to-three-lane relief roads could be added. The £2.8 billion plan, spread over 12 years, is the biggest single addition to the roads programme since the M25 itself.

Pro-roads groups want to see over the next few years:

An east coast motorway linking the M11 at Cambridge with the A1 south of Middlesbrough.

(Source: Daniel John, *The Guardian*, 23 September 1991)

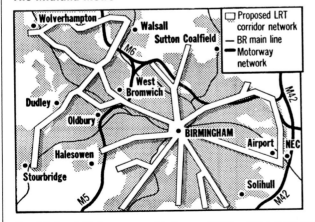

The Midland Metro

Proposed LRT corridor network
— BR main line
■ Motorway network

Wolverhampton
Walsall
Sutton Coalfield
M6
West Bromwich
Dudley
Oldbury
BIRMINGHAM
Airport NEC
Halesowen
Stourbridge
M5
Solihull
M42
M42

The Midland Metro concept is for an £800 million light rail network (LRT) with 200 km of track across the conurbation. The rolling stock will be single-deck, articulated trams, capable of 70km/hr and carrying 170 passengers.

Costing the coast road

A feasibility study into the proposed £1 billion east coast motorway puts forward a powerful case to the Department of Transport for its construction.

But while supporters of the 400 km road claim it would greatly improve traffic flows, boost local economies and bring 60 000 jobs to areas along its route, its impact on the environment would be very damaging according to TEST (Transport and Environmentalist Studies).

The proposed motorway, promoted by a consortium of county, district and town councils, the CBI and major companies, would extend the M11 northwards from Cambridge to Teesside via the Wash and the Humber Bridge.

Using two projections of vehicles using the motorway – 50 000 and 70 000 every 24 hours – TEST estimated that between 9.5 billion kilometres and 13.3 billion kilometres every year would be clocked up, of which cars would account for 7.85 billion kilometres and 11 billion kilometres.

A railway along the same route would generate a third of the estimated 4.8 to 6.8 million tonnes of carbon dioxide likely to be produced by road traffic.

Rail would consume between a half and three-quarters less energy than road traffic. Noise levels would be lower with rail, but both forms of travel would use large amounts of land, leading to inflated land prices, urban sprawl and the development of secondary transport corridors.

(Source: Daniel John, *The Guardian*, 1 March 1991)

CASE STUDY 9.1 *Getting in and out of London*

Background

The progressive outward spread of homes and the persistent central concentration of jobs generate powerful morning and evening commuter flows. These surges are at their most extreme in large metropolises such as London, moving in varying proportions along road (private cars and commercial buses) and rail networks. To this we may add the flows for shopping, entertainment and professional services, plus the huge volume of related commercial traffic. As a result, it is generally accepted that roads alone cannot cope: no matter how much is spent on roads and parking facilities, traffic jams or 'gridlock' seem to get worse even in wealthy countries dedicated to the production and use of motor vehicles (resource 9.6).

This realisation is not new. The first London 'underground' line was opened in 1863 and the first deep-tube, electric railway in 1890. Note that the claimed speed for an end-to-end journey along that 5.25 km line in 1890 was 24 km/hour (15 mph), the same as the average speed of central London tube trains in 1990! The famous Buchanan Report of 1963, called 'Traffic and Towns', showed that the private car will inevitably clog up central cities. It concluded that the only effective way to control car usage is 'the provision of good, cheap public transport, coupled with the public's understanding of the position'.

Yet despite mounting evidence, the tables in resource 9.5 show that government policy in the UK has continued to favour private road transport. The figures demonstrate the unabated expansion of roads and road traffic and progressively heavier goods vehicles, alongside the slow growth or even contraction of railway usage. Resource 9.7 shows that while the 1980s saw an increase in numbers carried on London's rail network, the quality of the experience deteriorated (more passengers, no more rolling stock) and the fares went up (increased

revenue) (resources, 9.9, 9.10 and 9.11). When nightmarish travel tales are so commonplace, it is difficult to persuade people to abandon their cars. Yet government policy has forced the rail companies to become self-supporting: 'Our duty is not to run a service that is desirable – it is to run a service that is profitable'. (Chairman of British Rail, 14 December 1990.)

This case study argues for a **coordinated** and **balanced** approach by showing that it is really no quicker to travel by car into

London. Journey speeds by both rail and car seem to settle down to about the same level. As further road building is likely to release suppressed demand and hence quickly fill up the extra capacity (as has happened with the M25 motorway), greater emphasis should be placed on upgrading the public transport system. Using the concept of a journey as consisting of three elements, (resource 9.8), key proposals for improvement are made.

9.5

The UK's public road system (Length in km to nearest '00)

Type	1978	1983	1988
Motorway	2400	2700	3000
Trunk road	12 000	12 200	12 500
Principal road	34 200	34 800	35 000
Other	287 200	236 000	303 900
Total	338 200	345 700	374 000

Road traffic in the UK (billion vehicle km)

Type	1978	1983	1988
Cars and taxis	202	231	295
Two-wheeled Motor vehicles	6	8	5
Buses and coaches	3	4	4
Good vehicles	45	45	58
Total	256	288	362

Road and rail goods transport in the UK (thousand million tonne km)

Type	1978	1983	1988
Road	99	95	130
Rail	20	17	18

Road goods transport in the UK by type of vehicle (thousand million tonne km)

Weight of Vehicle	1978	1983	1988
Less than 25 tonnes	793	622	682
More than 25 tonnes	627	658	971

Rail traffic in the UK

Type	1978	1983	1988
Passenger journeys (million)	724	694	825
Freight (million tonnes)	172	146	150
% consisting of coal and coke	55	60	53
Length of track (kms)	17 900	17 000	16 600

A city's limits

The transport history of Los Angeles could serve as an object lesson to anyone who still believes that the motor car is a blessing.

Shortly before World War II, the city's streetcar system, one of the best in the USA, was bought out by a consortium of General Motors, Standard Oil and Firestone – and promptly closed down. The consortium was convicted of conspiracy in 1949 but by then the damage was done. The next 20 years saw massive road-building programmes and a transport policy which saw the car as the ony means of transport. The result: a vast, congested urban sprawl.

For the next 20 years, car ownership and use continued to grow steadily. So did congestion. And so did road-building, designed to relieve the congestion. Today, there are only 10 nations which have more cars than Greater Los Angeles. The citizens of LA are acutely aware of the problems posed by unrestricted growth in motoring. The city's air is clearly in breach of the 1977 Clean Air Act, and its traffic problems seem insurmountable. After years of widening freeways, only to see the traffic jams expand to fill them, planners recently considered double-decking the freeways – only to be told by their computer that even then the roads would be full to capacity within 15 years. Now all the planners can hope to achieve is 'balanced congestion'.

They are now considering more radical transport solutions, from reviving the public transport system to pioneering the electric car. Not only do they have to do so in order to reduce air pollution: they also have to do so in order to keep the city moving.

(Source: *The Observer Magazine*, 15 April 1990)

London Regional Transport railway traffic

Type	1978	1983	1988
Passenger journeys (million)	568	563	799
Passenger km (million)	4510	4350	6300
Receipts (£ million)	177	285	417
Rolling stock (Seating capacity in thousands)	172	165	170
Length of track (kilometres)	383	388	394

The commuter trek

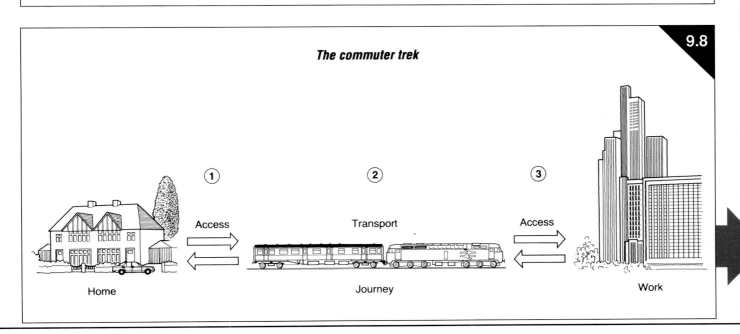

① Access
② Transport
③ Access

Home   Journey   Work

9.9

Tube Highgate to Victoria

Twenty years ago the London Evening Standard ran a series every night for a week about the horrors of travelling on the 'Misery Line'. Regular underground commuters will know at once it was the Northern Line. It still is. The second most maligned line is apparently the Victoria. To sample both, I plotted a journey between Highgate and Victoria, changing from northern to Victoria line at Warren Street. Naturally I did it in the rush hour with the baby.

At 7.42am I turned into Highgate station, carried the pushchair down 51 steps and queued for a ticket. The man ahead was buying his annual season ticket to Ruislip and looked as if he was paying for it with 2p pieces. Down escalator broken; carried pushchair down 141 steps, offers of assistance from two OAPs. Eleven-minute wait for train. Very crowded. Ask armpit next to me if this is a City or Embankment train. Change at Camden, advises armpit. Everyone spills out at Camden Town; everyone cranes neck to see indicator screens. Indicator screens not working. Fourth time this week it's happened, groans City-suited gent. So how do we know which train is coming? You stand in middle of subway connecting the two platforms ascertain from direction of cold wind which platform train is approaching, then run like hell to see destination board on front of train. It doesn't always work because sometimes the trains say they're going

straight to Kennington but then decide to go East instead. Play waiting, listening, running games with several hundred other passengers for 10 minutes before Embankment train shows up. Hard to find carriage with space fo pushchair. Desperate squash, baby in danger of asphyxiation between pinstriped legs. Lift baby up. Koochy koo, says man reading *Independent*. Baby shrieks. Warren Street. Change for Victoria Line. Down escalator broken. Carry pushchair down 90 steps. First train impossible to board. Flattened commuters fall out when doors open and hurl themselves in again. Second, third and fourth trains just as full. This is ridiculous, it is past 8.30am. Force entry on to fifth train, using pushchair as battering ram. Baby, surprisingly fast asleep. Oxford Circus. Caught in current between outgoing and incoming passengers, almost lost pushchair. Green Park. Train doesn't stop. Passengers bang on windows, no announcement. Another fire scare probably, says woman beside me. Ever since King's Cross they have around a dozen a week. Victoria. Total chaos. Down escalator broken so descending passengers monopolise stairs. Only one up escalator to handle backlog of trains full of furious Green Parkers. Official with megaphone trying to herd everyone on to one side like the Good Shepherd. Reach mainline station 9.07am. Verdict: nightmare.

(Source: Sue Arnold, *The Observer Magazine*, 15 April 1990)

9.10

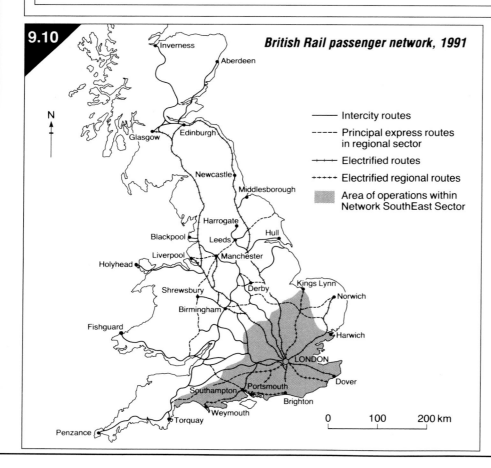

British Rail passenger network, 1991

— Intercity routes

---- Principal express routes in regional sector

+++ Electrified routes

++++ Electrified regional routes

▓ Area of operations within Network SouthEast Sector

0   100   200 km

Key understandings

◆ An equilibrium in journey speeds is established between road and rail trips to central areas in congested conditions.

◆ Central accessibility can be improved only by better rail services into and across inner London.

◆ Improvements in the 'access' elements of the commuting journey are the best ways of improving accessibility.

One over the eight per cent

As the Government pours more money into roads and postpones vital decisions on improving the rail network, the South-east of England faces a transport paralysis with disastrous consequences for the environment and the economy.

Many now think that industry, which has increasingly focused on the booming South-east, will be forced to relocate in the Midlands and North or go to Northern France because its workforce will not be able to reach their place of employment.

Rail commuters – some already crowded on to trains running at 160 per cent capacity – will get some relief in the next few years from new rolling stock and longer platforms, but real solutions will only come with a change in Government policy.

Police are already used to control the numbers going into some London tube stations at peak times and with many trains running at over 100 per cent capacity this is likely to become a regular feature of commuting life.

The crisis in transport in the South-east has been growing for the last five years. From the way the Government has reacted – allocating money to road building – it would seem that lack of tarmac was the key to the problem. But roads are carrying fewer and fewer people to work in London while rail traffic is booming. Some 77 per cent of commuters arrive by rail, 41 per cent by Network SouthEast and the rest by tube.

Network SouthEast's two million passengers a day makes it Europe's largest commuter network with a train arriving in London every 11 seconds in the rush hours. Without advertising, BR increased commuter traffic by 17 per cent in the four years to the end of 1988.

Mr Chris Green, director of Network South-East, is the first to admit that this boom in traffic, which started in 1985 after the slump of the early eighties, took them by surprise. Since then, he says, they have been struggling to catch up. He describes the situation on some lines as 'horrendous'.

Public transport policy in Britain is heavily weighted against a subsidised rail system. In Paris only 40 per cent of the cost of the service is paid for by the passengers in rail fares – in London it is 90 per cent. The extremes are Italy where fares make up only 30 per cent of income and Tokyo where there is no subsidy.

Commuter growth in the South-east is expected to grow by another 1.5 per cent a year between now and the end of the century. Network South-East cannot look to the London tube network to soak up much of this increase. Tube lines are already working at maximum capacity with trains every two minutes during the rush hour and the length of trains limited to the size of stations constructed by the Victorians.

British Rail have come up with three tunnelling schemes to ease the problem and decisions on all of them have been postponed. The most promising was a Paddington to Liverpool Street service with stops on the way at Bond Street, Tottenham Court Road, and Farringdon. It would have relieved the Central and Circle lines and allowed trains to cross London. Sadly for British Rail it could not demonstrate an eight per cent return on new assets which would cost £1500 million.

No doubt many of the employers on this route and stores like Selfridges would have felt the benefit, but, unlike the French who have a local employers levy system, the Government has no mechanism for charging them for the service.

The second scheme put up for Government go-ahead this autumn but shelved by the government was the £300 million metro link. This would require new rail flyovers in south London for extra tracks. British Rail faced a fight from Southwark residents who would have lost the characterful Borough Market and a number of listed buildings as well as some well loved pubs, but as value for money this again failed to meet the Government criteria. In terms of passenger numbers it would have increased peak hour service from south London to King's Cross from 4000 to 13 000 passengers an hour.

Next year British Rail wanted to add a north-south tunnel linking King's Cross and Victoria which would have made it possible to go from Dorking and Croydon to Milton Keynes and Stevenage. This would have relieved the nightmare of the Northern and Victoria lines. The price is £1500 million and cannot show an eight per cent return.

British Rail is making investments in new rolling stock and stations. This is classed as replacing existing provision and £820 million is planned to be spent. A new type of train called the Networker, made of aluminium with 16 per cent more seats and faster acceleration because of its light weight, is now being built. This will speed journey times. In addition, the existing platforms lengthened 20 years ago to take 10 coach trains will be lengthened again to take 12. The existing capacity of the fleet on this line will rise from 86 000 to 113 000 passengers.

This transformation will take some painful years to work through and barely keep up with demand.

South of London trains run so close together in the rush hour that 'if a commuter drops his umbrella between two trains' the whole system collapses like a pile of dominoes.

North of the river the situation is better. With more coaches on order and longer platforms planned, the capacity can be improved although there are still hiccups. One of them is British Rail's switch to one man operation. Guards, with their days numbered, are thin on the ground as they find other jobs. Train cancellations due to staff shortages are up to eight per cent on some lines. The short term solution of paying staff extra has been rejected by British Rail. Driver- only trains gain reliability by the simple device of paying the driver £7 a shift for turning up. It's called a productivity bonus.

New rolling stock, new signals, new staff are all part of British Rail's plan to catch up and temporarily overtake its booming passenger traffic but that will only be enough to keep it up with the game to the mid-1990s. Only a change in Government policy which would allow a railway building boom on a scale not seen since Victorian days can save London from reaching overload after that.

(Source: Paul Brown, *The Guardian*, 24 November 1989)

London – an acute case of strangulation

Commuting into London by rail is by two essentially separate networks, one focusing upon the main line termini south of the River Thames, e.g. Waterloo Station and the other upon termini north of the river, such as Euston (resource 9.12). To cross or move through the central areas, whether you have arrived by underground – the 'tube', or train, you change to the inner-city train system. This interchange takes, on average, five minutes, platform to platform in crowded and confined conditions. Then there is the tube journey itself (resource 9.9), followed by the struggle to reach the street and the final walk to your place of work. Resource 9.12 shows some proposed solutions to this problem. However it may be a number of years before they are implemented

It is hardly surprising therefore, that a key factor determining where people choose to buy or rent property, is the proximity to a direct rail line to their place of work. Little wonder too, that people are reluctant to abandon their cars for commuting. Indeed, until the late 1980s, road traffic entering central London was increasing steadily, as a result of a series of desperate traffic management schemes. By 1990 however, saturation point seemed to have been reached and both government and the public now accept the futility of trying to pour more people and their vehicles into the central area.

Surveys taken in the period 1962–1982, during the morning rush hours (0700 hours to 1000 hours) show that the journey speed for commuting to central London (defined as an area with a 6 km radius from Piccadilly) is approximately the same for car and public transport (resource 9.13). A report published in 1987 concluded:

'It seems that road network speeds settle to an equilibrium such that the average journey speed door-to-door by road equals that for the equivalent journey by the fastest public transport mode available'.

What seems to happen is that road traffic rapidly expands to fill the extra capacity provided by an improved or new road, and traffic clogging is as severe as ever. A classic example of this release of suppressed demand is the M25 orbital motorway around London – by Autumn 1991, the government were proposing a parallel relief motorway for the M25 (resource 9.14). Thus, travellers who are attracted to the new route to achieve shorter travel times, quickly fill it up, and soon travel speeds sink back to the old level.

A first step in studying the rail commuting problem is to identify the three main stages of the journey: (i) access from home to the station, (ii) station to station, including change of trains where necessary and (iii) access from station to work (resource 9.8). As the graphs in resource 9.15 show, the total access time, i.e. the time it takes to get to the train from home, and from the train to the workplace is approximately 30 minutes, 15–20 minutes from origin (home) to train and 10–15 minutes from train to

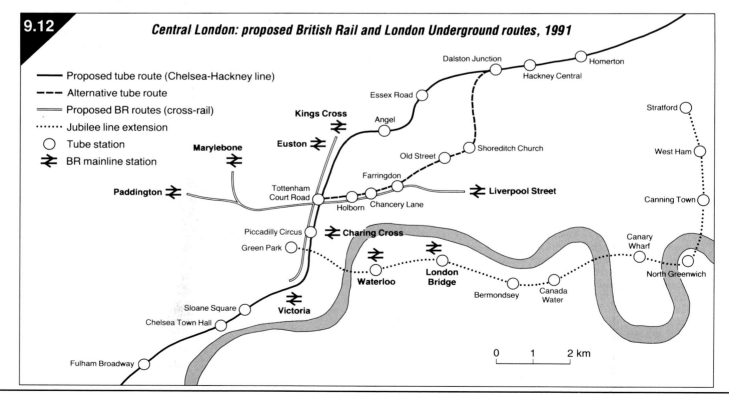

9.12 *Central London: proposed British Rail and London Underground routes, 1991*

— Proposed tube route (Chelsea-Hackney line)
--- Alternative tube route
= Proposed BR routes (cross-rail)
···· Jubilee line extension
○ Tube station
⇌ BR mainline station

Stations shown: Homerton, Dalston Junction, Hackney Central, Essex Road, Stratford, Kings Cross, Angel, Shoreditch Church, West Ham, Marylebone, Euston, Old Street, Farringdon, Liverpool Street, Canning Town, Paddington, Tottenham Court Road, Chancery Lane, Holborn, Piccadilly Circus, Charing Cross, Canary Wharf, Green Park, Waterloo, London Bridge, North Greenwich, Bermondsey, Canada Water, Sloane Square, Victoria, Chelsea Town Hall, Fulham Broadway

0 1 2 km

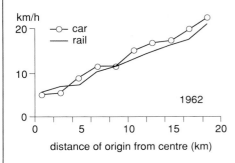

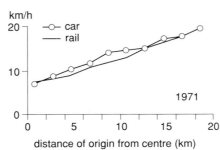

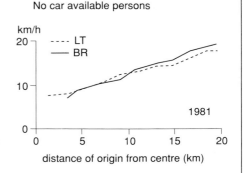

Direct journey speeds in the morning peak for journeys to central circular area (6 km radius) by distance of origin from centre

1962

1971

No car available persons

1981

destination (workplace). Notice too, that the distances covered and the speeds achieved on these access journeys are only slightly greater for those who commute from the urban periphery. The graph in resource 9.15 (c) tells us that for journeys of up to 20 km, the rail travel time ranges from approximately 20 minutes to 60 minutes. It is easy to see therefore, how the commuting trek can take an hour or more, each way, each day.

It is possible, of course to reduce the need for commuting by policies such as dispersal of job opportunities, but intense commuter flows are certain to continue. In seeking improvements in public transport we must distinguish between bus and rail travel. Surveys show that bus passengers tend to travel relatively short distances (average 5 km) from inner London to central London, and to work on that edge of the central area nearest to their home. Because of the flexibility of bus routing, and frequency of stops which ease access, it is the journey element rather than the access elements of the trip which offer scope for improvement. For instance, average journey speed by bus in central London has dropped to below 10 km/hour. Thus, the increased provision of bus-only lanes and more severe restrictions on the

Daily traffic congestion makes better rail services an ever-greater priority

use of private vehicles are likely to enhance bus travel speeds.

Rail passengers on the other hand, tend to travel longer distances and to be more likely to change to a second mode, e.g. tube or bus, on reaching their central rail terminus. The laying of new rail tracks is expensive, space-consuming and hence unlikely, with the possible exception of a line linking the Channel Tunnel with central London. The Jubilee Line is the most recent major rail investment, and while a substantial shift of

passengers took place immediately, the full impact on traffic flows took about seven years to evolve. This is because people change jobs and homes to match the new opportunities available to them. These changes vary according to the stage in an individual or family life cycle, e.g. on average, people change jobs every two-and-a half years and homes every seven.

As traffic density on existing lines has reached capacity, there is limited potential for increased services. As a result, most transport planners agree that for rail travel, it is the access elements of the trip where improvements might be found. For example, at the 'origin' end of the trip, improved bus services to the station and enhanced parking at the station. At the 'destination' end, one of the critical weaknesses is the awkward change from train to tube or bus to move through the central area, especially if this means crossing the River Thames. The most commonly recognised need is, therefore, for the building of cross-centre lines linking the major termini such as Waterloo and Euston (as with the cross-Birmingham line between Lichfield in the north and Redditch in the south). This would reduce the necessity for a change of trains, and so improve access times. As a 1987 study concluded:

CASE STUDY 9.1 *Getting in and out of London*

'This is not a matter of improving interchange at the main railway termini … The only way for the position for BR passengers to be improved is for the termini to be done away with, and for through-running schemes between a former terminus on one side of the central area and an appropriate former terminus on the other side to be built, with perhaps two intermediate stations, i.e. cross-centre lines.

'Such schemes have been considered many times in the past, in particular in the London Railway Study in 1974, but the only scheme to be given the go-ahead is the Thames-Link Scheme, reinstating a disused connection between Farringdon and Holborn Viaduct along the Fleet River. This Fleet Line runs from some 6 km and will eventually connect Bedford and Luton Airport with Croydon, Sevenoaks and Gillingham. In many continental cities, such schemes have been implemented, connecting rail systems on each side of the city centre. The main parallel with London is that of Paris. The decision was taken in 1971 to interconnect with a cross-rail scheme the main suburban services of the Gare du Nord and Gare de Lyon, and the new east-west Regional Express Line'.

Since this study was published, pressure has mounted, with BR and a variety of planners and consultants presenting proposals based on the cross-centre concept. Resource 9.16 compares the road and public transport problems and policies of London and Paris, making it clear that London is by no means unique.

(Source: adapted from M J H Mogridge, 'The use of rail transport to improve accessibility in large conurbations, using London as an example', *Town Planning Review*, 58(2), pp. 165–182)

9.15

Access times, distances and speeds for journeys to central (6km radius) area in morning peak by distance of origin from centre. Left: from origin to railway station; right: from central railway station to destination.

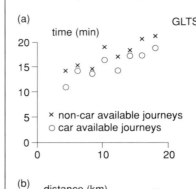
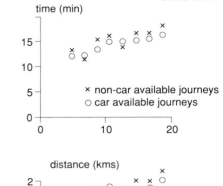
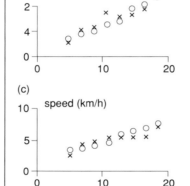
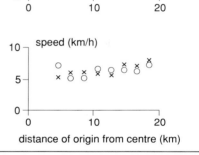

Activities

1 Outline the reasons why it is the 'access' elements of a journey that planners see as the most practical way to improve passenger travel.

2 With a partner, discuss the main problems which are likely to occur in efforts to improve access at:

a the origin, and

b the destination end of a journey.

(Try to identify who would be involved in making decisions about such changes, e.g. local government, central government agencies, private landowners and developers, transport companies, and what their roles might be.

3 Explain why travel speeds on road and rail routes in metropolitan areas tend to settle down to about the same level, even if new or improved routes are not introduced.

The Paris solution: would it work in London?

There is one depressing fact that unites the great cities of Paris and London: it is virtually impossible to cross either capital any faster in a souped-up Ford Sierra today than it was in a horse and cart 100 years ago.

The average speed of traffic in Paris has slowed to 6.2mph and in London to 11.2mph. On a bad day, with roadworks and breakdowns, it can take up to two hours to cross either capital.

Over the years motorists have borne these tribulations stoically while watching many grand schemes disappear in a welter of political bickering. Great debates have been waged about whether cars should be banned from inner cities or more roads and parking spaces provided.

But now there is a difference between the two cities; Paris is planning something spectacular to alleviate its problems. Three projects are under consideration and one seems certain to be adopted.

Jacques Chirac, the mayor of Paris, is looking at two proposals to build a network of tunnels beneath the city which will have cars speeding at 40mph beneath the Eiffel Tower while pedestrians stroll on a Champs Elysées free from the blight of traffic. Instead of two hours, it could take 15 minutes to cross Paris in subterranean motorways whose overall length would exceed the Channel tunnel.

Chirac is also considering another proposal to build a steel flyover on top of the existing ring road, the périphérique, though this may run into objections from residents.

Either way, the schemes, which have the backing of Michel Rocard, the prime minister, are part of a bigger project to develop the infrastructure of the French capital.

All this would take years to build, though a decision is due next year and the city may hold a referendum to make its final choice. One important factor is that the projects, which will cost billions of pounds, will be privately financed.

Until recently Chirac's policy was to cram more cars into existing space rather than force them out of Paris. But last week he announced a 10-year plan to ban parking on main city streets and create 5000 underground parking spaces a year.

In the first phase of a tougher anti-car programme, parking fines were doubled. Offenders now have to pay £90 for parking in a bus lane, £200 for not paying in the specified period, and £250 for the national pastime of jumping the lights. The city plans to 'remove' 60 000 illegal parking spaces, add more bus lanes and establish no-parking stretches on the boulevards.

Despite this crackdown, polls show that Parisian motorists are prepared to do and pay almost anything to drive in the city.

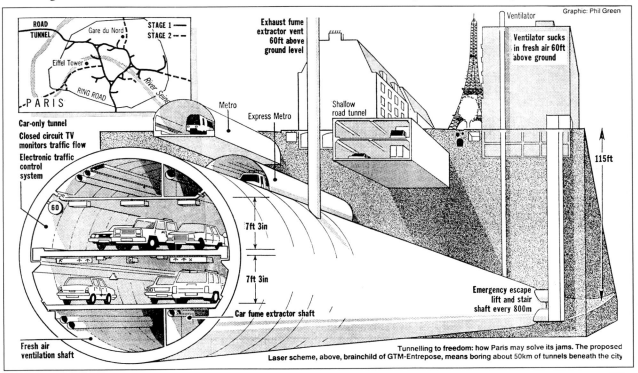

Tunnelling to **freedom:** how Paris may solve its jams. The proposed Laser scheme, above, brainchild of GTM-Entrepose, means boring about 50km of tunnels beneath the city

Up to 2.8m cars enter Paris daily while vehicles of inner-city residents add another 1.4m. There are only 720 000 legal car spaces for these 4.2m cars, and it is difficult even to find illegal parking.

The government consensus is that something has to be done, and nobody doubts that the French can undertake such massive projects. Of the two competing tunnel schemes, the one called Laser (Liaison Automobile Souterraine Expresse Regionale) is the furthest advanced, with a proposed 50km of subterranean motorway with numerous entry and exit points inside the city. So far it has the edge over a rival scheme that would improve links between Charles de Gaulle and Orly airports.

Laser is the brainchild of the GTM-Entrepose company, an offshoot of the Dumez construction giant working on the Channel tunnel. French banks have guaranteed the financing – £1.6 billion – for the first stage, with £2.2 billion committed overall.

The idea is for a central underground ring road linking the main business districts and train stations. It will have five branches from this ring, leading to 20 exit and entry points within the city and 10 more on the fringe. The toll for each car will be £2 and the system will be managed by Cofiroute, the company which has financed 425 miles of French autoroutes.

Entry will be computer-controlled and elaborate safety measures are proposed, with assurances that the tunnels could be evacuated in 10 minutes in an emergency. Large vans will be banned, partially for safety reasons and because this will mean smaller tunnels.

A spokesman for Cofiroute said that 'at the moment Laser is halfway between science fiction and reality. I should say political fiction, because that is where the real problem lies. Technically, there is nothing stopping this project.

'Advanced Japanese drilling machines can bore a precise 9.45-metre diameter tunnel. There are a lot of existing tunnels under Paris, making it look like a gruyère cheese. But at 35 metres, it will be below the other tunnels.'

Critics of Laser claim that the scheme will be a disaster because it will suck even more cars into Paris.

Two factors work in favour of the tunnel schemes. The plan for another flyover is likely to face strong resistance, and for once there is no big election on the horizon. This could allow politicians to push through what may initially prove an unpopular measure.

(Source: Alan Tillier and Paul Beresford, *The Sunday Times*, 12 November 1989)

CASE STUDY 9.2 *Motorway impacts – the case of Banbury and the M40*

Background

Motorways have two basic goals: the improvement of the flow of passenger and goods vehicles between major cities, and the removal of unnecessary through traffic from within the fabric of settlements (resource 9.17). There is, however, a third characteristic, that of enhancing the accessibility of settlements adjacent to the motorway, especially those large enough to justify junctions and sliproads. Such improved accessibility may attract industry, property developers, commuters and shoppers, and will increase land values. These spin-offs would, at first glance, appear to be to the benefit of such towns. However, the reality is much more complex, with both costs and benefits, when measured in economic, social and environmental terms.

This case study allows us to identify and assess these costs and benefits through a study of Banbury, a medium-sized town in Oxfordshire, midway between London and Birmingham (resource 9.18). It lies astride the dangerously overused A41 trunk road and adjacent to the new M40 motorway, intended to reduce pressure on the A41. (In a wider context, the M40 draws some traffic away from the M6/M1 Midlands – London route.) As the

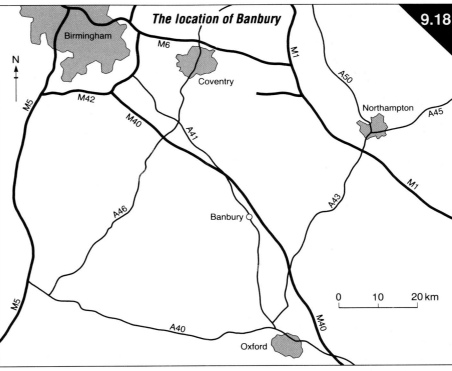

The location of Banbury 9.18

materials show, the impacts of the coming of the motorway fall into two main categories: (i) the effects upon the land and people along its route, (ii) the pressures for change within and around the town itself. e.g. in September 1990, Coca Cola was given permission to build a large bottling plant, after a long planning controversy – trade union officials pressed for jobs and residents protested at the loss of amenity.

As you work through the materials, note especially the impacts and changes, the perceptions and attitudes of various groups involved, and where the power to make decisions about environment lies.

The four viewpoints in resource 9.19 highlight the issues.

Key understandings

◆ Motorways are intended to improve accessibility and mobility.

◆ Motorways have significant economic, social and environmental impacts upon settlements and communities along their routes.

◆ Whether the impacts are beneficial or detrimental to your quality of life depends on who you are. Different people hold contrasting viewpoints about the coming of a motorway, and there are 'winners' and 'losers'.

◆ Much of the decision-making may be out of the hands of the local community.

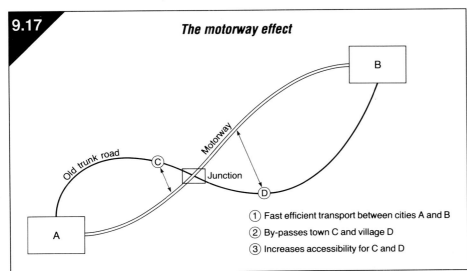

9.17 **The motorway effect**

① Fast efficient transport between cities A and B

② By-passes town C and village D

③ Increases accessibility for C and D

9.19

A farm divided

Mike Stevens (right, with his daughter Emma) drew the short straw twice. The M40 cuts in half two of the three farms he runs on the Banbury town boundary (he owns one and rents the other two from New College, Oxford). Life since the contractors arrived on site has been a nightmare: 'Grandfather started farming here in 1935. Part of me has gone with that motorway. No one prepared me for the devastation of these contractors moving in and ripping up land I had farmed all my life, He should, he said, have employed someone to replace him on the farm while he grappled with motorway business, on which he estimates he now spends half his time. 'The pressure has been enormous, not only on me, but on my family and the other workers. My wife will tell you that I am a different person, on a short fuse and a lot harder than I was.' But he added that he had learned who to deal with: 'Go to the top. I get on to the bosses; if you shout loud enough, you'll get things done. But it is no good being bloodyminded and standing there with a shotgun.'

Each farmer keeps a day-book in which he enters his problems. Martin Nichols, one of Mike Stevens's neighbours, showed me column after column cataloguing escaped animals, severed water pipes, and – all summer long – dense flying dust. 'It's like brown fog,' said his wife. What upsets the farmers is that they have to fight hard and long over trivial amounts to keep their farms in shaky business, while millions are being spent at the bottom of their fields. A land agent said: 'The contractors and the department will quibble over a drop in the ocean. If you go along the road you will see tremendous waste.' He cited an occasion on which three loss adjusters had travelled from London to consider a claim for £670. 'A farmer will (say) spend £70 installing a trough so that his cattle do not die of thirst. The contractors' attitude often is: Why not move the cattle? But why should he? Farmers would be far more M40-friendly if the other side didn't take such an unyielding attitude. They find themselves dealing with bureaucracy at its worst. The people who control the money are far removed from the hardship suffered by farmers. To them it is just another job.'

One temporary bonus Mike Stevens does enjoy is the use of the embryo motorway as a country lane between his farms. As we drove at a jolting 10 mph over the hard core, he pointed out where a duck pond had been and where, until a few months previously, they had driven the birds on to the only shoot on his land.

What makes the despoliation particularly galling is that neighbouring farmers lucky enough to have their land designated for development are making literally millions. I mentioned a man who had planning permission for a golf course on his land. 'Dear Fred,' sighed Stevens, 'is going to make a fortune.' His eyes narrowed as he spotted barrels of liquid aluminium on the motorway verge. Maybe that was blowing on to his crops and pasture. A few hundred yards on, we encountered an engineer, who adopted a pained expression at the sight of Mike Stevens. The battle between farmer and contractor was joined once more.

Guarding his vision

Brian Cornley, the chief planning officer of Cherwell District Council (which embraces Banbury) is, said one of his admirers, the town's 'guardian'. As a young man he lived in New Zealand, sustaining a vision of 'what I'd left behind and what I might go back to – which was always to an English market town as I had remembered it as a child; a street market for sheep and pigs and a covered market for veg. That's what I saw as the best of English life. The size was right. It was friendly. The community had almost everything that was needed, a decent supply of education, culture and shopping.' He sees Banbury, despite its rapid growth in the last 30 years, as such a community, worth defending with the powers vested in him against what he would consider to be the predatory ambitions of the developers: 'You can still grasp the whole of Banbury, feel it all, walk around its little, funny-shaped streets on any visit you make. Banbury just hangs on to these attractive characteristics. If you allow or cause it to grow much bigger, they will be

eroded or disappear fairly quickly.' What is needed, he argues, is some clear thought. What are the objectives set down for the M40? Relief of the M1; a fast through road from the south coast to the Midlands; the relief of existing communities who suffer appalling environmental damage. 'It is not one of the stated purposes to facilitate development within the Cherwell valley.'

He is, he believes, thoroughly in tune with what the average citizen wishes for the town. 'The local paper reflects the noisiest people. What they say gets wide coverage, and the planning authorities are seen to be dragging their feet. I suppose that I seem to be out of step with most of the commentators, but in step with the vast majority who live here.' The motorway's local purpose, he contends, is to enhance the quality of life for those who already live in and around Banbury, not to swamp town and villages with tens of thousands more people and acres of concrete. He makes a firm distinction between those with an axe to grind, those who can benefit in a business sense and the ordinary resident, who may now have the opportunity to visit the West End theatre and get back again in the same evening. Seizing every development opportunity as some business people

want, would, he argues, restore the traffic about to be removed by the motorway and devour the countryside.

He adds: 'I am misunderstood. I am not saying pull up the drawbridge and keep everyone out. I am advocating organic growth.' He believes that Banbury's existing, mainly new, industries will need what space there is in town to expand in order to survive. As they grow, they'll leave smaller premises behind them enabling new businesses to start. 'The growth in relative terms will be substantial.' If the developers converted their wildest dreams into action, the population of Banbury might reach 100 000 by the end of the century. 'That would be quite crazy,' he said. 'I'm not saying that my vision will be fulfilled, only that it can, if you, you and you stick together,' and he stabbed the air at an imaginary audience.

Going for growth

John Harper, a chartered surveyor with Chestertons, was brave enough to produce a blueprint for Banbury postulating a population some 25 000 more than that envisaged by the official town plan. It earned him instant fame among like-minded business people who want Banbury to go for growth, and notoriety among the protectors of the 'market town' ideal. 'Oh, you must go and see John Harper,' everyone said when I arrived in town, and their tones of voice unerringly betrayed where they stood on the issue of the motorway.

'Organic growth', as favoured by chief planning officer Brian Cornley and the majority of Cherwell Council, should, said the Harper paper, 'be replaced by a more positive programme of planned expansion'. (He made organic growth sound like something that only a planning wimp would advocate.) He painted a picture of Banbury collapsing under the weight of its existing problems – severe traffic congestion, rapidly

rising house prices, a chronic shortage of land – unless the planners threw a ring road round the town and released several hundred further acres for development. The council policies, he claimed, 'do not adequately address the pressures nor the potential pressures that the construction and subsequent opening of the M40 will undoubtedly bring'. He pointed to High Wycombe and Swindon as towns that had successfully exploited their easy access to motorways – thus bringing a shudder to all those who believe that Swindon is exactly what Banbury should not be.

'Banbury could accommodate with relative ease between 8500 and 9500 new houses in addition to existing commitments,' he wrote with happy insouciance. 'This number of houses could provide accommodation for an additional 22 000 to 24 500 people. The land identified for industrial and commercial development could provide (between) 15 000 and 18 500 jobs.' At least one critic was surprised that John Harper had not suggested an international airport.

Before I met this scourge

of planning 'wets', I had been expecting some fierce Visigoth, and was rather disappointed to find myself in the presence of a mild and middle-aged, slightly overweight, country professional gentleman. The real movement in town had started, he said, two years earlier. In the mid-Eighties there had been a million square feet of industrial space and 100 000 sq. ft of office going begging. Now there was nothing. 'Major companies have identified this place as an area to expand into,' he said. Prices had gone from £100 000 an acre to £1

million. He almost sighed with frustration at the thought of the developers who were beating a path to his door and had to be sent away empty-handed. He contrasted the 'old guard', who wanted things to stay much as they are, with the 'progressives'. He pointed with gloomy joy to the recent successful appeal by Tesco against the council's refusal to grant planning permission for an out-of-town-centre store. There were, he suggested, more such well-merited defeats ahead.

9.19

From wheat to golf

John Hunter has achieved what many farmers would now give their eyeteeth for. A sign at the end of the drive that leads to his 207-acre farm at Kirtlington, a few miles south of Banbury, proclaims: 'FOR SALE: farmland with consent for golf course, club house and hotel.' Farmers (especially small ones) are suffering. The days of fat Common Market subsidies are over – and, while costs rise inexorably, the price of farmers' produce remains pegged. The arrival of the M40 has raised hopes among farmers in a wide area around Banbury that they can either sell out to leisure-industry companies or themselves diversify. The Banbury office of the estate agents Savills has 28 projected conversion schemes on its books – 18 of them for golf courses. (Other notions include a minitheme park, tennis centres, clay pigeon shooting ranges, and a 'grown-up Butlin's', which requires 300 to 400 acres of woodland with planning permission.) Permission for a golf course will double the value of the land (which stands roughly at £1500-an-acre in the Banbury area); for golf course and hotel it can quadruple it.

John Hunter is lucky. His farm has access to a major road. It is relatively poor quality; his fields are gently undulating, and the soil is suitable for golf all the year round. He has 150-year old scheduled stone barns which are ideal for conversion into a small hotel and restaurant. When I met him, the farm had been on the market for a month, and interest was being shown by investors from all over the world. Brochures, said Hunter, were going out 'like confetti'. He is now past 60 and close to retirement, and is not, as are some farmers, sentimental about his farm: 'Land is to be used; it is better that it should be a golf course than not used at all.'

The path is not always as smooth as it has been for John Hunter. A few miles to the south, farmer Adam Besterman, having abandoned an ambitious proposal by a 'major PLC' ('They were talking megabucks') for a clay pigeon shoot so as not to aggravate his neighbours, is running into fierce local opposition to his application for a golf course. Although the M40 will slice through his land, and he believes that the golf course – liberally planted with trees – will actually enhance the environment, he has been caricatured, he complains, as 'a large developer moving in to capitalise on the area's grief.'

Is the M40 making Banbury cross?

In its most extreme, emotive terms, the arrival of the M40 faces Banbury

9.20

Banbury. How will the M40 link affect the town's individuality and the quality of life of its citizens?

with a choice between becoming the fastest-growing community in Britain, with all the upheaval that entails, or remaining – as several citizens put it – 'in the dark ages' as traffic, hastening between the nation's first and second cities, pounds past its slip-road. With the road complete, Banbury is one hour from the West Midlands and an hour and a half from London and Southampton. From being a community with an air of remoteness, Banbury faces a future as the hub of southern Britain.

The implications have thus far been reported almost exclusively in terms of economic aggrandisement. Newspapers – local and national – have run advertisement-packed supplements. Banbury is on the development map; hurry, hurry, while limited stocks of precious land and honey-stone cottages remain!

Any community touched by a motorway undegoes changes that reach into every aspect of life.

Banbury's individuality is already under assault: in come yet more multiple stores, volume house builders, national hotel chains. And in, also, come people without roots in its rich loam and with no historic attachment to its narrow 16th-century streets (resource 9.20). The country roads, which have long been dangerous, now bear a stream of speeding cars. A local public school reports an upsurge in applications; village schools struggle to keep going, and village shops close. New estates with leaded panes and two-car garages spring up on the town's margin.

A farmer said: 'I used to move my sheep along the road; I get rude gestures now – everyone is so cross. The police come along: 'How long are you going to be? And how far are you going?' Soon 50 cars build up. I may be within my rights, but I don't feel very comfortable.'

It had seemed, when the hotly contested route of the M40 was settled, that the section between Oxford and Birmingham might be Britain's final great motorway adventure, and Banbury the last substantial community to find itself stretched between a desire to grab the golden opportunities and a fear that, in doing so, it was entering a contract that would cost it, if not its soul, at least its character.

But in 1989 the Government announced a £12 billion, 10-year plan to barrel ahead with the construction of a further 2700 miles of new or widened roads, including several more motorways. For a motorway is now recognised to be as much the catalyst for economic expansion as the railways were in the last century. East Anglia blossomed once the M11 was completed; the M4 created Britain's most prosperous industrial corridor along the length of the Thames; and even the jammed M25 has transformed a vast swathe of the inner Home Counties.

Banbury suffers horrific blight from the nose-to-tail trucks grinding down the Oxford road and past the Victorian cross (replacing the original of nursery rhyme fame, destroyed in 1600). The ground perpetually trembles as if an earth tremor threatens. A relief road had been promised for 30 years, so Banbury might be supposed to be in the throes of an anguished debate about how to cope with an opportunity which – if it is poorly handled – bears within it the seeds of civic disaster.

Banbury is as near the centre of England as it is geometrically possible to gauge. If sound planning were the yardstick that determined the routes of motorways, the M40 should have been hurtling vehicles north and south since at least the late Sixties. Now that the road is coming, the development that would have been spun out over a quarter of a century will be compressed into three or four years.

The town had a small Victorian industrial heritage. However, the first major manufacturer, now British Alcan, only arrived in the Thirties – a watershed moment for the town – and during the Second World War employed 4000 people making aluminium sheeting for aircraft. But after the hostilities Banbury was restored essentially as a market town, basing its prosperity on agriculture.

Into this reticent, stratified community of 20 000 in the early Sixties were added 7000 'over spillers' from London and Birmingham, arriving to live in sprawling red-brick council estates and to take semi-skilled factory employment, e.g. Bird's Custard moved from central Birmingham.

Today Banbury's population is nearly 40 000, to whom must be added the several thousand more who live in the Horton-stone villages and farms that dot the countryside. The debate over how the town should respond to the motorway is now concentrated on how large this population should become.

Forty-two thousand by the year 1996, say the planners. An impracticable and dangerous limitation that would unnaturally stunt Banbury's growth, say the town's would-be developers. 'It's a joke,' said one property agent. 'I don't think the planning department has quite grasped the demand that there is.' Developers look to a population of between 60 000 and 70 000 by the end of the century.

The raw figures are symbols in a conflict that reaches back to the mid-Sixties, when the then town council – on the casting vote of the mayor – decided to reject a target figure of 70 000 for the town.

Everyone knows what he wishes the town not to become – variously a Coventry, a Milton Keynes, a Swindon, a Reading. The figure of 42 000 represents historic continuity with the concept of a small market town, in which most people know each other and can walk to work or to the shops – 'It's good,' said a small town advocate, 'to be able to go down the street in Wellingtons and not feel embarrassed.'

The larger population figures envisage a 'Silicon Valley' community, ringed by gleaming high tech business parks, and more amply provided with culture and recreation than a smaller town is ever likely to be. To the expansionist camp, the market town – 'Twee streets where the gentry do their shopping,' said one jaundiced man – is an outdated, romantic notion that threatens to constrain Banbury within a straightjacket.

The expansionists believe – despite a county structure plan that places severe restraint on growth throughout Oxfordshire – that they have the inevitability of momentum on their side. The tensions that face Banbury, they argue, will ensure that the council's restrictive decisions will be overturned at planning inquiries – 'They will get egg on their faces time and again,' said one – and will therefore lose local control over how Banbury grows. This, they contend, would be the worst possible consequence of the M40.

Even those with no axe to grind point to giant companies like Marks & Spencer, jostling either to come into town or to expand, and argue that these businesses know from national experience when a community is about to take off.

One section of Banbury's business community anxious to advertise its virtues are those who run cafes and hotels. For years they have watched tourists pause only long enough to take snaps of the Cross, treating the town – in the words of one – as a 'tea and wee' stop, before they hasten towards nearby Stratford and Oxford. 'It's a small town, steeped in history, and should have people queuing at toll gates to get in,' said Councillor Cowan, who manages the High Street Wimpy bar.

Banburians who love their town dearly feel like tearing their hair from time to time. A former schoolteacher said: 'There is in

Banbury a feeling that you cannot challenge the system. People are compliant. The extent to which pupils in secondary school are dead from the neck up is overwhelming. You have to shake them to get life out of them.'

Defensiveness lies also at the heart of local response to the sleek entrepreneurs arriving to exploit the M40. One Banbury businessman said: 'Developers do try to steam-roller locals. They offer low prices and an arrogant approach. 'Here we are,' they say, 'and we're going to buy your land. We're the best thing that ever happened to Banbury.' They come here and think that we have straw growing out of our ears. We might have done 30 years ago, but things have changed.'

Bretch Hill, is an overspill estate where a quarter of Banbury's people live. There is on Bretch Hill an unenviable concentration of social problems which belie the market-town image of Banbury's centre. At one school, almost half the pupils belong to single parent families. As the children of the first generation over-spillers grow up, there is gross overcrowding – often six or seven adults to a small council house. The vast majority of young people leave school at 16, disqualifying themselves from well-paid jobs in Banbury's modern industries.

The elected representatives of this underclass find themselves in an unlikely alliance with the developers. Labour county councillor Jack Steer, who lives on and represents Bretch Hill, said: 'The English country town is lovely for those who can afford to be there, but if you live on Bretch Hill, increasing industrial activity means that you've got a chance of at least earning a living and maybe actually getting your own home.'

Government policy is for local authorities to become enabling agents, encouraging the private sector to build low-cost housing rather than providing it themselves. There will be a crucial interlude between the end of the old system

and the start of the new. Meanwhile, argue Jack Steer and others, Banbury's boom could be aborted by the lack of cheap housing.

Pressure on housing will intensify as high-tech firms lure professional staff to the town – a third of the workforce in one company was recruited outside Banbury. Veronica Spencer, who runs a fistful of companies including two recruitment firms, said: 'I'd love to tell you that the whole place is booming, but it is not true. This town is not ready for the M40.'

There has been a jump in professional jobs: to meet the need, she has opened an 'importation' recruiting office in Coventry where wages for skilled people are 30 to 40 per cent lower than in Banbury. But life at the bottom remains wretched: she said that hourly-paid staff working for small, non-unionised companies were often treated 'incredibly badly'.

Time and again people complained about the lack of amenities. Banbury has a cinema and pubs. David Thomson, vicar of St. Paul's parish on Bretch Hill, said that most people's idea of a night's relaxation was 'a video and a six-pack'. His parishioners, many of whom survive on an accumulation of 'funny hours' jobs, are not the kind who say, 'Gosh, we're only 18 miles from Stratford-Upon-Avon!'

At the other end of Banbury's social scale, John Bridgeman, the managing director of British Alcan Enterprises and one of the town's chief movers and shakers, argues that there is such a thing as 'critical mass', which is needed to encourage and sustain a town's amenities.

Banbury, he said, has a thousand square miles of Britain dependent on it as a shopping centre and focal

point. 'It is a very tall order to expect a population of 40 000 and a relatively small industrial base to support the quality of infrastructure required by such an area.'

Leighton King is an American who first came to Britain with the US Air Force, liked what he considered to be the civilised quality of life, and returned, eventually to start Tech-Nel, a now thriving company.

Mr King, who lives a few miles to the north of Banbury in sight of the M40, believes that the motorway's coming should be seized on to kindle the local imagination. He said: 'It's not realistic to cherish a horse-and-carriage notion of Banbury. There is too much geographic importance to where we are for that.'

(Source: R Chesshyre, 'Banbury's cross roads', *Sunday Times Magazine*, 17 September 1989)

Activity

1 **Group discussion:**

   a Identify the 'winners' and 'losers' and summarise what they 'win' or 'lose', and hence why they support or oppose the motorway.

   b Is there an alternative to what is happening? If so, what is it, and how could it be organised?

2 Identify the individuals and groups who appear to have the power to make decisions and those who seem to be powerless to influence what is going on. How might this situation be changed?

3 Summarise how the M40 issue illustrates the concepts of 'accessibility' and 'mobility'.

4 Analyse the materials within the structure of this matrix:

	Economic	Social	Environmental
Benefits			
Costs			

CASE STUDY 9.3 *Transport networks in command economies – the examples of Moscow and Budapest*

Background

Under communist regimes, the state has frequently been the provider of public transportation, although the recent changes towards democracy may permit competition to replace this state monopoly. Under the communist system, car ownership levels remained lower than is common in western capitalist societies. This, combined with the emphasis placed by the authorities upon the provision of public transport, means that relatively high proportions of city dwellers rely on buses, trams and railways. The capital cities and metropolises of Eastern Europe and the CIS (formerly the Soviet Union) are generally historic cities whose modern expansion has given them a radial-concentric morphology, with residential and industrial sectors encircling the traditional core. The transport networks reflect this structure with a radial system connected by one or more ring links. As we have already seen in the case of London, the continued spread of residential areas and the persistent centralisation of jobs, places increasing strain on such a network.

Moscow and Budapest each have well-developed public transport systems combining bus, tram and rail. In both cases, population and economic growth has meant that continued additions to the networks capacity are required. It is particularly interesting to note how each type of transport serves a different purpose and hence has a different pattern. Note too, the influence the physical characteristics of the sites have upon the patterns and functioning, e.g. main rivers and hills.

Following the 1917 Revolution, Moscow replaced St. Petersburg as the capital and attracted large numbers of migrants. The city became overwhelmed, with older residential districts of the inner city

becoming seriously overcrowded. Long-term plans to restructure the growing metropolis were introduced in 1935 and again in 1970–71. Both plans involved massive housing projects, increasingly in peripheral

locations. In the 1980s alone, among a population of over eight million, one million people moved into apartments on the peripheral estates, despite a government policy of restricting further migration into

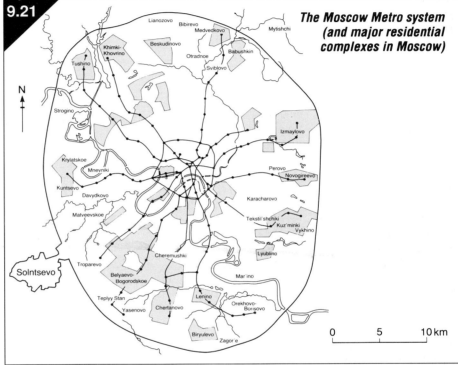

9.21

The Moscow Metro system (and major residential complexes in Moscow)

0   5   10 km

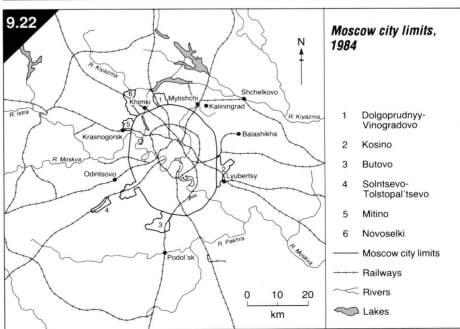

9.22

Moscow city limits, 1984

1   Dolgoprudnyy-Vinogradovo
2   Kosino
3   Butovo
4   Solntsevo-Tolstopal'tsevo
5   Mitino
6   Novoselki

────── Moscow city limits
┼┼┼┼┼ Railways
〜〜〜 Rivers
▨ Lakes

0   10   20
km

Moscow. In 1960 the city's boundaries were expanded to the new ring motorway, MKAD (resource 9.21), to which six further areas were added in 1984 (resource 9.22). Within these boundaries a radial-concentric metro system has been developed, linking the principal residential districts with the central and other employment areas (resource 9.21).

Budapest, the capital, is very much the primate city of Hungary, with a fifth of the country's population and one-quarter of the labour force. It is the hub of the national road and rail system and over 400 000 people enter the city daily. Since 1945, a single municipal body, the Budapest Transport Authority (BKV) has developed a complex system of public transport using bus, tram and train (resource 9.26).

Key understandings

◆ Socialist societies tend to place heavy reliance upon public transportation in their large cities.

◆ Different transport modes serve different purposes.

◆ Transport systems are dynamic over time.

◆ Transport systems reflect a combination of physical, historical, economic, political and social factors.

Part I: Moscow

Daily circulation

Although the city plan embodied the intention to move 337 factories and offices, with 130 000 employees, out of the centre, it remains the employment base to a very large extent and also the focus of most shopping, cultural and recreational activities for Muscovites as well as for visitors to the capital. At present only about one-tenth of the city's jobs have been relocated in the outer districts and construction of new industrial and commercial premises lags behind housing developments. Consequently, travel to work within the city itself now frequently occupies more than an hour in each direction and the urban transport network still has to bear a considerable strain of carrying commuters between suburb and centre at an average rate of 16.5 million journeys every day throughout the year.

The capacity to perform that service falls chiefly on the famous Metro system, now extending over some 217 km with 129 stations and used by nearly 7 million passengers daily. Recent additions to the network have probed southwards in the direction of the newest housing complexes, but geological problems and the increased cost of deeper tunnelling have meant that every kilometre built involves twice the

investment required in the early 1970s. The same flat-rate fare of 5 kopeks (5 pence), irrespective of journey distance, applies to all types of municipal transport and almost 6 million Muscovites use the bus services, in spite of their relatively slow speeds and less direct routes when compared to the Metro. In fact thousands can only reach a Metro station in the suburbs by first taking a local bus. To alleviate the extra costs incurred by passengers obliged to split their trips in this way, to meet the augmented demand of about 9.5 million inhabitants by the end of the century and to reduce journey times generally, plans exist to expand the Metro lines to 300 km in due course. Far fewer people (2.4 million) regularly patronise the less widespread and slower trolley-bus fleet, which operates best on direct axial routes rather than along tortuous city-centre ones. Short-distance trips by the residual tramways, mainly in the eastern parts of Moscow, total only 1.4 million per day. Smaller numbers of residents, among whom private cars are owned by only one in ten households, are prepared to pay the higher fares charged by taxis and the faster minibuses which ply between fixed stopping points on prescribed routes. As the demand for mobility in the city has increased, from 3.6 billion to 6.0 billion passenger journeys per annum between 1960 and 1985, substantial changes have occurred in the breadth and balance of the various transport modes (resource 9.23), reflecting not only local conditions but also wider Soviet policies. For example, under the Five Year Plans from 1961 to 1985 there were commissioned in Moscow 138.5 km of Metro line, 135.5 km of tramway and 873.8 km of trolleybus line (resource 9.24), with the result that electrified forms of transport, favoured for ecological reasons, now account for 64 per cent of all passenger traffic, two-thirds of that total being taken by the Metro. Meanwhile the Russian motor vehicle industry has expanded enormously, not least at the

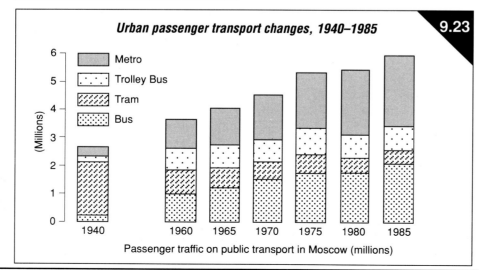

Urban passenger transport changes, 1940–1985 9.23

(Millions)

Metro
Trolley Bus
Tram
Bus

1940 1960 1965 1970 1975 1980 1985

Passenger traffic on public transport in Moscow (millions)

9.24	Newly-commissioned electrified urban transport capacities in Moscow, 1961-85				
	961-65	**1966-70**	**1971-75**	**1976-80**	**1981-85**
Double-track Metro line	36.0	30.3	26.6	20.7	24.9
Single line tramway	35.0	52.3	17.2	13.3	17.7
Single line trolley-bus route	268.4	209.4	159.0	168.8	68.2

Likhachev factory in south-eastern Moscow, so that the city's bus capacity has been able to cope with a doubling of demand since 1960, from 990 to 2150 million passengers annually.

An increased volume and spatially extended population circulation in Moscow itself has thus been created by the city's growth by natural increment and inward migration, by residential moves and the consequent lengthening of daily journeys to work as suburbs mushroom but employment stays fairly firmly established near the centre. Consumer travel needs, too, have been conditioned by the introduction of improved and more widespread transport facilities and a traditional orientation on central services and amenities, despite the building of numerous alternative retailing, educational and cultural complexes. Suburban families with friends and relatives still living near their former homes retain a high degree of loyalty to past behavioural patterns. Teenagers, too, have distinctive activity fields which usually combine two types of locality, integrated in their own experience by axial transport media. The first represents a familiar space centres on the home and school neighbourhood; the second, almost invariably focused on the heart of the city, perpetuates the attraction of that area to all Muscovites.

Two other aspects of human movement complete the picture of the Russian capital's relationship with its surrounding region. The first is the daily influx of people for employment, shopping, social and leisure purposes from beyond the city limits. Such a flow, now exceeding 600 million passenger journeys per annum by suburban electric trains alone, can also be explained in part by the magnetism exerted by any established metropolitan centre, but supplemented in this case by the city's internal labour deficit. The target population of 7.0 million envisaged in the 1970 plan guidelines had already been exceeded by that year, yet the shortfall in numbers available to participate in the required workforce meant that in the early 1970s there was a net gain of over half a million commuters from the hinterland to the city every day, and with similar numbers prevailing at the present time these people represent between 10 and 15 per cent of the total employment in Moscow. The scale of external commuting has grown rapidly at between 1 and 3 per cent per annum over the past 25 years. Whereas in 1960 the influx of 0.38 million was offset by an outflow of 90 000, in 1984 the numbers were 0.60 and 0.14 million respectively. These extra-urban passenger movements usually coincide in both time and direction with those generated inside the city – almost three-quarters are heading for destinations inside the Sadovaya Ring – thereby intensifying the congestion at rail-Metro junction stations at peak periods in the day. Including those who travel in to work or to study at the innumerable prestigious institutions of further education, Moscow's residential population of 8.7 million is thus increased to a normal daytime population of about 11 million by workers from the Greater Moscow region, travelling on average at least one and a half hours in either direction beyond the MKAD, enabled to bear the extra cost by obtaining the above-average wages offered in several sectors of the city's economy.

Simultaneously, these inhabitants of neighbouring towns or rural settlements benefit from lower living costs and the possibility of providing some of their food requirements on their own private plots of land in the countryside. In recent years, much critical attention has been drawn to the negative effects of long-distance commuting, for example in cost to the worker, in uneven use of transport media through the day, and lower labour productivity, but current planning assumptions accept that the process will continue in all large Russian cities despite a general desire to curb its further growth. By the end of the century it is expected that all the reserve areas within the MKAD will be fully urbanised, and that dispersion should proceed to 3 new satellite towns which will be self-contained in their employment capacities. Specific proposed sites have yet to be approved.

Periodic movement

The final interaction, between Moscow's resident population and the Forest Park Zone, LPZP which surrounds the MKAD, is by means of recreation trips in summer or at weekends. In addition to the 150 000 people who travel out from the city to work each day, it has been estimated that about one-quarter of Muscovites make periodic excursions into the LPZP, three-quarters of which retains its designated rural function as forest, fields and lakes. The less urbanised quality of the LPZP encourages many of its residents not only to seek work in Moscow but also to make use of the capital's higher level of service provision and cultural facilities, accessible from distances of up to 80 km by fast regular rail connections. On average people living within that radius of the MKAD

Daily passenger traffic entering Budapest using transport		9.25
Mode	**No. of passengers**	**%**
State railway (MAV)	98.300	39.9
VOLANBUS	56.650	23.0
BKV Bus	52.314	21.3
BKV HEV	38.974	15.8
Public transport total	246.238	100.0
Public transport	246.238	61.0
Arrivals by private car	157.500	39.0

make fortnightly visits to the city for social or cultural reasons, while such trips are a weekly feature in the lives of those residing less than 50 km away. Conversely, Muscovites themselves view the LPZP as a recreation zone to which they resort for fishing, camping, water sports and other individual or organised leisure activities, for example to their dachas (weekend cottages). Outward moves of this type extend over shorter distances; 70 per cent travel no further than 30 km beyond the MKAD. For that reason, they often find it preferable to use private transport that allows them greater flexibility to explore more varied natural or historical sites than if they were constrained by train timetables and fixed destinations. Groups and organisations usually hire buses to take them longer distances over the good road network, for example to the picturesque and protected forest-lake landscapes to the west of the city.

(Source: C Thomas, 'Moving Moscow's millions', *Geography*, 73(3), June 1988, pp 216 – 225)

Part II: Budapest

Budapest has a distinctive physical geography which has strongly influenced the evolution of its public transport (resource 9.26(a)). The River Danube divides the city into two for some 32 km, separating areas of contrasting relief. On the western side (Buda and Obuda) a series of hills reach 500 m: these are

heavily dissected by many steep valleys, level ground is rare and the geology is faulted. This hilly topography has influenced land use and severely restricts the modes of

public transport that can be employed. On the eastern side (Pest) the land is flat, only reaching 200 m at the city boundary 25 km to the east (the River Danube runs at about 100 m). The underlying geology of soft sediments on the eastern side presents little obstacle to movement above or below ground.

To serve the growing city several modes of transport services were established from the mid-nineteenth century on. Trams operated from the 1860s, the first underground line commenced operation in 1896, surburban railway lines were constructed between 1887 and 1914, regular bus services began in 1921 and the first trolley buses entered

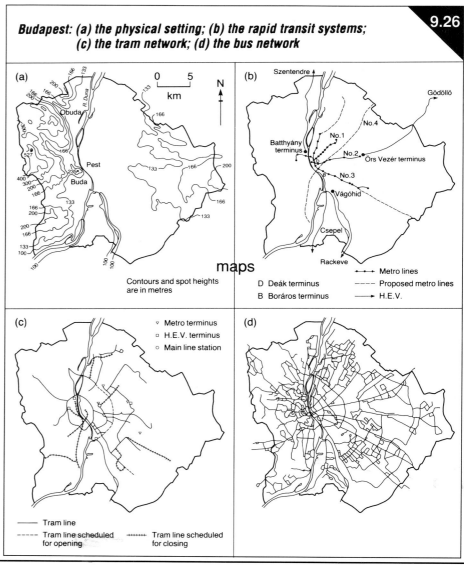

Budapest: (a) the physical setting; (b) the rapid transit systems; (c) the tram network; (d) the bus network

9.26

Mode	% of network	% of runs	% passenger/km
Metro	2.3	18.1	16.8
HEV	6.3	5.3	11.2
Tramway	14.0	24.6	15.8
Buses	67.3	45.7	52.4
Local boats	5.4	0.6	0.1
Other	4.7	5.7	3.7

Modes of public transport in Budapest — 9.27

service in 1933. However the modern period of the development of Budapest's public transport began at the end of the War. The city's public transport networks and services were almost totally destroyed in the battle for Budapest in 1944–45. Budapest's public transport today is the modified result of centralised planning which integrated transport with other changes proposed for the city. These firstly concentrated on repairing war damage but then proceeded to wholly new ventures such as extensive housing estates, industrial development and the transport links between them. In 1968 the BKV was established from the seven enterprises that had existed since 1949: the Metro was incorporated in 1973. The city's integrated transport services are heavily subsidised, to the tune of 70 per cent (the British equivalent is 12 per cent) and run frequent timetables, many for more than 19 hours a day and ten for all 24. The services are very inexpensive, at two *forints* (about two pence) for the buses or three *forints* for all the other modes – irrespective of the distance to be travelled. Tickets are pre-purchased (season tickets are available) and a personal punch ticketing system is used on all services.

The backbone of the public transport service is a rapid transit system using the Metro and electrified local railways. This conveys passengers around the central districts and between the city centre, suburbs and Greater Budapest. These services are supplemented by bus, trolly bus and tram services which act as feeder

lines, by ferry services which close 'loops' across the Danube, and by a number of unusual urban modes such as a funicular railway, the Pioneers' railway, a cogwheel railway and a cableway (resource 9.27).

The Metro or underground railway consists of three lines (resource 9.26(b)). Line No. 1 (the 'Millenium Underground') was opened in May 1896, making it the oldest on the mainland of Europe. It runs between Vörösmarty Square, close to the Danube, 3.75 km to the east: although small (each carriage contains only 16 seats) and shallow (the tunnel height is 2.75 m) it is incorporated into the rest of the system at the central station. This station, like many others on the system, is where the integration of above and below ground services occurs. Lines No. 2 and No. 3 are modern and have been opened in stages between 1972 and 1984. The stations are also of that pattern and the line is graded up to and down from the stations, facilitating braking and acceleration. Consequently the service is fast and frequent, varying between a peak headway of 2 minutes 7 seconds and 4 minutes 30 seconds off-peak. Line No. 2 is the only Metro service to drive under the Danube, its deep level tubes connecting the southern mainline station of Déli (to the west of the city) with the eastern station of Keleti. Line No. 3 runs parallel to the Danube and is finally intended to terminate at the city boundaries, so connecting Budapest's international airport (Ferihegyi) in the south and the proposed housing estates of Káposztásmegyer to the north of the city centre. For many years further

lines have been planned but the capital cost of such schemes, in spite of the contribution made to the city's transport flow (about 341 million passenger journeys in 1985) by the existing Metro, will mean that new construction is linked to the condition of Hungary's economy.

The suburban electric railway (HEV) consists of four lines totalling 97.6 km and is operated to serve the settlements of Greater Budapest (resource 9.26(b)). One line begins at Batthyány tér (where there is also a Metro station and bus terminus) and runs north along the Danube bank through Obuda to Szentendre, a commuter, tourist and weekend recreation centre 20 km to the north. A second line commences at the Metro station at Örs Vezér tere and runs 26 km north-east to Gödöllö. The third runs from Boráros tér onto the island of Csepel: while the fourth begins at Vágóhid south of Boráros tér, to run 42 km south on the Pest bank to Dunaharaszti and Ráckeve which is a major recreational area.

There are 172 km of tram tracks in Budapest carrying 30 main routes (resource 9.26(c)). An inner circular line links Pest and Buda across the Margit-hid Margaret bridge and Szabadsaghid Freedom bridge from which lines fan out to serve the inner suburbs and residential districts. Overall the length of track has been diminishing under pressure from district renewal, road improvement schemes and substitution by bus, trolley bus and Metro services but some new lines have been opened to serve new housing areas. Future developments will continue to provide precise feeder services for the rapid transit system, but it is also proposed to provide a new express tramway from Arpád híd to Vágóhid using a dedicated way along a ring road about 5 km from the city centre, the Hungária Körút.

The bus network is 824 km long of which 755 km are in the city and 70 km in Greater Budapest (resource 9.26(d)). Punctuality is assisted by the many bus-only lanes and on 41 of the 170 city routes there are limited-stop services in addition to normal schedules. The buses are made in Hungary (Ikarus) and this sizeable home market underpins substantial export sales. The buses are single-deck, one-man-operated vehicles. On the more heavily used routes articulated buses are used. Buses are a flexible form of public transport and provide services in areas where other modes cannot be operated. Thus they are particularly important in hilly Buda. BVK's bus service is complemented by a second company. VOLAN, which provides feeder services and direct routes for commuters beyond the city. Despite their operating advantages, buses are a major source of pollution and as traffic levels rise in the city are increasingly subject to delays caused by congestion. Trolley buses are also subject to these delays but cause no pollution and so make a valuable contribution to services in the inner city (resource 9.28). Their network is limited with only thirteen routes over 57 km. Earlier plans to end the service have been opposed on environmental grounds.

9.28

The Budapest tramway

The 'unusual' modes within the public transport system are the Szechenyi hill cog railway, the Pioneers' railway, the Zugliget hill cableway and the ferry services. The first is regularly used on a daily basis in an especially hilly part of Buda, but like the others also has an important tourist function. The ferries also have a regular use carrying people and vehicles across the river stretches where there are no bridges, for example south of Csepel.

The provision of this complex transport system is planned in the context of change in the population, employment and settlement patterns in Greater Budapest. Many of these changes are promoted by the government itself and the BKV as a municipal authority plays a vital integrating role, ensuring that new industrial and residential developments are incorporated into an effective city-wide transport system. Specifically the plan has centred on the development of a rapid transit system, with the other modes interleaving with that primary network, so allowing the distinctive features of each mode to be exploited given the routes to be operated. However agents other than government have also propelled change, reflecting the very special blend of socialism that has existed in Hungary since 1956 and the economic difficulties the country has endured in the last decade.

Chief amongst these non-governmental agents has been the substantial level of private enterprise which is permitted in Hungary and which has flourished in Greater Budapest and thus run counter to the government's own decentralisation policies. This enterprise, and the affluence that came with it, substantially increased private vehicle ownership in the city putting enormous pressure upon the centrally conceived transport plans. The number of private cars in Greater Budapest probably already exceeds 400 000, a tenfold increase

since 1960. As a result the number of passengers on public transport has declined. It has also become necessary to develop car regulatory schemes such as meters, one-way systems, bus lanes and pedestrianised streets. These measures have done little to solve the problems of pollution, congestion and on-street parking and so plans to segregate transit, commuter and local road traffic and to facilitate traffic flow have resulted in new road and bridge building programmes. In capital terms these are expensive projects and may act to further postpone the development of the rapid transit system. The final addition to this unhappy forecast is to note that the difficulty of reconciling BKV's services with the private car mirrors the fundamental tension between any collective and private provision of services. As a result the private car owner may well resent the expense of the lavish, subsidised system and the collective planners will find it hard to seriously tackle a problem caused by private consumption.

(Source: P Machon and A Dingsdale, 'Public transport in a socialist capital city: Budapest,' *Geography*, 74(2), April 1989, 159 – 162)

Activities

1 Summarise the patterns of Moscow's and Budapest's public transport systems, and how they have responded to changing conditions

2 What are the principal problems faced by the two transport systems, and how do they illustrate the accessibility/mobility limitations imposed by a radial-concentric urban structure?

CASE STUDY 9.4   *The changing ports of England and Wales*

Background

As a densely populated island with a highly indented coastline, Britain has a large number of ports. In 1986, there were 70 ports handling over 100 000 tonnes a year each, of which 35 exceeded 1 million tonnes (resource 9.29). For many years, these ports relied on traditional technology for general cargo handling, based on a labour-intensive system of cranes and manhandling of a vast range of individual items from the ship's hold to the shore facility. This 'break-bulk' system had a low productivity, and kept a ship berthed in port for between 50 and 60 per cent of its life. The slow cargo-handling speed also limited the size of ship.

There was considerable uniformity in ship size and design, and in the berths that held them. For instance, with the exception of the small number of large passenger-vessel berths, most docks could accommodate ships with a maximum of 10 000 DWT (dead-weight-tonnes). The open quay and the transit sheds rarely exceeded 0.5 hectares for a single berth. Such a berth would, at best, have a throughput capacity of 100 000 tonnes a year. Thus, to achieve a large capacity, a port would need a considerable number of berths and associated facilities.

As recently as the 1960, British trade was still dominated by the historical trading relationships with North America, Africa, Asia and Australasia.

'It was normal for ships in these deep-sea trades to do a 'milk-round' of home ports so that discharge and loading took place as near as possible to the destination and origins of the imports and exports … The average land haul for the mainly lower-value bulk imports amounted to 58 km and for the higher value exports 106 km'.

Thus, land transport costs were kept down and each port had a well-defined hinterland. However, a ship might spend several weeks loading, unloading and moving round the coast.

Since the 1960s, rising labour and port costs have created pressures for lower cost, and faster handling methods to minimise ship port time and reduce labour demands. Ship size has also increased and layout has become standardised, to benefit from the economies of scale. These changes, when combined with the major shifts in the orientation of Britain's sea trade, e.g. the evolution of the EC, and changes in land transport infrastructure, have brought fundamental changes to port location and structure. This case study outlines the main aspects of this 'revolution'.

Key understandings

◆ Technological and economic changes have caused a revolution in the location of ports and the way they operate.

◆ Small, well-located and efficiently managed ports can prosper while large, old ports may have difficulty in adjusting to change.

◆ Technological change has created severe job losses in port industries.

How technology has affected the ports of England and Wales

The technological revolution

The term 'revolution' has been often applied to the changes in cargo handling and maritime transport that have taken place in the last 25 years. Three principal areas of technological change can be identified: (i) developments in

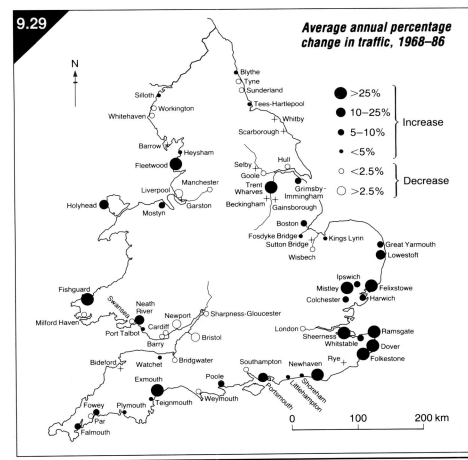

9.29

Average annual percentage change in traffic, 1968–86

>25%
10–25%
5–10%   } Increase
<5%
<2.5%
>2.5%   } Decrease

Blythe
Tyne
Sunderland
Tees-Hartlepool
Whitby
Scarborough
Silloth
Workington
Whitehaven
Barrow
Heysham
Fleetwood
Selby
Goole
Hull
Liverpool
Manchester
Trent Wharves
Grimsby-Immingham
Holyhead
Garston
Beckingham
Gainsborough
Mostyn
Boston
Fosdyke Bridge
Sutton Bridge
Kings Lynn
Wisbech
Great Yarmouth
Lowestoft
Ipswich
Mistley
Felixstowe
Colchester
Harwich
Fishguard
Swansea
Neath River
Newport
Sharpness-Gloucester
Milford Haven
Cardiff
Port Talbot
Bristol
London
Ramsgate
Barry
Sheerness
Whitstable
Dover
Bideford
Watchet
Bridgwater
Southampton
Newhaven
Rye
Folkestone
Exmouth
Poole
Portsmouth
Littlehampton
Shoreham
Weymouth
Fowey
Plymouth
Teignmouth
Par
Falmouth

0   100   200 km

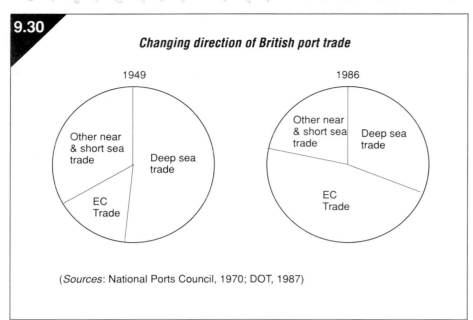

9.30

Changing direction of British port trade

1949

Other near & short sea trade

Deep sea trade

EC Trade

1986

Other near & short sea trade

Deep sea trade

EC Trade

(*Sources*: National Ports Council, 1970; DOT, 1987)

9.31

Terminal costs at England and Wales ports (1982)

	Traditional technology	Deep – sea container	Small – ship container	Ferry ro/ro
Annual throughput:				
Weight (tonnes)	70 000	960 000	540 000	1 200 000
tonnes/man/year	1 000	10 440	24 540	17 140
Total costs/tonne (£)	6.84	2.36	1.07	0.59

generation container ships of 750 TEU (Twenty-foot Equivalent Units) approximated in size to the conventional general cargo ships (180 m length, 9 m draught), but recent buildings have capacities of 4000 plus TEU and with lengths of 290 m and draughts of 13 m are very large in comparison with traditional vessels.

Cargo handling methods have become both more sophisticated and much more varied and specialised vessels now exist for carrying packaged timber, forest products, pallets, containers, barges and vehicles.

The impact on ports

Not surprisingly, these innovations in cargo handling have been reflected in the character and spatial pattern of port activity. As a consequence, there has been greater selectivity with respect to site and situation and greater differentiation with respect to the facilities provided and the trades serviced at an individual port.

In the case of the bulk and container trades the high cost of the ships and shore-side facilities can still bring great reductions in unit cost in comparison with conventional handling but only if the throughputs are maintained at very high levels. There are therefore strong arguments in favour of concentration and these are reinforced by the much smaller number of vessels and terminals that are needed to handle any given volume of cargo. The contrasts may be outlined as follows:

Conventional technology

- Labour intensive
- Low level of mechanisation
- Low man/gang/berth output
- Slow ship turn-round
- Small ships
- Many ships
- Numerous uniform berths
- Port dispersion

materials and cargo handling methods; (ii) increasing ship size; (iii) improved ship design and vessel specialisation. These three are inter-related and together have brought profound geographical consequences. Vast areas of traditional dockland have been rendered redundant, many other areas have been transformed, new ports have been created and whole new trading patterns have emerged.

The changes in cargo handling are best described by the term 'unitisation' or the grouping of individual items of freight into standardised units by *packaging* (crating, strapping together of sawn timber), the use of *pallets* (wooden or metal platforms on which goods can be consolidated and strapped), the use of *containers* and the RO/RO movement of lorries and trailers by *roll-on/roll-off* methods. The unit size will be such that mechanised handling can be maximised and wherever possible the unit will be moved from origin to destination without breaking of bulk and intermediate handling. Transfer is facilitated and at the port the cargo handling productivity is improved and where ship turn-round was once measured in days or even weeks, it is now measured in hours.

Increases in ship size have been most dramatic in the bulk trades with a few oil tankers now in excess of 450 000 DWT and many in the 250 000 to 350 000 range. Many dry-bulk carriers are from 150 000 to 200 000 DWT with a few even larger. Likewise in the general cargo trades, the greatly increased speed of cargo handling has removed the major constraint on ship size. The first

Unitised traffic through ports in England and Wales 1970 – 86

9.32

	1970	1980	1986
(i) By type (million tonnes)			
Road vehicles	3.5	19.9	31.7
Rail wagons/barge	0.84	1.1	0.98
Containers	11.4	18.0	24.4
Other RO/RO	1.2	2.8	3.1
Total	16.9	41.7	60.2
(ii) By trading area ('000 units)			
Deep sea	257	852	962
Near-and short-sea (Europe)	1271	2395	3218
Internal coastwise	492	472	548
Total	2021	3719	4728

New technology

- Capital intensive
- Highly mechanised
- High man/gang/berth output
- Rapid ship turn-round
- Larger ships
- Fewer ships
- Fewer specialised berths
- Port concentration

The resulting concentration may be illustrated in a variety of ways and at different levels. Thus, at the level of individual ports, large parts of the fabric have become redundant and cargo handling is concentrated in a relatively small part of the dock area. London provides a supreme example with all the up-river docks having closed to traffic and with Tilbury now handling almost as much cargo as all the dock systems did previously. A similiar trend can be seen at Liverpool and Southampton.

Concentration of activities at a smaller number of ports can also be observed; for example, Britain's leading container shipping company, P & O Containers, now uses only one British port for each of its principal services (Southampton for Far East and South African services; Tilbury for Australasian and Indian services and Felixstowe for East African and Gulf services), where previously most of the major ports would have been involved. Tilbury now handles about 80 per cent of all Britain's trade with Australasia. It follows that, far from being regional, these ports or load centres have hinterlands that are national in character with the shipowner absorbing the additional costs of land transport. Port proximity is no longer a matter of concern.

It is clear that for containers and bulk cargoes the arguments run strongly in favour of concentration of port activity but the reverse may well be true for RO/RO trade. Simple RO/RO berths or link spans can be provided at no great cost and newer RO/RO ships are increasingly given their own ramps thereby eliminating the need for costly shore-side facilities. The relatively low construction and operating costs mean that investments are soon paid for, risk is limited and it is easy to enter the market. Many more ports have become involved and the technology has allowed dispersion and encouraged the use of the nearest port to reduce land-haul costs.

The top-ranked individual ports for containers and RO/RO traffic, Felixstowe and Dover respectively, handle about the same proportion of the traffic by that mode, but at lower levels of ranking the containers are markedly more concentrated than the RO/RO traffic, yet more small ports are involved in RO/RO than containers. The rapid expansion of the unitised traffic is demonstrated in resource 9.32.

Port concentration – container and RO/RO, 1986 (Percentages of foreign and coastwise trade)

9.33

	Container traffic	Road goods vehicles
First rated port	30.2	30.5
Top three ports	59.3	42.4
Top five ports	70.4	52.5
Top ten ports	86.0	72.6

Source: calculated from Department of Transport (1987)

Deep-sea transhipment in Antwerp and Netherlands, 1976 – 1984 ('000s tonnes)

9.34

	1976	1980	1984
Transhipped imports			
Bulk	2292	5433	5107
Container	357	475	823
Other	1326	1001	1303
Total	3975	6609	7233
Transhipped exports			
Bulk	25	20	363
Container	410	475	1198
Other	243	270	617
Total	678	765	2178
Percentage			
Of total imports	3	7	13
Of total exports	6	4	8

CASE STUDY 9.4 *The changing ports of England and Wales*

The pattern of port activity for an island such as Britain will be strongly influenced by the direction of national trade and this has changed significantly over the last 25 years. Whereas in 1969 deep-sea trade accounted for 51.7 per cent of the total it had declined to 30.9 per cent in 1986 and short-sea trade had risen from 48.3 to 69.1 per cent with EC trade alone increasing from 15.1 to 47.5 per cent of the total. This trend was apparent even before Britain joined the EC but was greatly magnified after. Irish, Scandinavian and Baltic trades have held their shares, Iberian and Mediterranean trades have declined markedly in relative terms while trade with the near-continental neighbours increased dramatically.

While the west coast ports had a geographical advantage in servicing the deep-sea and Iberian/Mediterranean trades, with the changing direction of trade they found themselves on the wrong side of the country. Much of the growth traffic is ideally suited to movement by container or RO/RO and the statistics (resource 9.33) clearly demonstrate that it is the east and south coast ports that have been advantaged. The ports of the south-east and Wash/East Anglia together account for 70.3 per cent of the total RO/RO traffic while all east and south coast ports account for 84.8 per cent.

The traffic between Britain and mainland Europe comprises two distinct elements – there is direct trade between the areas and there is also British trade with third parties that is routed via European ports. The pressure to tranship increases with ship size on the trunk haul especially when only a small part of the cargo is destined for Britain. Transhipment will only be favoured where the freight rates are such that it is cheaper to ship via a mainland port than ship direct. For example, if the difference in freight rates from Rotterdam and Hull to the Far East is greater than that of shipping between Rotterdam and Hull, a transhipment is likely to take place. Clearly the critical factor will be the short-sea freight rates. All too frequently the freight rates from British ports are higher than from their continental rivals as a result of lower operating efficiency and lower levels of port subsidy. British ports have to bear the cost of all their dredging and pass on light dues to the user whereas, at continental ports, these costs are assumed by the State, which also covers far more of the capital investment costs for port development. The mainland market is far larger than the British market, and can therefore support a wider range of carriers.

In the late 1960s and early 1970s transhipment made up only a small proportion of British trade, fluctuating between 2.8 and 5.2 per cent a year. For example, in 1973, 550 000 tonnes of British non-fuel imports from the United States were received by way of Rotterdam, Amsterdam, Antwerp, Ghent and Le Havre (in that order of importance) while 127 000 tonnes of the exports to the United States went by way of Antwerp, Rotterdam, Amsterdam, Le Havre, Bremen and Hamburg.

There has been a dramatic increase in transhipment traffic. In 1984, transhipment through Belgian and Dutch ports accounted for 13 and 8 per cent of imports and exports respectively (resource 9.34). Rotterdam and Antwerp were the most important transhipment ports with coal, animal feed, grain, mineral ores, machinery and other manufactures as the main import commodities and barley as the principal export.

The changing port system

Port ranking (resource 9.35) may be used as an indicator of change. In terms of the total tonnage handled, the ranking in 1965 was very much a list of the historical, conventional general cargo ports, but by 1986 several of the ports have slipped

England and Wales port ranking — 9.35

1965 Total tonnage	1986 Total tonnage	1965 Non-oil imports	1986 Non-oil exports	1986 RO/RO	1986 Containers
1 London	1 London	1 London	1 Felixstowe	1 Dover	1 Felixstowe
2 Liverpool	2 Grimsby/Immingham	2 Grimsby/Immingham	2 Tees	2 Fleetwood	2 London
3 Southampton	3 Tees	3 Tees	3 London	3 Harwich	3 Southampton
4 Manchester	4 Milford Haven	4 Port Talbot	4 Dover	4 Felixstowe	4 Hull
5 Tees	5 Southampton	5 Dover	5 Grimsby/Immingham	5 Medway	5 Ipswich
6 Hull	6 Felixstowe	6 Felixstowe	6 Southampton	6 Grimsby/Immingham	6 Liverpool

down the hierarchy (Liverpool, Manchester) or disappeared from the top ten (Bristol) to be replaced by new oil ports (Milford Haven, Medway) and the new 'unitised' ports (Felixstowe and Dover). The non-oil import ranking reflects both general cargo (London, Dover) and bulk traffic (Immingham, Tees, Port Talbot), while Felixstowe has leapt to the top of the export list by virtue of being the leading container port and also having a considerable RO/RO traffic. The specialisation is reflected in the rankings for container and RO/RO traffic with previously insignificant ports such as Fleetwood, Harwich, Portsmouth, Ramsgate and Dover getting into the rankings.

From 1965 to 1985 the total trade of England and Wales increased by 10.4 per cent but that of the ten main ports of 1965 declined by 31.8 per cent. The regional breakdown further illustrates this trend. In the Thames/Kent region, London's traffic has declined by 20 per cent since 1965, but the other ports, including Dover, Ramsgate, Folkestone, Colchester and Brightlingsea, together increased their traffic by 580 per cent. In the Sussex/Hampshire region the Southampton traffic increased by a marginal 3.2 per cent from 1965 to 1985 while that of the other regional ports, headed by Portsmouth, Shoreham and Newhaven, increased by 75 per cent. In the West Country the major ports (Bristol and those of South Wales) suffered heavy decline while the other ports showed a modest increase of 22 per cent with Poole, Exmouth and Teignmouth showing considerable gains. Even excluding the former high ranking ports of Liverpool and Manchester fails to produce any growth for the north-west ports, clearly the heaviest losers from the changing direction of trade. The position on the north-east coast and on Humberside has been greatly distorted by North Sea oil traffic, but small ports along the Rivers Trent, Ouse and Humber have together shown a 98 per cent increase in traffic. Undoubtedly, the

9.36

Is small beautiful? Unloading at Colchester Dock at high tide

spectacular growth has been in the Haven ports of Felixstowe, Ipswich, Harwich and Mistely, which together grew by 650 per cent over the period 1965 to 1985, and to a lesser extent in the ports of the Wash and northern East Anglia (115 per cent).

It is clear that a number of ports that in 1965 were insignificant or of relatively minor importance have moved into the top rank and many small ports have attracted considerable traffic growth in contrast with their larger neighbours (resource 9.29). Felixstowe provides the supreme example. In the early 1960s it was just a small dock with about 30 dockers handling limited amounts of coastal and short-sea traffic. Almost continuous expansion of container and RO/RO facilities brought it to sixth rank overall in 1986 and the first port for non-oil exports and container traffic. Over 1000 are now employed and enterprising private management has been able to capitalise on the advantages of historic backwardness, favourable site for development and changing geographical values.

On short-sea hauls the proportional contribution of port costs increases crticially and operators must therefore seek ports which offer the highest productivity, rapid ship turn-round, flexible operational practices,

good labour relations and lack of restrictive practices. It does not follow that these will be found at the port offering the lowest charges but to the extent that the shipowner can satisfy some of these requirements he will be able to reduce his overall costs. In Britain, a basic distinction could be made between 'Scheme' and 'Non-Scheme' ports. At the Scheme ports the labour was registered and regulated by the National Dock Labour Board which came into existence in 1946 in the particular conditions of that time. Effectively, the Registered Dock Workers (RDWs) were guaranteed employment and could be re-deployed but not made redundant except on a voluntary basis. When the government phased out the Scheme in 1989 over 60 ports still operated under Scheme conditions and although the number of RDWs was reduced from 65 128 in 1965 to 11 168 in 1986, a number of the larger ports still found themselves with surplus labour and at a considerable cost disadvantage in comparison with the Non-Scheme ports.

A number of the small ports have increased their traffic by becoming the bases for high-frequency ferry operations on the short-sea routes – Dover, Ramsgate, Harwich,

Portsmouth and Poole provide obvious examples. In some ways of greater interest are the many small ports at which the growth has been dependent on the 'tramp' market particularly for the bulk and semi-bulk trades with mainland Europe. A number of these ports develop particular links which become served by regular sailings. For example, Colchester has weekly sailings to Hamburg and Delfzyl (resource 9.36).

Improved ship design

The success of so many small ports has in large measure been the result of improved designs of coastal and short-sea vessels. The traditional coastal and short-sea traders rarely had a cargo capacity (DWT) of more than 600–700 tonnes and many were in the 200–350 DWT range. Economies of scale required vessels of higher DWT but preferably with no greater draught than traditional vessels so that they could get into smaller ports. Since much of the traffic consisted of bulk (grain, ores, scrap) and semi-bulk (timber, forest products) commodities there were also advantages in having obstruction-free box-shaped holds and full, open hatches to allow speed of loading/unloading and versatility in types of cargo that could be carried. During the 1970s, many mini-bulkers of this type were constructed with DWT in excess of 1250 tonnes.

A further refinement was the construction of mini-bulkers with low profiles which allowed inland penetration under bridges and other overhead obstructions. Shallow draught (3–4.5 m), low-profile (air draught up to 6.0 m) vessels with full sea-going capability, appropriately called river-sea vessels are now frequent visitors to many smaller British ports, and are able to provide direct links to inland locations in Europe such as Basel, Strasbourg, Duisburg, Liège, Brussels and Paris.

Conclusion

It is clear that an understanding of technological change in maritime transport, operating in several distinct ways, is basic to any analysis of Britain's changing port system and, more particularly, to any explanation of the decline in many of the former principal ports and the associated rejuvenation at a large number of small ports. Containerisation of deep-sea general cargo trades and increasing ship size in bulk trades have resulted in concentration of activity at fewer ports. An associated increase in transhipment through ports in mainland Europe combined with a general redistribution of British trade in that same direction has resulted in a dramatic increase in the trade of many smaller ports, especially those favoured by an east or south coast location. This increase has in places taken the form of container or RO/RO traffic, but has also been in the form of big increases in bulk and semi-bulk commodities. The recent development of vessels able to serve small ports and provide an element of inland penetration and yet move cargo in economically viable loads has clearly been the basis of small port success.

(Source: D Hilling, 'Technology and the Changing Ports of England and Wales', *Geography*, 1989, pp. 117–127)

Activities

1 Make a list of the principal changes which have occurred in British ports, and against each change, give a brief explanation. Think in terms of location, mode of operation, labour requirement, type of trade and direction, technology.

2 **Group discussion**

What is the likely impact of the opening of the Channel Tunnel upon the location, character and prosperity of English ports? (Reflect upon the factors influencing the port system illustrated in this case study.)

CASE STUDY 9.5 — Transport networks in the developing world – the example of Zaire

Background

Inefficient and poorly integrated transport networks are one of the main constraints on development in many developing countries. There is usually a mixture of river, road and rail components which involve expensive break-bulk transfers from one mode of transport to another. This is particularly significant for those countries which rely upon the export of bulky minerals and agricultural products, and the import of capital and consumer goods. Often, the transport network is a legacy of the colonial era, when the colonial power and its commercial companies built railways and/or roads to link ports with raw material sources (resource 9.37). Such a skeletal network may not be an effective basis for the more broadly-based development programmes of post-colonial governments. Furthermore, much of the rail infrastructure (track and rolling stock) is now old and in need of replacement, at great expense.

Zaire, the focus of this case study, illustrates a number of these characteristics. It is one of the major countries of equatorial Africa, with a population of 34 million people (1987 figure) (resource 9.37). It is almost landlocked, with only a narrow corridor to the Atlantic Coast. Its main resources are coffee, cotton, timber, copper, cobalt, diamonds and, off the Atlantic coast, oil.

Traditionally, the Zaire River and its tributaries have provided the main highways, with some 15 000 km of navigable waterways. On to this have been added 5000 km of railways and 15 000 km of largely poor quality roads, only 3700 km of which have an asphalt surface. The two main ports are Kinshasa (the capital, population 2.6 million) and Matadi, with Brazzaville and Pointe Noire nearby in Congo also being used. There is a second ground transportation system which is external and connects interior Zaire by road and rail to the Indian Ocean ports of Mombasa, Dar es Salaam, Beira, Maputo, Durban and East London, and to the Atlantic port of Lobito via the Benguela railway. This reliance on transport links across other countries clearly makes Zaire vulnerable and the government is trying to reduce this dependency.

The fragmentation of the rail network and the escalating maintenance problems have resulted in increasing proportions of freight being moved by road. This, in turn, is having a serious impact upon the

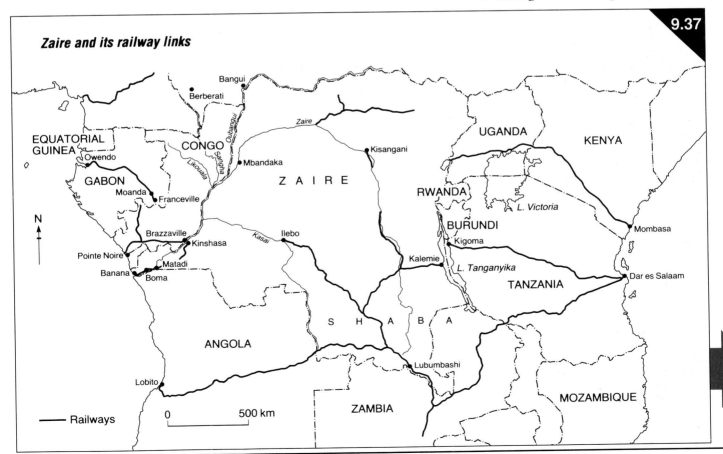

9.37

Zaire and its railway links

— Railways

0   500 km

Key understandings

◆ Fragmented and outdated transport networks are a major constraint to development.

◆ Construction and maintenance of an efficient transport infrastructure is essential, especially for countries which rely heavily upon marketing of bulky materials.

◆ The number of break-bulk transfers should be minimised and need to be efficient.

◆ Readily available energy supply is a critical element in a transport policy.

◆ It is dangerous for a country to rely on transport links which cross neighbouring countries.

road network which is not built to withstand such heavy traffic. In consequence, the government is encouraging the upgrading of the rail system in an attempt to transfer much of the bulky raw material traffic away from the roads. A key element in this policy is the availability of electricity from the Inga HEP scheme on the lower Zaire River, which is currently being used at well below its full capacity.

Zaire struggles to improve the transport network

Approximately two-thirds of Zaire's export earnings come from copper and cobalt. Copper is by far the more important, and is mined in Shaba province, in the south-east, far from the coast (resource 9.37). Until 1965, most of the exports went by the 2100 km Benguela railway through Angola to the port of Lobito, a journey which took 10 days. Since 1975 however, this railway has been out of action because of the war of liberation against the Portugese and the subsequent civil war. This has meant that Shaba's copper has been rerouted through Zaire's one Atlantic port, Matadi. This 2700 km

route, known as the **Vote Nationale** or national way, is in fact three sections: 1600 km by rail from Lubumbashi to Ilebo, 700 km by barge along the Kasai river to Kinshasa, 400 km by rail to Matadi. The two break-bulk points, delays caused by low river levels and shifting sandbanks, and the deterioration of the railways, mean that the journey during the 1980s was taking 50 days, compared with 20 days in 1970. Despite its inefficiency, the government has insisted on using this domestic route in preference to alternatives though Tanzania or South Africa. Nonetheless, by the late 1980s, this route was taking only 55 per cent of the exports, the remainder going via Dar es Salaam (Tanzania), 10 per cent, and South Africa, 35 per cent, despite the distance (3500 km) and high cost.

Kinshasa, the capital of Zaire, is the main transhipment point for all materials and goods leaving and entering the country via the port of Matadi, and handles around 600 000 tonnes a year. Physical geography gives us the reason for this importance: upstream of the deep Malebo pool at Kinshasa lie the long navigable reaches of the Zaire river, while downstream the river descends 270 m in falls and rapids over a distance of 350 km. The HEP potential of this stretch is enormous, as the Inga project indicates (see resource 9.38), but it is not navigable. As a result, a railway winds its way through the Crystal Mountains for almost 400 km between Kinshasa and Matadi. Kinshasa's 1100 m of quays handle minerals, petroleum products, palm oil, timber and containers, plus a busy ferry traffic across the river to Brazzaville, the Congo capital.

The port of Matadi (population 150 000) is vital to Zaire, as, although the country has 9000 km of land frontier, it has only 40 km of coastline, and is almost landlocked. Yet Matadi has significant site problems, for it is built on a narrow strip of land on the southern bank of

the river, backed by steeply rising valley sides. This site leaves little room for expansion, and residential areas now sprawl upwards to higher ground. Furthermore, the port lies 133 km from the open ocean and the lower Zaire river has unstable sandbanks, sharp bends and swift currents, limiting ships to 10 000 tonnes if fully loaded. Some 60 km downstream is the smaller port of Boma, where some cargo is unloaded so that ships can ride higher in the water and so reach Matadi, the off-loaded cargo then being taken by road to Matadi. This is clearly a very inefficient system.

There is a dock facility at the mouth of the Zaire river, but it is for oil and petroleum products only. The Moanda oil terminal can take tankers of 100 000 dwt (dead weight tonnes) and handles Zaire's 1.5 mt offshore production of crude oil. In addition it feeds imported oil to the associated refinery.

Efforts to improve the infrastructure

One priority has been to try to overcome the port bottleneck. Because of Matadi's site and situation limitations, a modern port near the open ocean has seemed desirable. One problem is that Matadi is on the south bank of the river, but downstream, the Angola border reaches this south bank of the Zaire river. Thus, in the 1970s a plan was produced to bridge the river at Matadi and construct a railway along the north bank of the river to the fishing port of Banana, at the mouth of the river near the Moanda oil terminal. A new deepwater port was to be built at Banana, which would be a free trade zone, i.e. free from taxes and tariffs, to encourage trade. With the aid of Japanese capital, the bridge was completed in 1983, but only as a road bridge, as the estimates for rail traffic could not justify the expenditure.

The second priority has been to try to upgrade the Vote Nationale. The deterioration of the road and rail sections, partly through poor management, makes transport costs and hence the price of the copper and agricultural products higher than necessary. Rehabilitation of the route began in 1987 and is due for completion in 1994. As the cost will exceed $350 million, assistance has been received from the World Bank, the EC and the African Development Bank. The aim is to reduce the journey time for the copper from Shaba to Matadi to 20–25 days, and to further lower the costs by increasing the capacity of the route. For example, on the 300 km rail section from Lubumbashi to Ilebo, completed by 1990, there is new track, electrified line with new rolling stock, improved communications and signalling, and the copper is containerised. On the river section between Ilebo and Kinshasa, there will be extensive channel dredging and new navigation lights to permit night-time transportation; new, larger pusher barges and pilot boats.

At Kinshasa the port capacity is being increased, onshore equipment is being upgraded and shipyard and navigation systems modernised. Similar improvements are under way along the Kinshasa-Matadi railway, where the carrying capacity is likely to reach 1.5 mt of copper ore a year. Remember that only one-half of the trade between these two cities is by rail, the rest goes by road, and this road is being upgraded. Thus, although there will still be the two break-bulk points caused by the rail-river-road mode transfer, overall efficiency should be improved, i.e. the friction of distance should be reduced.

A third direction of infrastructure improvement is to the east. First, there is the all-rail route via Zambia and the Tazara railway. Second, there is the railway from Shaba to the port of Kalemie on Lake Tanganyika, then by lake steamer to Kigoma and on to Dar es Salaam by rail. The effectiveness of this route depends, of course, upon how well the Tanzanian rail and port improvement programme develops.

Two further developments to watch for in the future are the re-opening of the Benguela railway, but this will require enormous investment after lying unused for almost 20 years. Second, there is the long-held dream of building a Ilebo-Kinshasa railway, so eliminating the river section. During the late 1980s the former Soviet Union was approached for financial and technical assistance, but events since then have killed any such possibility.

(Source: adapted from D Fair, 'The Atlantic parts of the Zaire river basin', *Africa Insight*, 19(2), 1989, pp. 103–108)

Note

Since 1989, when the schemes outlined here were discussed, there has been severe political upheaval in Zaire. Thus, a number of these plans may well take longer to complete.

9.38

The Inga Scheme

At independence, 72 per cent of Zaire's electricity output was accounted for by four small HEP stations supplying the Shaba copper mining region. In addition, isolated plants served the larger towns such as Kinshasa, as well as scattered mining areas in Kivu and Kasai provinces. The vast potential of the Inga scheme, estimated at 40 000 MW, was not seriously exploited until the later 1960s. It lay nearly 2000 km from Shaba, the main centre of demand, too far to justify the cost of its construction. At the site chosen, the Zaire River falls 102 m in a 15 km tract. The first Inga station was completed in 1972. Its output was sufficient to serve Kinshasa, but justification for a second station built in 1982, had to await the construction of a power-line to Shaba. This 1725 km long connection was completed in 1983. Shaba continues to account for 69 per cent of Zaire's electricity consumption with 27 per cent taken by Kinshasa and Lower Zaire.

Inga's installed capacity, officially put at 1750 MW is in excess of present consumption needs. In 1985 only 20 per cent of the capacity of the Inga stations was being utilised. Attempts were made to develop an aluminium smelter at the port of Banana, utilising imported bauxite, and to establish an industrial 'free zone', but these potentially large consumers have not materialised. However, Belgium is backing the electrification of the 366 km Kinshasa-Matadi rail line, with Inga as the power source.

Being the vast country that it is, it would be uneconomic at this stage to distribute Inga power throughout Zaire over a national grid system. Instead, most of its smaller centres continue to be served by small (mainly HEP) plants.

Activities

1 What is meant by break-bulk transfer? Give examples of the inefficiencies caused by such transfers and what is being done to reduce them in Zaire.

2 List and illustrate the main problems of the existing transport network.

3 What are the main products carried in Zaire, what are their characteristics, and what mode of transport is most economic for their movement?

4 How will schemes currently being developed make the transport system more efficient?

5 Why is the Inga HEP scheme so important for Zaire?

CHAPTER 10

Aspects of development

Introduction

The term 'development' has been defined in many ways. In books and articles written in the 1950s it was often equivalent to 'economic growth': if Gross National Product (GNP) was expanding, then development was taking place. During the 1960s and 1970s, it became accepted that this was an inadequate description. For instance, if the additional wealth generated by the economic growth benefitted only a small élite, leaving the majority of the population unaffected, then genuine development could not be said to be occurring.

Thus, factors such as the distribution of the extra wealth and its use to improve the welfare of the population were built into the definitions. Development came to mean *the progressive improvement in the standards of living and quality of life for an increasing proportion of the population*. Development becomes measured by various social, health and educational indicators, e.g. number of health clinics, percentage of population with secondary school education, as well as the economic growth indicators, e.g. GNP, or numbers employed in manufacturing industry.

The 1980s caused yet another rethink, triggered by two crucial realisations: first that 'development' was still a far off dream for millions of people (resource 10.1); second that the combination of population growth and misguided growth and development policies are causing serious environmental problems.

10.1

The development gap

The purpose of development has been defined as the ability to offer people more options. One of the primary options is access to income – not as an end in itself, but as a means of obtaining a better quality of life. Other options include a longer life, political and personal freedom, community participation and a guarantee of human rights. The developing countries have made progress towards human development in the last thirty years. Averages of progress in development conceal disparities within countries – between urban and rural areas, between rich and poor and between men and women. As the following list shows, any gains are balanced by a still startling inequality between the developed 'North' and the developing 'South', most particularly in terms of poverty and standards of health, rather than in personal development.

• **Life expectancy**
In 1960, life expectancy in developing countries was an average of 46 years. In 1987, this had risen to 62 years. The mortality rate in children under five has halved in the past thirty years. But 14 million children still die each year before their fifth birthday. The maternal mortality rate in the South is 12 times thath in the North – the largest gap of any social indicator.

• **Adult literacy**
In 1967, only 43 per cent of people in the developing world could read. Twenty years later, 60 per cent of people could.

However, nearly 900 million adults are still unable to read or write. Literacy rates for women are still only two-thirds of those for men.

• **Health services**
Nearly 1.75 billion people do not have access to safe drinking water.

Rural areas have on average only half the access to health services and safe drinking water that urban areas have, and only a quarter of the access to sanitation services.

• **Population**
The share of the developing countries in world population is expected to grow from 69 per cent in 1960 to 84 per cent by 2025, with a corresponding decrease in population in developed countries.

• **Poverty**
Some 800 million people go without sufficient food every day. The average per capita income in the South in 1987 was only 6 per cent of that in the North. 150 million children under five (one in three) are malnourished.

The poverty of the developing nations poses one of the greatest threats to the environment. Choices are made because people's immediate need is to survive, not because they lack concern for the future. Therefore, any plans of action for environmental protection must include programes to reduce poverty in the developing world.

Our common future

'Ten, or even five years ago, a survey of people's anxieties about the future of human civilization might have put fears about their military security, focused on a threat of East-West conflict, or on nuclear holocaust, close to the top of the list.

'Such a survey today would be more likely to show such fears being replaced by concern over the global environment. People all over the world are increasingly worried not only about their own and their children's future. Atmospheric and water pollution, a rapid extinction of plant and animal species, and the emerging spectre of global warming and climate change, have created a deepening anxiety about the future of this planet.

'The gross mismanagement of our planet has much to do with an inequitable distribution of the benefits of development. Perpetuating this inequity can only mean a continuing drawdown on the world's natural resources and the environment. After a century of unprecedented growth, marked by scientific and technological triumphs that would have been unthinkable a century ago, there have never been so many poor, illiterate and unemployed people in the world, and their number is growing. Close to a billion people live in poverty and squalor, a situation that leaves them little choice but to go on undermining the conditions of life itself, the environment and the natural resource base.

(Source: extracted from a talk in 1989 by Gro Brundtland, Prime Minister of Norway and Chairman of the 1987 report *Our Common Future: From One Earth to One World*)

There has been growing criticism of projects funded by international agencies and rich nations. Throwing money at the problem does not always provide the answer, despite the huge sums involved.

For example, blame for some of Amazonia's disasters has been laid upon the World Bank, while Japan's use of her enormous wealth has dangerous implications. Thus, the environmental dimension has been built into the definitions. Resource 10.2 sums up the position.

The need, therefore, is seen to be a strategy which links growth and conservation. It is based on the concept of **sustainable development**.

The report, 'Our Common Future' offered the notion of sustainable development as a way to meet the new challenges facing us. The Commission defined sustainable development as meeting the needs and aspirations of the present generation without compromising the ability of future generations to meet their needs. It requires political reform, access to knowledge and resources, and a more just and equitable distribution of wealth within and between nations.

Sustainable development includes two key elements. One is the meeting of needs, and in particular the needs by those who have been left far behind in a century of extraordinary growth. The second element concerns the limits which world society must now impose to protect the resource base of our environment, both locally and globally. Therefore sustainable development imposes standards of consumption which must be met within the bounds of ecological possibility.

The sustainable development approach includes these characteristics:

1 **Interdependence** The acceptance that human and natural elements of environmental systems at all scales, are vitally interconnected.
2 **Long-term perspective** Development must be based on ecological, not solely economic, i.e. next year's profits, and political, i.e. the next election, timescales.
3 **Humility** Acceptance that there are limits to our understanding and control of natural environments.
4 **Counting the true costs** Estimates and accounts must build in the costs of environmental consequences, rather than seeing environmental resources as 'free'.

5 **Remembering the poor** The vulnerable poor are often the first to suffer, to be displaced, or simply to be ignored in existing policies.
6 **Broader perspectives** Narrow nationalistic thinking needs to give way to wider international perspectives, e.g. introducing ways of maintaining world prices of the primary products upon which developing countries depend and of controlling their debts.

(Source: G H Brundtland, 'Sustainable Development: An Overview, *Journal of SID Development*, 1989, nos 2/3, pp. 73 and 14)

A further debate concerning development in countries of the developing world focuses upon how it can be achieved. At one extreme there are the large, multi-purpose schemes involving United Nations agencies, international banks, 'rich' countries, – the 'top-down' approach, where change is imposed from above. At the other extreme are small-scale 'self-help' projects involving the local people directly in the decision-making process, – the 'bottom-up' approach. The projects set out in this chapter vary in scale, purpose, organisation and the degree to which they fulfil the requirements of 'sustainable development'. They make it clear that no single model provides the answer: project character must be appropriate to the society and environment within which it is taking place.

As you read the case studies, pay particular attention to (i) who is taking the decisions, (ii) the aims of the project and how they are being implemented, (iii) who benefits and who loses, (iv) the environmental impacts. (NB Urban development in the Third World is covered in Chapter 4, while issues connected with tourism development arise in Chapter 8).

CASE STUDY 10.1 *Balancing development and*

Background

The accelerating loss of tropical rainforest in Amazonia is well-known (resource 10.3), and the outcry surrounding the destruction grew steadily through the 1980s. Protests have tended to focus upon the ecological value of the forests, land rights and the forests as the home of 'traditional' societies, and the effects on world climate. Recently, however, a fourth wave of interest has centred upon the development alternatives for the region: development is accepted as inevitable, so the key issues are: can development and conservation co-exist, can development be sustainable, and who will be in control of the development?

In 1989, a West German government official involved in development aid wrote: 'The Amazon is at an extremely critical phase of its development. To what extent this development can be steered depends, among other things, on the type and amount of support Brazil is offered'. He sees these aspects as important in any decisions made:

(i)   Scale and character.
(ii) Causes of deforestation.
(iii) Government policies.

Key understandings

◆ Development in Amazonia is inevitable. The critical issue is the **character** of that development. Will it be sustainable and ecologically sound?

◆ Increased energy generation is an inevitable part of development.

◆ All forms of energy generation will affect the rainforests. Decisions about whether to minimise impact and maximise generation will be difficult.

◆ Decisions about development involve international agencies, national and regional governments, and local people.

◆ International agency and government policies to encourage development may have unexpected and damaging consequences.

This case study highlights these aspects and their relationship to sustainable development. Part I focuses upon the expanding energy demands that are inevitable if economic development and related social change are to take place. Massive HEP schemes along the Amazon system are shown to have enormous environmental impact and to be inefficient, but the alternatives each have their problems. Part II examines the limitations and effects of a range of well-intentioned government policies, and recommends how they might be strengthened.

Part I: Power plants and politics

The international organisation known as the World Bank has been the largest single source of financial aid to countries of the developing world, especially for large-scale projects. For example, in Brazil it has helped to fund the road network based on the Trans-Amazonian Highway, which is making Amazonia more accessible. The World Bank has been severely criticised for failure to assess and keep a close enough watch on these 'penetration road' projects. It has taken part of the blame for the accelerated deforestation in the State of Rondonia, caused by the influx of settlers along the penetration roads (resource 10.4). As a result, a massive US $500 million loan to Brazil was agreed in 1989 only after long negotiations about the allocation of the money and the supervision of how it will be used. The loan is linked to the Brazilian government's 'Our Nature' programme, announced in April 1989, which has ambitious environmental aims within its development policies, e.g. short-term halting of timber exports and tax reductions on agricultural and cattle breeding schemes until ecologically sound plans have been drawn, control of the use of machinery in gold panning, the reform of forestry laws to encourage hardwood plantations, the setting up

Deforestation in Amazonia		10.3
State	**Percentage of state cleared**	
	by 1978	**By 1988**
Acre	1.6	12.8
Amapa	0.1	0.4
Amazonas	0.1	6.8
Goias	3.6	11.6
Maranhao	2.8	19.7
Mato Grosso	3.2	23.6
Para	0.8	9.6
Rondonia	1.7	23.7
Roraima	0.1	1.4
Total	1.5	12.0

of a national environmental fund.

Some of the US $500 million is to be spent on the Amazonian jungle, where the world's largest network of rivers harbours Brazil's huge energy reserves. According to expert estimates, 76 power stations with an installed capacity of some 100 000 MW can be erected in the green wilderness, which would then generate twice as much electricity as Brazil's present turbine capacity provides or twenty-one times more than the turbines of the Aswan Dam in Egypt. Owing to the low gradient in the Amazon, huge dams up to 65 kilometres long would have to be built holding in reservoirs of over 80 000 km², thirty-one times the territory of Luxembourg.

The management of the government electricity corporation Eletrobras is trying to placate the opposition with the assurance that they only want to construct another 31 power plants in addition to the four already standing. Up to 2010 in fact, they are only planning to set up fourteen with an output of just about 50 000 MW. Even if all 31 schemes were implemented, this would only mean the inundation of 100 000 km² of land, a mere 2 per cent of the Amazonian region. In the opinion of

Eletronorte President Miguel Nunes three hundred and forty people (only) would have to be relocated for the contested power station Cararo Xingu, 286 of whom are 'isolated Indians with no tradition'.

The champions of the Indians of course see things quite differently. They maintain that the Xingu dams would drive 40 tribes and 70 000 Indians, out of their villages. The Xingu region, where countless Indian tribes have sought refuge also supports a uniquely rich flora and fauna.

Ecologists feel that their concern is borne out by Eletronorte's record. When building the largest forest power plant, the US $5 billion Tucurui project at Rio Tocatins, the clearance was proceeding too slowly, so Eletronorte had an area of forest of about 2500 km² immersed. As a result, the Tucurui Dam, whose turbines will generate a capacity of 5280 MW, encloses 60 million tonnes of rotting wood, which is poisoning the water with sulphurous gases and methane. Today, four years later, the water is undrinkable.

Balbina, too, is like a red rag to the Greens. The half-finished hydro-electric plant north of Manaus has put 'another Luxembourg' under

water, depriving the Wairmiri of a part of their hunting grounds, and all for a 'ridiculous' 250 MW.

The Greens of the world may protest, but Brazil has no choice but to keep to a growth path and hence to build more power plants, if it wants to give food and work to the three million people who are added each year to Brazil's population. For the next decade, experts reckon with an annual rise in energy consumption of six per cent. Far too little has been expended on infrastructure over recent years so a 'blackout' is looming for the beginning of the next decade. Without the Itaipu power station lots of lights would have already gone out in Brazil, but the reserves of the world's largest power station (12 600 MW) on the border with Paraguay will be exhausted in three years after the installation of the last turbines. Where is the extra energy going to come from?

Coal is available only in the south of Brazil and it is of low quality and can only be treated locally. The exploitation of the 310 000 tonnes of rich uranium deposits has been resisted by the environmentalists for years. Since they are also opposed to barrage weirs with locks on the Amazon river, they must ask themselves what alternatives they have to offer. Their inability to provide an answer underscores their dilemma. Pressure from outside is hardly likely to stop the Brazilians from exploiting their jungle resources. Unofficially, the opinion has been voiced that Brazil cannot be expected to abstain from developing for the sake of preserving the ozone and carbon dioxide balance (resource 10.7).

At best, the protests of politicians, parties and parliaments of Western Europe and North America can see to it that the billion dollar projects to exploit the energy resources of the Amazon are subjected to economic scrutiny prior to startup and are monitored for ecological impacts during construction work. Even this doesn't really help all that

10.4

Land cleared for cattle ranching in Brazil. Notice the charred tree stumps stretching into the distance

much though: the Amazonian forests are not so much in danger of being destroyed by dams and sluicegates; the threat comes more from the proliferating networks of roads zig-sagging westward.

(Source: M Gester, 'Power Plants and Politics in Brazil', *Development and Co-operation*, No. 3 1989, pp. 6–8)

Part II: Impacts of development policies.

A study published in 1989 jointly by the World Bank, the World Wildlife Fund for Nature and the Conservation Foundation claims that policies to encourage development have played an important part in much unnecessary and environmentally undesirable forest clearance. The following is a summary of the viewpoint presented by the study, and five recommendations for an effective programme of sustainable development.

Government policies designed to open up Amazonia for human settlement and to encourage certain types of economic activity have played a key role in the deforestation process.

Tax incentives for settlers in the region, along with subsidised agricultural credit and essentially unregulated resale of land, have been making it profitable to clear forests. These economic incentives have contributed to the destruction of about 600 000 sq. km of forests in Brazil's Amazonia region, which comprises nine states or territories.

Many of the country's current deforestation problems can be traced back to the mid-1960s, when the government launched a campaign to develop Amazonia. The physical isolation of Amazonia – and the protection this provided to the rain forest – came to an end in 1964 with the completion of a 1900-kilometre all-weather highway that connected the new capital city of Brasilia in Brazil's heartland with

Belem at the mouth of the Amazon River.

Large numbers of migrants in search of land and employment entered the region of the new road. Firms interested in starting cattle ranches and taking advantage of cheap land and generous tax and credit incentives also flocked to the area. There can be no doubt that the surge of migration and economic activity stimulated by the Belem-Brasilia highway contributed to widespread deforestation.

Starting in 1966, the government moved ahead with other development efforts that included an ambitious road-building program and additional tax and credit incentives for private enterprises entering the region. These moves led to further deforestation.

In the mid-1970s, new tax incentives and access to free or low-cost land attracted a wave of immigrants to the Amazonian state of Rondonia, where deforestation is taking place at a 'truly astonishing' rate.

But settlers arriving in Rondonia quickly discovered that the land they cleared for farming or cattle-raising was so fragile that it became useless after only a couple of years. So to keep their farms going, many cleared new land.

To stem the tide of destruction, the government launched in 1981 the north-west Brazil Integrated Development Programme, known as Polonoroeste. The programme, supported by a World Bank loan, aimed to reduce forest clearance on land with little long-term agricultural potential by promoting sustainable tree-crop farming. The programme included the construction of roads and other infrastructure to accommodate the anticipated growth in the region's tree-crop industry.

Deforestation in Rondonia became catastrophic as thousands of new migrants arrived after the government's paving of a major road cutting through the state in 1984.

But population growth alone can explain neither the extremely rapid pace of deforestation nor farmers' preference for pasture formation over the cultivation of tree crops. Several government policies made the problem worse.

First, the government agency in charge of forestry development has not been able to enforce laws requiring settlers to keep half their land forested. And second, the development of tree-crop farming planned under the Polonoroeste programme was based on the assumption that farmers would have access to credit to buy fertilisers and other goods needed for maintaining land once it had been cleared.

But subsidised agricultural credit dried up soon after the programme began, and many farmers could not afford to buy the fertilisers they needed to make their tree-crop farms flourish. Just as in the 1970s, farmers cleared more forests as their old land became useless for farming or herding. And, tax breaks continued encouraging destruction of forests – even by people who could afford to buy fertilisers.

Despite rapid migration to Rondonia and other parts of Amazonia – and all the deforestation that accompanied that migration – the region continues to suffer economically and contributes little to the national economy. Amazonia still accounts for only an insignificant 3 per cent of the national income.

The study recommends five policy changes that could slow the rate of deforestation in Amazonia, especially the state of Rondonia.

- The government might consider eliminating financial incentives for livestock production in Amazonia. More than two decades of experience have shown that livestock projects have been responsible for much environmental damage and yield little in the way of production or employment.

- The government could declare a halt on funds given out for projects that depend on charcoal derived from rain forests as a main source of energy. Such a move is especially important for the Greater Carajas area in eastern Amazonia where pig-iron plants are now being constructed (resource 10.5).

- Brazil's National Institute for Colonisation and Agrarian Reform could modify its policy of recognising deforestation as a form of land improvement and, as such, as grounds for granting rights of possession. This policy has encouraged felling of forest in areas with little or no agricultural potential.

- Brazil's Institute of Forestry Development could abolish its rule requiring settlers to preserve forests on half of their land. The rule has been shown to be unenforceable in a frontier region and provides little, if any, protection to the environment. Instead, legislation should be enacted to require the formation of 'contiguous block' reserves equal to 50 per cent of the total area being used for agricultural purposes in a given region rather than 50 per cent of each farmer's lot. Such reserves would help to maintain biological diversity, benefit agriculture, and increase the number of migrants who could be settled on better soils in already occupied areas.

- The government should intensify its efforts to improve the administration of taxes, which, if duly collected, could have beneficial effects on land use. A progressive rural land tax has the potential to improve land-use patterns by penalising those who engage in environmentally unsound activities.

(Source: 'Deforestation in Brazil's Amazon Region', *Development and Co-operation* No. 3, 1989, pp. 8–9)

10.5

Forests Going up in Smoke

The Grande Carajas programme devised in 1980 is aimed at developing the eastern sector of the Amazon region industrially and agriculturally. It embraces 900 000 km^2 or 10 percent of Brazilian territory. The plans are extremely controversial and it is questionable, partly for economic reasons, whether they can be fully realised. As a result of government incentives though (settlement of smallholders, cattle breeding, aluminium works and other industries), the programme has unleashed a monster which has already devoured half of the rainforest in the core territory.

A key component of the programme is the exploitation of iron ore, manganese ore and other mineral deposits in Carajas by the partly state-run CVRD company. US $3.5 billion were invested (credit from the World Bank, EC, among others). Operations have been running since 1985 (output 25 million tonnes a year), with environmental factors catered for in model fashion. The indirect effects, though, are posing serious problems.

Electricity is supplied by the 7800 MW hydroelectric plant at Tucurui which was erected at the same time and which also supplies the rapidly expanding industrial centre of Maraba established with the help of government subsidies. However, this also includes 15 government approved iron-smelting plants which burn charcoal. Two of these were started up in Maraba in 1988.

Together they have four blast furnaces. Planned annual output is 360 000 t of pig iron. Due to insufficient afforestation, 30 000–60 000 ha of natural forest have to be felled per year in order to provide enough charcoal – that's as much as 160 ha daily. The projected consumption of all 15 plants is 1.2 million tonnes of charcoal or 90 000–200 000 ha of forest a year. A lot more wood is constantly being burned wastefully in the agricultural sector; however, independent burners obtain their charcoal through the cheapest means available. In other words, they don't bother to use wood obtained from the clearing of land for agricultural purposes. The devastating results of this were realised when it was too late. The production of pig iron is only worthwhile when charcoal prices are low. Government regulations on forest conservation stipulate that the proportion of charcoal obtained through own afforestation should be 25 per cent in the 6th year of operation, 50 per cent in the 10th, and 100 per cent from 1997 onwards. However, experience has shown that charcoal from plantations cannot be produced for less than US $80 per tonne. Since no afforestation has taken place so far either, and since the period of growth is at least seven years, the above deadlines cannot be met. In other words, pig iron production with charcoal is patently inefficient; it can only survive through overexploitation. Clearly, the mining industry is banking on being able to circumvent existing regulations until the investments have been written off and plants can be shut down easily.

The Brazilian authorities express the vague hope that in future technological improvements will lead to a reduction in charcoal consumption and that its production will not cause any ecological problems thanks to afforestation, 'rational utilisation' of the primary forest areas, and recourse to land in the agricultural sector which has been cleared anyway. However, experience in Minas Gerais has shown that afforestation either fails or isn't carried out under the same legal and administrative conditions. There, some of the charcoal has to be procured from the fringes of the Amazon region, sometimes 1000 km away.

(Source: H P Schipulle, *Development and Co-operation*, No. 5, 1989)

CASE STUDY 10.1 *Balancing development and conservation in Amazonia*

Activities

Pair discussion topics:

1 Outline the cases for and against the development of HEP in the Amazon basin, and assess the alternatives in terms of social, economic and ecological impacts.

2 Why is it proving so difficult to introduce sustainable development in Amazonia? (Use resources 10.5, 10.6 and 10.7.)

3 Why is Brazil likely to resist the 'help' of outside agencies such as the World Bank, World Wildlife Fund for Nature, etc.?

4 Identify who is involved in making decisions in Amazonia, and who you think *should* be making the decisions.

10.6 Issues and answers

The world cannot just sit back and await the uncertain outcome. The Amazon is in an extremely critical phase of its development. To what extent this development can be steered depends, among other things, on the type and amount of support Brazil is offered to help master its economic problems. Decisions made in connection with this should account for the following:

● The Amazon region, covering more than 5 million km^2, is the largest tropical rainforest region in the world, whose importance for the regional and world climates as well as for global biological diversity is unique. About 75 per cent of this area (3.7 million km^2) belongs to Brazil. In 1975 it had only decreased in size by about 1 per cent. Since then the destruction has taken on progressively drastic dimensions. The World Bank estimated a depletion by 1988 of 12 per cent (600 000 km^2).

● The primary causes for this are known: short-term economic interest in the exploitation of mineral resources, wood, water power and arable land, which in turn is a result of the country's economic plight (domestic economic failures, external economic problems, debts), unmanageable structural changes (agricultural modernisation, urbanisation) and the resulting demographic pressure: foreign policy and strategic interests towards neighbouring states and thr of losing sovereignty through foreign intervention play a role.

● Largely, the casal relationships between government policy and the destruction of the forests are clear: tax and subsidy incentives, poorly implemented land reform, infrastructure divorced from land use, mistakes in forestry policy and in the granting of timber concessions. These then, are concrete areas where changes in policy should be made.

(Source: H P Schipulle, *Development and Co-operation*, No. 5, 1989)

10.7 A Brazilian viewpoint

Amazonas' controversial governor, Gilberto Mestrinho, says he values the lives of people more than those of animals and plants.

When you have a nation as large as Brazil, with so many diverse areas, you can't group the whole country under one general environmental code. What's true in the south or in the coastal states is not necessarily true here in the Amazon, so it makes sense that each state determine its own environmental policy.

The problem is that anytime somebody talks about doing anything at all in the Amazon, there is this wild hysteria from the rest of the world and from certain sectors in Brazil telling us we can't cut down a tree. The fact is, the Amazon is the least destroyed place in the world. Since the arrival of the Europeans some 500 years ago, only 8.5 per cent of the Amazon has been deforested. In my state of Amazonas, only 1.24 per cent has been deforested. These are the facts. And the people here are living in misery, but nobody cares about them. All you hear is "Save the Amazon, save the animals." Environmentalists care more about trees and monkeys than people. It's absurd. I have my priorities straight. I value the lives of the people more than those of animals and plants. Only after we have improved the lives of humans can we begin thinking of the fauna and flora.

I'm a conservationist, not a preservationist. The Amazon is not a museum – as many foreigners want it to be. There are almost 17 million people living in the Brazilian part alone, and you can't expect them not to interact with their surroundings. We are not monkeys in a zoo. But we can develop the Amazon while conserving it. It is vast and can accommodate many different types of activities, including the controlled exploration of minerals and wood.

Developed nations, which have used their resources to become rich, now expect us to live in misery. The Amazon has one of the richest mineral deposits in the world. A mine causes very little destruction to the environment but can bring in lots of revenue to the state. The same with timber, if done properly through forest management, where only the valuable hardwoods are taken out and seedlings are replanted. But we are not even allowed to export logs.

Most environmental groups are defending economic interests, not nature. They are being used by multinationals and cartels to prevent us and other Third World nations from cutting into the developed world's profits. It was only in the '60s and '70s, when Brazil began to explore the natural resources of the Amazon and foreigners saw that we could extract the resources at a very low cost, that the whole campaign to preserve the Amazon began. We weren't destroying the forests; they know that. But we were threatening foreign businesses. They continue to fabricate stories and exaggerate the facts, say we are torching the Amazon, that there will be a greenhouse effect. The truth is, the amount of carbon dioxide released from forest fires is insignificant, while the more than 500 million motor vehicles of the world emit 56 per cent of the carbon dioxide in the atmosphere.

(Source: *Time*, 16 September 1991)

CASE STUDY 10.2 *Rural self-help and foreign aid – examples from Pakistan*

Background

One of the obstacles to generating effective development is obtaining the support and enthusiasm of the local communities who will be affected by development projects. It may seem obvious that people will be less enthusiastic about a scheme which they see as imposed on them from above – the 'top down' approach. Yet the 'bottom-up' approach, whereby the responsibility for a project belongs to the local community themselves, also has certain critical problems. These include the lack of financial and technical resources, an absence of the sort of organisational structures which can take the necessary decisions, a poor infrastructure, in particular roads and water supply. In most cases, therefore, outside help has been inevitable, from both the national governments and foreign agencies. There is perhaps a natural tendency for these external bodies to think that they know best or to wish to retain control of how money is spent, and so to impose their

preferences upon the local people. There is the question too, of what happens when the project funding ends and the 'experts' leave.

Governments and aid agencies have become more sensitive to such issues, are more skilful in obtaining the genuine involvement of local people and in trying to ensure that the development is sustainable in the longer term. The examples in this case study illustrate the 'self-help' approach adopted by a West German aid agency (GTZ) in two districts in Pakistan (resource 10.8). In both cases the fundamental principle is to help the villagers to help themselves and for the developments to be run successfully after the aid projects have ended. In the Pattoki district scheme described in Part I, the aim is to add a viable commercial element to the economy based on dairy cattle and milk marketing. In the Mardan project of Part II, infrastructure development is given first priority, supported by environmental improvements such as water management and

afforestation. Notice the concern in both examples for the future of the schemes, and whether they can stimulate similar developments elsewhere.

Key understandings

◆ Development is more likely to be effective when the decision-making is in the hands of local people.

◆ The role of foreign aid agencies should be to help local communities with resources, with organisation and skill improvement, and then to withdraw, having provided the basis for self-sustaining development.

◆ Fundamentals for successful commercial development must be sound infrastructure, regular supplies of reliable quality products, and an efficient marketing system.

Part I: Building a farmers' organisation in Pattoki

Pattoki is a small town in the Punjab province, about 85 km south of Lahore. It lies in a predominantly rural area, although in the last few years, a number of industries have sprung up along the road to Lahore. Farmers in the area produce rice, wheat, sugarcane, cotton, and a variety of fruits from their irrigated fields. Livestock plays a relatively minor role. Buffaloes are kept mainly to provide milk for the family with surpluses being sold to the local market. Bullocks are used as draught animals, while goats and sheep provide the meat for the family diet.

The GTZ first moved into the area with a research project on animal production, marketing of milk and meat, and animal breeding in 1979. Four years later, an agreement was signed between the governments of Pakistan and the Federal Republic of Germany which laid the basis of the

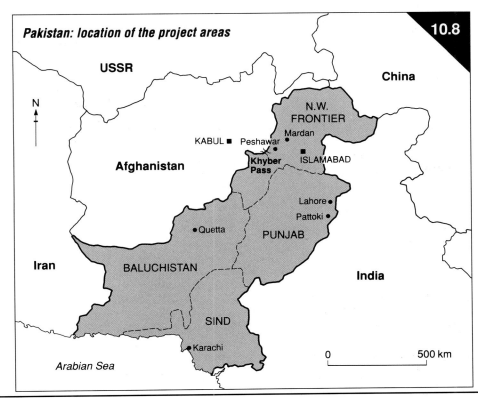

Pakistan: location of the project areas   10.8

USSR

China

N

N.W. FRONTIER

KABUL ■ Peshawar Mardan

Afghanistan

Khyber Pass ■ ISLAMABAD

Iran

Lahore ●
Pattoki ●

● Quetta

BALUCHISTAN

PUNJAB

India

SIND

● Karachi

Arabian Sea

0   500 km

Pattoki Livestock Production Project. The aim of the project is to increase the incomes of farmers from livestock production and to establish a farmers organisation – Idara-i-Kissan – which will be able to carry on the activities of the project when the German advisers will be withdrawn.

By 1989, five years after the first veterinary services were offered to the farmers in the project area, considerable progress has been achieved through a package of integrated measures, and financial benefits are accruing to the farmers from the milk collection, processing and marketing scheme. Traditionally, marketable surpluses of buffalo milk are collected by the local dodhi, or milkman, who goes around the village on his bicycle and then sells the milk to a contractor who in turn will sell the milk either to a dairy plant or to a retail outlet. The drawback for the farmer is that the dodhi is often also the moneylender and will bind the supplier by advances for a whole season. Prices paid to the farmers fluctuate with demand and supply and are not tied to fat content, i.e. the quality of the milk. Also, dodhis often cheat while measuring the milk, and further dilute it with water to the detriment of the consumer. Conditions at collection points are extremely unhygienic: ice blocks dumped on the ground among cow and donkey dung are crushed and filled into the containers to cool the milk. No care is taken to keep the milk clean of flying straw and dust.

To improve this situation, the German team has completely reorganised the milk collection system. In 35 villages around Halla, the centre of the operations, milk is collected directly from the farmers and then brought by donkeycart to the chilling unit in Halla. From here, it goes to a specially constructed dairy plant in Pattoki from where it is marketed locally and in Lahore.

We watch the milk collection at Badhana, a village of 600 households a few kilometres from Halla. At eight o'clock in the morning, most of the 110 farmers who have joined the scheme, have already delivered their milk. Now, in winter, is the peak milk season. Each farmer sells between 5 and 7 litres per day, the rest is kept for home consumption. The Village Milk Collector (VMC) takes a sample of each pot for later analysis of its fat content. Farmers are paid not only by the quantity, but also by the quality of their milk. Daily deliveries are carefully entered in a logbook as a record for the weekly payments. At half past eight, all the milk has been collected. The containers are stored on a donkeycart which immediately sets out on the untarred road towards Halla and the chilling unit. Speed is essential, because the milk will spoil within hours in the day's heat.

10 o'clock at the central collection point in Halla. Donkeycarts from the neighbouring villages begin to arrive. The milk is first tested for taste and then poured through a linen cloth into a larger container. 10 000 litres are collected on an average day. After chilling, the milk goes to the dairy plant in Pattoki where it is pasteurised and filled into plastic bags of varying sizes. Because of its high quality and undiluted taste, it has already captured a market in Lahore where it is transported every evening by lorry.

In what way do the farmers benefit from this scheme? First of all, they receive a better price of their milk. Secondly, because they are paid by fat content of the milk, they have an incentive to improve the health and the quality of their livestock. They are helped in this by the veterinary section of the project. Mobile teams of veterinarians are going around the villages and offer treatment for the animals and advice on animal husbandry for the farmers. Village extension workers provide farm inputs like fertilisers, feed-concentrates, minerals, and fodder-seeds. As a result, the animal mortality rate has fallen from 8 to 2 per cent, the cows give more milk, and are worth more when they are sold. Incomes from livestock, especially in the villages near the Ravi river where agriculture is less important, have started to rise.

The question is, however, what will happen to the scheme once the substantial material and personal assistance from the German side ends. Progressively during the course of the project, local staff have been involved in the various activities at village level. Besides the Village Milk Collector and the Village Extension Worker, there is a Village Veterinary Assistant and a Female Village Worker who are paid for their performance through commissions based on turnover of their respective activities. Recently, village representatives – 'nomaindas' – have been nominated and trained to control all programmes at the village level. They will represent their villages in the Idara-i-Kissan (IK), the village organisation, formally established in 1989 and which is expected to carry on the project activities as a private non-governmental company. Eventually, it is hoped, the IK will be economically viable and self-sustaining so that outside assistance is no longer needed.

Problems remain. What, for instance, is to happen to the considerable assets such as vehicles and equipment brought in by the Germans? Is it justifiable that the IK as a private company just inherits these assets although they were given as part of a government-to-government agreement? The Livestock Department of the provincial government in Lahore is looking with hardly more than lukewarm enthusiasm at the establishment of IK and seems reluctant to spread the idea elsewhere in the Punjab. In the villages, too, there is opposition. The traditional dodhis resent being thrown out of business by the new collection scheme. This brings new divisions to communities which are already often split into hostile groups and unable to unite in one village organisation.

It is thus still too early to judge whether the Pak-German project in the Pattoki area will eventually succeed, and – what is more – whether its success can be sustained. A positive sign is that villages in the adjacent areas have applied on their own to join in the scheme. An expansion is welcome because the dairy plant can only be used to capacity if more than the present 10 000 litres daily are processed. But expansion also means that the distance to the chilling plant in Halla is becoming too large and that a second unit must be installed. And the larger the area served by IK the greater the need for transport and infrastructure if veterinary and extension services are to be maintained. There is still a long way to go before IK will be a viable self-help organisation.

At present, only camels and donkeycarts like this can make the journey to the nearest market. Improvements in the roads will mean new income opportunities for the farmers

Part II: Promoting self-help in the Mardan District

After leaving the main road near Rustam, our four-wheel driven jeep is heading towards the mountains. The stony road winds around rocks and into dry river valleys, crosses a shallow stream, and climbs up steep embankments eroded from the last rain. A breathtaking view compensates for the bumpy ride: yellow mustard fields interspersed with a few isolated trees stretch all the way to the foot of the bare and rugged mountains, the first chain of the mighty Hindukush.

The first goal of our journey comes into sight: the mountain village of Zorabad, a dense cluster of mud houses sheltering 240 families. Zorabad is one of the villages in which the Pak-German Integrated Rural Development Programme Mardan (IRDP) is active in trying to promote development through self-help. The project area in the Mardan and Swabi districts of the North-Western Frontier Province was selected on criteria such as lack of infrastructure, and irrigation facilities and its general backwardness and underdevelopment. The principal aim of IRDP is to involve the population in determining developmental priorities and activities to which the project can make a contribution.

In Zorabad, the visitors are awaited by an assembly of the Village Development Organisation (VDO), a branch of the self-help groups that the Pak-German team are trying to set up in each village of the area. 168 households in Zorabad, or 70 per cent of the total population, have signed up for membership and paid their 5 rupee membership fee. This gives them the right to participate in the election of the three VDO leaders and the Village Organising Committee comprising 10 to 15 members. Meetings are held every fortnight to discuss ongoing and proposed projects.

The members of the village assembly in Zorabad explain to the visitors what benefits they have so far derived from the project. Two new deep wells are being dug, concrete linings for two existing wells will be put in place. Water is a major problem during the long dry season. In spite of the closeness of the mountains, the groundwater table is extremely low. Deforestation of the steep hillsides is one of the causes. It is also the cause of disastrous torrents bursting into the valleys when the monsoon rains set in. The next project which the villagers of Zorabad want to tackle, therefore, is the construction of a dam for flood protection. A nearby river, now completely dry, threatens to erode the hillside on which the village is built.

Another priority is the improvement of the road. At the moment, only camels and donkeys can make the journey to the nearest market. When improvements in agriculture bring higher yields of wheat, barley, mustardseed, and maize, better access to the village would also mean new income opportunities for the farmers. Up till now, they have hardly any surpluses which they could sell.

We continue our tour through the project area. On the banks of a dry river bed, work is in progress on a road which will link several of the isolated villages with the market town of Rustam. The banks are fortified against flood damage and culverts are constructed to drain off rain water. Near another river bed, a deep well with a water table 80 metres below the surface will be lined with concrete and a diesel pump will be installed. The project is financing the pump while the villages using the well will be responsible for operating costs and maintenance.

In Cheena, a village of some 300 households near Rustam, another meeting of the local Village Development Organisation is in progress. About 55 per cent of the villagers are VDO members. A Youth Development Organisation has also been created. Projects already carried out include the installation of streetlights, the pavementing of village streets, and a social forestry scheme. A demonstration field for spring potatoes and wheat has also been established and a livestock extension worker employed.

We want to know more about the afforestation project. With pride, the villagers report that the survival rate of the 11 000 seedlings planted last summer on a communal plot near the village was much higher than in an unsuccessful government scheme earlier on. A guardian is being paid to protect the plants from goats. Now a little hut will be constructed as shelter for the warden. In the future, the villagers plan an extension of the afforested plot.

Another priority is once again a road to link up Cheena with Rustam. The problem is that a neighbouring village whose territory is crossed by the road has no interest in the improvement which would mean additional competition from Cheena. Land disputes such as this one often impede the work of the development workers. The district government, which could settle the dispute, is often indifferent – a frustrating experience for the remote villages which depend on better roads for a better life.

The establishment of the VDOs could mean that things will change in the future. One aim of the project is to make villagers more aware of their rights and to enhance their ability to approach government departments and development agencies to promote their own

interests. the key word here is 'institution building at village level'. A VDO is only accepted as a partner by the IRDP when at least 50 per cent of all village households are represented. Projects not only have to be approved by the majority of members, but as far as possible the work is executed through self help with as little outside assistance as possible.

Nevertheless, the support given by IRDP to the VDOs is substantial: field officers assist in the formation of project committees for priority schemes, training of office bearers, supervision of project committee activities and the solving of village conflicts; technical and financial inputs include feasibility studies, design, provision of materials and tools, technical work supervision and funds required in addition to self-help contributions. In 1989, 87 per cent of IRDP's budget will be provided by the German Agency for Technical Cooperation (GTZ). The contribution by the Pakistani partners is only 13 per cent.

Once again, as in the case of the Pattoki project, doubts remain. Previously, government officials rarely found their way into the remote villages at the foot of the Hindukush. Badly paid and without transport, they have no incentive to leave headquarters to face the complaints of the village people. In contrast, IRDP is well staffed with five foreign advisers, some 60 Pakistani staff, and a sufficient number of cross-country vehicles to enable them to work regularly at the village level. But can such a project become a model for other parts of the country? Replication will be very difficult indeed without a comparable input of external resources, i.e. foreign aid.

Both the Pattoki and Mardan projects show that it is possible to reach the rural poor and build self-help institutions at the grassroot level. But doing it with foreign governmental assistance is extremely

costly and requires millions for just a few villages. A replication of the experience on a nation-wide scale is, therefore, out of the question for a poor country like Pakistan. All one can hope is that at least in the project areas, sustainable development will continue and the villagers will have learned to help themselves once the foreign helpers have returned home.

(Source: D Brauer, 'Rural self-help and foreign aid. Two German projects in Pakistan', *Development and Co-operation*, No 1, 1989, pp. 10–13)

Activities

1 Outline the characteristics of (a) the traditional system and (b) the introduced system of dairy production in the Pattoki district. Why were the changes necessary, and why was there opposition?

2 Why was infrastructure improvement given first priority in the Mardan project?

3 How do the Pattoki and Mardan projects illustrate the importance of infrastructure, organisation and self-help as bases for successful development?

4 What are seen as the crucial problems when the aid agency teams leave?

5 **Pair discussion:**

In what ways do these two projects help you to explain what is meant by 'sustainable development'? (Think carefully about definitions of 'development' and 'sustainable'.)

CASE STUDY 10.3 *Is the price of development right? Alternatives in India*

Background

It is generally accepted that a crucial foundation of development in a developing country must be a sound agricultural system. Despite rapid urbanisation, many developing countries are likely to remain, for the foreseeable future, essentially rural societies. With both rural and urban populations expanding, food supplies must at least keep pace with demands. Improving the quality of life for the rural population has been a major goal of development programmes. Schemes involve housing, education and infrastructure improvements, but above all, they need to increase agricultural outputs in terms of both quantity and quality. This can be achieved by raising the productivity of existing farmland and by bringing new land into cultivation. Where possible there needs to be a balance between subsistence and commercial products. A further goal of agricultural development may be land re-allocation to reduce the numbers of landless families.

In many parts of the tropics, the critical resource in success or failure may be water. Rainfall may be highly seasonal and unreliable. Thus in purely rain-fed agriculture, both crops and animals endure a long dry season, with food and fodder being stores to sustain people and animals. Alternatively, some products may be traded and the money used to buy food during the dry season. Such systems often leave a narrow margin between survival and starvation, especially when population numbers are growing. The basic answer to these hazards is to upgrade the water supply: to improve its reliability and to make it available for more months a year, i.e. to save some of the rainfall. Many societies have evolved such storage and irrigation schemes over hundreds of years, using simple technology but a thorough understanding of their environment and how to use the water efficiently (resource 10.10).

10.10

Agricultural terracing, as here in Bali aids the efficient use of water and helps preserve the precious soil surface

The various traditional approaches are largely effective in subsistence economies with slow rates of population growth and hence moderate environmental pressures. Today, the situation has changed: populations are expanding rapidly; individuals and governments strive for higher standards of living; there are drives for commercial products with which to enter world trade and earn foreign currency etc. The results are intensified environmental pressures and demands upon water resources. Thus, one of the most controversial development issues in many countries has been how to utilise water resources to benefit the maximum number of people at the lowest possible cost.

At one extreme there is the high-tech answer. This involves massive multi-purpose dam and reservoir projects, copied from the west and financed by international banks and agencies such as the World Bank, e.g. the Kariba Dam, Zambia; the harnessing of the River Indus in the Punjab. Mounting criticism of the cost, time-scale and effectiveness of such vast schemes has led to what is known as the appropriate technology approach, use a level of technology

and a scale of project appropriate to the society and economy. This approach gives control of the schemes to local communities, and the schemes are often based upon water management strategies with which they are already familiar.

Nowhere are the dilemmas of development, and which route to follow more vividly illustrated than in India: a massive country, with highly seasonal rainfall, a rapidly expanding rural and urban and a desperate shortage of food. The case study sets out the social, economic and environmental benefits and

---

Key understandings

- There are alternative approaches to the development and management of water resources.

- The alternative approaches have different social, economic and environmental impacts.

- Expensive, 'high-tech' projects may not be the answer to development problems.

- The issue of 'appropriate technology' as a development strategy.

costs of alternative approaches to water management and poses the fundamental question: what is the best way to improve the quality of life of a rural family?

India's troubled waters

The Sardar Sarovar dam is huge. It is Gujarat's answer to the equally huge problem of recurring drought. Like large parts of India, the state has had little monsoon rain for the past four years. Rain was so scarce in 1988 that the worst-hit areas received water for only 15 minutes every two days. Throughout the driest fortnight the government of Gujarat supplied Rajkot district with nearly 3 million litres of water each day at a cost of £1.8 million. The government claims a loss in agricultural production of £20 billion because of the drought.

The dam, 1210 metres long, will rise 139 m above the river bed. With a width of 750 m, the main canal coming off the reservoir will be the largest in the world. The canal will carry water from south Gujarat into Rajasthan, 445 km to the northwest. The Gujarat government estimates that the stored water will irrigate 1.8 million hectares, supplying 3.5 billion litres of drinking water

every day and producing 1450 megawatts of hydroelectricity. To do all that, and much more, says the government, the dam project will cost more than £3.5 billion and will take 22 years to complete.

Droughts are never far from the thoughts of Gujarati farmers. The last four dry years have increased the government's drive to build the Sardar Sarovar dam across the Narmada River as quickly as it can, yet opposition to the dam has never been stronger.

The Sardar Sarovar Project will destroy the homes and lands of 70 000 people in Gujarat, Maharashtra and Madhya Pradesh. It will drown almost 14 000 hectares of forest land and, inevitably, much of the wildlife that inhabits it. The dam will create pockets of stagnant water that will increase the prevalence of malaria in the vicinity of the dam. The reservoir will also destroy important temples and shrines.

Indian environmentalists claim that irrigation on such a large scale is bound to cause waterlogging and a build-up of salt in some of the soils in the area to be served by the dam. Soils vary considerably in the amount of water they can hold. Organic matter holds water well.

Soils that are rich in organic matter and little else may be prone to waterlogging. Sandy soils hold little water and very clayey soils may be impermeable. A good soil has a balanced mixture of sand, clay and organic matter.

Environmentalists criticise the Gujarat government for pressing ahead with the project even though it has studied the potential for waterlogging in only one-fifth of the soils in the area.

About 240 kilometres further south, people have come up with a strikingly different solution to the problem of drought. From the top of a hillock near the village of Adgaon you can see fields of sunflowers. There would be nothing remarkable about them except that, in midwinter at least, Adgaon's fields stand out like a green oasis in a vast expanse of dry, scrub land.

Adgaon village, in the Indian state of Maharashtra, was as dry as its neighbours four years ago. It receives an average rainfall of about 500 millimetres a year. Most of the rain falls between July and mid-October. Even then, the number of rainy days within the wet season may be fewer than 10.

In 1987 the area received only 300 millimetres of rain. The water in Adgaon's 153 wells had all but disappeared and surveys showed that there was no water to be found even 90 metres below ground. From 1972 until 1986 the government of Maharashtra had to supply drinking water to Adgaon during dry spells. The streams were drying up and soil erosion was increasing. Government officials estimated that about 3 tonnes of soil disappeared each year.

A volunteer group called Marathwada Sheti Sahya Mandal encouraged villagers to use small-scale methods of conserving soil and water. It taught them to build small earthen walls, or bunds, along the contours of the fields, plugging the gulleys carved out by soil erosion and building small dams across streams.

10.11

The Sardar Sarovar Dam. Is a large-scale solution like this the only answer to the problem of recurrent drought?

The idea is to trap water where it falls and to keep it in the soil for as long as possible. Villagers agreed not to let their animals graze on land newly planted with trees. Four years later Adgaon has peaceful, shady avenues and plots of acacia, neem, ber, eucalyptus and banana trees. The wells have water. Men and boys once again net fish in the main stream to the south of the village, even in December when it used to be dry.

Adgaon's modest attempts to save water and soil has cost about 1.7 million rupees in its first three years. The Swiss Development Corporation, a governmental aid agency, provided just over half of the money and the rest came from the Indian government. The project at Adgaon forced no one to sacrifice house and land. It destroyed no forests and no temples. Nor did it increase the prevalence of malaria or any other disease in the area.

Adgaon and Sarovar are as different as they could be. Yet the two projects share the same aim. How they tackle the common problem of drought illustrates the radical difference of opinion on what development really means in India today. The government claims that small-scale methods could not provide enough water for India's growing population. Opponents of large dams say the government has not even investigated that possibility.

Sardar Sarovar Narmada Nigam Ltd (SSNNL) claims that its dam employs the most sophisticated technology which fully addresses the social and environmental issues. The entire length of the main canal will be lined with concrete to prevent water from seeping into the soil and waterlogging it. Only two other irrigation projects in the world employ computers to control the delivery of water. Gates every 10 to 15 kilometres along the main canal will open and close by remote control. The operators will similarly control the delivery of water to 37 main branches of the canal.

Piezometers in wells dotted around the command area will record fluctuations in the water table and will alert the operators to the risk of waterlogging. If the water table rises too far the operators will pump water out of the wells and into the main canal.

Salinisation, or the damaging build-up of salts, can occur when too much surface water is fed into the soil and the water table rises. As water evaporates, salts that were once dissolved in the water crystalise at the surface. Vegetation dies back to reveal a salt desert. In some areas saline water underlies aquifers containing fresh water. Surface irrigation can result in saline and fresh water mixing. In this case the aquifer as well as the soil may become contaminated.

According to SSNNL the water available for irrigation is so meagre that there is no chance that the twin problem of waterlogging and salinity would arise. However, the project includes a system to monitor fluctuations in the water table. The idea is to force farmers to use both canal water and ground water for irrigation. The amount of canal water allocated will depend not only on the type of crop grown but also

on the level of the water table in an area.

One reason why irrigation projects have failed in the past is because farmers regard the water as free and use more than they need. That problem rarely arises in small projects such as that at Adgaon where water is collected and stored where it falls and so remains under local control.

The best that science can offer?

At first glance, the Sardar Sarovar Project seems to be a well-researched project whose design exemplifies the best that science and technology can offer. However, many people in India's growing environmental movement say that the SSNNL has merely paid lip service to the problems that large dams present. Nor does the history of large dam projects in India inspire much confidence that such a comprehensive scheme for managing the water resource of the Narmada and that of Gujarat will ever be implemented.

The then Prime Minister, Rajiv Gandhi, drew attention to the sorry state of affairs in his speech to state

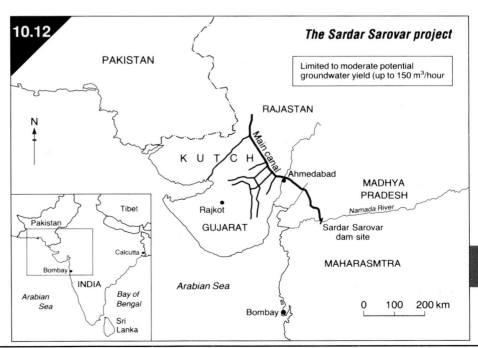

10.12 **The Sardar Sarovar project**

Limited to moderate potential groundwater yield (up to 150 m³/hour)

PAKISTAN

RAJASTAN

K U T C H

Ahmedabad

MADHYA PRADESH

Namada River

Rajkot

GUJARAT

Sardar Sarovar dam site

MAHARASMTRA

Arabian Sea

Bombay

0   100   200 km

Tibet

Pakistan

Calcutta

Bombay

INDIA

Arabian Sea

Bay of Bengal

Sri Lanka

Farmers in the Adgaon area have found small-scale water conservation as beneficial, and perhaps more so, than many large-scale schemes

ministers of irrigation in 1986 when he said: 'The situation today is that, since 1951, 246 big surface irrigation projects have been initiated. Only 65 of these have been completed and 181 are still under construction. We need some definite thrusts from the projects that we started after 1970. Perhaps we can safely say that almost no benefit has come to the people from these projects. For 16 years we have poured money out. The people have got nothing back, no irrigation, no water, no increase in production, no help in their daily life.'

Indian environmentalists are convinced that even if the dam and its 72 000 km of waterways were built according to plan, even if its sophisticated, computer-controlled system of water delivery worked flawlessly, the dam would not last long enough to make it economically worthwhile. Rivers carry sediment and reservoirs eventually become silted. It is no great problem for farmers to maintain small dams, such as those built at Adgaon. there, farmers regularly dig the fertile silt out of the pools and gulleys and spread it back on the fields. In contrast, when a large reservoir such as the Sardar Sarovar becomes silted there is little to do but pack up and go home. Dredging is sometimes possible if the reservoir is shallow enough but the costs may be prohibitively high. The question is: How many years does it take for the

sediment accumulating in the reservoir to reduce its storage capacity to such a degree that it is more economical to decommission the dam than to keep it in operation?

Feasibility studies carried out before the construction of the dam began, estimated that the dam should work for at least a century. Again, history suggests that this is wishful thinking. According to a report of the Irrigation Commission, the assumed rates of siltation seldom tally with observed rates (resource 10.14).

Dams silt up even more quickly if the catchment area of the river is devoid of trees. Forests help to hold soil and protect against its erosion. The Narmada River is 1300 km long. Its catchment area lies not in Gujarat but in the state of Madhya Pradesh, hundreds of kilometres to the east. Thus Gujarat has no control over the treatment of the catchment area of

the river that feeds the reservoir of the Sardar Sarovar dam.

Even if the government of Madhya Pradesh did everything it could to maintain and protect the forests of the Narmada catchment area it is unlikely that its efforts would be successful. Anil Agarwal, one of India's leading environmentalists, says that forests thrive only when managed by people who have a personal interest in their survival. 'If somebody else is going to come and green the land, even if it be the government, the people will look upon this as the government increasing its property, but not theirs. They are not going to cooperate. The result will be very low survival rates of the trees being planted.'

The Sardar Sarovar Project will submerge almost 14 000 hectares of forest land. The SSNNL claims that only a third of this is true forest. The Conservation of Forests Act, passed by the Indian government in 1980, says that if forest land is to be used for something other than forest an equivalent area of land must be planted with trees. However, the Ministry of Environment claims that this rarely happens. The SSNNL says that it will plant 30 million trees in 'less dense and non-forest areas'; more than 600 000 trees in the vicinity of the dam and almost 12 million trees in an area equivalent to the size of forest that the project will destroy. The equivalent amount of land has been found in Kutch, in north Gujarat but, says Agarwal: 'Ecologically it makes no sense to

10.14

Annual rates of siltation in selected reservoirs in India (in million cubic metres)		
Reservoir	**Assumed rate**	**Observed rate**
Bhakra	28.36	41.27
Maithon	0.84	7.37
Mavurakshi	0.66	2.47
Nizamsagar	0.65	10.76
Panchet	2.44	11.75
Ramganga	1.34	5.38
Tungahadra	12.08	50.62
Ukai	9.18	26.83

destroy forest in one region and find land in a totally different ecosystem. In any case, the ecological role of new forest is very different from that of the original forest.'

The Sardar Sarovar Project is only one part of the largest development scheme for a river valley that India has ever planned. The entire Narmada Valley Development Project (NVDP) is probably the largest scheme of its kind in the world. It entails building 30 major dams, 135 medium and 3000 minor dams on the Narmada river and its tributaries over the next half century. Environmentalists estimate that the completed project would cost 25 billion rupees (£960 million) to irrigate 4.8 million hectares. It will also submerge about 600 000 hectares of land and displace more than a million people.

Large dams have a short and troubled history. In India they go back only 70 years or so. Engineers admit that there is still much to learn about their construction and, particularly, their safety. Geologists recognise that impounding large bodies of water can, and often does, trigger earthquakes, a phenomenon called reservoir-induced seismicity. The Koyna dam in southern India is 103 metres high and its reservoir can hold nearly 3000 million cubic metres of water. By 1963, when the reservoir was less than half filled, the frequency of seismic shocks greatly increased. The epicentres of the shocks were all near the dam or under the reservoir. In 1967, one big seismic shock killed 177 people and injured 2300 others in the village of Anagar.

Kumar Singh, a geologist who works for Eklavya, a quake action group based in Bhopal, in Madhya Pradesh, is particularly concerned about the risk of earthquakes from new dams proposed in the Narmada Valley Development Project. Singh remains unconvinced that the project authorities have taken into account the cumulative risk of seismicity given the proximity of the Sardar Sarovar dam.

The project, by virtue of its scale, its dependence on loans from the World Bank and other international development agencies and its seemingly blind faith in the superiority of technology, has becòme a symbol for what many in India regard as 'wrong-headed' development. Smitu Kothari of Kayan, an independent Indian group studying development, believes that large dams only widen the gap between rich and poor. 'We question the very logic of projects like this. Who benefits from them?

Officials of the Central Ground Water Board, part of the government of India's Ministry of Agriculture and Irrigation, emphasise that the project is not the complete answer to drought-proofing Gujarat. They point out that during the recent drought, the water supplied to drought-stricken areas of Gujarat came from properly located and properly maintained wells in Gujarat itself. It is important to note that while Gujarat suffered drought, so too did the catchment area of the Narmada river, in Madhya Pradesh. The board maintains that only parallel planning and management of ground and surface water will provide a lasting solution. Groundwater is ignored at a high price.

Resources go into huge projects while very little is spent on studying smaller, more 'people-centred' alternatives. 'There have been hundreds of requests to the government of Gujarat for small amounts of money to deepen tanks, improve rain water collection and storage and for water management schemes in general. We need these small and medium-sized schemes rather than gigantic projects whose impacts are still not yet scientifically understood,' Smitu Kothari says. 'It is only through the recovery and regeneration of the degraded

ecosystems of Gujarat that you can ensure sustainable development. It is only with a comprehensive programme which involves people at all levels of society and that is evolved in close collaboration with the local people that one can have sustainable development. All other forms of development, according to me, are top-down approaches by people who do not adequately understand people's cultures, their relationship to their environments, and who are not that concerned about long-term sustainability.'

(Source: O Sattaur, 'India's troubled waters', *New Scientist*, 27 May 1989, pp. 46–51)

Activities

1 Why is there need for projects such as the Sardar Sarovar dam in this region of India?

2 What are the aims of the project?

3 How does the project set out to achieve these aims?

4 Compare the Sardar Sarovar and Adgaon approaches to water management, using the following headings as a basis:

- Financing and cost.
- Technology and scale.
- Decision makers and controllers.
- Time-scale.
- Effects on people, quality of life, and environment.

5 In what ways do the materials illustrate the idea of 'appropriate technology' as an approach to development?

6 Carry out an evaluation of the project, using the following matrix structure (use also the summary of the issue in resource 10.15 overleaf):

	Economic	Social	Environmental
Gains			
Losses			

10.15

Dam unlooses green tide in India

Peasants and environmentalists in an obscure central Indian town condemned to death by drowning will today protest against what has been called the world's largest planned disaster.

The demonstration will be held in Harsud, a town of 15 000 souls in Madhya Pradesh, India's biggest state. If the planners and politicians have their way, the state will boast, in a few years, the world's biggest artificial lake. A network of more than 3000 dams will trap the waters of the mighty Narmada River and spread them over more than 300 000 acres of farmland and forest.

The project will displace at least 300 000 people – some estimates say a million – many of them tribals. It will threaten rare species of animals, including tigers, panthers, sloth bears, and wild boar.

It will, say its admirers, bring prosperity to a drought-prone land, spreading drinking and irrigation water deep into Madhya Pradesh, Gujarat, Maharashtra and even the desert state of Rajasthan to the north.

Supporters of the dam stoutly deny that the flooding of the Narmada Valley will bring inevitable hardship. Mr R C K Koshy, secretary of the Narmada Development Department, insists that the government has prepared 'one of the best rehabilitation packages in the world', with guaranteed land grants and special assistance for the dispossessed.

Such claims are derided by environmentalists like Mr Baba Amte, who accuse bureaucrats and politicians of making grand but empty promises.

In a scathing open letter to the then Prime Minister, Mr Rajiv Gandhi, he wrote that politicians made such promises to ease their consciences. 'It is really quite another matter, and one well beyond the capacity of your government to ensure that the three lakh (one lakh is 100 000) people are properly rehabilitated.'

He added that the Prime Minister had heard the arguments against the Narmada project not once or twice but hundreds of times. 'You have chosen to respond in the only manner you seem to know; by not responding at all,' he wrote.

Mr Amte and others dispute the government's claims of the benefit of the Narmada development and say it is technically and financially unsound, environmentally destructive, and will rob hundreds of thousands of their homes.

A good deal of the anger of the anti-dam movement has been directed at the World Bank, which is contributing up to £300 million towards the cost of one main dam and part of the canal system. But the total cost of the construction and of installing power generation equipment, will be many times the World Bank contribution. Already, in 10 years, the price of harnessing the Narmada has gone up at least tenfold.

The government says that the project will be cost effective in terms of the new prosperity it will bring. At present, just 4 per cent of the river's potential is used for irrigation. Should the Narmada, they ask, be allowed to empty itself into the Bay of Cambay, on the Arabian Sea, or should it be used to improve countless wretched lives?

Baba Amte, dismisses the argument. He points out that the Narmada Sagar dam, which has just been sanctioned, would submerge nearly quarter of a million acres of cultivable and forest land.

'Thus we have the unbelievable situation of a state having to spend thousands of crores rupees (a crore is 10 million) to submerge as much of its territory as it is going to irrigate through the projects.'

Claude Alvares, an environmental specialist writer, who has described the Narmada project as the world's largest planned disaster, believes that it will become the launch pad for the young Indian Green movement. He wrote in a recent issue of the Illustrated Weekly of India: 'The Harsud meeting is expected to be a turning point in the country's experience of development. Participants intend to serve notice on the planners that such large, destructive projects, inhuman and antinatural in their consequences, will no longer be permitted, whether supported by the World Bank or not.'

In Harsud today, pride of place will go to leaders of the local village communities whose lands are livelihoods are threatened. That in itself is a breakthrough in a country whose teeming poor rarely get a chance to speak, let alone be heard. And in 30 other Indian towns, including the capital, there will be smaller rallies to protest against large-scale prestige development projects, like dams, mines, heavy industries and big power stations. An action committee formed by several environment groups said yesterday that the Harsud rally would be attended by representatives from several other threatened communities.

They included those facing displacement from the proposed national missile test range in Orissa, and a nuclear power station in Karnataka.

The committee said that the Sankalp Mela (pledge rally) at Harsud was the first attempt to build a common platform for the various regional campaigns against 'giganticism' in development planning, which had forced 20 million Indians from their homes since independence in 1947.

(Source: Derek Brown, *The Guardian*, 1990)

CASE STUDY 10.4 *Losers in the development game –*
an example from Zimbabwe

Background

Measuring the success or failure of a development scheme must take into account the social and environmental as well as the economic results. 'Who wins and who loses?' is a crucial question. Lake Kariba dam in north-west Zimbabwe holds back the waters of Africa's largest artificial lake. When completed in 1956, it was regarded as a technological wonder and a 'jewel in the crown' of high-tech development schemes. Its HEP generators still provide over 50 per cent of Zimbabwe's electricity requirements. The lake itself supports the country's major fishing industry. The hotels, game parks and beaches scattered along its shoreline attract large numbers of tourists and income. These are substantial benefits, but the people displaced as the valley was flooded have been clear losers. Their losses need to be added to the debit side of the balance sheet when evaluating the Kariba project.

Key understandings

◆ Economic benefits of a development project may be offset by social and cultural losses.

◆ Development projects need to give careful consideration to the future of existing communities and take their wishes into account.

◆ Benefits from development projects may be unevenly distributed.

The impact of the Kariba project on the Tonga people

For the country as a whole Lake Kariba has been a development boon, but as is the case with the construction of many other dams throughout developing countries this success has been at the cost of others. For the indigenous inhabitants of the river, the Tonga people of the Zambezi valley, the flooding of the river in the late 1950s and their subsequent removal from their homelands has brought about a social, cultural and economic disaster. 'Quite simply,' claimed one of the older inhabitants of the region, 'the 60 000 people who used to live along this stretch of the river have seen little of the benefits that have come with Lake Kariba and more of the problems. For us it has been a disaster rather than a blessing.'

The indigenous people of the Zambezi valey, the Tonga, are an ethnic group who inhabited this stretch of river for many centuries. their main economic activities were centred around fishing and an agriculture geared to the seasonal flooding of the Zambezi river. Their eviction from the region in 1956 by the then Rhodesian Government to make way for the dam resulted in their displacement to the lands overlooking the valley, in many places a bleak, inhospitable range of hills and mountains which some environmentalists consider can only support a small percentage of those who were eventually resettled. A glimpse at the small dilapidated huts which now compose their villages, the thin, ragged animals, the cracked fields with occasional patches of maize would seem to support this opinion.

Claimed one resident in a report published a few years after the resettlement programme, 'We can remember the life we led before the dam and the life we led after it. There is no comparison. We knew that our removal from the river would bring us hardship, but what could we do. One day our chiefs came and told us that the white man had ordered us to move. Some tried to oppose them but we were removed by policemen with guns. On the other side of the river men were shot. In less than a year the land that we inherited from our grandfathers and their ancestors was taken away from us and what was given in return did not replace that loss.'

The hardships that the Tonga endured since their removal have been many and varied. Accustomed to an agriculture which could depend on the rich alluvial deposits of the river their resettlement among the poor, fragile soils of the uplands proved disastrous. There was very little attempt by the colonial administrators to retrain farmers in new agricultural techniques, needed to survive in a harsher environment. Crops withered during the many drought years that have taken place over the last few decades, and with no access to irrigation the Tonga could not become self sufficient in food production. These regions were also heavily populated by wild animals, and many farmers lost their lives protecting what crops did survive the drought against marauding elephant and buffalo. At the same time any Tonga caught killing these animals, even for purposes of defending their fields were accused of poaching and received heavy fines and prison sentences.

The region could not even support cattle. The highlands above the Zambezi are heavily infested with tsetse fly and the only livestock that will survive are donkeys and goats. Furthermore the resettlement areas were too far from the lake. Lack of crops, meat and fish meant that starvation occurred frequently and malnutrition became endemic.

Benefits went to others

The expected spin-offs from the construction of the dam – electricity, revenues from tourism, cheap fish, irrigation – also did not materialise for the indigenous population, who received few of the guarantees given to them by colonial administrators on their eviction. The fishing industry that grew up around the lake was set up by outsiders, most of whom preferred to employ their own workers from other regions of the country. When the Tonga did receive employment it was generally at a menial level with low rates of pay and no employment protection rights. At the same time the catches of kapenta (small sardines) fished from the lake were purchased by middlemen from the towns and cities of Zimbabwe at prices that the local people could scarcely afford.

Furthermore the wild animals that caused such destruction and havoc to local farmsteads attracted numerous foreign visitors and with them large amounts of money, but once again these revenues flowed out of the region into the pockets of hotel proprietors, tour operators, game hunters and the Government Treasury. 'We were prevented from killing wild animals even for purposes of defending our fields,' remarked one Tonga, 'yet the tourists dined on wild game in the hotels of Lake Kariba. We watched thousands of them come into our region to take photos of the elephant and buffalo that were causing us to starve. We began to feel that those animals were more important to the Government of this country than the men, women and children who had to live here. 'Under these conditions there was very little for the Tonga to do but to emigrate and during the first decade after the construction of the dam it was estimated that about a third of the resettled population fled the region for possible employment elsewhere.

The cultural and social effects of resettlement on the Tonga, as a separate group with their own identity and traditions, have matched the grave economic consequences resulting from their move. Old clan ties were broken with the resettlement of different families in different areas, with no easy transport facilities to maintain previous contacts. Chieftainships were broken up and the old system of community courts and councils of elders were gradually destroyed. With the flooding of the waters it also became impossible for people on one side of the river to visit their friends and relatives on the other. Previously there had been frequent interchange between Tonga communities separated by the Zambezi, but the Zambian and Rhodesian authorities began to insist on passports and other regulations.

Economic hardships also had a profound effect on the social relations that had bound communities together for many years. In particular the emigration of young people from the region in search of employment deprived the Tonga of their more active population who might have campaigned for development and their economic and social rights. The resulting disillusionment among those who remained has resulted in high levels of alcoholism and drug abuse. The main factor that keeps these people together now, claimed one observer, is not their shared history but their common poverty.

Despite the fact that the post–independence government has been much more concerned about the development of the region and has embarked on a policy of building schools, clinics, improved transport facilities etc, the Tonga still remain a marginalised community with no voice of their own and little input into the decisions that affect them. The teachers, doctors, administrators, politicians and extension workers who are now trying to improve their status are predominantly outsiders and while their concern is genuine and sincere, without local representation the Tonga will not emerge from the historical backwater and oblivion to which their resettlement condemned them.

Cultural alienation

Children are taught in Shona and English, claimed one inhabitant of Mola, a small village in the resettlement area. They read history books which do not discuss the evolution of the local people: they are given an education which can only be satisfied by moving to the towns and cities outside the region. the political decisions that affect the Tonga are made by men and women who have limited access to what the people really want. But changes in these areas will only occur when local people themselves begin to demand them, and the signs at present are that this is not happening. 'Our generation,' claimed one older inhabitant of the region, 'was destroyed by the resettlement. Perhaps it rests with our children to regain something of what we have lost.'

The tragedy is that this need never have happened. In the rush to construct its 'technological wonder' the Rhodesian government largely ignored the wishes and aspirations of the people who would be most affected. Improved training for farmers, access to irrigation and other agricultural inputs, access to wildlife revenues through controlled killing of animals and jobs associated with tourism, employment opportunities for locals in the lucrative fishing industry might have prevented the resulting disaster that befell these people. The Tonga are not saying that the dam should not have been built, concluded one resident. The benefits are there for all to see. But where development ignores the lives of some people, especially those who are displaced as a result of such projects, then it is much less than the success it could be.

(Source: C McIvor, 'People of the Lake', *Development and Co-operation*, No. 1, 1989, pp. 16–17)

Activity

Group project

A proposed dam will flood a valley currently settled by farming and fishing communities. As part of the development plan, make recommendations for the future of these people, in the light of the experience of the Tonga people in the Kariba scheme.

Index

Acknowledgements

Photographs

The publishers are grateful to the following for permission to reproduce the following photographs (resource numbers are in brackets). If any acknowledgement has been omitted, this will be corrected at the earliest possible opportunity.
AGE Fotostock: p.191 (8.28); American Airlines: p.197 (9.1); Aspect Picture Library: p.57 (3.22) (Tom Nebbia); Prodeepta Das: p.242 (10.11); Ruth Dunne: p.220 (9.28); Edifice: p.130 (6.9); Mark Edwards/Still Pictures: p.1, (1.2), p.70 (4.1), p.76 (4.7), p.233 (10.4); Ekistics: p.86 (4.21), p. 87 (4.22), p.88)4.24), p.91 (4.30); Ford: p.92 (5.1); Robert Harding Picture Library: p.20 (1.30); Antonia Hussey: p.187 (8.24), p.189 (8.27), Hutchison Library: p.244 (10.13); The Image Bank: p.96 (5.8) (Colin Molyneux), p.171 (8.1); Impact Photos: p.239 (10.9); Richard Mildenhall: p.150 (7.9); More Land for Homes Campaign: p.54 (3.20); Jeff Morgan: p.98 (5.10); Network: pp.210–212 (9.19) (Homer Sykes); Oxford Picture Library: p.31, (2.11) (Chris Andrews); Robert Prosser: p.3 (1.4), p.38 (2.20), p.47 (3.6), p.53 (3.18), p.58 (3.24/3.25), p.95 (5.6), p.100 (5.14), p.143 (6.28), p.146 (7.5), p.147 (7.7), p.148 (7.8), p.168 (7.27), p.174 (8.5), p.174 (8.6), p.176 (8.9), p.182 (8.18/8.19), p.192 (8.32), p.225 (9.36); Chris Ridgers: p.123 (6.4), p.124 (6.5); Sealand Aerial Photography: p.24 (2.14), p.55 (3.21), p.172 (8.2); South American Pictures: p.74 (4.6); Tony Stone Worldwide: p.212 (9.20); p.241 (10.10) (Hilarie Kavanagh); Topham Picture Source: p.184 (8.21), p.205 (9.14).

Artwork and tables

The resources listed below were taken from the following sources:

Chapter 1
1.3: World Development Report, 1984, Table A1, p.187.   1.7: In DFW Cross 'Counterurbanisation in England and Wales: context and development', King's College, London Department of Geography, OR, 8 May 1987.   1.8: (a) and (b) Cross as above, (c): 1991 Census of Population,   1.9, 1.10: Cross *as above*,   1.11: In AG Champion, 'Recent changes in the pace of population deconcentration in Britain, *Geoforum*, 18(4), 1987.   1.12: Cross *as above*, from Cloke and Edwards 1986,   1.13: Cross *as above*,   1.15: Figures for graph from Stewart K Fraser, Centre for Comparative International Education, La Trobe University,   1.17: Education Guardian, September 10, 1991, graphic by Paddy Allen/Line and Line. Figures: source IPPF,   1.18 – 1.21: In B Werner, 'Fertility Trends in the UK and in thirteen other developed countries, 1966–86', *Population Trends*, 51, Spring 1988, pp.18–24,   1.22: *World Resources*, Basic Books 1986,   1.24 – 1.26: In HRJ Davies, 'Population change in the Sudan since independence', *Geography*, 73(3), June 1988, pp.249–255,   1.28: In MB Gleave, 'Changing population distribution in Sierra Leone, 1974–1985', *Geography*, 73 (4), October 1988, pp.351–354,   1.29: Gleave as above,   1.31 – 1.35: In RC Jones, 'Causes of Salvadorean migration to the United States', *Geographical Review*, 79 (2), April 1989, pp.183–194

Chapter 2
2.1: Figures from the House Builders Federation,   2.12: In 'The Green Belt', *Which*, August 1989, pp.388–391,   2.13: *Which, loc cit*. Map Crown Copyright, reproduced by permission of Her Majesty's Stationary Office,   2.15 – 2.18: From SCI SFRP (1976), 'The Improvement of London's Green Belt, in AM Blair, 'Future landscapes of the rural-urban fringe', in DG Lockhart and B Ilbery (eds) *The Future of the British Rural Landscape*, Geobooks, 1987,   2.26: In CD Adams, AE Baum and HD McGregor, 'The availability of land for inner city development: A case study of Inner Manchester, *Urban Studies*, 25 (1), February 1988, pp.62–76,   2.28: Adapted from Adams et al, *as above*.

Chapter 3
3.1: Source for graphs, Building Societies Assocaition in *The Sunday Times*, 15 October 1989,   3.2: In *Regional Trends*, 24, HMSO, 1989, Table 5.6, p.71,   3.3: In *Regional Trends*, 24, HMSO, 1989, Table 5.2, p.70   3.4: In *Regional Trends*, 24, HMSO, 1989, Table 5.13, p.74,   3.5: Graph and pie chart in *New Statesman and Society*, 3 November 1989   3.7: Source: Housing and Construction Statistics, HMSO,   3.11 – 3.14: Source: Housing Investment programme returns, in MP Kleinman, 'Where did it hurt most? Decline in the availability of council housing in England', *Policy and Politics*, 16 (4), October 1988, pp.261–276   3.19: Source: Housing and Construction statistics, various sources,   3.26: Based on map in *The Sunday Times*, 3 January 1988,   3.27 – 3.29: Source: The Building Societies Association and the Department of the Environment in C Hamnett, *The Royal Bank of Scotland Review*, 1988,   3.30: Source: information from the Halifax and Nationwide Building Societies, in *The Sunday Times*, February 1992, and Roy Brooks Estate Agents in *The Sunday Times*, November 1989   3.31: Hamnett, *as above*.

Chapter 4
4.2: From O Rondinelli, *Third World Planning Review*, 4 (4), 1982,   4.3: Figures from the World Bank 1985, in World Development Report, Washington DC,   4.14: From S Pornchokchai, 'Bangkok slum and squatter settlements', *Planning and Administration*, 16(2), Autumn 1989, pp.104–114,   4.17 – 4.20: Based on C Rakodi, 'Upgrading in Chawama, Lusaka: displacement or differentiation?', *Urban Studies*, 25, 1988, pp.297–318,   4.27 – 4.29: From Yang Binhui, 'Hongshan: a new village on the banks of the Qiantang River', *Ekistics*, 322, January/February, 1987.

Chapter 5
5.2: From *The Guardian*, 8 February 1992,.   5.3: From G Humphreys, 'Changing places', *Geography*, 73(4), October 1988, pp.298–307,   5.6: Humphreys, *as above*,   5.11: Source: Asian Development Bank in *The Guardian*, 24 November 1989,   5.14 –5.16: From: B Heppell, 'Pacific sunrise: East Asia's newly industrialising countries', *Geography Review*, March 1990, pp.7–11,   5.17: Based on map in *The Guardian*, 10 January 1988   5.18: Humphreys, *as above*,   5.22: From *The Guardian*, 13 December 1989,   5.23 – 5.30: From A Mair, R Florida and M Kenney, 'The new geography of automobile production: Japanese transplants in North America', *Economic Geography*, 64 (4), October 1988, pp.352–373,   5.34 – 5.37: From DW Edgington, 'New strategies for technology development in Japanese cities and regions', *Town Planning Review*, 60(1), 1989, pp.1–26,

Chapter 6
6.10 – 6.17: From RDF Bromley and CJ Thomas, 'The impact of shop type and spatial structure on shopping linkages in retail parks', *Town Planning Review*, 60 (1), January 1989, pp.45–70,   6.18 – 6.26: From CM Guy and N Wrigley, 'Walking trips to shops in Britain cities', *Town Planning Review*, 58 (1), 1987, pp.63–79.

Chapter 7
7.2: Source for figures: RH Best, Department of the Environment,   7.3: Source for figures: European Community,   7.4: From *Development and Co-operation*, No 1, 1989, p.32,   7.10: From D Grigg, 'Types of farming in England and Wales', *Geography Review*, 1988, pp.20–24,   7.11 – 7.13: From JE Wrathall, 'Recent changes in arable crop production in England and Wales', *Land Use Policy*, April 1988, pp.219–231 updated to 1990,   7.14: B Ilbery, *Geography*, 1990,   7.15: Drawn from *New Scientist*, 8 October 1988, p.51,   7.17: From J Conrad, in *Land Use Policy*, April 1988, p. 209   7.18: Figures from Water Authorities Association, 1987,   7.19: MAFF/WOAD December Census, Water Authorities Association 1987,   7.20: Meteorological Office MORECS System, Water Authorities Association, 1987,   7.22: From *Geofile*, No 92, April 1987, Part (a) after Kirkby and Evans in Kirkby and Morgan 1980,   7.23: From *Geofile*, No 92, April 1987, after Wilson and Cooke in Kirkby and Morgan 1980.

Chapter 8
8.11 – 8.12: From Wagtendonk, *Leisure Sciences*, 4(3), 1981,   8.13: US National Parks Service (Yosemite National Park Management Zoning Plan),   8.14: Wagtendonk, *as above*,   8.15: Data from the Countryside Commission's National Countryside Recreation Survey, 1985,   8.22, 8.23, 8.25, 8.26: From A Hussey, 'Tourism in a Balinese Village', *The Geographical Review*, 79 (3), July, pp.311–325,   8.30: Source: Pearce, 1987 after Mignon and Heran, 1979,   8.31: From Lewis and Williams, *Geography*, 74(2), April 1989, p.158.

Chapter 9
9.5: From Annual Abstract of Statistics, HMSO, no 126, 1990,   9.12: Source: Department of Transport (1989) *Central London Rail Study*, London: Department of Transport,   9.13, 9.15: From MJH Mogridge, 'The use of rail transport to improve accessibility in large conurbations, using London as an example', *Town Planning Review*, 58 (2), pp.165–182   9.16: From *The Sunday Times*, 12 November 1989, graphic by Phil Green,   9.21 – 9.24: Adapted from map in C Thomas, 'Moving Moscow's millions', *Geography*, 73(3), June 1988, pp.216–225,   9.25 – 9.27: From D Machon and A Dingsdale,m 'Public transport in a socialist capital city: Budapest', *Geography*, 74(2), April 1989, pp.159–162,   9.29: From D Hilling, 'Technology and the changing ports of England and Wales, *Geography*, 1989, pp.117–127   9.30: Figures from National Ports Council, 1970, and Department of Transport, 1987,   9.32: Source: Department of Transport, 1987,   9.33: Source: calculated from Department of Transport figures, 1987,   9.35: Source: National Ports Council, and Department of Transport, 1987,   9.37: From D Fair, 'The Atlantic ports of the Zaire river basin', *Africa Insight*, 19 (2), 1989, pp.103–108.

Chapter 10
10.3: From *Development and Co-operation*, No 3, 1080, p.2,   10.11: From the Report of the Irrigation Commission: from the Centre for Science and Environment, *The State of India's Environment*, 1982, New Delhi, 1982, p.62.